SEEING FAIRIES

CONTENTS

Introduction
by Simon Young[*]

Seeing Fairies and Fairy Literature

Anyone with any interest in literature will know the tortured path that many works, even works later denominated as "classics," have had to follow to find their way into print. But very few books, good or bad, have passed through birth pangs as difficult as the ones experienced by the present volume. It all began in 1955, when the British author, Marjorie Johnson, then aged 44, began to put together the material for a book entitled *Fairy Vision*. She worked with the noted Scottish author and folklorist Alasdair Alpin MacGregor and got Quentin Craufurd, a man who defies easy definition but who had a long-standing interest in fairies, to write the introduction to her monograph. However, *Fairy Vision* matured more slowly than Marjorie had expected: first Craufurd died in 1957 (he had fortunately already written the introduction), then, in the same year, MacGregor dropped away from the project, though not before he had dedicated one of his finest volumes to Marjorie. The years passed and still the book was not completed. Marjorie, who was based in Nottingham, in the English Midlands, later referred to three major problems: health issues in her family; professional obligations (Marjorie worked full time as a lawyer's secretary); and difficulties with her eyes. There may have been some attempts to publish the book prior to the 1990s. But it was only in 1996 that a manuscript, the manuscript that is behind the present book, was finally typed up: Marjorie was 85. By then its title had changed to *Seeing Fairies: Authentic Reports of Fairies in Modern Times, A Book for Grownups*.[1]

Marjorie sent the impressive collection of fairy sightings and fairy material that she had amassed to publishers in Britain and in Ireland, but she had no luck despite the able assistance of Leslie

---

[*]   Dr. Simon Young is a British historian living in Italy. He has written extensively on the middle ages and on fairy lore and fairy belief.

Shepard, a fellow fairy enthusiast and an expert on Bram Stoker.[2] However, Leslie proved assiduous and the breakthrough eventually came thanks to him. He found, in fact, a home for *Seeing Fairies* at Aquamarin, a publisher based in, of all places, Germany. The result was that in 2000 *Seeing Fairies* emerged with an entirely different title. This time it was *Naturgeister: Wahre Erlebnisse mit Elfen und Zwergen*. One can imagine Marjorie's pride but also bewilderment as she, at 89, finally held in her hands her life's work in a language that she could not read. If this sounds like the universe playing a cruel joke, then the punch line had not yet been delivered. In 2004, when the author was 93, *Naturgeister* was translated into Italian as *Il Popolo del Bosco: i luoghi dove vivono gnomi, fate, elfi e spiriti della natura, un mondo di fascino e mistero*. Another book that Marjorie could not read. Marjorie died in 2011, aged 100.[3] She did not live to see her book brought out in English: but with her strong beliefs in the survival of the soul, she assumed that one day she would witness this happen "from the other side." The published version in English, with some minor changes, will doubtless make her shade smile: the final proof that the transition from imagination to the printed page is fraught with all too worldly problems.

Now but wait a moment, the reader might be thinking. Here is a book that took the best part of half a century to get into print (and then "only" in a foreign language). It was a book that was repeatedly refused by reputable Anglophone publishers and one that only slipped through the printing press in 2014, just shy of sixty years after its first drafting. Perhaps, the same reader may consider, this is a poor recommendation. Well, if you've bought this online or had the fortune to get it in wrapping paper, then, it is, to be frank, too late to protest. But just in case you are one of those twentieth-century types who actually look at books in bookshops, let's make the case for *Seeing Fairies* and make it as strongly as possible.

This book is special because it brings together an unprecedented number of fairy sightings, ranging from the late nineteenth to the late twentieth century. The fairy book market—which is not admittedly very broad—does offer rivals. Edmund Jones, in the eighteenth century, gathered a collection of fairy and ghost sightings in two volumes, best read today in a modern reissue (2003) as *The Appearance of Evil*. Some of Katherine Briggs works include fairy experiences, side by side with traditional fairy tales and fairy lore. Janet Bord's fascinating *Fairies: Real Encounters with Little People* contains several score of the same. Then, most notably, Evans-Wentz' classic *The Fairy Faith*, published just before the First World War, has a hundred plus fairy sightings from Ireland, Mann, Brittany, and the Celtic fringes of Britain. Marjorie Johnson trumps them all, however, in terms of numbers. There are here about four hundred sightings from around the world. In short, this is the biggest single collection of fairy experiences ever amassed.

If you are one of the minority who believe in fairies, then here you have the most substantial archive of accounts ever brought together: a work that does not supersede Bord's, Briggs', Evans-Wentz', and Jones' work, but that can stand proudly on the bookshelf alongside them as one of the great fairy books, with more discursive volumes like Jeremy Harte's *Exploring Fairies* and Lewis Spence's *The Fairy Tradition*. And what if you are one of that substantial majority who do not believe in fairies? Then you have the perfect data set to make your case against "the little people": five hundred fairy sightings waiting to be picked apart and analyzed. Whether fairies are out there (author points to wood, hedgerow and waterfall) or in there (author points to balding head of middle aged "witness") then they need to be explained. Marjorie gave us, in these pages, the tools to do just that. Yes, there is a lot of baggage in this book: particularly spiritualist and theosophical baggage, words we'll return to below... And for the twenty-first-century reader, even those like Marjorie who are believers in a non-physical dimension, this baggage can be a little hard to lift: a paragraph on bees from Venus stands out in my memory... But, particularly in the crucial early chapters (where the most interesting sightings are to be found), the baggage can be consigned to the left luggage counter and the accounts can be assessed on their own merits.

The Fairy Investigation Society, Spiritualism and Theosophy

The next question is: where did Marjorie get the material for the book? And the answer to this is, in large part, to be found in one of the most curious British organizations ever to have been dreamed into existence: the Fairy Investigation Society (FIS). The history of the FIS is a fascinating topic in its own right. But for present purposes we can reduce that history to the barest of outlines. In 1927 the FIS was founded in London by, among others, Quentin Craufurd, a brilliant retired naval scientist who had had, he believed, some success communicating with the dead and fairies by radio: this is the same Quentin Craufurd who invented the first remote radio device — the precursor of the mobile phone; and who wrote the original introduction to the present volume. He was joined by Bernard Sleigh, an artist specializing in wood engravings, who had experience with fairy themes and who had penned a series of fairy short stories, published in *The Gates of Horn*: happy the man or woman who can, today, find a copy of this rare book. Others were included in the magic circle. There was, for example, Claire Cantlon, a London medium, who acted as secretary of the FIS for a time and who had been prosecuted for her séances in a memorable trial in which Arthur Conan Doyle appeared for the defence. (There is no proof, at least none known to me, but Doyle, a fairy believer himself, may have belonged to the FIS; he certainly knew Craufurd.) There was also Nina Alida Molesworth, a shadowy figure from the British aristocracy again with links to spiritualism, and there was Jean Michaud, a Belgian publisher resident in the capital, who encountered, from time to time, the Great Beast, Aleister Crowley.[4] From 1927 to immediately before the war, the society met, discussed fairy matters, and carried out experiments. What brought these different individuals together in one room? The answer "fairies" is not enough, and a recurring theme in the biographies of the members, at least those that we can trace from this date, is an interest in spiritualism and even theosophy, an outgrowth of spiritualism associated with the notorious (or according to tastes, celebrated) Madame Blavatsky.

Say "spiritualism" to someone living in the modern west and they'll picture a man or a woman in their grandparents or greatgrandparents generation sitting in the semi-dark and trying to communicate with "the departed." But spiritualism was more than just table rapping and knocks and "ether." It was an attempt, honest in the case of most members of the movement, to open vistas onto a wider world beyond the physical realm. It was only natural that fairies were eventually appropriated by spiritualism as part of this wider spirit land: for all their *faux* modesty, spiritualists were empire builders. Traditional fairy-believing communities in the nineteenth century tended, if they thought about the meaning of fairies at all, to associate them with the dead; and it is even possible that fairies were originally born from an attempt to make sense of death. However, spiritualists rejected this approach. Spiritualists, in fact, would have seen any such idea as threatening the central beliefs of their movement, namely that the dead were in a heavenly realm, constantly bumping into Napoleon and Charles Dickens, and sending messages back to earth. Instead, fairies were recast, by spiritualists and particularly by theosophists, as nature spirits or even "elementals." This was not an original idea—in the Renaissance Neo-Platonists had played around with similar notions, there are even hints of this in *Midsummer Night's Dream*—but it was one that proved potent and went mainstream with remarkable speed. It is striking that Evans-Wentz' *Fairy Faith in Celtic Lands* in 1911 uses spiritualist terminology freely for fairies, as do—and this is perhaps more significant—some of his informants. The Cottingley Fairy photographs were publicized by Arthur Conan Doyle, a spiritualist, and Edward Gardner, a theosophist. Indeed, the Cottingley Fairies, who are so often sold as being the end of English fairy belief, are nothing of the kind. They mark the transition from the dregs of medieval fairy belief, which had survived in the rural corners of the UK, to a new spiritualized fairy, who tended to be both less dangerous and harder working.[5] The influence of this new model has been immense and is growing. If you take your child or a privileged nephew or niece to see fairies at the cinema today, you will find yourself watching the Tinker Bell films, in which a small community of fairies look after nature: teaching birds to fly and helping with the change of the seasons. Or you may see, if you are lucky, less well known but more powerful fairy flicks, including *The Secret of Kells* in which a fairy defends her forest, or *Epic* in which the fairies fight the boggarts to save nature from the forces of entropy. These films could never have been made in, say, the 1850s: first, because, obviously, of the lack of technology, but just as importantly because of very different nineteenth-century ideas about fairies, for fairies, then, were neither nature helpers nor even particularly nice (see further below).

Marjorie Johnson and Her Book

But what does Marjorie Johnson have to do with theosophy, the Fairy Investigation Society, or, for that matter, modern children's films? Here we have to trace, as best we can, the fairy beliefs of a Nottingham girl born in 1911, who was already seeing fairies in her infancy. Her first publication, when she was 25, was a letter in 1936, in *John O'London's Weekly* magazine describing how she had, aged seven or eight, seen an elf in her bedroom (*John O'London's Weekly* ran several letters at this date on the topic of fairies, all of which are collected together in chapter seven of the present volume). Many children see fairies, of course, something that is explained by sceptics in terms of imagination and by believers in term of innocence. But what is fascinating about Marjorie is that she continued to see fairies throughout her life, becoming, to use her own words, a "fairy seer." Indeed, she had what I can only describe as a series of fairy "familiars," as well as occasional contact with a "radiant being" who gave her, Marjorie believed, permission to write this book. Reading, in fact, Marjorie's biography, as it emerges in *Seeing Fairies*, I can't help thinking that had she been born in prehistoric Britain she would have been a "shaman," a tribal visionary. It goes without saying, meanwhile, that had she been born in sixteenth- or seventeenth-century England she would have attracted the attention of the local ecclesiastical court and any enthusiastic witch-finders in the area. She was born in the wrong time, though her time proved a safer one.

We have no proof that Marjorie belonged to the Fairy Investigation Society before the war and some hints that she did not. At this date the FIS was difficult to join for those outside a charmed upper middle class, bohemian circle in London: Marjorie, lived all her life in Nottingham and collected fairy accounts on her own in the 1920s and the 1930s. We do know though that, after a brief intermission in the Second World War, the society revved back to life, under the leadership of Craufurd. Perhaps already by 1947, when the FIS was certainly up and running again, Marjorie was a member. Certainly, she was secretary of the organization by 1950 and remained secretary into the early 1960s. The word "secretary" can, of course, cover many different roles, and its real meaning is dependent on a given organization. But, in the case of the FIS, the secretary was, at least by the 1950s, the organizer and administrator and, in all but title, the head. Marjorie fielded questions from new and potential members, and she also brought out an occasional newsletter, some examples of which survive. She received, too, questions about fairies from members of the general public — one little girl, for example, wrote in to ask what proof there was for the existence of the fey. She received as well accounts of fairy sightings from Britain, Ireland, and, indeed, from Africa, the United States, and the British Dominions (Australia, Canada, New Zealand and South Africa). Most of these accounts came from FIS members: to give some sense of how important these contacts were consider that of the 120 members in the 1950s, over half are thanked in this book for accounts and opinions.[6]

At some point in the mid-1950s, Marjorie got or was given the idea of widening her sample outside the rather narrow limits of the FIS. It was one thing to concentrate on accounts of believers, but if fairies existed then presumably members of the general public had seen them as well. Why not reach out to the general public and try and bring in these accounts that would otherwise be lost? Marjorie may have remembered her letter, twenty years previously, to *John O'London's Weekly* where she had been one of a rash of "Joe Publics" keen to share their fairy experiences. Alternatively, the idea may have come in conversation with the Scottish folklorist Alasdair Alpin MacGregor, another member of the FIS, who was not only a talented author but also a talented self-publicist. Certainly, in 1955, it was Alasdair Alpin MacGregor who took the lead on behalf of the duo in writing to *The Listener* (the major BBC magazine of the time) and *Folk-lore*, asking for fairy accounts for inclusion in a soon-to-be-published collection: "If any reader would care to submit an authentic account of his or her having seen, or been aware of the presence of, a fairy or fairies, we would certainly give it sympathetic consideration." The pair wrote, as well, to other publications, though I have been unable to track down any of these letters.[7]

The result was that Marjorie Johnson had two major sources for her collection of fairy encounters: (1) experiences of FIS members, hence the tweaked subtitle of the book; and (2) experiences of those who wrote in answer to her and MacGregor's press campaign in 1955. To this must be added two further sources that salted the collection: (3) accounts she came across in other publications or transmissions (there are some scattered references to radio programmes); and (4) some very few accounts she was given or that she came across herself after her resignation as secretary of the FIS (mid-1960s?), but before the final drafting of the book in 1996. Then, finally, we must remember (5) that Marjorie was herself a passionate fairy believer and regularly saw fairies: a gift she shared with other family members, particularly her sister, Dorothy, with whom she was extraordinarily close, and her mother, who was once scandalised when an elf looked through her bathroom window during her ablutions.

I regrettably never met Marjorie but in several interviews with friends it becomes clear that she was a *very* special individual. Time and time again friends spoke of her in reverence: for example, "They truly broke the mould when they made Marjorie, she was the kindest, gentlest, most interesting soul I ever met."[8] A simple perusal of the following pages brings this out: written style is, in my experience, an infallible guide to character and Marjorie's English is straightforward, considerate (see her discussion of the Cottingley photographs), and vibrant with conviction. Talking to those she knew, I had, despite my own scepticism about many of Marjorie's beliefs, a sense of someone capable of creating a space around her, in which the normal rules of life did not always operate. For example, one no-nonsense house-help, later a friend of Marjorie's, described her first day of employment: while doing the dishes, she saw a mysterious transparent blue light float over the sink...[9]

Fairy Sightings

A mysterious transparent blue light floating over the sink... And here we must turn from the history of the collection to the sightings in this book and the problem of fairy accounts more generally. Other fairies in the pages that follow save a child from punishment, soothe a dying woman, and help flowers bud. The worst that can be said about these fairies, in fact, is that some are rather insipid. There is certainly little to fear. Curiously, in one of the very few "nasty" fairy stories, Marjorie feels she has to justify its inclusion as it goes against the grain of other accounts.[10] It is a far cry from the fairies of earlier times when mysterious lights were a best-case scenario and where maiming and death were the rule. Take this story from Wales. The experience dates to the early 1700s: it gives an excellent sense of how fairies were seen in the generations after the English Civil War. Some children have run into a circle of mysterious dwarfish dancers in a field and the children are frightened.

> In the first discovery we began, with no small dread, to question one another as to what they could be, as there were no soldiers in the country, nor was it the time for May dancers and as they differed much from all the human beings we had ever seen. Thus alarmed we dropped our play, left our station and made for the stile. Still keeping our eyes upon them we observed one of their company starting from the rest and making towards us with a running pace. I being the youngest was the last at the stile and, though struck with an inexpressible panic, saw the grim elf just at my heels, having a full and clear, though terrific view of him, with his ancient, swarthy and grim complexion. I screamed out exceedingly; my sister and our companions also set up a roar and [my sister] dragged me with violence over the stile on which, at the instant I was disengaged from it, this warlike Lilliputian leaned and stretched himself after me, but did not come over.[11]

If that is not chilling enough, consider the following even more traumatic Irish episode, also involving children, the encounter dating from the 1850s, the account from c. 1910.

> One day, just before sunset in midsummer, and I a boy then, my brother and cousin and myself were gathering bilberries (whortleberries) up by the rocks at the back of here, when all at once we heard music. We hurried round the rocks, and there we were within a few hundred feet of six or eight of the gentle folk, and they dancing. When they saw us, a little woman dressed all in red came running out from them towards us, and she struck my cousin across the face with what seemed to be a green rush. We ran for home as hard as we could, and when my cousin reached the house she fell dead. Father saddled a horse and went for Father Ryan. When Father Ryan arrived, he put a stole about his neck and began praying over my cousin and reading psalms and striking her with the stole; and in that way brought her back. He said if she had not caught hold of my brother, she would have been taken for ever. [12]

It is difficult to be scientific about these matters, of course. How do you measure malignity or fear? But even a rapid browse through the fairy sightings in this collection suggest *far less* menace than was the fairy norm in the eighteenth and nineteenth centuries. I looked through Marjorie's book for an equivalent reference to a child meeting a scary fairy. The encounter I chose here is fascinating for various reasons, but no one would, I think, say that this is frightening. At very worst it might be described as eerie: note the refusal to make eye contact, the fairy escorting the child away, and the cool touch. We are in Kent and the girl was Felicity E. Royds.

> [Felicity] found she had left some object—her coat or a toy—in the rose garden, and was sent back alone to fetch it. The rose garden was surrounded by thick yew hedges, and at the end of it was a cast-iron gate leading

into a thicket of rhododendrons. The object, which she had gone to fetch, was on the grass near this gate, and she had just retrieved it and was turning away, fearful of what might come out of the bushes, when she saw coming through the gate a small man leading a light brown horse. The man was shorter than Felicity and appeared to be wearing a blue tunic with something white at the neck. His skin was very brown, browner than his hair. The pony was about the size of a Shetland but very slender. Although she did not feel frightened, Felicity did not look at the man directly, only out of the corner of her eye. He put his hand on her wrist, and his touch was cool, not cold like a fish or lizard but much cooler than a human touch. He led her out of the rose garden and onwards until they were within sight of the house, and then stood still while she went in. She said that she was not at all musical, but while he held her hand she seemed to be aware of a strain of music that was sweet and high but sounded rather unfinished.[13]

And this is as scary as Marjorie's fairy accounts get. Not only is this sighting not the equal of the examples above from Ireland and Wales, it is also atypical in the collection. Usually the fairies here are shown to be either unconscious of, or unconcerned with, the presence of children, or they are benevolent. The following example is a nice compromise between these two positions. I've stuck again with a child's perspective.

At the age of eight or nine [Miss Berens] lived in Worcestershire, and she was pushing her dolls' pram down a lane near her home when she met a man who was obviously the worse for drink. This frightened her, and she walked quickly with her pram to a gateway, where she knew she could open the gate easily. She went through into a field, and there, just inside it, on a big, moss-covered stone, sat a sad-looking fairy with folded wings and clad in greyish clothes. The child looked round to see if the drunkard had followed her, but he had not, and when she turned to speak to the fairy it had disappeared.[14]

Nor is behaviour the only difference between pre-twentieth-century and twentieth-century fairy sightings. Fairies in Marjorie's book are invariably associated with nature: theosophists, as noted above, believed that fairies were simply part of the natural process and that each flower, rock, and body of water had its own tutelary spirit. I haven't kept score but having read this book a number of times I would guess that half of the sightings are explicitly connected with nature in theosophist terms. Compare this now to eighteenth- and nineteenth-century fairies, who lived out in the countryside, but who did not (or at least were not seen) helping plants or making trees grow higher.[15]

Even appearances change with the years. Wings are everywhere in *Seeing Fairies*: about half of the sightings have fairies fluttering around bushes or gliding from branch to branch. Eighteenth- and nineteenth-century accounts sometimes described fairies moving through the air: or in some cases moving from place to place instantly. But wings were not there in tradition. They were inserted in fairy art late in the eighteenth century. The inspiration for winged fairies almost certainly came from the sixteenth-century *putti* or cherubs (the last stink bomb of the Renaissance), angel lore, and just possibly a line of Alexander Pope's *Rape of the Lock*. By the nineteenth century fairies were often pictured with wings (and without), but I know of no nineteenth-century *encounter* where a fairy is seen flapping around. By the early twentieth century, though, this starts to change—Cottingley is crucial—and by the 1950s, when Marjorie began her collection, wings were acceptable though not *de-rigueur* fairy-wear. Today, of course, wings are the *sine qua non* of fairies. No fairy-themed children's party would be complete without two-dozen, cheap strap-on sets.[16]

All this leads us to perhaps the most intriguing problem of all. Why do fairies change with the centuries? How is it that fairies in 1700 seem to have behaved and lived and looked differently from fairies in 1950, say? Having never had a conversation with Marjorie Johnson, I cannot be sure what her answer would have been to this question. Perhaps she would have replied that fairies do not change but that our perceptions of fairies do? Fairyists from a theosophist background argue that fairies create their bodies and their clothes from our ectoplasm (a word I've never really understood), sometimes copying human observers, a view Marjorie Johnson shared to judge by this book. Perhaps they also copy human expectations? A sceptic, of course, would argue that fairies change because they are simply human projections. The human mind has created fairies and, as a result, fairies mutate according to mutable human needs and expectations. Similar arguments are made about meetings with "aliens" and other "entities," of course, and the sceptics, be they right or wrong, have the neater, simpler argument here. Marjorie Johnson's book will not, in any case, resolve that problem; the slipperiness of this topic is such that no book or study ever will. But Marjorie's heroic, life-long effort to explain fairies provides one of the most powerful torches yet to shine into (delete as appropriate) the hidden world of faery/the cobwebbed corners of the human psyche.[17]

I should note that some folklorists would disagree with the utility of this book. A number, indeed, will argue that the fairy sightings gathered here don't really count because these fairies (with their wings, pollen, and lack of anger-management issues) are not traditional fairies. But nothing could be further from the truth. These are the *new traditional fairies*, the latest version of a supernatural or fantasy creature that has been evolving since the time of the Anglo-Saxon elves and perhaps since the time of the pre-Celtic peoples of these islands. Marjorie's fairies—the bastard children of Madame Blavatsky and Oberon of the Fey—don't, it is true, resemble eighteenth and nineteenth-century fairies. But, then, the fairies of Queen Victoria's reign were different from those of Chaucer's and Shakespeare's day, and the fairies of the twenty-third century will be different from those of our time. Personally, I find Marjorie's fairies less interesting than those running around the British and Irish countryside, c.1800, bringing chaos and sometimes luck in their wake, but the aesthetics of fairies is another issue altogether.

Last Things

I want to finish this introduction with a proposal, a justification of my editing policy and, of course, thanks. First, the proposal. The Fairy Investigation Society (then under Leslie Shepard) came to an end sometime in the early 1990s. In the past months I have attempted to start the organization anew. I cannot say "bring it back to life" (as Craufurd did after the Second World War) because, for one, there is no continuity of members between the original FIS and the remodeled version; and, also, because I have tried to set the FIS up on a slightly different footing. The original FIS was open to those who believed in fairies. The refounded FIS will be open, instead, to anyone who is interested in fairy lore, believers or otherwise: it is hoped that membership will stretch from hardened folklorists, through Forteans, to the outer fringe of modern "fairies" and fairy mystics. As well as an e-letter, there will be a forum and the sharing of expertise and knowledge. If you are interested, I would direct you to my website www.fairyist.com where you can easily make contact. I also intend, in 2015, to launch, a new fairy census fifty years after the Johnson-MacGregor survey. I hope that this will mean a database of contemporary fairy belief. I will be concentrating my fire on the United Kingdom and Ireland, but I would welcome any descriptions (first- or second-hand) of fairy sightings or encounters for eventual inclusion from anywhere in the world.

Next, a few words on how this book was revived in 2013 after so many years "on ice": not least because those quoting passages might want to take into account some of the textual problems I faced before they employ Marjorie's words. The manuscript was, in the autumn of 2012, in the hands of Heather Guy, one of Marjorie's heirs. For my own research and also in view of eventual publication, Heather very kindly scanned the entire manuscript and sent it to me in pdf, simultaneously using OCR software to email it as a word processed file. My job—and it has proved a surprisingly difficult one!—was to compare the original and the scanned file and to correct the inevitable mistakes that come about when an old-fashioned typewritten manuscript of several hundred pages is fed into a computer. I was helped extensively in this by Jeannie Lukin, whose final communication on her work included the sentence: "I enjoyed a lot of these stories, but my eyes did start bleeding a bit toward the end"; sentiments I came to share. It is important to be absolutely and emphatically clear that any errors of word recognition, e.g. "bad" instead of "had" or "then" instead of "them," are entirely my own fault, as I have been through the text repeatedly and was at no stage rushed by the publisher. If some have slipped through, I apologise profoundly to Marjorie and to the reader, both of whom deserve better.

While correcting OCR errors I gradually came to realize that there were also, as was to be expected, mistakes in the manuscript. In changing the original prose I gave myself two rules: (1) the would-Marjorie-approve rule and (2) does-this-help-the-twenty-first-century-reader rule. What has this actually meant? Well, I never changed the ordering of the book, despite strong temptations to do so: but I did frequently change paragraph breaks and punctuation. I shifted the boundaries, too, between some of the later chapters, but again never changed the sequence of accounts. I corrected grammatical errors, "typos" and spelling mistakes, which I suspect that Marjorie would have spotted during proofreading. I integrated the book's two footnotes into the main text changing the language slightly to make the prose flow. I have not, at any point, changed the substance of what Marjorie wrote, even if (very, very occasionally) I felt that Marjorie or her correspondents could have expressed themselves better. There is one exception: the dedication has been altered to take in the extra reference to Leslie Shepard present in the German translation but not in the English manuscript. I presume the German translation represents a later version in this respect. On three occasions Marjorie speaks of illustrations that were to appear in the book: once in relation to an ice tracing and twice in relation to fairy photographs. In two cases these were not available, and so could not be included: I removed then the reference to printed illustrations. One of these three illustrations, however, a magnificent photograph of Marjorie playing a pan pipe to "a materialising fairy," Heather Guy found in her attic and now graces the front cover. In the chapter on angels, a page was missing from the version passed onto me by Heather, and subsequent searches in the original manuscript, by then in the hands of Wendy Constantinis, proved futile. Luckily part of this page ("When I was down at the point..." to "but I felt so happy") had been previously published in the *Fairy Investigation News-Letter* 5 (1961). For the rest I, on Wendy's suggestion, went to the German translation and retranslated back from German into English with the expert help of Droo Ray. The words from "M.K.F. Thornley, a pilgrim..." to "...experiences with angels." are, in fact, my own, but should give the sense of Marjorie's now lost page. I might note here that the German translation seems generally to have been of a high quality, though it abbreviated some episodes. Square brackets contain very occasional editorial notes. Then, a last point: Marjorie wrote her own blurb for the back cover, which has been used.

I have tried to convey in the two paragraphs above difficulties in the preparation of *Seeing Fairies*. If any reader has the suspicion that I have either failed to spot an OCR error or, far more seriously, that I have overstepped my brief in re-editing and he or she would like to check for their own purposes, then I will be very happy to pass on a scan of the relevant part of the manuscript.

Turning now from difficulties to glory I want to finish this introduction by thanking all those who have helped me in finding the manuscript, with my work on the manuscript, and with my research into the Fairy Investigation Society more generally. I take great pleasure in repeating here some of the names above and of introducing others for the first time: Karen Averby, "Dr. Beachcombing's Blog," Janet Bord, David Boyle, Jean Bullock, Chris Charman, Wendy Constantinis, Nichola Court, Adrian Gallegos, Gus Gayford, Wade Gilbreath, Rose Gordon, Heather Guy (and family), Chris Hale, Jessica Hemming, Lesley Hall, Patrick Huyghe, Stephen Lees, Jeannie Lukin, Patricia Lysaght, Suzanne Michaud, Peter Michel, Maggie Michelle, Droo Ray, Bob Rickard, Ian Russell, Chris Savia, Richard Shillitoe, Paul Sieveking, Michael Swords, Stephen Taylor, Chris Woodyard, Yvonne (whose surname I lost, sorry!), Lisi and Lea and Valentina Young, and *Folklore*'s anonymous reviewer of my 2013 FIS article. The following pages represent the life's work of an intelligent, dedicated, and passionate woman: they deserve an English-speaking public and I like to think that Marjorie Johnson would welcome, fifty years overdue, the publication of her fairy book, while being tolerant of the trifling changes I have made.

— Santa Brigida, Italy, 15 May 2014

Notes

(1) Simon Young, "A History of the Fairy Investigation Society, 1927-1960," *Folklore* 124 (2013), 139-156 at 145-146; MacGregor dedicated his *The Ghost Book: Strange Hauntings in Britain* (London, Hutchins, 1955) to Marjorie.

(2) Heather Guy remembered the following in an email, 27 Mar 2014. I include it here because it gives some idea of how Marjorie operated: "The week before she received this good news [about publication with Aquamarin] she told me that she was giving up trying to find a publisher. Her actual words were 'I'm going to get the manuscript back and give it a decent burial!' The next week when I went to see her she told me of a dream she'd had the night before. She was struggling up a big hill and Dorothy [her sister] (who had passed away several years before) and groups of fairies were urging her to keep going to the top. I remember this very clearly as the *next* week when I called in, she said 'I have wonderful news!' and told me about Leslie Shepard's success in finding a publisher. She was convinced that this dream was the fairies way of telling her to keep going and the book would be published."

(3) Young, "A History," 146-147, and Simon Young "Necrolog: Marjorie Johnson," *Fortean Times* 292 (September 2012), 26-27.

(4) Young, "A History," 140-145.

(5) *Ibid.*, 139.

(6) *Ibid.*, 145-148, note that the date 1950 comes from the blurb (written by Marjorie Johnson) and included on the back of the present volume. The letter from the little girl appears in the *Fairy Investigation Society News-letter* 4 (Summer 1959). The membership lists are reprinted in Young, "A History," 151-153.

(7) MacGregor, "Letter to the Editor" in *The Listener* 53 (1955), 526 and *Folklore* 66 (1955), 302.

(8) An email from Heather Guy, 14 Feb 2014.

(9) This account came in a phone interview with Rose Gordon 12 Jul 2012: note that a similar account is to be found in this volume from another home-help, Maureen, who saw "a little shining thing" in Marjorie's house, p. 168.

(10) pp. 100-101.

(11) Jones, *The Appearance*, 65-66.

(12) Evans-Wentz, *Fairy Faith*, 72-73

(13) pp. 54-55.

(14) p. 45.

(15) A very rare exception to this is to be found in Simon Young "Three Notes on West Yorkshire Fairies in the Nineteenth Century," *Folklore* 123 (2012), 223-230

(16) A study on fairy wings is badly needed. The most interesting comment known to me appears in Katharine Briggs, *The Anatomy of Puck: An Examination of Fairy Beliefs among Shakespeare's Contemporaries and Successors* (London, Routledge and Kegan Paul 1959), 9-10. An intriguing early instance from semi-traditional (?) lore is to be found in Abraham Elder, "A Legend of Puckaster, Isle of Wight," *Bentley's Miscellany* 4 (1839) 368-380.

(17) For "entities" always stimulating (and occasionally outrageous) are the writings of Hilary Evans: *Gods, Spirits, Cosmic Guardians: A Comparative Study of the Encounter Experience* (Aquarian Press 1987); and *Visions, Apparitions, Alien Visitors: A Comparative Study of the Entity Enigma* (Thorsons, 1984).

For rich-veined Orpheus sweetly did rehearse
How that the seeds of fire, air, water, earth,
Were all locked in the vast void universe;
And how from these as firstlings all had birth...
— Virgil, Eclogue VI

DEDICATED

to my sister DOROTHY
who shared with me so many interesting experiences

And to
ALASDAIR ALPIN MACGREGOR
Who collaborated with me in collecting reports of fairies
during the years 1955-1957

And to
The radiant being who gave me the fairies' permission to
compile this book, and who helped me to obtain a few true stories
up to the time I met Alasdair Alpin MacGregor

And to
LESLIE SHEPARD for his extraordinary efforts in finding a
publisher for this book.

Foreword
by Capt. Sir Quentin C.A. Craufurd[**]

Fairies! Who am I to write a foreword to such a book? I have been asked to do so because I have approached the subject from a different angle. I have conducted a host of researches and have arrived at the conclusion that the so-called Fairy Race exists. Its Kingdom is very vast and embraces creatures of varying intelligence, some of which are very close to humanity.

I have no extended vision in the sense that is generally understood. So in place of clairvoyance I have had to lumber along with scientific instruments, those and the blinkers imposed on me by textbooks and a college training.

I was brought up to the Navy, and being of a scientific leaning I took a course of physics in Greenwich College. It has been my hobby, as far back as I can remember, to trace the action of mind upon matter, believing, as I do, that nothing is completely unconscious of its Creator. This biologist's study of material may be faultless, but the invisible part, which propels the mind of a creature, remains a secret.

One gets on intimate terms with wild creatures on shipboard. In the confines of a small cabin, little derelicts, which have lost their way on migration, settle down wearily and become happy in snug quarters. Very often it happens that a wild or frightened bird grows curiously content if it has slept close to you and you also have slept. What occurs during sleep, one does not know, but the desire to get on friendly terms penetrates the creature's armour so to speak, or it may be that contact is made with its group spirit in other regions. At least, that is the explanation given in the East. Through these der-

---

[**] Capt. Sir Quentin C.A. Craufurd, BT, M.B.E. R.N. (Retd.). F.R.S.A., F.I.N.T.P., A.M.I.E.E. etc., was president of the Fairy Investigation Society. He passed away on May 8, 1957, age 82, before the completion of this book. Since then, many other accounts have been added that were not from members of the now-defunct Fairy Investigation Society. — Marjorie Johnson

elict or injured wayfarers I made, as I believe, my progress towards Faerie.

When at last I had swallowed the anchor and retired to have a garden of my own, with time and opportunity I carried out private researches. With my electrical appliances I pushed on from warm-blooded, warm-hearted little creatures, who played about in my laboratory and workshop, and through the expanse of cold-blooded creatures and even insects, to the kingdom of the flowers, the Vegetable Kingdom.

I was well equipped to follow on the lines of Sir J. C. Bose, the eminent director of the Bose Plant Institute of Calcutta, India, and one of the earliest radio pioneers. I myself was early in radio about the time when Marconi brought his first experiment to England. Where Bose had paved the way, I could copy and explore. He traced the nerve response of animals down through the Vegetable Kingdom. In flowers he found responses that could be equated with pleasure, fear, and pain. You may detect the passing of living matter between two polarised plates of zinc. It may be visible: a casual bird assistant; a mouse prospecting for a tit-bit; or something strangely living that you cannot see. And so on, from mere echoes, or response to stimulus, until at last there comes reflection from some mind of will—a fairy call.

In my case I began with an electrical apparatus of my own design and a nearly worn-out torch-battery, and one day I heard fairy music, the sound of harps and bells. "Something" knew I was incredulous and yet delighted.

It answered to my voice. "Something" present in the laboratory could answer with intelligence; could be amused at my incredulity; could obligingly repeat the signals for a guest, so that two people heard the same thing in different telephone receivers.

There were, then, fairies who could find amusement in two human beings who did not believe in fairies! One of my early questions was: "Are there, then, such creatures as fairies?"

The reply came: "They are all around you."

"Then why cannot we see them?"

"Your minds are not tuned!"

"How do you mean 'tuned'?"

"Your ether machine is tuned and you are not."

"Ether machine? Do you mean that box over there?" I pointed to the wireless.

"Of course," came the prompt reply.

So that was that! We had to tune in to what was about us or remain ignorant.

Later they said, "We are under a different set of natural laws, but we can appreciate yours."

For five years, 1927 to 1932, nine of these little elves (they told us they were marsh fairies) played with us and other utterly incredulous visitors, who came to be converted or to attempt to expose some base illusion. The fairies triumphed. In the workshop and laboratory, in our drawing room or garden, they gave evidence of their mischief and their power. They also gave evidence of their knowledge. They would write for us and use strange words of ancient Saxon for which we had to find the meaning—words such as *blid*, the root of "blithe," meaning "full of life" such as a fresh-plucked flower, which they could delight in as against a bunch, which had been kept in water for some days. They also showed how they could affect and change the growth of flowers in a garden, and how they could pass through walls and closed doors. They also told of ancient remains buried far under the ground, in some cases confirmed where it was practicable.

My tame jackdaw could see them. They teased him, and he seemed jealous and regarded them with grave suspicion. Sometimes he would move his head about oddly, following something we could not see at all, and the fairies told us they had been dancing to the music of our wireless. At our request, they danced on the flowers by the cupboard and made them move in time with the music.

As I say, I had no psychic sight, but there were others who had clairvoyant vision and who could see them. One of these was Mr. Bernard Sleigh, who had written a book called *The Gates of Horn*, which was recommended to me by a psychic friend. Mr. Sleigh had conceived the idea of a "Society for the Investigation of Faery Fact and Fallacy," around which he had written accounts of fairy tradition, and so on. I liked the book and got into communication with him, and in 1927 we decided to form such a society to be called "the Fairy Investigation Society": he with fairy vision and I with a pair of crutches called modern science.

In those days certain religious communities were against us. But since then it has come to light that even some of the clergy and bishops have seen the fairy folk and proved for themselves that these are not, after all, evil beings, but are radiant little creatures working with humanity under the Divine Will of our mutual Creator.

Mrs. Claire H. Cantlon, a fairy seer, was then the Hon. Secretary, and a few of us met at first at a house in London. Those were the halcyon days.

It was the policy of the Society to remain rather secret, for we heard accounts from members who wished to hide their identity since they held high official positions, and we heard enough to know how strongly fairy-vision was established. But other members got restive and wished to move into publicity and on commercial lines, and there were a few rather foolish people drawn by a love of the sensational. We had not all the same motives and the same language, and the Society disintegrated like the walls of the Tower of Babel.

The original few held together until the advent of the Second World War, when meetings had to be abandoned altogether, and in 1940 the records in my possession were scattered by enemy action. Out of the salvage I was beginning to try to piece something together with the idea of a book when, by one of those chances that seem to be design, Marjorie T. Johnson and I were brought together. She had been collecting for some time just the very things we had hoped to collect for the Society's records, accounts from those who claimed to possess "the fairy sight," and she became Honorary Secretary of a resurrected Fairy Investigation Society.

In a book of this kind it is difficult to know what to present and what to withhold. My advice would be to withhold nothing. Let the reader pick and choose.

For myself, I have crossed the Rubicon. I know that fairies exist, and this book has my hearty approval and bears herewith my personal congratulations.

Introduction
by Marjorie T. Johnson

I would like to express my gratitude to all contributors, young and old, who have made this book possible. They have written from many parts of the British Isles and overseas, and the general tone of their correspondence has been one of mingled pleasure and relief, for many of these men and women have kept their fairy experiences a closely guarded secret owing to the ridicule and scepticism they received from their relatives and friends, or anyone to whom they had mentioned the subject. One lady wrote: "It is so nice to know that someone else has seen fairies besides myself. I saw them when I was a child, but I was laughed at so often that gradually I ceased to go where they were, and did not speak of them again, though my belief in them has never faltered."

This feeling is shared by hundreds of fairy seers, some of whom are now between 80 and 90 years of age, yet they still cherish the memory of their lovely visions of Faerie. As Mrs. Dorothy Jenner wrote in a letter to *Prediction* in 1971: "Only the most stubborn cynic would suggest that hundreds of observers were either mistaken or deliberately dishonest."

It must indeed have been an "eye-opening" experience for the angler in Australia who turned round to see quite close to him a tiny creature with a Desert Pea flower for a hat and leaves from the same plant for its dress; the lady who came upon a busy group of elves in the woodlands, collecting twigs and tidying-up their haunts; and the twin sisters who saw a fairy whose colouring was "of a delicate blue surrounded by tinkerbell light, and glowing like a little star in the evening shadows."

It is sad when parents refuse to listen sympathetically to a child's babble, for children at an early age are still closely linked with the invisible worlds, and the etheric part of their eyes is not yet fully co-ordinated with the physical, so they think there is nothing unusual about seeing fairies and perhaps playing with them.

My own belief in them was fully justified at the age of six, when

9

a friendly little elf invited itself into our house, and as I grew older I became filled with a burning desire to keep the Fairy Faith alive and to know more about this fascinating evolution that runs parallel to and merges with our own. I was helped in this by the kindness of the late Mr. S. Carlyle Potter, who put his library of antiquarian and modern books at my disposal, and from these I learned that a knowledge of the existence and work of these nature spirits was part of the Ancient Wisdom, and was extant in the literature and teachings of the Theosophical, Anthroposophical, Rosicrucian, and other Mystery Schools, esoteric societies, and certain religious organizations, orders, and trusts, including the White Eagle Lodge with its Publishing Trust and the Iona and Findhorn Communities. The Chalice Well gardens in Glastonbury contain many fairies and water spirits, according to the Founder of the Trust, the late Major W. Tudor Pole.

Fairy lore is certainly not a childish subject; it is deep and boundless, and the more one studies it, the more one realises how limited is one's knowledge of something that is so vitally important, not only to the human race but to the whole of creation. Thomas à Kempis spoke truly when he said: "If thou thinkest that thou understandest and knowest much, yet know that there be many more things which thou knowest not."

Paracelsus and the ancient philosophers classified these spirits of the elements of Earth, Water, Air, and Fire under four main groups—Gnomes, Undines, Sylphs, and Salamanders, respectively. There are, of course, many different kinds under the various headings, and the graceful little flower-fairies are a type of Sylphs.

All these beings are the manipulators of the forces of Nature. They are active in the Mineral, Vegetable, Animal, and Human Kingdoms, and play an essential part in the Divine Plan. Their bodies are fluidic and self-luminous, and they can assume different forms, but mostly imitate the human. They may also be seen as pulsating clouds of colour, or as tiny etheric lights. Some of them have wands, which are a symbol of authority in the Fairy World. All these nature spirits are part of the Angelic Hierarchy and evolve eventually into Angels.

Every flower and tree contains within it the archetype, or Divine Idea, of what it is to become, and it is the nature spirits who help to bring this into manifestation. They are ready and willing to cooperate with us in every aspect of human life if we will learn to obey Nature's fundamental laws.

Because our bodies are composed of the solids, liquids, gases, and ethers of the elements, there is constant action and reaction between us and this elemental life, which is all around and within us. I have been asked why it is that some people can see fairies while others cannot. The faculty is latent in everyone, but in many cases, for various reasons, it has not been unfolded or used in this present incarnation, so those who are able to "see" should not think that they have been endowed with a special gift that raises them above others!

Some have only transitory flashes of clairvoyance in times of stress or of great joy, or when they are thinking of "nothing in particular," which has been the case with several of my contributors. In others it has been developed through constant prayer and meditation, and there are also those who have direct intuitive spiritual perception.

It is always dangerous to try to force the psychic faculty, and my contributor Mrs. Emma S. King, whose accounts of fairies and angels are in this book, gave the following words of wisdom: "True occultism to me is living whole-heartedly what one learns from the daily tasks, no matter how difficult or monotonous they may be; and thinking steadily on a widening field of love and tolerance. Therein lies spiritual progression, and the best and surest means of opening the doors of clairvoyance and clairaudience safely, as and when a person is ready."

Mrs. King had full, conscious control of the inner vision, and she told me that when she had these experiences during a church service, she usually kept her full physical consciousness, although active and alert on the other planes. She looked inward from the mental body and noted what was happening astrally, while her physical body just sat quietly awake on the church seat.

We humans have free will, but the nature spirits' work is instinctual, and they joyously obey the Divine Intention. That is why they are nearly always seen to be smiling. In some of the little elves, pixies, and manikins this happiness is shown by a wide "grin," but in the higher types it is a smile of radiant joy and exaltation, which they can in some measure impart to the fortunate onlooker. It is interesting to note that a similar expression of bliss appears on the face of a meditating yogi when he reaches the state of union with God.

One of the loveliest sights is that of a flower fairy tending her plant. She rises above it to absorb the vital universal energy from the atmosphere about and, after pausing to assimilate it, she sinks back and pours it, together with her own life-force, into the plant, causing its etheric double to glow as it imbibes the power. During this oft-repeated three-fold process, the face of the fairy-guardian is full of ecstasy.

When the nature spirits wish to materialize at the physical-etheric level, in order to be seen more clearly by each other and by certain human beings, they can slow down the rate of their vibrations so that they are on a different wavelength, and when they want to vanish they increase the vibrations again, and so disappear from human sight into a higher dimension. (What a pity that all exploited birds and animals cannot do likewise when faced with their human persecutors.)

The fairies are not the only ones who are able to do this, however, for there are certain highly evolved people such as Masters and Adepts working for the good of the world, who have such a great expansion of consciousness that the vibratory rate of their atoms can be raised at will to dematerialize their earthly bodies and work among us unseen, or lowered to re-materialize them when physical contact is necessary.

Certain people refuse to believe in fairies because they remain invisible to them, so they think they must be figments of the seer's imagination. But in reality we ourselves are invisible Spirit, only seen by each other because we are materialized and individualized in a temporary physical body, in order to function on the Earth plane for a while. Our eyes can take in only a limited number of vibrations, so there must be countless beings around us who are invisible to us because they are on different wavelengths, and that might apply to some of the inhabitants of other planets, for they could possess bodies more ethereal than ours, and they might absorb their nourishment from the atmosphere or produce etheric food, like the fairies do. Humans and non-humans, we are all just different expressions of the one all-pervading Life.

It is said that cynics and sceptics do not like to believe in anything until they have proof, while others are content to remain unbiased until it is disproven. I hope my readers will keep an open mind, and then they might experience some of the fairies' radiant carefree joy, and perhaps regain that sense of wonder that is sadly lacking in the lives of so many people in the world today.

Chapter 1: Nature Spirits in Gardens and the Countryside

In the summer of 1955, Mrs. Beverley C. Milligan, an Australian living in Scotland, went picnicking with her Scottish husband on the slopes above Loch Duich. The time was about 2 p.m., and after the meal they were lying quietly in the sun in a grassy space among the bracken and heather, when Mrs. Milligan became aware of a movement at the corner of the clearing. Gently she drew her husband's attention to two small figures that had emerged from the bracken and were crossing the clear space towards a further stretch of bracken. Both of the wee folks were dressed in greenish breeches and short coats of a heathery shade. They were hatless, and one was darker than the other. They also varied in height, one being about ten inches high and the other two inches shorter. Between them they were carrying a bundle, which seemed to be very heavy, though they made no sound. Mr. and Mrs. Milligan were astounded and could hardly believe their eyes. They rose and walked in the direction in which the tiny pair had gone, and were lucky enough to catch another glimpse of them just going into a hazel thicket a few yards away. Needless to say, when this experience was recounted in the days that followed, it received little credence, but as Mrs. Milligan so wisely said: "It seems quite clear that when folklore the world over is so full of fairy beliefs, there must be some factual foundation for it all."

Her 92-year-old grandmother, who was of Danish birth, was brought up in the Queensland outback in pioneering days, and often she would tell her and the other grandchildren how she had, on a few occasions, watched the little people in lonely places in the Bush, when she herself was young. She was most emphatic about it when her grandchildren treated her story as a joke, and she described these fairies as tiny brown people wearing scanty clothes, like loincloths, the fairy women wearing the same kind of clothing

15

as the men. She had seen them by a creek, drawing water in what appeared to be small earthenware pots. She had also watched them seemingly at play, and again when they were dancing.

On the cold, clear, moonlit night of 24 December 1953, at about 11:35 p.m., Mr. G. was walking up a road in Ewell, Surrey, in company with two friends, Mr. C. and Mr. F., when a small misshapen figure about five feet in height ran across the road in front of them. "The face could not be discerned, but one gained the impression of sharp features. The clothing was undoubtedly bottle green, and a conical hat was worn, with an edging of fur. Knee-boots completed the rig." This dwarf, or gnome, never reached the other side of the road, but disappeared about two feet from the opposite kerb. "Unfortunately," said Mr. G., "Mr. F. maintains to this day that he heard and saw absolutely nothing. Mr. C., however, corroborates my story. We are all, without exception, teetotallers."

One hears many stories of thorn trees that are held sacred by the fairies. Here is an account from Mrs. E. C. Thomson, of Sydney, New South Wales, Australia: "When I was about twelve years old I went from my Scottish home in Peebles to spend a holiday in Ireland as the guest of my mother's cousin. She was married to the Rev. Joseph Moorhead, whose home was at a Manse near Ballymena, Co. Antrim. The grounds around the Manse were quite extensive, and my host told me that under a hawthorn tree on the way down to a stream, which ran past one side of the grounds, the fairies sometimes played, and he would like me to see them. 'We must choose a moonlit night and the grass must be dry,' he said. On three nights he took me to the place, but the grass was damp and we saw nothing. On the fourth night, however, things were ideal, and a very excited little girl saw about twenty fairies dancing under a white hawthorn tree. It was one of the prettiest sights I have ever seen, and I have never forgotten it."

Another contributor who was privileged to see a similar sight was Mrs. Andrew Crawford Fields, of Co. Derry, Ireland. She remembered that when she was ten years old she was standing on the side of an old fort called Lemon's Rock, near Newtownstewart, Co. Tyrone, and looking down into an adjoining field in which was a fairy thorn. It was about 8 o'clock on a bright evening in July, and as she stood gazing she saw a number of little folk dancing in a circle around the tree. They were dressed in different colours, and she watched them and heard the sound of singing and sweet music for about fifteen minutes, until a horse and cart came along the road at the top of the rocks, and the little folk disappeared. The fairy thorn was noted for having a brown ring around it on which the grass never grew. "And," said Mrs. Fields, "we were warned as children not to go inside this ring lest the little folk should take us. The Lemon family saw them dancing many times, but I saw them only on this occasion."

Mrs. Ada F. Constable used to live in a small bungalow alone in a field, some distance from the village of Walesby, Notts. One day her small son, aged three or four years, was looking out of the window on to the garden, appearing to watch something very intently, so she said "What are you looking at?" And he replied, "The funny little man." She asked what he was like, and her son gave her a fair description of what she associated with a dwarf or gnome, wearing a long, pointed cap with the point tapering towards the front. On her asking what he was doing, she was told with no surprise or excitement: "He's working in the beans, Mummy."

Four men, who wished their names and addresses to be withheld, thought they saw some wee folk near a large drain in Lincolnshire. The time was early evening and the sun was setting and casting reflections in the water, which at that period of the year was high and reached the top of the long grass at the sides. This made them wonder whether they were the victims of an optical illusion, the only repudiation being that not only one but all four of them were able to observe these creatures, whose clothes were of various colours: red jerkins and green breeches, yellow jerkins and mauve breeches. In height they were approximately nine inches, and both bodily and facially bore resemblance to humans. On seeing the four men, who were traversing the path near the water's edge, the little people darted into a nearby mustard-field.

The next account: "We were spending our summer holiday at the beautiful little fishing village of St. Ives," related the Misses O.

and N. Burnet. "It was a lovely summer. The weather was perfect; and, amongst other things, we had been revelling in the rugged beauty of the Cornish coast and the heather-clad moors. We decided that on the night of the full moon we would make up a party and drive by car along the moorland road to Lands End, there to partake of an *al fresco* meal on the rocks by moonlight. The day arrived, and we packed our hampers into the cars that were to take us along the coastal road to our destination, and set off. After a very short time we found ourselves right out on the moors. Not a sound was to be heard but the purr of the car engines. The moon lit up the road ahead of us like a white ribbon, and below us on the right lay the sea, sparkling in the bay. We had our meal and were returning along this same road, the silence still unbroken save for the snap of a twig as a wild moorland sheep or other animal scuttled out of the way, when suddenly across the track shuffled a small figure which stopped short, dazzled by the headlights of the car. My brother put on his brakes and drew the car to an abrupt standstill, and so did the driver of the car following, which was about to pass us. The figure resembled that of a little man barely two and a half feet high. He had a hairy face and very long arms, but the most striking thing about him was his very long, pointed feet, upon which he moved in a sort of shuffling manner. He wore on his head a hat of the same shape and shade as a mushroom, and his clothing, to which we did not pay much attention, was, as far as I can remember, of a darker shade of brown, and green. With terrified eyes, which shone in the light of the headlamps, he blinked and hesitated for a second or two, and, just as quickly and silently as he had appeared, he was gone. The two men in the car behind us got out, for they too had seen this strange figure for a fleeting second or two. We all looked over the low stone wall that bordered the moorland road, but there was no sign of him."

Mr. John Neary, of Houghton-le-Spring, County Durham, saw fairies on two occasions, but the second experience, which he had in 1954, was clearer in his memory. He was sitting in a wood on a hot day in July, reading some of Keats' poems, in preparation for a public examination, and had just reached the second verse of the

Ode to Autumn, when his attention was distracted by a light movement in a clump of bluebells. At first he thought it was a bird, but on looking again he saw that it was a fairy of indescribable beauty and lace-like delicacy. When he discussed this apparition with members of his family, they were sceptical, with the exception of his father, an Irishman, who affirmed that all his family had at one time or another seen leprechauns.

"We thought you might be interested to hear of an experience of ours," wrote Mr. J. L. Presland. "In August 1954, Mr. A. Malone and I were walking in the countryside near Caterham, Surrey, and presently we sat down under a tree for a smoke. We had been there some time, when suddenly I noticed a small head peering round the trunk of the tree. I gazed at it in amazement, but it disappeared before I could draw Mr. Malone's attention to it. We went to look round the other side of the tree, though my friend was laughing derisively. As there was no trace of it, I decided I must have imagined it, but as soon as we began to walk on, both of us saw a small figure dart out of a bush, run about ten yards, and then disappear into another bush. In size it was about nine inches high, with a body well-proportioned except for the head, which seemed too small and bore very little hair. It had a brownish-coloured skin, and did not appear to be wearing any clothes. We made a thorough search of the bush into which the creature had disappeared, and also an area round it, but we found nothing. We could not say definitely whether it was a fairy, for it had no wings, but we do not see what else it could have been. We are, however, quite certain that we saw it."

At their grandmother's house in West Sussex, Michal (later to become Mrs. Johnstone) and her twin sister, Peggie, saw a tiny figure appear for a few seconds beside them on the lawn. "We were agreed," she said, "that it was a female fairy. Our impression of her colouring was of a delicate blue surrounded by 'tinker-bell' light, and glowing like a little star in the evening shadows." The twins were only about six at the time, but when Mrs. Johnstone wrote in 1955 she declared that although sixteen years had elapsed, the vivid picture of that experience still remained with her and her sister, and they both could give an identical description of what they had seen.

Seeing Fairies

The first gnome that Mrs. L. F. Small, of Nottingham, saw was in Epsom Forest, off Friday Street. There was a dirty bit of rope round the bottom of a tree, and the little gnome was standing looking at it with an expression of extreme annoyance on his face. She received the impression it was his tree, and that he very much resented the rope being there. When Mrs. Small lived in Richmond Drive, she had some pink dwarf Canterbury bells on the rockery in her garden. One day she saw a lovely gossamer-winged fairy with the sweetest little hands, gently tending these plants. Her next experience was in 1940. She was sitting by her French window, which overlooked the garden where she had some outdoor tomato plants. She was not used to growing these, and the main shoots had been taken off in mistake for the side-shoots. As she sat looking out, she became aware of two little gnomes about one foot high, standing pointing to where the first crop of tomatoes should be. In their green and brown tunics, they blended so perfectly with the green plants and the brown wall in the background that they may have been there for some time before she noticed them. Their faces were puckered and they looked so distressed that she sent out thoughts of apology for damaging the plants, and they turned and looked at her very solemnly and then disappeared. A short time afterwards, when she was busy mending in her room, she became conscious of somebody at her feet, and on looking down she saw the same two little gnomes, holding between them a queer, flat basket of green tomatoes. They kept looking at her very seriously, and then at the tomatoes, and she felt they were trying to tell her something. She opened her mind to receive their message, which was to the effect that if she gathered the tomatoes at once, while they were green, and wrapped them up and put them in a dark place to ripen, she would still have a good crop. When they realised she understood them, they walked solemnly away.

Miss Mary Brameld told me that she and her sister Elizabeth often sensed the little folk when they visited the country, and on different occasions she had seen a gnome standing by her side, sometimes with a rake in his hands, and always smiling. She saw him "only in a flash," so never had a chance to observe all the details of his clothes. She knew he wore a pointed cap, a little jacket and trousers, and that the colours were red and green, but she wasn't sure whether the cap and jacket were red and the trousers green, or *vice versa*.

The next account came from Mrs. Carolyn E. Penny of Sholing, Southampton, who described herself as "a housewife with seven people to care for, so naturally not given to much dreaming." She was washing-up after lunch, looking straight through the window in front of her, when, in the sunlight, which was slanting between her house and the next, she saw a fairy flying slowly in an upright position, her wings working from back to front in a slow opening and shutting movement, as those of a butterfly do when it is sunning itself. Every forward movement hid her face from view. Her little hands were crossed and lying on her dress, which was knee-length and of a sparkling gauze-like material. Her wings were coloured in pastel shades, as also were her shoes. Her tiny feet "moved in a sort of walking way," and she looked like a very large fuchsia-flower travelling along.

Mrs. Penny was startled, and called to her children: "Quickly to the front door—here's a fairy." They all rushed out, and of course the fairy was nowhere to be seen. "I was told it was not April the first," she said. But in spite of being teased by her family, Mrs. Penny maintained that it was not a dragonfly, a butterfly, or a bird that she saw. She knew that she really had seen a fairy and would believe in fairies until her dying day.

A civil servant in South Africa, Mr. Leslie Spence said he thought he must have possessed some psychic faculty in his early childhood, as he had a distinct recollection of seeing a group of some half-dozen little men, clad in brown tights and jerkins and wearing brown hats, doing a stiff-legged dance around a hummock of earth: "I was with some adult (probably my father) at the time, but he did not seem to see the little men, and I was too young to be able to tell him about them. I was not too happy about my safety, and I held tightly on to his hand and urged him to move on."

Miss Ann R. Boote, of Cheshire, wrote that she had seen fairies of all descriptions in natural surroundings and had watched them

21

working on the flowers and trees in her garden. From her own experience she found that the fairies appear to those who give out a sympathetic vibration, and from this they seem to build up their form, which they are able to vary at will. Their general appearance, she said, "can change in colour and shape in just a 'blink of the eye'." She confirmed the opinion of many seers, that fairies are best seen in bright sunlight, when their actions become stronger and their appearance clearer.

In 1935, Mrs. Emma S. King, of Australia, was living in a Queen Anne villa situated in a big landscaped garden on the corner of two busy streets. She loved this home and garden, every brick and flower of it; every tree and blade of grass. The gardener came one day a week, and they worked well together, for she was willing to learn all he could teach her, and he had found someone who loved every flower he grew. Consequently his work became a joy, and often he went for two days instead of one each week. "How that garden appreciated being loved and worked for," she told me, "and how it bloomed. Not only was it beautiful itself, but it gave such an abundance of lovely flowers for all the rooms, as well as for friends who had no gardens." One morning, Mrs. King carried in a big flower-basket of dahlias, which she had cut to arrange for the house. They were large blooms, the size of a plate, and the head of one fell off, so she put it flat in a wide soup-plate on the kitchen table under the window. After she had arranged and carried the last vase into the drawing room, she walked back quietly down the long hall to the door of the kitchen and stopped in amazement. There, on the flower head in the soup plate was an exquisite fairy, almost a living, breathing extension of the flower and of the same lovely tints and sheen, only more radiant. Mrs. King watched it for a while and then, being alone in the house except for the big old watchdog, prepared her lunch on the end of the table and ate it while she gazed at the lovely creature. "The members of my family, when they came home, were very much interested," she told me. The boys asked her innumerable times, "Is it still there, Mum?" The fairy stayed with the flower until it faded. On the second day it seemed to lose its sheen as the life in the flower receded. Then it disappeared.

The next experience was in the drawing room, a big, bow-windowed room, where Mrs. King went for a quiet read and short meditation each day about 11 a.m. Her eyes were drawn to a tall, slender, pink vase on the top bracket of the mantelpiece, containing one large dahlia. There, clinging to the flower and breathing and vibrating as an extension of it, was another exquisite fairy of the same order, about nine-to-twelve-inches tall. She looked at it and admired its beauty for a few minutes, then was called away and forgot it for a time, but like the other one it disappeared as the freshness of the flower faded. Mrs. King found that grass fairies were quite different: "Almost like animated, flowing blades of grass; tiny little fellows more like gnomes than fairies." Her attention was drawn to another order of nature spirits one morning when she was weeding a row of early bulbs before they came through the earth. There was a humming rhythm that she knew and felt came from the bulbs with the returning life of spring. "This humming rhythm ceases," she explained, "when the first green tips of the new shoots break through the soil." Beside the front gate was a large, white-flowering, plum tree in which lived a nature spirit of a higher order, almost four feet tall. "I loved that tree, and the being who lived in it," she said, "but when the North gales tore at the branches, whether I could see them toss and sway or not, I ached in my body with the tree and the stress of the storm."

Another contributor writing from Australia was Mr. J. Boris Robertson, who had the following experience in October 1955, while staying in Cloncurry, Queensland: "When fishing recently, north of here (in the Leichhardt River), I was fortunate enough to make my first acquaintance with a fairy. I had been some hours at this rather secluded spot and was lost in thought, when something made me turn round and there, quite close to me, was a quaint little thing not six inches tall, with a Desert Pea flower for a hat, and leaves from the same plant forming the rest of its attire. I made a sudden move, which seemed to startle the gentle creature. It fled into the bush, and I now regret that in my amazement I made no attempt to follow it. I need hardly say that I have never before discussed this matter with anyone for fear of incurring adverse comment."

Seeing Fairies

Mrs. J. Hanley related that while on a visit to Wales as a girl of about eighteen, she had been trout fishing in a mountain lake about Betws-y-Coed with a young man friend. As the light was too bright for them to hope to catch anything, they set off for home about 3 o'clock. It was a lovely afternoon of brilliant sunshine, with not a breath of wind. "Our track," she said, "was a grassy path about the width of a farm cart and lay between banks of heather, with now and then an outcrop of rock or an old thorn tree, or some bracken and gorse, to break the outline. The mountaintop was level and one could see a good distance in all directions. As we walked along talking, I began to have that sensation most of us know at some time or another, the feeling that there was someone walking behind me. I turned instinctively and saw a little man about two feet high, who looked rather as if he had been put together out of sticks or the twisty roots of gorde. He seemed to me to be swaggering along, mocking us, I think, as a small boy might do. I turned to my companion to say 'Look, quick!' But even as I turned, I realised that I had seen something extraordinary, and that if I made him look and there was nothing there to see, I would feel a fool. I thought I had better take another look myself first and did so, but the little figure was no longer visible, so fearing to appear childish or silly, I decided not to say anything after all to my companion. Nevertheless, I had the feeling that there were others, still watching us, to whom we were objects of derision, and that I had just happened to be quick enough to have seen one of them, caught him unawares, in fact."

Like the previous contributor, Commander T. A. Powell was trout fishing in Wales when he had a strange experience, but in his letter to me he wished to make it clear that he was not the type of man to see visions. Here is his story: "It was about 11 a.m. on a summer morning, in a place where a river flowed below a large area of wild moorland. I was fly-fishing for trout on the left bank, casting to the opposite bank, as there were streamers of mud in midstream, which made it difficult to land fish. I hooked a half-pound trout, and, while playing it clear of the weeds, I became aware of an excited chatter in a high-pitched voice on the far bank slightly upstream of me, i.e. some 45 degrees away from the direction in

24

which I was fishing. It was the typical staccato speech of a Welsh-
man talking English, and as far as I can remember the words were
'Catch him, Tommy; I like to eat trouts, Tommy man; give him to
me, Tommy.' I glanced up (foolishly, as the trout took this opportunity of getting tied up in the weed), and saw that my visitor, though
not tiny enough to be in the Little People category, was small and
looked like an oldish man of, say, 65, hatless, with wisps of grey hair
and a short, grizzled beard. He was in his shirtsleeves (colour forgotten) and had very bright green trousers, which came high up his
waist. He was dancing about and waving his arms. I was naturally
astonished and annoyed, as fishing is, for me, a solitary vice; but I
said 'All right, but I haven't got him yet,' or something of the sort.
He paid no attention to this remark, but kept on with his gabble: 'I
like trouts, Tommy!' I concentrated for a few seconds on extricating
the fish from the weed. During that time I was delighted to notice
that the gabble had ceased. As I drew the fish into the shallows, I
looked up and my visitor had evaporated. This really did give me a
shock, and my heart missed a beat. He had disappeared completely
in open ground, as he could not have regained the stile at the end of
the road-bridge some 150 yards away and uphill in the few seconds
during which I had looked away. I made enquiries in the village,
but nobody knew or had seen anyone in any way like the visitor I
had described. *How did he know my name?*"

In view of the foregoing account, it is interesting to note that in
1921 the late Dr. Thomas Wood, Mus. D., heard a clear, faintly-
mocking, high-pitched voice calling "Tommy! Tommy!" and again,
nearer, "Tommy!" when he was sitting in a lonely spot on Dartmoor
in steamingly hot weather composing the music to Miss Clemence
Dane's *Will Shakespeare*. None of the other people in his camping party ever called him Tommy, and although he searched, and
looked through his field-glasses, there was no sign of any human
being. He received a clue to the mystery on the following day, however, for while he was sitting in the same place he heard fairy music, which he wrote down and included in his autobiography *True
Thomas* (Jonathan Cape, London).

When Miss Barbara M. Pleydell-Driver was at boarding school

in Bawdsey, Suffolk, there was a music mistress who told her that she always saw fairies and elves in the very early morning when the dew was on the grass, and that she watched them collecting the dewdrops. Of course the schoolgirl Barbara longed to see them and begged the mistress to allow her to go to her bedroom at 6 a.m. "This I did, full of great expectation," she said, "only to find I could not see them, but could only listen to her wonderful description of the scene on the lawns."

M.B., a rector's daughter, recalled the day at Pomeroy when she and her mother and sister decided to go to the village, and as they were setting off down the rectory avenue, laughing and talking as they went, she noticed a tiny man standing between the avenue gates. She pointed him out to her two companions, but they couldn't see anything although she saw him quite plainly, even his little face. She said he was wearing a brown pixie cap, a red coat, and brown trousers, and he stayed there for several minutes before he disappeared.

Miss Gladys Rowlett, of Sussex, saw fairies frequently during her childhood, and in 1949 she caught a glimpse of one about eight inches long, with large, gauzy wings, flying through the garden by harvest moonlight. It was surrounded by a radiant glow and was very lovely.

At the age of six, the journalist Miss Rosemary Meynell stayed for a few weeks at a cottage in Worsley, near Manchester, with her aunt and uncle and a young cousin of her own age. While she was there, another guest in the house (the late Mr. A. A. Naylor) said that he would show them some fairies. A great many preparations were made, including the carrying of a concave mirror into the garden and the burning of incense, and Mr. Naylor indicated the exact spot where the children, and the grown-ups with them, ought to see the fairies. They saw nothing. Later, when the cousin had gone to bed, Mr. Naylor suggested that Rosemary should go and look in the copper beech trees at the edge of the garden, which he claimed were great favourites with fairies. It was there she saw them: "small people (some coloured green and others the colour of copper-beech leaves) sitting on the leaves and twigs quite high up in the branches." She had the impression that they were scrambling about busily, intent on their own business. She had no idea how many there were; perhaps a dozen seen indistinctly and one or two quite recognisable little men, their clothes, faces, hands, etc., all the same colour. "I had been looking," she said, "for the more picture-book conception of a fairy (with gauze wings, etc.) and these little people were a surprise to me. I tried very hard to see them the next day, with Mr. Naylor and my cousin, but I never saw them again."

Miss Meynell's aunt, Mrs. Iris Strick, told me that when living in Devon her younger son, Arthur, saw a little man in a tree there once. "Arthur was in his pram and pointed it out to me," she said, "but I could not see anything. I believe he *did* see it because his eyes had changed focus in just the same odd way that Mr. A. A. Naylor's did when he was looking at something on another plane. We lived at one time in part of the old Governor's House, Edinburgh Castle, and when my son John was a very small child he pointed suddenly to something invisible to me moving across the drawing-room floor. 'Ook, ook,' he cried, 'tiny baby, tiny baby!' and followed it with his finger pointing. Questions were very little good; he was too young. Mr. Naylor thought it might have been a gnome out of the great rock on which the Castle is built." The clearest thing that Mrs. Strick herself had seen in Scotland was a small brown creature peeping over a tree-stump. She and others were sheltering from the rain, and Mr. Naylor had burned some incense to attract nature spirits, but without immediate results. Then, when they were not trying to see anything, Mrs. Strick saw this prick-eared elf, eighteen inches or more high, stalking them from the tree-stump.

From Rugby, Mr. J. D. Watkins-Pitchford, A.R.C.A., F.R.S.A., (also known to many as "B.B.") wrote that a friend of his, while motoring along a Devon lane at night when the snow was on the ground, was startled to see in the light of his headlamps six little people about eight inches high, carrying a ladder across the lane. "They seemed very perturbed, and there was a bit of a scramble when they reached the other side, as the bank was steep. But two of the little men clambered to the top of the bank and hauled away until they managed to pull the ladder out of sight through the hedge."

ie Second World War, there happened to Mrs. Doro-
hat she referred to as "just one of those unforgettable
ie's life." Living then at Gillingham, she and a friend
went walking in the Darland locality of that Kentish borough. They
had not travelled far along the Darland Banks when, owing to the
excessive heat of the day, they sat down to rest. It was a particularly
still day; not a breath of wind disturbed the hot, summer air. As the
two of them tarried there in relaxation and contentment, gazing
across the intervening country towards the village of Luton, Mrs.
Mayo noticed a little brown, fluffy ball, about the size of a ten-
nis ball, speedily ascending the steep banks towards them. When
it reached her left side (her friend, by the way, was seated to her
right), it popped open, affording her a very brief glimpse of a gnome
or pixie within.

"Did you see that?" she asked her friend, turning round sharply
towards her in amazement.

"See what?"

Mrs. Mayo pointed with some urgency to the spot at which she
had seen the fluffy ball open to disclose its tiny occupant, but no
longer was anything of the kind visible. "I had never heard at this
time of the Deva Kingdom or anything of that sort," she declared,
"and so what I did see was not imagination in my case. It all happened so quickly, but it happened!"

One very still evening, about the year 1921, while sitting on a
seat in Westcliff, Essex, with her two sons, aged nine and eleven
years respectively, Mrs. F. M. A. Southwell could hardly believe her
eyes when she saw a number of gnomes in a large tree. They were
about seven inches high and were very busy gesticulating and pointing to each other, completely unaware of the human trio in their
vicinity. The little creatures and their clothes were colourless, yet
the jackets appeared darker than the trousers. The latter seemed in
one piece with the soft-looking shoes that they wore. They had also
some kind of headgear. The tree was very old with many branches,
but the gnomes seemed to be treading on air between, underneath,
and above the branches. Mrs. Southwell did not fear them at all, yet
did not find them attractive. "I kept opening and shutting my eyes,"

she said, "in case it was all illusion. But there they were, absolutely distinct." During this time, she had been sitting in amazed silence. Then the nine-year-old child said, "Let us get away from here."

"Why?" she asked.

He replied: "I seem to see little people in that tree."

Mrs. Southwell then turned to the other boy. "Do you see anything?"

"No," he answered.

She told me: "So far I had not said that I had seen the gnomes. I found it curious that one, and not the other, of my boys had seen them."

The ceaseless activity of these beings, which were observed by Mrs. Southwell and one of her sons, tallies with the perpetual motion of some brown elves that my sister and I saw in Pannett's Park during a holiday at Whitby, Yorkshire, in July 1956. We were relaxing peacefully on a seat after an enjoyable but rather strenuous walk, when I noticed some considerable movement in a tree that grew at the foot of a wooded slope facing us. It was swarming with elves, and when I drew my sister's attention to it, she could see them too, but neither of us had any idea what they were doing so busily. In common with Mrs. Southwell's gnomes, these elves seemed to be moving quite easily above, below, and between the branches. This strange feature was confirmed by a trained seer, who said that tree manikins seem quite unaffected by the law of gravity.

A contributor who described herself as "a lover of nature" was walking through a lane in Lancashire when she saw something blue flashing into a bank in the distance, but on reaching the spot she could find nothing. A few weeks later she was in the same lane and a little figure came running from the opposite side at the same spot, this time within a few yards of her. It was about one foot in height, and in its left hand it held something white, like a mushroom or an egg. Its wings, which were a lovely shade of blue and silver, seemed to reach the ground. On seeing her, it paused, and then continued running across the road. She could not find out where it went but concluded it had run through to a field a short distance away, where there was an old tree-trunk.

Seeing Fairies

A strange adventure befell the late Mr. Hugh Sheridan in the first week of February 1953, and Mr. Willie Monks has kindly sent me this summary of his friend's statement: "I was going home as usual across the fields from where I work at Messrs. J. McColloch & Sons, Gerrardstown, to my home at Bettyville. Both these places are in Ballyboughal, and the distance between them is about a half mile. I was alone. It was duskish—about 6:30 p.m.—and when nearing the corner of one of the fields I heard a tittering noise 'like the titter of someone going to play a joke on you.' At first I thought it was some of the other men who had gone on before me and who might be intending to play some prank. However, I noticed immediately afterwards what looked like a large, greenish tarpaulin on the ground, with 'thousands of fairies' on it. I then found there were a lot more around me. They were of two sizes, some about four feet high, and others about eighteen or twenty inches high. Except for size, both kinds were exactly alike. They wore dark, bluish-grey coats, tight at the waist and flared at the hips, with a sort of shoulder cape. As all the fairies kept facing me, I could not be sure if the cape went around them, but the ends stuck out over the shoulders. The covering of their legs was tight, rather like puttees, and they appeared to be wearing shoes. I started on the path towards home, and the fairies went with me in front and all around. The larger fairies kept the nearest to me. The ones in front kept skipping backwards as they went, and their feet appeared to be touching the ground. They seemed to be wearing hats rather like a raised beret in shape, with a jutting-out top edge. There were males and females, all seemingly in their early twenties. They had very pleasant faces, with plumper cheeks than those of humans, and the men's faces were devoid of hair or whiskers. I did not specially notice their hands. As I moved along the path, one tall fairy kept before me all the time. This was a girl, and a man kept near her. They seemed to have partly fair, wavy or curly hair. None of the fairies had wings. They tried to get me off the path towards a gateway leading from the field, but just before I reached it I realized they were trying to take me away, so I resisted and turned towards the path again. At about 40 yards from the gateway, I was going along by the ditch when I fell or got into it, but I do not know very clearly how this happened. While I was in it, the fairies remained around, and I could see others coming out of the bushes and briars. I got out of the ditch and continued towards the path until I reached it again. I moved on towards home with the fairies around me, and they kept up the tittering noise all the time. In the end I got to a plank leading across a ditch from one field to another, and suddenly all the fairies went away. They seemed to go back, with the noise gradually fading. At one time I had reached out my arms to try to catch them, but I cannot be sure whether they skipped back just out of reach, or whether my hands passed through them without feeling anything. They were smiling and pleasant all the time, and I could see their eyes watching me. When I got home, I found I was about three-quarters of an hour late, but I thought I had been delayed only a few minutes. While the fairies were with me, I had a rather exciting feeling 'like being on a great height,' but I was in no way afraid. I would very much like to meet them again."

Mr. Willie Monks' cousin, the late Michael Flynn of County Dublin, told him that he saw a fairy on one occasion while he was crossing some fields on his way to school (probably in the early 1900s). In a nearby field, which was separated by a small stream from the one he was in, he noticed a figure about the height of a child of eight or nine years old, but in appearance it was like a very old man clad in knee-breeches, who seemed to be carrying something in his hands. He was wearing some sort of headgear, but Mr. Monks could not remember how his cousin described it.

Mrs. Doris Poole recalled an experience she had at the age of nine or ten, while living at Tuffley, a little village on the side of Robin's Wood Hill in Gloucestershire. She was sitting in a field close to a tree, when about seven little people approximately eight inches tall looked over a bluebell bank, then climbed over and came quite near to her without apparently noticing her. They reminded her of harebells blowing in the wind, but they had long, flowing hair and their dresses were in pastel shades of mauves, pinks, yellows, and blues, falling softly from their shoulders to below the knees. A little fellow dressed in red came last, carrying something in front of him. They all seemed in a hurry and disappeared behind the tree.

Other fairies were seen in Gloucestershire by this correspondent when she was in a primrose wood on the edge of Painswick Beacon. They had wings, and their hair was darker than that of the field fairies. Their dresses were of similar style, but in brown, green, and lemon shades. They were in among, and taller than, the primroses, and were looking down on them. Now and then one would touch a flower or a leaf and peep underneath, as though searching for something. "I was so entranced," wrote Mrs. Poole, "that the last one had gone before I realised it. My niece's teacher told her there were no such things, but I know I wasn't dreaming, and I have never forgotten them."

In a little Norfolk village, at the age of seven, Miss Kate Allen was going on an errand during the August school-holidays when she encountered a little blue-eyed man about eight-inches high, wearing a green coat and a pointed hat. As he gazed up at her, she saw that his mature face was in strange contrast with his fair, youthful complexion. His appearance was only momentary, but she knew she had not imagined it, although at that time she had never heard of such beings as gnomes. One of a family of ten children, she was not encouraged by her mother to have many flights of fancy, and no fairy books were ever allowed in the house. Miss Allen was over 80 at the time she wrote to me, but her childhood experience still remained fresh in her memory.

The following account was kindly written out for me from the notes of the late Mrs. Mary Barclay, by her friend Mrs. Hughes: "Mrs. Barclay had an unhappy childhood and was very lonely. She used to go to the woods, where she could see the elves. One day, in great distress and fear because she had spoiled a clean apron and knew that she would be punished when she arrived home, she went further into the woods and sat down weeping under a large tree. Presently she heard faint music and saw a company of small beings with musical instruments. They played and danced to amuse and cheer her. She went home happy and saw that her apron had become quite clean. In later life she could still become aware of elf land if she could get away to the woods and be quiet for a while, but the complications of wartime life in Edinburgh in 1940 made it impossible to get this release, and she missed it very much."

The fairies seem to be better at cleaning aprons than at sewing, according to this experience concerning Madame H. P. Blavatsky and Colonel H. S. Olcott, co-founders of the Theosophical Society in New York. They were, at the time, in the Society's flat called the Lamasery, when a little elemental pulled Madame Blavatsky's dress desiring to be set some small service. The Colonel made the joking suggestion that it be set to hem some new towels, and Madame Blavatsky, after first declining to act on the suggestion, at length consented. They locked the towels, needles, and thread inside a bookcase and left the elemental to do its work. In about an hour and twenty minutes the little creature was back at Madame Blavatsky's knee and making a little piping sound, something like a mouse's squeak, to reveal its presence. The bookcase was unlocked and the towels were taken out. They had been hemmed, but according to the Colonel, "in a fashion that would disgrace the youngest child in an infant sewing class!" I came across the account in the November 1933 issue of World Theosophy, USA, which ceased publication the following month.

Mrs. Mary Oliver, writing from the Aeolian Islands, Sicily, said that she saw many fairies in her infancy. She had a Norwegian nurse who took this for granted and, while not encouraging it, she did not discourage it. "Then," went on Mrs. Oliver, "after my brother was born and the nurse did not have so much time to give to me, I had an extremely ugly gnome with a beard right down to his toes, who attached himself to me. I was absolutely terrified of him and would scream every time I was left alone. I think he must have been one of the Norwegian trolls, but our Negro cook told me that he was a bogeyman and that he followed me because I had been naughty. Then one day my mother heard me having hysterics and said 'How long has this been going on?' She was told that it had been for some months, and although I was only two and a half years old she used shock treatment on me; she told me that no such thing existed, and she thrashed me soundly. After that, I did not see him more than once or twice in the space of ten years, but I could smell him. He had an odour like fungus."

Seeing Fairies

When Mary Oliver was eleven years old, she saw a little fairy man. Her family had an island in the Muskoka lakes in Canada, and on this island was a brook spanned by a bridge. Her mother used to send her to the other side of the island at sunset to fetch the evening mail, and she had to pass through the woods as it was getting dark. Always she used to feel frightened when nearing the brook, which sometimes had moonlight reflected in it. She would be seized by an inexplicable feeling of terror and would return to the camp incoherent with fright. Even in the daylight she was afraid of this wood and the brook. Then, one very hot day at noon, she was so frightened of crossing the bridge that she fell down on the path and just lay there, too weak to get up. With her head pillowed on a mossy bank, she looked up at the sky through the trees, and finding that she was very dizzy, she started to go to sleep when right in front of her nose a little man, wearing a wintergreen-berry on his head, came out of a hole in the ground. He made an effort to talk to her, but she could not understand what he said. He seemed to be very cocky and proprietary about his little hole, and she could see she was not welcome. She marked the place and went home feeling quite happy. After seeing the little man, she was no longer frightened to cross the bridge. In fact, she used to leave the camp specially to go and look for him, but although she found the hole she never saw him again.

Nor did she see another fairy until her first night in a boarding school in Germany in 1926. Hearing a strange sound of music, she looked out of her window into the Thuringian forest, and saw a band of gnomes marching round a tree in the snow beneath the window. The next day, she told her head-mistress, Baroness von Bornburg, about it, and the Baroness was very much interested.

"They do exist here," she admitted. "My sister saw them and my grandmother used to see them, but no one except you has seen them since the war, although there are many people in the village who would not work here in the castle because of them. There is a tale, although I daresay it is only a tale, that in my great-grandfather's youth the cat brought one into the kitchen once."

"The music was so wonderful," Mary told her.

"Yes," she replied. "I have heard about that music. When a boy in the village hears it, it is supposed to mean that he is going to make a fortune!"

About a year after her marriage, Mary Oliver and her husband were returning home late from a party and were driving through the Roehampton Gate into Richmond Park, where their home was, when Mrs. Oliver saw a deer in front of the car and shouted "Be careful!" Her husband said, "It's all right. I saw the reflection of the headlights in the deer's eyes." He stopped the car, and the deer went slowly across the road in front of them. On its back was a little man about three feet high, clad in a jerkin and hose. He had a turned-up nose, and feet that looked like potatoes.

"What is it?" said Mrs. Oliver.

"Ssh!" her husband replied. "He's a leprechaun! Well, I never expected to see anything like that here, so close to the Star and Garter Hospital."

The next day, Mrs. Oliver mentioned the incident to a friend, who made the strange comment: "Don't be cheap."

She told this to her husband, and he replied, "When we go to see James Stephens on Sunday, you can tell him, and I know he won't consider it is cheap." And James Stephens didn't. He told them of many other such instances.

After the death of her husband, Mrs. Oliver went to live in a very beautiful house in Cornwall, which was not expensive because it was reputed to be haunted. She was alone, with no electricity in the house, and one night when she needed another log for her fire, she went from the library without a lamp and passed through the kitchen to the wash-house where the logs were kept. "I got down on my knees on the tiled floor," she said, "and reached under the wash-tub to dislodge a log, when I heard a noise like a scolding squirrel—'Chit-chat, chit-chat'—and there, on top of the logs and surrounded by a green light, stood a furious little man who looked like an artichoke but was only as big as my thumb. His face was ugly and frog-like, and he was shaking his fists at me, ordering me off his property. I grabbed a log and tore back to my fire, which I banked with coal. I was terrified." After this incident, Mrs. Oliver met the owner of the property and a previous tenant, both of whom told her that there were "pixies" in the house, and they laughed when she told them about the little man who had been so angry and rude to her. A few weeks later, when the weather turned very cold, Mrs. Oliver left that house and went to France, never to return to Cornwall.

Reverting to Mrs. Oliver's account of the old gnome with the odour like fungus, this may be typical of some of the ancient, very "earthy" gnomes, for it reminds me of a forbidding one we had in the garden of our previous house when I was young. He never actually materialized in his gnome-form, but I was fully aware of him and knew that he guarded a very large clump of semi-wild, dusky-red peonies, which grew in a shady corner of the orchard. He seemed so possessive over his precious plant that I never dared to pick or touch any of the fine blooms, and I always sensed when he was there because of his fungus smell.

While staying in Edinburgh in 1940, Mrs. Olive Mytton Hill saw two gnomes, approximately seven inches in height. They were bearded and wore red caps, brown shoes, and green tunics with collars of a faint coffee shade. Mrs. Hill was travelling in her astral body at the time, and as soon as the speed slackened she opened her eyes and felt herself gently raised to a standing position. It was then she saw the gnomes, and she started to glide about one and a half feet above the short, velvety grass. She went slowly past these little fellows, one of whom appeared to be much older than the other and had his spade in the ground at the foot of the tree against which he and his companion were standing. They turned to stare at her, both of them making a hissing noise; and she said to herself: "Oh dear! They don't care for me to be here." When she told her family about this episode they thought it a huge joke, but she still remembers it very clearly after all these years.

A nature spirit known to be very common in some parts of Scotland is the little brown gnome, and Capt. Sir Hugh Rhys Rankin, Bart., Hereditary Piper, Clan Maclaine, saw one standing on a wee tumulus on the edge of the Creagan-side drive at Barcaldine House, Oban, Argyle, in 1932. His wife, Lady Rankin, wrote that she, too, had seen these brown gnomes when in Scotland.

Another account of fairies in Scotland came in 1949 from Mr. David Thurston Smith of Argyle, who began by explaining: "I am one of the lucky ones whose range of vision is above normal. I do, therefore, on occasions see not only fairies but other beings invisible to the majority. I have seen many little people about three to four inches in height, as delicate as wind-blown leaves. I catch frequent glimpses of them in the house and in the woods. Here in Scotland, as in Yorkshire, there are gnomes of about three feet in height, of a most remarkable physical activity, capable of running at amazing speed through the woodlands, which seem mainly to be their particular habitat.

"I have oft-times wondered at the physical force of small men, but never so much as at that of a gnome I saw in a plantation near my former house in the Pickering Valley of Yorkshire. About two feet in height, and of sturdy bind, he was rummaging about among fallen leaves as though he had lost something. On perceiving that I could see him, he rushed away at a most surprising speed, leaping over fallen boughs and brambles."

Mr. Smith found that lamb riding was a popular game for gnomes, and he liked to watch them when dusk was falling. "The mother sheep do not seem to mind," he said, "and I am sure the lambs enjoy it. The little people like the turnip fields. They sit on toadstools in the rows during the hot weather, and watch the partridges run by. It is cool in there, and they can generally get a shower-bath of crystal-clear water by shaking the leaves."

Mrs. I. Morrison, also of Scotland, recounted an experience she had in the "blackout" during the Second World War. She had alighted from a bus, feeling very anxious to be home because the air-raid sirens had sounded, and although she had not far to go she wondered how she would manage to get across the street in the pitch darkness. Just at that moment a light descended on her shoulder, moved in front of her, and spread itself out. It was a lovely little fairy dressed in silver and green, and it floated before her, lighting the way. Shouting to some nearby wayfarers to follow her, Mrs. Morrison kept her eyes on the glowing figure, and they were all taken across the road in safety. After she had been in her house for a little while, a friend, who was passing by when the bombs started falling, called in and said she thought she and Mrs. Morrison ought to go to the air-raid shelters. Mrs. Morrison said, "Well, we are quite safe," and she related her experience with the fairy, but her friend did not believe in fairies and remained sceptical. When the time reached 11 p.m., Mrs. Morrison told her friend she thought she should be getting home, although the "all-clear" had not yet sounded and the bombs were still falling in the distance. She walked with the friend along the road, but when they had gone a good part of the way Mrs. Morrison heard a voice telling her that her friend could turn back, and the fairy appeared again and went in front of her friend. "Look!" Mrs. Morrison said. "That's the little fairy was telling you about, and it is going to take you home." She told her friend to follow the fairy, even if it became just a tiny light. The next morning the friend came to see her, thrilled by the experience, and she declared she would never doubt again. This same fairy seemed to attach itself to Mrs. Morrison, for after that experience it was seen by her quite often.

Another nature spirit who acted as a guide was seen by "H" of Buckinghamshire, whose accounts of his many other experiences appear elsewhere in this book. He said: "I went out for a car ride with a young lady, and on the way home a fairy, of whose presence my friend seemed quite unaware, was fluttering just in front of the car for several miles. We were doing 45-50 miles per hour, but the fairy (in a frilly tutu, and with big butterfly wings) kept up with us without any effort. Incidentally, we weren't sure of the way, and the young lady kept asking me which turning to take. I took my bearings from the fairy, and as soon as my companion said she knew where we were, the little creature vanished."

When Miss Eva Jack, of Rosshire, was asked by her cousin, Miss Annie Jack, if she had ever seen a fairy, she admitted she had not, whereupon the old lady replied: "Well, I have" and proceeded to tell the following story. One lovely summer evening in the 1940s, when she was about 70, she was returning home through a wood with her sister after attending a. Sabbath service in Culbokie School. They had just crossed the stile, which brought them into a field, when they saw a vision that remained with them all their lives. Not very far from the knoll known as the Fairies' Hill, which is in the wood above Culbokie Loch, they saw rows of little people dressed in brown, dancing up and down. Later, one of the sisters told Miss Eva Jack that although it was impossible to say for certain that they were fairies, she couldn't think of anything else to call them. They were not children from the village, for it was too far away, and these little people were all of the same size, and all dressed alike.

Mrs. Kathleen Fryatt, a teacher of elocution, was born in Northern Ireland but was living in Essex at the time of the following experience, an account of which she sent in 1952 to the *Braintree & Witham Times*. In the summer of 1951, she was out for a walk with her husband, in Witham, and, having decided to take a shortcut home through the fields along the Foulkbourne Road, they entered a field known as The Walk. (Mrs. Fryatt was told afterwards that this used to be a monks' walk leading to a monastery.) The path was lined with old trees, and noticing that one of them was hollow, she stopped and looked into it. To her utter surprise, she saw in the bark the faces of three or four grotesque little men with large noses and ugly mouths, and lying on the ground inside the tree was a little old lady of seven or eight inches in size, with a sort of Welsh hat and a long, full skirt. Mrs. Fryatt told her husband, but when he looked he could see nothing. "You are imagining them," he said, and picking up a stick he pretended to poke the old lady, but his wife called out: "Do not dare to touch them!" When he realised she was serious, he put down the stick, and they tried to continue their walk. "I say 'tried'," she explained, "because we found that the path was no longer a shortcut, as corn had been grown at the end of it. My husband said, 'Now look what your fairies have done.' We retraced our steps and, as the fairies were still there when we reached the hollow tree, I apologised to them for my husband's behaviour, explaining that he came from Essex and did not believe in fairies. When we reached home, I decided to boil an egg each for our tea. My egg was perfect, but my husband's egg was completely bad. I boiled another one for him, and it, too, was bad. The strange thing is that never before nor since has either of us had a bad egg. Were the fairies having their revenge on a disbeliever, or was it just coincidence? I never expected to see these little people, but I would swear in any court of law that what I say is absolutely true."

My thanks go to Mrs. Wm. Tait for sending the following account of an experience related to her by her cousin, Miss Elizabeth Johnston. "In 1896, when Miss Johnston was about five years old, she left her home at 'Columbus,' Bridge of Walls, in Shetland, one Sunday afternoon to visit a neighbouring family, who lived in a house about 100 yards away. She was in a hurry because she knew the family would shortly be leaving for church. It was a lovely summer day, and too hot to run all the way, so she walked up the steep bit past the gable of her home. A rough grunting sound suddenly directed her gaze towards the turf dyke at the back of the house and she saw clearly, lying on top of the dyke, a little man staring belligerently at her. His clothes seemed to be all dark brown, and he had a long beard of much the same colour. His gaze never left her face, and his only attempts at communication were two or three loud grunts, which seemed to convulse his whole body. She stood transfixed for a few minutes, then took to her heels." It is interesting to note from the next account that this gnome was not the only one who grunted.

"We have a very fat, green gnome who lives here and grunts like a pig," wrote Mrs. Claire H. Cantlon, of London, in 1933. "He seems rather bad-tempered, as he growls at the children and runs away when they see him. I have not seen him, but I have heard the noise that he makes. Our black Persian cat plays with a fairy that teases him, and he makes bird noises to it. You can see that it flies round and round just out of reach, and puss puts up his paws and tries his best to catch it, and then looks all round to see where it is. He then has to wait until the fairy returns, and then the same thing begins all over again and will go on for 30 minutes or more. It is most entrancing to watch. One day, at tea, my eldest girl saw a fairy on the bookshelf. I could not see it, but the dog did and flew at the books and barked. All my children are able to see fairies and gnomes about the house and garden, and also in the woods and country places that we visit. They take them as a matter of course."

During the Second World War, Mrs. M. A. Rodliff occupied her aunt's house in Harrow. She had many psychic experiences, but none so wonderful as that relating to the fairy vision she had there. On a night when the moon was full, she saw from the threshold of her back door what appeared to be glow-worms in the neglected wartime garden, but as she stood watching them they began to move in a manner that glow-worms never do. They had become a dozen or more gnomes, skipping merrily on the tops of the Brussels sprouts. In height they ranged from a foot to roughly twenty inches and were dressed as if for a party, some in green coats and hats, some in red coats and hats, others in mauve. "They were definitely having such fun," she said. "Soon they left the Brussels-tops to dance on the lawn close at hand, and to run hither and thither in great elation. Though I was transfixed with surprise, I was truly delighted to see them. There was such merriment that I, too, felt happy and couldn't tear myself away from the back door." Mrs. Rodliff added that this vision remained with her as clearly as any experience of her life, and she could recall the sense of wellbeing and joy it instantly communicated. Her sole regret was that those to whom she related this unique experience were apt to laugh at her, "and this," she said, "is why I'm glad to pass on my account to anybody sympathetic enough to accept it."

Mrs. Edna F. Wilson mentioned the following experience in a letter to *Prediction* magazine, and I wrote to her for details. In November 1946, she moved from Birmingham with her husband and three children to a very isolated and lovely little valley in Hertfordshire. On the estate of 43 acres was a sixteenth-century mansion and two lodges, far back from the road. Everywhere was overgrown when the family moved in, and no one else lived on the estate, the owner being abroad. The house was on a hill with a dense wood at the back, and during the hot summer of the following year Mrs. Wilson used to love to sit in this wood and was very much interested in the flowers in the grounds. "Quite suddenly, I became clairvoyant in several ways," she said, "and the first fairy I saw was sitting in a red rose and had beautiful wings like those of a butterfly. I was amazed, of course, and after that I used to look for fairies, and they were everywhere. The wood was swarming with them, and I would watch them floating up around the trees. They were never more than four inches in size, and were always smiling. Like some of the little people in fairy tales, they were wearing long, flowing gowns with jewelled straps across the shoulders and sometimes a band around the head with a star in the centre. I liked to sit and gaze at them in the afternoon, when they were continually float- ing about the flowers. I watched them, too, in the peach house, floating up and down amongst the peaches, and also amongst the tomato plants in the greenhouse. They were on the cut flowers that my little girl would bring into the house, though she never could see them. When evening came, I used to sit just inside the wood, and they were all dancing in circles, quick as lightning—gnomes and fairies and pixies all together. They seemed to be floating down from everywhere to join in the fun. Though I listened for music, I was always disappointed. First I was aware of lights moving about in the grass. In fact, I always saw the lights first, and had to use a cer- tain amount of concentration, which was why I sat in solitude. But the queer thing was that at night, when I was watching them danc- ing, I became so interested and absorbed in them that everything seemed to come to life, even the blades of grass, and I actually felt as if I were in Fairyland."

In 1951 I received permission from the Aquarian Metaphysi- cal Institute of Colour Awareness to quote this description, written by their founder, the late Ivah Bergh Whitten, of some tiny green elementals at work perfecting clover leaves. "These tiny creatures work in squads with a sort of military precision. These squads form almost the perfect outline of a four-leafed clover and keep a perfect drill formation. Those working at the heart of the leaf (if this is the object worked upon) deliver all their force, then step back allow- ing fresh elementals to take the brunt of the task though they, be- ing now in the second row, shove or pull as the case may be, then step into the third row where still less effort is required of them. In the fourth row they do nothing but work their way to the fifth row. When they reach the outer curve, they again return to the centre to perform their task and again drill through the next leaf of clover in like manner, repeating until the leaf is complete. At the end of the last one, if the task is not finished, they start all over again at the drill. The Green Elementals are joyful, radiant, and work with a vim and zest, tinting, polishing, dusting, toning-up, and perfecting the tree, shrub, vine or fern."

Mrs. Veronica Maxwell of Devonshire, an artist who painted celestial subjects, could sense, but not see, fairies. She had a friend whose mother, when a child, lived in Ireland, and one day this child was holding the pony while her own mother visited an old cottage. As she waited near a large granite boulder, two of the "little people" about fourteen inches high emerged from under the stone, smiled at her and clapped their hands, then vanished. When Mrs. Maxwell was staying on a wild island on the Bay of Donegal, she met several people who had actually seen fairies, including a General's widow, who watched them dancing on the lonely sands in the sunset; an Archdeacon who, from his boat, saw them flitting about on the shore in the moonlight; and a friend who had an estate on Dartmoor and used to watch them down by the streams, among the bog-myrtle and cotton-grass. Mrs. Maxwell also met someone in Devonshire whose cousin was one day sitting on an old log in the dense woods of Berry Pomeroy Castle (on the edge of Dartmoor), when "out of the corner of her eye" she saw something move at the end of the log. It was a pixie, wearing a little cap and jerkin, and he looked very annoyed at seeing her there. Suddenly he sprang up, ran along the log, slapped her face, and disappeared!

"It is often said that the fairies do not appear in cities," wrote Mrs. B. E. Rushton, a Theosophist living in Birmingham. "My experience in the spring of 1961 has disproved that idea for me. We have a minute spot of garden behind a four-foot wall on one of the busiest roads in the city. Buses pass every few seconds and it is difficult to cross at all during the day. I planted a couple of dozen bulbs, most of them tulips, and passing them out or in would carefully count each one. I would talk and laugh and recount and put my hands gently around the smaller ones. They were very real to me as I have poor health and they are a glimpse of the country. One day, I was very depressed and had a bit of a headache, so I lay down in one of the noisiest rooms in the house as we had a guest in my room. I lay on my back, listening to the traffic, when I felt an electric charge in the air. This always means I am to have a 'visitor' or become 'projected.' It was a 'visitor.' A 'presence' wafted in at the door and there was laughter all around me. It went to my feet and followed the line of my body to my head. I felt a bulb 'kiss' my mouth several times and a voice in my head said 'Because you love them so.' There was much happy chatter in the air and I was re-energised. I can feel the soft touch of the dry skin of that bulb whenever I think of it. The voices were not bell-like or chirpy as those I had heard before in the country. There seemed a greater intelligence and the ability to communicate. I have felt in the country that the beings were examining me rather like the Lilliputians did when they found Gulliver. This was different. I felt their personal feeling for me."

One morning Mrs. Rushton saw a gnome, or elf, on a hill at Clent, in Worcestershire. As soon as she had formulated the words "Well, he's real" and turned to look directly at him, he had disappeared. It was at Clent, too, that she and her daughter heard strange music approaching, and saw leaves and dust gyrating in the air swiftly towards them. According to tradition, these eddies of wind and dust are occasioned by hosts of fairies travelling to a new dwelling-place. "We were caught up in a real singing whirlwind," she said, "and our skirts and scarves went with it till it continued over the edge of the hill. There it met an uprush of air from below, and died to our ear on the instant. It was a wonderful experience, and one which I was thrilled to share with my daughter, who was then about eighteen. She said afterwards, 'It is fun going out with you, Mummy. Unusual things seem to happen.' Clent Hills are full of magic. Once, I lay down to bask in the sun, and dozed off. A voice in my ear said firmly, 'Time to go down now,' and when I opened my eyes there was not a soul in sight. The sky had darkened, and just as I reached a bus shelter over a mile away, a storm broke. But for the warning I should have been drenched to the skin, at the very least."

An incident that occurred when she was about five and a half, and living in Kent, was recalled by Miss B. M. Berens. She and her

44

older sisters had been out to tea and were proceeding to collect their pet goat, which was tethered in a field. Their way lay along a path between a garden and an orchard, and her sisters, seeing that she was lagging behind, told her to wait by the gate while they fetched the goat. Dusk was falling, and she was feeling rather frightened. Glancing up at a tree, which seemed rather light, she noticed several fairies sitting on the branches and looking down at her; nine to twelve inches high, they were dressed in blue, pink, and green, had long fair hair and wings like gossamer. As she watched them, all her fears left her. Then she saw her sisters coming along with the goat, and when she looked up again at the tree, the fairies had vanished.

At the age of eight or nine, she lived in Worcestershire, and she was pushing her dolls' pram down a lane near her home when she met a man who was obviously the worse for drink. This frightened her, and she walked quickly with her pram to a gateway, where she knew she could open the gate easily. She went through into a field, and there, just inside it on a big, moss-covered stone, sat a sad-looking fairy with folded wings and clad in greyish clothes. The child looked round to see if the drunkard had followed her, but he had not, and when she turned to speak to the fairy it had disappeared. Miss Berens pointed out that on both occasions she had been frightened until she saw the fairies, and they had dispelled her fears and brought her comfort.

"I never fail," wrote Mrs. Frances E. Cotton, of Tasmania, "to marvel at the variety of forms that spirit builds about itself." And she went on to tell me that a friend of hers, Mr. J. Green, Senr., of Hobart, saw a gnome-like manikin sitting cross-legged under a bush in open heathland, busy over something in its hands. Its clothes were dull red, green, and brown.

Another friend, Mrs. Britta Adams, told her that in October 1925, when she was a child in Wellington, New Zealand, she saw on some rhododendron blossom several semi-transparent, long-robed creatures, each wearing a sort of narrow, trailing stole, back to front. With her were her young sister and a cousin, but they could not see the fairies, although their attention was drawn to them; and the fairies themselves seemed busy and quite uninterested in the children.

In 1922, when Miss Penelope C. Storey was seven years of age, she was living with her people in an old cottage in the Buckinghamshire village of Great Missenden, and it was there she saw her first fairy. She had been put to bed on a summer evening and was lying awake with the curtains undrawn, gazing out at the gathering twilight. "Quite suddenly and entirely unexpectedly," she said, "I saw, floating down slowly past the window, a perfectly proportioned miniature female form, so far as I could judge between twelve and thirteen inches high, with long hair, and clad in some filmy drapery. Her arms were outstretched sideways, and her feet gracefully together. In the dusk, she looked colourless-grey and white in effect. No wings were visible—and this is worth noting, as all the childhood fairy books on which I had been nurtured depicted fairies with wings. She simply floated, quite slowly, vertically downwards through the air. I felt a certain sense of excitement, but no great surprise, and did not even think of getting out of bed to see if I could see anything more.

"Shortly afterwards, my Mother came in to see if I was still awake, and eagerly I told her what I had seen. Of course she refused to believe me and said it must have been an owl. But it was no owl that I watched, and I remember telling myself solemnly that I must never forget that on that night I had seen a fairy. The episode has indeed remained imprinted on my mind with far more vividness than most childhood memories."

Another reader who cherished an unforgettable experience was in her thirties at the time. Miss Dorothy M. Tomkins was walking down the garden path when, for no reason at all, she turned her head to the left, towards the lawn, and there, at a distance of several feet from her, was a brightly coloured fairy two- to two-and-a-half inches in height. She could see the tiny being's head and its wings, which were folded down. "I remember distinctly," she said, "standing absolutely still and saying to myself, 'This is *not* a butterfly or anything else, it is a *fairy*. I am *absolutely* sure, and nothing and nobody must ever make me doubt it.'"

The fairy that Miss Christine Hutchinson saw was also very

small. When she was eight years old, she had a fairy house at the bottom of the garden at her home in Leeds, and every morning on the table in the little house she found a sweet, together with a note wishing her a happy day. She believed they came from the fairies until she discovered that her mother put them there.

Then one morning her faith in fairies was truly rewarded. As she was walking down the garden path, she saw something that she thought at first was a kind of fly, though not a moth or a butterfly. She was surprised at its extraordinary brilliance, and then, to her great delight, she saw that it was, in fact, a tiny, bright yellow fairy. When relating this in 1957, Christine told me that, although she had reached "the sobering age of sixteen," she still believed firmly in the existence of fairies after that childhood experience of hers.

Miss Towen, of Monmouthshire, saw her first fairy in that county about the year 1945 on a very hot day in June, while the bees were humming amid the fragrant blossom of the lime trees. She and two young friends, David and Margaret, were quietly admiring a group of very large, scarlet antirrhinum flowers when suddenly one dropped forward, opened, and out came some twirling tissue veiling, which passed close to Miss Towen's head. Rising gently into the air was a bright blue fairy, with arms outstretched her beautiful face clearly visible. "A fairy!" said Margaret. "A blue fairy!"

"A girl fairy," said David. She was, most decidedly, a lovely figure, and they watched her soaring higher and higher until there remained just a very faint, shining wisp. The two children were so enthralled that when they went to school they told their mistress in front of the whole class and were made fun of in consequence, though the teacher agreed there might be such things as fairies; but the mother of Margaret was furious, and the poor child was forbidden to mention the matter again. Miss Towen had her next visitation after she had been stuffing a rag doll with kapok. She placed the remainder of the down in a cardboard box, which had a lid without sides, and left it under the window for quite a long time. One spring morning in 1949, she went to the box and was lifting some of the kapok when, with a whirling motion, out floated three fairies, each of them in a different hue, yellow, bright green, and deep rose pink. In both of these experiences Miss Towen noticed that the arms of the fairies were elongated, and seemed to be used to guide them as they rose. They had no wings, but very fine gossamer veiling, which seemed to come from the back of their necks, leaving their faces and heads free.

"Last spring," wrote Miss Marjorie A. Thompson, of Australia, in November 1955, "two of my friends (Barbara Diprose and Jill Major) and I spent part of our holidays at my parents' home in Traralgon, Gippsland, Victoria, and during our stay we took several trips to the Strzelecki Ranges. In these hills there is some of the most beautiful scenery in the whole country. Tree ferns fill the gullies, and on the hilltops the giant gums of the Australian bush stand erect. In the midst of this magnificent country are two reserves where the beauty of the bush is indescribable. They are known as Bulga Park and Tarra Valley. The former boasts a swing bridge, which crosses a deep gully of tree ferns, and it was here that we saw the elves. In our search for unusual wild flowers, we were a little off the beaten foot-tracks at the time, and were among a clump of tree ferns, towards the centre of which was a small clearing where only a few bracken ferns no higher than three inches were growing. Before our astonished eyes, three minute creatures resembling aborigines emerged on the far side of the clearing and began to speak to each other, though we could not hear what they were saying and they may have been using some means of communication known only to themselves.

"This part of Victoria was originally inhabited by aborigines, and there is now a Mission Station for this diminishing race at Lake Tyers. The elfin aborigines, seen simultaneously by the three of us, were approximately nine inches in height, and each was clad only in what seemed to be a piece of bark. One carried a didgeridoo (the music-pipe used by Australia's aborigines), and each of the others had a woomera (a throw-stick). As you can imagine, we were dumbfounded, and gazed at them in awe. We had time to take note of their appearance before they parted ways and went back into the ferns, the one with the didgeridoo accompanied by the shorter of the other two, the third retiring by himself. Naturally, my parents did not credit our tale and we were unable to prove anything to them, so we again visited Bulga Park, taking with us our cameras, but despite an afternoon spent in waiting we had no success."

One bright summer evening around the year 1923, near Skerries, Co. Dublin, Mrs. A. Freda Young caught a glimpse of an elfin creature. It was on a road bordered by grass, a ditch, and a hedge, and she saw it jump from the hedge across the ditch and disappear in the long grass. It went out of sight too quickly for her to observe the details of its dress, but it seemed to be clothed from head to foot in dead-leaf colour, and had no beard, and no wings that she could see. Mrs. Young said that as she was about eighteen years old at the time it is unlikely that she imagined the vision. Moreover, it caused her some surprise because the figure was approximately two feet high, much bigger than she would have expected a fairy to be.

Miss Bay Kirkaldy, of London, related the following experiences of fairy vision: "My childhood was spent at Harlow, Essex, in one of the manor-house type of dwellings for which the county is well-known. When I was about twelve years of age, Edward, our garden boy who had recently left school and taken up work for us, called me and said he wished to show me something interesting. At the back of the house we had two kitchen-gardens, the newer of the two dividing the older from an orchard. At the orchard boundary a Christmas tree had been planted and was flourishing. It was simply crowded with fairies about the size of dragonflies, perfectly recognisable as to sex and seemingly quite indifferent to our presence. I remember it was a bright mid-morning in June, and the sunshine seemed to enhance their shining, almost luminous, appearance. We watched them for some time, the young lad telling me that he had seen them often. He cautioned me not to go too near, as the fairies would all disappear if we did, so we watched them across a stretch of kitchen garden. I should guess that we were about ten or twelve yards away from them. Our observation was interrupted by a housemaid who called me in to lunch. Edward told her he was showing 'Missy' the fairies. She said something to the effect that that wasn't unusual but I had better not say I had seen them or grown-ups wouldn't believe me and would say I was fibbing: I remember she said to Edward, 'We've often seen them, haven't we?' or words to that effect. Then she touched her lips with her fingers as if to say 'Don't let anyone know.' When I went back in the afternoon they had vanished, leaving no trace, but what I had seen that morning left a very deep impression upon me."

Bay's next experience was in 1924, when she was still twelve. She was walking one summer evening with a friend in St. James's Park. They entered from the Mall and strolled slowly round the right-hand side of the lake. The path curved thereabouts and there were some beautiful flowerbeds. Just before these came to an end, there was a kind of semi-grotto running back into the shrubs. The evening sun was shining into it and here again the place was alive with the little people. The men-fairies seemed to be wearing tight-fitting trousers with red, blue, or green jerkins, and a kind of fisherman's cap. The ladies seemed to wear a kind of shining white garment and had the same luminous quality as the fairies Bay had seen on the Christmas tree. The wings of both males and females were iridescent, though smaller and not so obvious in the males, who did not seem to fly around so much. They appeared to move incessantly, sliding up and down the grotto rocks and the branches of the shrubs. They kept up a perfect babble of conversation that only came to Bay's ears as a rather melodious twittering. She noticed that all the fairies seemed to be quite oblivious of a little crowd, which had collected to watch them, though some of the people obviously could not see them at all, despite the efforts of their friends to point them out. So far as she can recollect, their appearance was reported in the press.

At the time she wrote to me, her home was a small, pleasant, detached house, which she shared with two friends. It faced on to a secondary main road, beyond which was a large open space leading to the Welsh Harp. Their garden at the back was secluded, and the fence at the end was covered at flowering-time with "Paul's Scarlet" roses. She and one of her friends had often noticed that on perfectly windless days the standard roses in front bent in a peculiar way, as if suddenly bearing a weight. One day in 1956, when the roses were in bloom, she was gardening and felt that someone was watching her. It was a little old man wearing a bright green doublet, tan "breaks," and a pointed cap. "Hello," she said, and he smiled most sweetly at her, climbed down a rose-stalk, and disappeared.

From Bulawayo, Southern Rhodesia, Mr. Stuart W. Wright wrote that many years ago he had a little daughter who used to chase fairies from flower to flower. She would run excitedly from one part of the garden to the other, calling to her father to look at some particular flower on which a fairy was perching for the moment, and she could not understand why he was unable to see any of these sprites. "Mary Stuart was a most lovable child, just like a fairy herself," he concluded. "She passed on when she was eleven. I would love to have the gift that she possessed."

One autumn evening, when Mrs. A. Commins, of Cornwall, went upstairs, to draw the bedroom curtains, she glanced out of the window and saw a little patch of mist, which gradually cleared to a light like neon-lighting, but ball-shaped, and then, fascinated, she watched what she called "the glitter of the fairies," mauve, blue, green, orange, yellow, red, and white lights brighter than any gems, going around in a little circle, then darting backwards and forwards. She hurried downstairs to fetch her little daughter to the window. The child looked in the direction in which her mother pointed, and then drew in her breath and said: "Oh, Mummy, isn't it beautiful." They both stood spellbound, and then the daughter whispered: "Let's go down and see if we can see them outdoors." They went very quietly, but the opening of the door must have disturbed the fairies for they had gone. Mother and daughter searched with a torch around the place where they had seen them, and they noticed that the blades of grass and the leaves of the flowers looked as if they had been trampled on in a ring about one foot across in each direction.

Mrs. Commins had had previous experiences, and she described the speech of fairies as "high-pitched, quick, and very clipped." She used to see what she called "working-party elves" in groups of five or six very industrious little fellows tidying up the twigs, which had fallen from branches, and stacking up leaves. Their dress consisted of knee-length boots like Wellingtons; light fawn trousers; dark

brown or khaki-green jerkin; black belt and collar; and brown pointed cap. Their faces were flesh-pink but "very grubby-looking." She
described the costume of gnomes of the "cobbler" type as slightly
different, with a green ruffle round the neck, and shoes with pointed toes. Each fairy-cobbler wore a leather apron, and carried a little
pack on his back, and she always knew when one of those was about,
for his hammering had a definite rhythm: Tap tap tippity-tap. Tap
tap tap. Tap tap.

Mrs. Commins recalled that when she was fourteen years old
her father was appointed to the Coastguard Station at Dartmouth,
and one October day in his spare time he took her into the country
and left her sitting on a large stone in a woodland bower while he
went shooting. The first thing she saw was a snake coming out from
under a stone. It wriggled away from her and went into a clump of
bushes. Looking round, she saw a space in the bushes, and standing there in the dim light was an animal, which she thought was a
collie dog. She was used to dogs, so she jumped to her feet saying
"Here, Boy; come on; come on; Boy," and was going up to stroke
it when her attention was distracted by what appeared to be a large
blue butterfly. It was flying up and over and under the branches of
a tree, and as she watched it out of the corner of her eye its colour
changed from blue to white, and then to mauve, and she realised
it was not a butterfly but a lovely fairy. Just as she was thinking this,
it vanished. At that moment her father came dashing through the
opening in the bower shouting, "Are you all right, Rene?" for what
she had thought was a collie dog was a huge fox, which must have
been frightened by the sound of her father's gun and had crept into
the bower for refuge. Her father had returned just in time to see the
animal slinking away from there, and he thought if the child had
innocently cornered it and touched it she might have been bitten.

"When I told him about the fairy," said Mrs. Commins, "he
replied that it must have come to protect me, and that I must always
believe in fairies because they had helped him lots of times." Her
father then went on to tell her that in his younger days he was coming home one evening when he saw what seemed to be a beautiful
broken flower lying in the lane, and he thought what a pity it would

be if some person or a horse should step on it. He picked it up and placed it on some grass, but when he had walked on for a few steps, he thought "That's queer: that flower seemed like a living being," so he went back and straightened its petals and put it further towards the hedge, realising that the fairy spirit of the flower was still with it. At the same time he made a wish, not for himself but for his two sisters, one of whom had always longed to live in Paris, and the other to be a titled lady. "My father's wish, at that time, was fantastic," said Mrs. Gamine, "but within a year Aunt Edith was living in Paris and Aunt Anne had married a Count."

At the time of writing to me, Mrs. D. Van der Molen was a capstan operator in London, working nine hours a day. "So" she said, "I have no room for imagination." Before the 1939-45 war, she met an interesting family of cliff-dwelling pixies in a village a few miles from St. Austell, Cornwall. Her husband's boat was there frequently, so she made many visits. The first of these pixies to be seen by her was almost two feet in height, very lithe, and chatty. He had abnormally large ears, of a deep brown colour, and between the tips of them, just above the forehead, was a conical-shaped growth, which was semi-hard to the touch. This he called his "lump of knowledge." His lady was long, dark brown in colour, and covered with short hair similar to that of a horse. From the ankles to the shoulder blades, and from the wrists to the shoulders, were round bands of yellow-coloured hair, which gave the impression of zebra markings. The face, neck, hands, and feet were very dark brown, more like leather than skin. The toes were extremely long, just like fingers, the big toe being wide apart like a thumb on the hand. When working, these pixies used both hands and feet with extraordinary speed and agility. Mrs. Van der Molen had to knock a pre-arranged number of times on the cliff when she wanted to see them. She assured me that communication with them was not telepathic: she conversed with them in the ordinary way, and was able to see them plainly.

Since childhood Mrs. A. Campbell, of Queensland, Australia, had been able to see things that were unseen by others who were present, and consequently she used to receive many scoldings for "telling falsehoods." In 1929, while she was sitting resting in the Botanical Gardens in Sydney, New South Wales, she noticed a movement in a bed of aster daisies, and thought it strange on so mild an afternoon. As she watched the flowers in motion, a small head of fair, curly hair popped up, and its smiling owner, sheath-like in form and covered in green, stepped partly out of the flowerbed.

Her second experience was in 1933. "I was arriving home (quite sober) at about 10:30 p.m.," she related, "and this creature, which I am about to describe, must have heard me walking down the garden path. It was coming backwards down a branchless tree-trunk, and in shape it resembled a large-sized ape. Its body had a dark leaf covering; its neck was short and I saw no hair but a dark green head with a cap-like covering. Its feet were flat with nails like claws; its hands had small hooks. When it reached the ground, it did not turn round but slunk round the tree trunk, and I was not brave enough to go after it with a torch." Some time later, in the same garden, she saw among the trees a forest nymph that she reckoned, in comparison with her own height, would be about four feet tall. She did not notice its feet, but its legs were bird-like. Its body resembled that of a butterfly, with folded wings, which scintillated colours. The back of its head was also butterfly-like, with curled antennae, but its face was human. It was standing perfectly still. She met several other people who had seen these wonders, but they refused to say much about their experiences on account of being thought queer. A bush naturalist, who collected specimens of flora and fauna for that country and overseas, told her that it was a common occurrence to see these forms, but that if she were wise she would keep the knowledge to herself or she would be called a crank.

The house in Kent in which Felicity E. Royds lived as a child was modern but had been built near a knoll, where, she said, "We often found prehistoric flint implements, and there was a sunken ditch running through the garden, which according to tradition was the track of an old British (not Roman) road." It was one cold, grey summer evening when Felicity, aged eight or nine, had returned home late along with others after visiting some cousins who had been frightening her with ghost stories. She found she had left some object—her coat or a toy—in the rose garden, and was sent back alone to fetch it. The rose garden was surrounded by thick yew hedges, and at the end of it was a cast-iron gate leading into a thicket of rhododendrons. The object, which she had gone to fetch, was on the grass near this gate, and she had just retrieved it and was turning away, fearful of what might come out of the bushes, when she saw coming through the gate a small man leading a light brown horse. The man was shorter than Felicity and appeared to be wearing a blue tunic with something white at the neck. His skin was very brown, browner than his hair. The pony was about the size of a Shetland but very slender. Although she did not feel frightened, Felicity did not look at the man directly, only out of the corner of her eye. He put his hand on her wrist, and his touch was cool, not cold like a fish or lizard but much cooler than a human touch. He led her out of the rose garden and onwards until they were within sight of the house, and then stood still while she went in. She said that she was not at all musical, but while he held her hand she seemed to be aware of a strain of music that was sweet and high but sounded rather unfinished. Some nine years later she again heard the same strain coming from the knoll, but although she went out to investigate she was unable to see anything.

Miss Doris G. Stephens of South Wales told me that an old man who was caretaker of the Castle at Laugharne, in Pembrokeshire, saw some "little white elfin maidens" in the ruins. She also spoke of her young niece who used to see a fairy man. He would come and sit on the windowsill of her playroom, and she called him Orton, or referred to him as "the little white man." She first saw him when she was four, when she shouted to me in her Grandpa's garden, "Look, Auntie, there is the little white man," but I could not see him. "He has gone now," she said, "across the field, but he will be here again soon." She told me he was dressed in a white teddy-bear suit, which also covered his head, and he had "something to do with the daisies." "Later in the year, when winter came on, I asked her, 'Where is Orton now?' and her reply was: 'He has gone to live underground.'" Miss Stephens remembered that in fairy legends the Little People go to live in their homes underground, or in the

Irish raths or Little People's hills, in the winter, and she supposed that the child had obtained many of her facts about Fairyland from the books, which her nurse had read aloud to her. "But," said Miss Stephens, "when the nurse was questioned she avowed that the child had not been told any of those things from books. The information could only have been given to her by her fairy friend. When she was seven she gave up speaking about him anymore."

The setting for this next account is in a wild part of a garden of many acres in Ootacamund, Nilgiris, S. India, about 1889. The nine-year-old child Muriel (later to become Mrs. Armitage) used to lie on the rough grass by an underground water-channel—a natural outlet of a small pond between two hills, where she could hear water gurgling below. Further down, the water disappeared completely, but above this point were two peepholes in the grass. Through these could be seen miniature waterfalls, and on the mossy ledges were minute black frogs less than an inch in size. One morning, unable to ride before breakfast, she climbed on to a lichen-covered rock and sang about the frogs and insects. She did this only when alone, and the tune consisted of what she called "the four nature-notes." Three fir trees (plump and thick-set, and hideous in her eyes because they did not belong, as did the age-old sholah with moss-covered branches) grew below the rock. In the middle of her song, she saw what she thought was a small, queer-looking, red and green bird on a lower branch of the nearest fir tree. She slid down, climbed a branch and, above her head, was a little red and green man with a long grey beard, big nose, rosy cheeks, and peaked cap, laughing down at her. He was not much larger than an English sparrow; his jacket was red, and he wriggled his legs as he sat on the branch. She climbed after him as far as the tree would allow, but then he was gone. Bitterly disappointed, she had to admit that the he-fairy was not like Oberon, whom she had seen when she was Titania in Tableaux Vivants, when four years old. She said she knew nothing of Grimm's Fairy Tales, nor of Hans Andersen's, being unable to learn to read or write either English or French. She thought that the four notes of the nature-song, sung on the old rock, must have enticed the he-fairy to show himself. "Could he have come with the fir trees, which may have been imported as saplings from Europe?" she wondered.

Mrs. Mary Walton, a Buddhist living in Birmingham, recounted an experience she had at the age of seven, while on holiday at a farm near Dundee. The day was lovely and warm, and she sat facing a large elder tree, running her fingers through a clump of bluebells and, childlike, "listening to hear them ring." In the stillness, she fancied they were giving out a tiny tinkle. She stopped playing with them and rested her chin on her hands, "wool-gathering." First she saw what looked like a patch of mist, and then she heard music. Fascinated, she sat motionless, scarcely daring to breathe, as little fairies and elves began to dance and jump about to the music of a fairy fiddler who sat astride a swaying dog-rose. Everything was in perfect miniature, "like looking at a ballroom scene through the wrong, end of a pair of opera-glasses." After her experience she met an elderly lady and told her about it. "Yes," came the answer, "strange things are seen round about." When Mary remarked that the music nearly made her dance, the woman said: "It's a good thing you did not. You are a fay child, and when you are a lot older you will understand that those are elementals and are as real as you and me. Perhaps some day…" Then she stopped, and looked at her long and earnestly: "Don't tell anyone what you saw, but sit there again, and you may again see them or hear their music. When I was a child like you, I often heard it." Unfortunately the young seer was unable to return to the same spot, for the school holidays ended a few days afterwards.

One of my contributors, Mr. J. H. Craigen, kindly put me in touch with Mrs. E. Niven, of Ireland, who gave me the following account. Her husband's uncle was once crossing over some mountains outside Dublin with a friend, when they reached a fence and were suddenly accosted by a most peculiar little man who gave both of them a very uncanny feeling. He got in between them and chatted away until they came to another fence, where he mysteriously disappeared. The two men were terrified, and afterwards they could not remember one word of the conversation they had exchanged with their strange companion. Mr. Craigen was told by a Wesleyan minister, of Co. Antrim, that in one place where he was stationed, a number of people who were going to mass on a Sunday morning stood on the roadside and watched some wee folk dancing around a tree.

The aunt of a friend of Mr. Craigen's, when young was helping her father to gather potatoes in a fields, and just as they were about to stop work they lit a fire with the potato tops. When they went into the house, her father found he required the graip and sent her back for it. On reaching the field, she was surprised to see a number of little folk dancing around the brightly burning fire. She was so frightened, she ran home without the graip. When the mother of this aunt was doing some washing at the side of a stream one day, she could hear the little folk up in a tree laughing at her.

A similar experience came from Mrs. Esther Gardner, who related that when her late husband was gardener of the extensive natural Questhaven Retreat in California, he had a little gnome friend "of grandfather age," who adored him and wanted to be just like him. The great Angel Guardian of the area communicated this information to the leader of the retreat, the Rev. Flower A. Newhouse, author of *The Kingdom of the Shining Ones, Natives of Eternity, Rediscovering the Angels*, etc. The gardener never saw the gnome, but was often aware of his nearness and his helpfulness. One day he distinctly heard someone laugh at him when a root on which he had been heaving suddenly gave way and he rolled over and over. He jumped to his feet to see who had been watching him, and laughed as he chided the gnome, for no human being was in sight.

Miss Stella Watson of Surrey, an artist and modeller in clay, had seen fairies all her life but never when they were in the act of flying, "My fairies seem to come out of holes in banks," she said, "and I believe they also live high up in the trees. I think fairies and birds have a lot in common." During her travels she saw fairies in Canada, France, Ireland, Italy, Ceylon, etc., But none in the North Island of New Zealand. She was very young when she was in Canada, but she remembered there were fairies who looked like Indians in among the birch trees on the Prairie edge, while the fairies seen in Ceylon were "small and very sweet, and they seemed to be sucking something," though she could not see what it was. In England she had watched the nature spirits playing follow-my-leader down long blackberry sprays, and noticed that the thorns did not seem to hurt them at all. She had observed them on overhead wires and described their colours as green, grey, or blue, with an iridescent sheen. Sometimes she heard their voices "very high-pitched and chirpy." As a child she would come upon them sitting under nettles, with their backs against the stems. They seemed to have small pipes in their mouths, for there were tiny puffs of something like smoke rising into the air. She was puzzled by the fact that she had noticed flocks of fairies on the big main roads, and the explanation she tried to give herself was that they must be living in the remote past, before such roads were made, and were therefore oblivious to the noise. Another explanation could be that they were in an entirely different dimension, to which Miss Watson was lucky enough to be able to tune into.

Once, when cycling from Oxford late in the night, she ran into a large procession of them under some beech trees. She alighted and stood among them, but they took no notice of her and seemed to pass through her when they wanted to. During the summer months, she used to sleep out in a hammock near a lake, and often when she awoke she would see the little people "all over the place." One April afternoon in 1935, she was in the woods with a friend much younger than herself, when both of them saw groups of fairies all around. "They seemed to be going to a meeting," she said, "but very soon my companion spoilt it all by screaming with excitement."

When she was driving home one summer evening with a sealyham named Jenny by her side, the dog looked up suddenly and barked. A magpie was flying over the car, and in its claws was a tiny figure, which appeared to be struggling. As the bird passed, the little "captive" looked directly at Miss Watson. "I shouted and hooted," she told me, "but the bird flew on, and the result was that my car ran up a bank and I bit my tongue, an incident that left me with a very painful memory." Of course, the magpie would not really harm the little creature, but nature spirits love enacting these-scenes for the benefit of certain human beings.

At intervals Miss Watson used to stay at her lonely cottage high up in Llanfrothen, Penrhyndendraeth, Merioneth, North Wales, and she said that while there she heard talking constantly at dusk and dawn. There were high voices and low, and music like a Jews-harp. The sounds always seemed to be in the ground beneath her. A few days before Midsummer Day in 1959, she heard a voice near her say "Good evening" quite clearly, then something else and the words "...very thirsty," so she put out a bowl of milk and some water. Sometimes she thought she heard galloping horse or pony, although none had been up there for many years. It may have been a Welsh Pwca, a shape-changing sprite similar to the Irish Pooka and the English Puck. Miss Watson's unusual account of a water fairy is included in another section of this book.

One morning in November 1949, Miss Ruby D. Johnson of County Kildare was seated in the Dublin-bound bus that leaves Poulaphuca (a Gaelic place-name signifying Pool of the Pooka, or Puck's Pool) at about 7:30 a.m. Just as the bus was starting off, she glanced idly through the window and was amazed to see a tiny child busily gathering something from the nettles and weeds that fringed the roadside. It was dressed entirely in whitecap, coat, and leggings. Miss Johnson's amazement was due to the fact that the child was about the size of a seven-month-old baby, and yet was able to walk. She was also very surprised that such a small child should be allowed out in the bitterly cold semi-darkness of a wintry morning. "I clutched my companion and tried to draw her attention to the little figure," she said, "But my companion could not see it at all, and the other passengers in the bus began to eye me strangely!"

From Captain E. A. MacKay, of London, I heard of a fairy seen from the window of a railway carriage by his Godmother, Mrs. Hyndman, of Wick, near Bournemouth. About the year 1933, Mrs. Hyndman was travelling in a train from Bournemouth to London on her way to attend the funeral of an acquaintance of hers. She was sitting in a corner seat, idly watching the scenery when, a short while before reaching Basingstoke, the train drew to a standstill in a cutting, and a slight movement in the grass on the embankment caught her attention. There, literally within a few feet of the window, she saw a small being sitting on the grass with its knees drawn up and its elbows resting on them. Its face was cupped in its hands. Dressed in a non-descript drab costume and wearing a sort of cap on its head, it seemed to her to be scarcely interested in the train, and she had the impression that it was just tolerating its being there. So surprised was she at seeing this minute creature that she couldn't say a word. She just sat and stared at it during the short interval before the train moved off again, and then she turned her head and watched the little being receding from sight. Although Mrs. Hyndman had had one or two psychic experiences of another kind, she told her godson that she had never seen a fairy before, and had not seen one since.

When Capt. MacKay sent me his godmother's experience, he told me he had some of his own to relate. At the age of eleven he used to do a lot of bicycling around the Wiltshire countryside, and on a lovely day in spring one of his trips took him to Bratton in the Downs. He was wheeling his bicycle up a steep lane bordered by hedges, which were covered with fresh green buds, when he came to a small field on his left and was suddenly aware of activity—not of rabbits or other small animals—in the near corner just beyond the hedge. Stopping to peer through, he saw several faint little figures, who seemed to be running round and round and frolicking. As he laid his bicycle down on the grass verge and peered closer, the movement suddenly ceased, and although he waited for several minutes all was quiet and deserted.

On the next occasion, he was using a hazel twig to locate a reputed buried treasure in the garden of an old house outside Reading, when his search took him up to a thick shrubbery of laurels and other bushes. He was just wondering if he would have to search this too, when, from between the leaves, he saw a small, rather naughty looking little face peeping at him. "I could hardly believe my eyes," he said, "but as I looked, the face withdrew." For many years, when Capt. MacKay was sitting in his chair, he used sometimes to feel a definite pressure and warmth on his left knee, as if a child were sitting there. Several independent sensitives mentioned to him that a gnome had attached itself to him and favoured his knee as a resting-place, though he himself was never able to see the little fellow. When he and his sister were very young (she being about five years old), they lived in Wiltshire in an ancient house, which was reputed to be haunted. His sister repeatedly saw fairies there, and one, for whom she had an extraordinary name, often used to come to her early in the morning and talk to her.

When Mrs. E. Heath was living in County Antrim, Ireland, she saw a fairy dressed in a red peaked cap and a green jacket. Her hair was flaxen and curly, and she wore shoes with pointed toes. Another fairy, which appeared in a farmhouse a short distance away, was also dressed in red and green, with pointed shoes, which had silver buckles. She sat on a "creepy stool," but did not stay long. "There was a fairy glen at my uncle's farm in County Monaghan, and a fairy tunnel below one of his fields," said Mrs. Heath. "He often talked about the lovely music he used to hear at a late hour of the night."

My next contributor, Mrs. Jane Dowie, was a district nurse, and after her retirement was county councillor for the Earlston Division of Berwickshire. Her account is also of a little red and green creature. In August 1934 or 1935, she and her two sons were on a hiking holiday in Skye, staying at Youth Hostels. They had reached Dig—she cycling while the boys walked—and after visiting Flora MacDonald's monument Mrs. Dowie set off ahead of her two sons for Duntulm Castle, where they all proposed to meet and have lunch, which they carried in their knapsacks. It was a pleasant, sunny day, and she was cycling along enjoying the scenery and idly wondering how far the boys were behind her and how long she would have to await their coming. She was, perhaps, two miles short of Duntulm Castle when quite suddenly, to her startled gaze, a little creature, which might have been two inches high, ran across the road in front of her. She had a momentary vision of green and red, and thought at first that it must be some rare bird but, when she jumped off her cycle to see where it had gone, there was nothing but sheer rock, with not a crevice visible where it could be hiding. She went to Duntulm Castle feeling very much disturbed and fervently wishing her sons had been with her to have beheld the creature, but they had visited the Tweed Factory and then returned to the Youth Hostel, so never came that way. Mrs. Dowie cycled back by Staffin and was not again on that road, but neither at Dunvegan nor Glen Brittle—where she met many other hikers—had anyone seen this small creature, although they had passed that way.

A similar being was seen in the spring of 1947 by D. Saunders, who wrote as follows: "While walking in the oak wood at Ballathie, Stanley, Perthshire, I saw under one of the trees a tiny figure. Treading softly on the mossy path, I approached it cautiously, and even as I drew nearer this figure became smaller and smaller, till by the time I reached the spot where it had stood, it had vanished, leaving no trace of its presence. I returned to the same spot at the same time week after week, but never saw it again."

Max Heindel, in his book *Nature Spirits and Nature Forces* (Rosicrucian Fellowship, Oceanside, California), tells us that at the summer solstice, which falls on 21 or 22 June, the veil between the human and the fairy kingdom grows very thin; and that on this night the fairies hold a great festival at which they bake and brew their etheric foods and dance with joy at having served their important purpose in the economy of Nature. Many people look on Midsummer Day as the 24 June, the date of the Quarter Day, and claim to have had experiences then instead of at the summer solstice, but it is quite possible that the fairies continue to hold celebrations in their own territories for several days during that period.

I was privileged to attend one of these celebrations and was taken to stand outside a wood to await the fairy procession. I could see it coming when it was some distance away, as all the figures were self-luminous. As they drew near, they smiled and greeted me, and I was aware that I was the same size as they were—or they had become the same size as myself. It was an Alice in Wonderland situation that has been experienced by "H" of Buckinghamshire and other seers. I noticed that most of the pixies were in smart tunics, and their hats were of the same shape as toadstools. Strange though as it may seem, I can't remember what the fairies wore. A gate leading into the wood was opened and they all passed through. One of the fairies, who had been talking to me, invited me in, but I'm ashamed to say I suddenly felt afraid and refused the invitation. I think I was worried about the etheric food, which they would have offered me, and which it would have been unwise of me to accept. Some years later I had the same fear when I was "pixie-led"—but that comes further on in this book.

Mrs. Constance Carpenter, of Ryde, Isle of Wight, told her daughter Judith, who was four years old and very interested in fairy stories, that the fairies always came out to dance on Midsummer Eve, and for this purpose they liked the circles made by toadstools. Imagine the delight and surprise of both mother and child when they went into the garden on the morning of Midsummer Day and found there two complete circles of toadstools. The late Sir Arthur Conan Doyle said that, although these "fairy rings" are produced by fungi such as *agaricus gambosus* or *marasmius oreades*, he had to admit that they have always been associated with the little people and make a charming course for a circular dance.

There was one child, however, who derived no pleasure at all from such a spectacle. Richard Edward, when seven or eight years old, was playing in a meadow late in the evening when he heard the most beautiful music, and on turning round he discovered about a dozen little people dancing around a "fairy ring." Feeling very frightened, he ran home to his mother and told her what he had seen. His face was ghastly, and he was crying so much that she had great difficulty in comforting him. I was told this by his niece, Mrs. S. C. Roberts of Caersws, Mont., who had often heard her father speak about his brother Richard, and he said they were always being warned not to play in that meadow lest they be drawn into the fairy ring. No wonder poor little Richard was so scared! Mr. Tom Charman said that fairies love sitting on toadstools and climbing about them; and many a time he had seen some most charming circles of fairies playing round them.

Mr. Richard Byrne, of Co. Leix, Eire, was twelve years old when he saw a troupe of fourteen fairies dancing round a fairy ring. Eleven years later he again saw fairies, but this time they were too numerous to count. They were dressed in red and gold, and were all on little white ponies and kept him with them until morning. They invited him to return to them on the following night, but he was afraid to go. Miss Maria Bradfield told me that one Midsummer Eve in her adult years, she had an exquisite vision of the dance of all winged creatures, extending from the turf on which she stood up to the brilliance of the setting sun.

A little fairy house constructed of several layers of frilly-edged fungi was seen by Mrs. Ellen Hilton, of Lancashire, a lecturer, writer, and spiritual healer. The house was at the foot of a dead tree near a stream flanked by green banks, and she noticed it first in May 1955 on the day of the Wesak moon, the Buddhist festival. Then she had to leave for Palestine, but on her return she went over the stream to see how the little folk were getting on. She found the house was a paradise of rhythm and music, and there was great activity because it was still not quite complete. It was, however, ready by Midsummer Eve, and looked very beautiful. Mrs. Hilton was the author of *Therefore with Angels* (printed privately) and *Glimpses of Life Eternal* (Regency Press Ltd., London), and she went on some of the pilgrimages with my contributor Mrs. M. K. F. Thornley, who said of her: "She sees into the other world continually. Like Clara Reed, another contributor of yours, she saw fairies in my garden."

The garden to which Mrs. Thornley referred was in Cornwall, and possessed a "cairn," just a pile of stones and mossy concrete blocks beside the little overflow of surface water, which, she surmised, probably ran down by her boundary to the sea a million years ago. In 1948 her seer friend, Mrs. Clara Reed, saw two large fairies there. She said their names were Trindy and Frieta, and the cairn was their home. Within the last few years a wonderful white strawberry plant had appeared, and Mrs. Thornley had gathered its fruits from early summer to November.

It was during the Midsummer of 1943 that Mr. Roy Morgan, a robust Mancunian residing in Kensington, saw in a garden at Hendon a fairy and an elf. His friends had left him alone in the garden so that he might wander round at leisure. He was not thinking of anything in particular but happened to be admiring an almost

breathtaking profusion of roses on a large bush when, to his astonishment, he saw poised on a rose leaf a female fairy. She was six
inches in height, perfect in form and face, and dressed in gauze of
yellow and faint blue. She continued to smile at him for several seconds, and as he watched her there appeared beside her on another
rose leaf a little elf, four inches or so in height, clad in brown and
green raiment. Then both of them faded away as quickly as they
had come. As is so often the case, the many friends to whom he
mentioned this experience were more amused than believing. "It
wasn't a case of clairvoyance," he said. "That explanation I ruled
out entirely. Nor was it a butterfly or anything of that sort. It was a
wee person like an exquisite doll." He revisited the garden hope-
fully, on many occasions, and although he never again saw so magic
a spectacle, it had convinced him that fairies were real and not just
figments from a land of make-belief.

Several contributors have seen fairies in or around roses. My
sister Dorothy saw a semi-transparent figure on our rose bed, near
the "Rapture" rose. She said it had long, narrow wings, but only
one of them was fully materialized. Later, both she and I saw this
small being on several occasions, and once I watched it following
her down the garden path. It was of the elfin type. I was looking
through the window at the garden one day when I saw a fairy standing at the side of a rose bush, which was not yet in bloom. She was
dressed in yellow and was about eight inches high. As my sister had
been resetting the rose bushes in different parts of the garden, I did
not know which one this was, so I pointed it out to her. "Oh, that's
a yellow rose-tree," she said. Eight days later I saw the little figure
standing there again, and this time the yellow roses were coming
out and were the same shade as her dress.

Mrs. Erica R. Forty, of London, told me that when she was young
she saw a fairy near a rose; and Miss Irene Barron, of Queensland,
Australia, caught sight of a tiny fairy in a rose, during her early
childhood in England. "It was very tiny," she said, "and lay curled
up asleep in the middle. I just stared, hardly daring to breathe, but
then, silly-like, I walked away, and when I came back it was gone.
I have not seen one since." A rose fairy was also observed by Miss

Mary McGowan Slappy, a professional writer and artist, of Washington, USA, when she, too, was a child. "I saw her there," she said, "on the first red rose to bloom in our garden. No one else saw anything but the rose, but my fairy was there."

The poet and writer on mystical subjects Miss Maud Baynes wrote to me that when she lived in Ealing she picked three or four yellow roses in her garden one very warm summer afternoon, and took them up to her bedroom where she placed them in a vase on a little table by her bed. As the weather was so hot, she lay on top of her bed to rest for a short while. "I was quite awake," she assured me, "there being no question of my being even near sleep, when, glancing at the roses, I saw them distinctly begin to shake as if in a dance. The shaking and dancing continued in a rhythmic manner, and I was aware of 'personalities' within them. It was as if they wished to draw my attention to something, and although I could not actually see the figures I was intensely aware of great friendliness, persistence, magnetism, and happiness. I have had many similar experiences, and once heard with physical ears their sweet laughter. I have also heard music."

In a letter written in 1957, Mrs. G. K. Evason, of Kent, reported that she had seen a gnome wheeling a tiny garden wheelbarrow. "He is interested in the front garden, which is cared for by the lady tenant of the flat above me. He is taking himself and his work very seriously, for the garden is not thriving too well and he is helping to clear away old roots, etc." This busy gnome must have been clearing the way for one of the garden sylphs, for in December another letter came from my correspondent: "On waking at the usual early hour, I became aware of a pink cloud in what appeared to be a small rose tree in its winter garb, that is, no foliage or blooms, just bare branches. Then the rosy glow dissolved and a dainty pink fairy became clearly visible. She appeared to be tending this little tree, which is in the front garden here, so I hope it will bloom well after being treated so lovingly." The sequel came in August of the following year, when Mrs. Evason wrote: "Do you remember my account of the fairy tending the rose bush? Well, the front garden has a number of these bushes, six pink ones in a row, and many others of different varieties round the garden. All of them bloomed, and some continue to bloom most gloriously, so evidently the fairy really did help, as this is the first time that they have been so successful." I think the gnome, too, deserves a share of the praise for preparing the ground.

These little earth-folk can be very helpful, as Mrs. Clara M. A. Clayton, then living at Stapleford, Notts, discovered one very hot, dry afternoon when she was trying to hoe the garden ready for some seeds, which she wanted to sow. The ground was parched, and she couldn't pull the weeds out. Feeling hot and tired, she was still struggling when she saw a little brown gnome watching her. He had his arms folded and was laughing at her efforts. "Don't stand there laughing at me," she said to him, "but help me with this hard ground." Immediately, he disappeared, and she stood there fascinated as she saw the ground moving and the soil throwing up the weeds until a large patch, much bigger than she had needed for the seeds, had been thoroughly loosened. "There could have been more than one gnome working on it," she said, "for within a fraction of time it was ready for me, and all I had to do was to gather the weeds into a bucket and get the rows ready for sowing. The earth was beautiful to work in, and I kept thanking the little brown gnome and letting him know my pleasure and appreciation for what he had done. I didn't see him again, but I knew he was there, and I felt that he shared my happiness.

"The gnomes are also the guardians of the minerals within the earth," continued Mrs. Clayton. "They are form-builders, and they work in stone metal, etc. Without them we should have no beautiful jewels or precious metals. They guard carefully the secret of their life work, but on certain occasions it is revealed to a member of the human race, if such a one has a great love for all these unseen workers of nature and a firm belief in their existence. These two things I have always had since childhood. And so, one day, I found myself in the presence of a little green gnome on a hill. His face was serious, and he looked anxiously from side to side. Then he beckoned to me, and as he went suddenly through the ground like a fish swimming through water, he changed to the colour of earth and he moved easily through soil, rock, etc. I followed him with my inner vision until he ceased his downward journey and showed to me his particular place of work. He was busying himself with metal of some kind, I thought, but he was able to put his hands through it and enter into it and, as he worked within it, he beat it and moulded it and then pulled a piece out just as if it had been a bit of soft clay. The creative force working through him was fashioning that part of Mother Earth, and he could do anything with that particular substance within it. He showed the piece to me and then rubbed it and seemed to wash it in an underground stream. Suddenly I knew it was silver. It appeared whitish-grey in the earth, and he grinned and seemed delighted that I knew what it was, for now he held it close to me and it gleamed like pure silver. Then he stiffened and became alert, as if he heard the approach of his co-workers. All at once, everything went dark and I saw him no more, but I thanked him in my heart for showing me his secret workshop."

Near Mrs. Clayton's previous house in Stapleford is a huge, isolated mass of rock with layers of harder stone protecting the softer red sandstone below. This ancient sentinel is called the Hemlock Stone, and according to Arthur Mee's *Nottinghamshire*, it is 70 ft. round, 30 ft. high, and is said to weigh over 200 tons. "When I've gone to it alone," said Mrs. Clayton, "I have been aware of its great Guardian, which has been with it throughout the ages and will be with it until it has crumbled away in the distant future. To me, it is hallowed ground where this strange stone stands. I have drawn into its very heart, uniting my life with the One who lives within it and whose aura extends a long way into the surrounding area. This noble Rock Spirit is silent and withdrawn, yet aware of my presence and of my gentle touch upon the stony surface. Little gnomes are working under and around it and in the adjoining wood. They are very busy, but nowadays have an air of resentment towards the folk who visit the place and the children who constantly set parts of the wood on fire near it. The great stone has been for some time encircled by an iron fence, but the children burrow a way beneath it and try to deface the rock. Before I left the district I definitely felt a change in the atmosphere of the place, and the nature spirits were working further below the ground."

Mrs. Clayton has seen at various times the sylphs, or air spirits, and describes them as "brilliant creatures, swift as lightning in their movements. I have also been aware of fairies in my garden," she said. "They are lovely creatures of varied colours, their shining auras more light and delicate than the most beautiful flowers in the garden. These flower fairies, which may be a variety of sylphs, have wings; the wings really being forces that come out of them. I used to bend low among the flowers and enter into the life and beauty that surrounded me on all sides. I would see certain flowers lighting up with a most delicate radiance. This was the aura of the little fairies, flashing a golden-yellow herd, a pale pink there, a lovely violet, blue, and green in other parts. Wherever they concentrated their vital force, those particular flowers seemed to grow lovelier and more radiant for the time being. Little gnomes, too, were busy among the flowers. It was truly a fairyland of beauty and enchantment. So much work was being done, the nature spirits being used by the higher beings to imbue the flowers with their life force."

Mrs. Clayton was born in Wales, and when she was nearly eighteen years old she used to go as often as she could, on fine days, on a lovely wooded slope, which was part of the Snowdonian range. The spot she visited had beautiful grassy slopes, and to the left could be seen the Menai Straits. "I used to take sandwiches with me," she said, "also a book which I had on my Confirmation Day and the New Testament. I always sat on the same grassy slope with a wood behind me, quite away from the path unseen by anyone. Then I would read for a while and meditate, and try to enter into the heart of Nature, whose bounty surrounded me on all sides. In my soul I spoke to the God of that mountain and felt his presence very strongly. I knew he brooded over the place and was ever watchful — a Being full of Peace, Strength and Beauty. I felt he was aware of all forms of life which existed in and on that mountain, including me.

"During these visits, which became even more sacred as they went on, I was aware of little beings watching me in the wood, which was behind me, possibly tree nymphs and wood elves, but I felt they were very shy and would not come out from the wood. I was also aware of small creatures, light and airy, dancing in the sunshine on the slope beside me, and I felt, rather than saw, the fairies scampering over my knee and alighting on my shoulders. Shrill music was sometimes heard close to me, and then in the wood behind. In this wood was a great Presence, the Spirit of the trees, who stood tall and still, with folded arms, guiding and directing the work of the wood elves and tree nymphs, and his aura filled that area. What I experienced on that mountain has lived with me to this day."

Mrs. Minnie Higgs, of Morden, Surrey, said that one summer evening late in 1938 she and her child were riding with her husband on his motorcycle and were about to enter Forest Row, East Grinstead, when a strange feeling of being surrounded by a fairy host made her touch her husband and say, to his utter astonishment, "Drive the motorcycle quietly, as anything could happen here."

Writing in 1955, Mrs. Higgs said that the two other members of her family had both passed on, but she still went to Forest Row and the feeling she had at first was always strongly with her.

Miss Christina L. Bain, of Blackley, Manchester, is another contributor who senses the presence of fairies and knows when she is in their surroundings. When she was 30, and staying at Kents Bank, Grange-over-Sands, she joined a group of friends for a walk over the hills. On the wooded crest of one hill, the group stood "stock-still" when she said, "Hush! The fairies!" To her, their presence was very real. At a later date the leader escorted another group over the same spot, and a friend told Miss Bain that he halted the party there, saying: "Here live the fairies."

"On another occasion," said Miss Bain, "my sister motored me slowly down the by-lanes of Warwickshire and we came to a ring of trees. Here I cried: 'Look, a fairies' ring!' To me they were there, and I still feel the atmosphere of the fairies when I recall these experiences."

Writing about the flower fairies in her garden, Mrs. D. Goddard, of Hampshire, wrote: "They are so tiny and luminous that the very air seems lighter as I sense them. They seem to me to have slight little bodies with gossamer wings. I feel they pass on some of their lovely colours to the flowers as they open, as one would paint the hues on a painting. They are too wonderful to describe in our language because the brilliance of their presence makes physical things only half beautiful in comparison. I feel they play an important part in God's creation."

When she was young, Mrs. Caryl Haynes, of Shropshire, used to spend hours alone with Nature. The lovely fields, and a dingle with a brook and waterfall, provided a playground that could not be bettered, for it was peopled with creatures that she wouldn't have changed for any other playmates. She remembered the name of one little fellow, because her mother tried to make her say "Arthur," when she insisted he was called "Hartha." He stood about eighteen inches tall, and his dress seemed part of him. This varied with the seasons, although she couldn't remember seeing him during the winter, when there was snow on the ground. His speech was like the sighing of wind in the fir trees and had a fascination for animals. "That's how I came to play with the rabbits and the birds," explained Mrs. Haynes. "The rabbits came and sat at my feet, and the birds, on my hands."

As she grew older, her mind became filled with mundane matters, and she did not see any of her little friends until many years later, when she and an aunt were walking in the country. The aunt was chattering away, when Mrs. Haynes saw the head of a nature spirit peep out of the hedgerow. She couldn't resist it; she whispered "A rabbit!" and, putting her hand in the hedge, she brought out a fine baby bunny, which had been popped into her hand by the little being whose head she had seen. She showed it to her aunt before letting it go free, and her aunt was thrilled. She thought her niece had some power of a kind that brought rabbits out of hats, and Mrs. Haynes said she never would be able to explain to her aunt what really happened.

Mrs. Maybelle Gillespie's son, Thomas, used to see fairies in his native Galloway, mostly near the house and in the garden. Especially he liked the "lady fairies," as he called them, and the way the fairies helped to show the birds where to get food and berries in wintry weather. On one occasion, at the age of ten, he brought Mrs. Gillespie some flowers and explained that a fairy had said: "Give these to your Mother."

Many years ago, when Mr. George E. Rice and his late wife lived in Middlesex, they were invited to spend an afternoon with Dr. Outram, a lady doctor of philosophy, at her home at Shenley, in Hertfordshire. Dr. Outram had been told by a well-known London medium that she had a fairy dell in her grounds, and this interested her because her lodge-keeper's little son, aged four, kept on telling his mother that he played with the fairies. Having heard that Mr. Rice's wife was a gifted medium, Dr. Outram was eager for her to see the fairy dell, so thither Mr. and Mrs. Rice went with their younger daughter a few weeks later, and they and their hostess sat close to an old oak tree and waited. The dell consisted of a double line of trees with grass instead of a road between, and the little party had been there about two hours when Mrs. Rice exclaimed: "I see them; they are little brownies, and they are coming out of that hollow tree over there." She pointed to a tree on the other side of the grass-way. "They are bringing out a Maypole. They have set it up and are dancing round it, inter-twining the ribbons and shouting just as children do." Dr. Outram sat wide-eyed, staring in amazement at Mrs. Rice, then in awed tones she said: "That is exactly what my lodge keeper's little boy has been telling his mother."

When Miss D. L. Voss-Bark was exercising her dogs in the woods near Minehead, in Somerset, she saw two pixies rushing away at her approach. They ran into a hole leading to a hollow oak. "But," she said, "They are really very human. They forgot to duck their heads, and so off flew their hats and went rolling in the pathway. I was luckily able to obtain the two small hats and bring them back with me, and so I am able to convince my friends of the truth of the tale." Miss Voss-Bark had mentioned this in an article in the *Dog World Annual* of 1938, and I wrote to ask her what the hats were made of. She replied that they were perfect little cones of wood.

"What a pity," declared Mrs. Agnes Taylor of Cornwall, "that you never met Nellie Sloggett of Padstow, alias Enys Tregarthen and Nellie Cornwall. Under one or other of these names she wrote her books of Cornish fairy stories, several of which were based on the old legends, which have been handed down for many generations. Often, when I visited her, she saw fairies on my shoulders."

A well-known children's psychiatrist, who for professional reasons preferred to remain anonymous, told me that she had seen fairies all her life, and that she and her twin brother used to spend many hours observing the little people in the country round their home, which was in Southern Ireland and was on the verge of a great bog. "The little elves loved the peat-fires," she said. "They would sit cross-legged on the nursery hearth, holding out their tiny hands to the blaze, and chuckling to each other when the sparks flew and the turves fell in the warmth of the flames. As far back as I can remember, there was always a baby in the heavy-hooded oak cradle by the fireside, and Sarah, our Irish nurse, sat and sewed by candlelight in the soft Irish dusk. For nursery tea we had cake one day, and jam or golden syrup the next. On golden syrup days the slices of bread were cut in the kitchen early in the day, spread with syrup and stacked on the plate so that the syrup soaked right through the bread. I remember joking with my brother at the sight of a little gnome sitting on the edge of the plate, holding his mouth open to catch the drops of syrup from an overhanging slice of bread. There were the Christmas tree fairies, the Easter grotto fairies, the fairies who guided folk through the bog, and the undines who danced in the waterfalls. They were all quite different from each other. They were busy all day, and their movements were swift and sure. They were like children in comparison with those greater beings, the angels, who moved with such dignity and light.

"Then came a time when my father decided to go and live in England. The hustle of moving hardly reached the nursery until the day when we all boarded the ship in Cork harbour to begin a new life among strangers. My mother was a harpist, and the great instrument, in its green baize cover, stood beside us on the deck. It was difficult to settle down in England. My mother missed the warmth of the Irish people, the rough country scenes, and the soft Irish rain. She became ill, and one day just before my seventh birthday, Sarah took us all into the room to say goodbye. Although it was a winter evening, the room was strangely light. A soft radiance flooded my mother's face and enveloped the tiny face, which was all we could see, of the baby lying in the crook of her arm. We (the six children) waited in silence beside Sarah. My father stood as motionless as a statue by the side of the bed. My mother beckoned, and Sarah went forward and lifted the baby from her arms. She murmured 'Goodbye,' then held out her hands to my father, who clasped them in his own until my mother's smile faded and she was at rest. At that moment, fifty or more fairy people, holding a shimmering blue cover, came instantly forward and drew the wonderful gauze over the bed and the still figure. The light faded and the room felt cold. Then from the corner came the clear notes of my mother's harp. Baby Michael grew into a quiet, dream-boy. He had a love for all living things, and it was he who pointed out to us the fairies in the herb walk, and the gnomes picking the fruit off the low bushes and quarrelling with the birds for the best specimens. I do not see the fairies now as often as I did, but they do pay me a visit occasionally."

Another instance of fairies being seen round a deathbed was related to me by Capt. Sir Quentin Craufurd, Bt., M.B.E. His wife's grandfather was, he said, "as confirmed an old sceptic as you would want to meet," but he had a fairy rath in his garden and would never allow anyone to interfere with it. Just before he passed away, the Wee Folk gathered at his bedside, and he said that although he knew it could not be true, he could see the little fellows quite plainly and was very glad they were there!

When Mrs. Margaret Nailard was living at Feltham in Middlesex during the Second World War, she had a very lovely flower garden in which she used to sit and watch the little flower fairies smiling at her. There were also pixies and gnomes with their pointed hats, and they would all form a circle and go dancing round and round. She said it was a beautiful sight, and she looked forward to seeing them each day when the weather was fine. A born clairvoyant—as were her mother and grandmother—she was still able to see the wee folk in her old age, and she told me that shortly after the arrival in England of the Jamaican immigrants, she had seen some delightful fairies of the same type.

I am indebted to Mr. Michael F. Kelly Mor, late of the Royal Engineers and Ordnance Survey, for sending me Mr. Colgant's account of the fairy hurlers, or hockey players, seen in 1886 in a field adjoining the main road near the village of Mullagh in County Galway, some six miles from the farm on which Mr. Kelly Mor then lived. As they had been seen playing in that same field a few years earlier, news that they had turned up again spread like wildfire through the Galway countryside. The incident passed entirely out of his mind, as he had left the locality a year or two later and did not return to it for more than half a century. In 1940, the year he took up residence in Galway city, he received from a friend a letter mentioning that Mr. Hugh Colgan, a well-educated and prosperous farmer who was related to the friend, had had an accident and was in Galway hospital. The friend suggested that Mr. Kelly Mor might be good enough to visit the patient there and, perhaps, take him some light reading matter, so Mr. Kelly Mor duly arrived at the hospital taking with him a magazine he had purchased at random. Mr. Colgan gratefully accepted it and glanced in a casual way at its contents. On noticing that they included a ghost story, he was prompted to say that he himself could relate a curious experience. The visitor encouraged him to do so, instantly realising that this man was one of those who, in 1886, had witnessed the fairy hurlers in the field.

"One evening," began Mr. Colgan, "when returning home from school in company with five other youngsters, boys and girls, we stopped to watch a lively game of hurling. It was being played by a number of little men with their coats off and wearing white shirts. After a while the ball landed within a few feet of the low fence by the roadside, and I jumped over the fence into the field to throw it back to the hurlers, but, to my astonishment, there was no ball. Neither were there any hurlers to be seen. My five companions declared that they all vanished the moment I cleared the fence. I should add that I was thirteen, the oldest among us, when this happened." He went on to say that the field in which the hurlers were playing was a large pasture, several acres in extent, devoid of any ditches, trees, or hedges, which might have concealed them. When he and the other scholars dashed home to tell parents and villagers of their experience, they were greeted on every side with the offhand observation, "It's not the first time the fairies have been playing there."

Mr. Kelly Mor said there was a sequel to this. In the 1950s the same Mr. Hugh Colgan and a number of other farmers were sitting smoking and reminiscing by the turf fire in a house some miles away from Colgan's, and in the course of the evening Colgan related his boyhood experiences with the fairy hurlers in the field near Mullagh. He was concluding with the remark that not one of those who had shared it with him was now alive, when a voice in the background contradicted him. It was that of the elderly housewife who had been listening to him while baking her bannocks. "You are mistaken," she interposed, "for I was there also. There were six of us, you remember…"

Again through the kind help of Mr. F. Kelly Mor, I received Mr. Michael A. Nevin's account of what occurred one Midsummer evening in the year 1917. Mr. Bernard McMahon was driving his uncle's cows to a field beside the fox covert in Thaula, about four miles from Loughrea in Co. Galway, and Mr. Nevin was accompanying him. On reaching the gate leading into the field, they were letting the cows in when a big blaze shot up in the centre of the covert, and one of the men remarked what a terrible thing it was that someone had set it on fire, covered as it was with furze and gorse bushes and trees, which extended over three acres. The flames rose high for several minutes, then died out suddenly, and the two onlookers were just expressing their relief that the person who started the fire had extinguished it, when it blazed up again, and they watched it for another few minutes until it died down again as before. This was repeated about ten times, but each time it flared up it remained alight for a shorter period, until the final blaze just shot up and died away on the instant. Then, from the same spot, out came hundreds of little men on their hands and knees. They crawled along by the fence until they came to a point about a hundred yards further on, and as each one reached it he disappeared. The two men watched this strange procession for at least three minutes, and still it went on, so they decided to rush to McMahon's uncle's house, where the neighbours gathered in the evenings, and bring them all up to see this queer sight. The neighbours returned with them, running as fast as they could—the total distance being 400 yards—but when they reached the covert there was no trace of the little people, or anything unusual. Naturally, they were disappointed and rather angry, and some of the boys accused the men of playing a joke on them. The scene of the fire was revisited the next day, but not a trace of any ashes could be found, and not a blade of the long grass seemed to have been disturbed. Yet Mr. Nevin and Mr. McMahon had stood only 100 yards from the phenomenon, and had seen it quite clearly in the twilight just after sunset. Twenty years later, again at twilight, a young woman named Mary Alton, who had never heard of the previous occurrence in the covert, was returning home after visiting a friend's house. While she was walking along a lane by the same field, she saw a similar display of shooting flames, but unlike the other witnesses she did not stay long enough to see any little people appear. She was so frightened that she fled straight back to the house she had just left and remained there until morning!

A journalist who came to interview me confessed that he himself had seen fairies. His childhood had been spent in Glamorgan, Wales, and one day, when playing with a group of boys, he hid from them in a thick shrubbery. While there, he suddenly became aware of a path leading through it, which seemed to have been trodden by little feet. Following this path, he emerged at last to find himself on a small, green, sun-drenched plateau, at the far end of which were gaily-coloured hollyhocks and delphiniums. He gazed entranced at what he believes were fairies, prancing about in the flower beds. He thought at first that he was dreaming, but eventually convinced himself that he was actually witnessing a fairy scene. To his great regret, when he grew older and developed more courage for revisiting the area, he was never again able to find the path to the green plateau, nor, despite persistent searching, any trace of the fairy people.

Miss Katie Richardson had an experience in May 1942, which was "so lovely and so wholly unexpected" that it was often in her mind. It occurred in Lippin Wood in the village of West Meon, Hampshire, when she was 43 years old, and I quote her words: "I was taking a walk in this peaceful spot when suddenly, on reaching a shallow, saucer-like depression in the ground, flanked on one side by a tree, I saw a group of very disgruntled-looking little men engaged in tidying-up. They were collecting the tiny twigs and leaves (which I could scarcely see) and after sweeping them up with little brushes they placed the rubbish in a neat pile at one point of the hollow.

"If this surprised me, it was nothing to what followed, which made me almost afraid to breathe, for from the proximity of the tree there appeared a number of fairies dancing about out of sheer happiness. They were from eighteen to twenty inches in height, and were dressed in varied shades of pink. One of them made a sign to the little men, who were standing apart from them, and a tiny round table and some chairs were brought and placed where the fairies directed. Next, the fairies produced a delightfully lacy table-cloth, and after shaking it out they spread it over the table. They then disappeared, and I wondered what was going to happen next, but in no time at all they appeared again, carrying between them a perfectly lovely-looking cake, a two-tier affair, with a most artistic decoration in icing. (As a professional cook, I've often longed to reproduce the design, but it's beyond me and, I think, anyone else except the fairies.) When it was placed and, with a great deal of fuss, all was arranged to their liking, they disappeared once more, and this time when they reappeared it was as maids of honour and train-bearers to the Queen herself. She was taller than the others, and her dress was of a deeper shade of pink than theirs. The skirt of it was full, like a miniature crinoline, and covered her feet. She had a crown on her head and carried what I can only describe as a wand. On reaching the table they all curtsied to her before taking their places. The cake seemed to me to be in the nature of a surprise for her, and she showed great pleasure at seeing it. When she cut it, I saw that it was yet another shade of pink throughout. Two pieces had been cut out, and I found myself wondering whether the little men would be given any, when I heard a very faint sound, at least, it was faint to my very acute hearing, but it was enough to send the fairies hurrying away and out of sight. In no time at all, the little men had whisked away the table and chairs, and then they, too, had gone. Later on I saw the fairies again, but this time they were without their Queen.

"Before my experience in Lippin Wood, I'd had great doubts about the existence of fairies, but I've never doubted since. My next sighting was at Warnford, a tiny hamlet next to West Meon. There was a small horse-chestnut tree growing on the roadside, and while I was looking up, admiring the flowers, I noticed a little fairy balancing on one of them. My thought 'Oh, fancy a fairy in a tree' was answered with 'I am a tree fairy;' and then when I showed surprise she added 'Only the ones with flowers on.' She seemed more solid than the other fairies I had seen and was quite bold in comparison. I think the method of communication was mental.

"I saw fairies again in the village of West Meon in late June 1943. I had offered to help pick fruit in a garden attached to a large house there. I did not know the lady of the house and had only seen her once or twice. After we had finished fruit-picking, she said, 'I'd like you to see my special garden, one I made in memory of my son after he had passed over.' We entered it by a wrought iron gate, and I found myself standing in a very lovely walled garden, which was peaceful and secluded, and ablaze with colour. The atmosphere was so wonderful that I often recapture it. Soon I became aware of numbers of fairies tending the flowers and moving swiftly amongst them, and also some little men who were paying special attention to the roots. My companion turned to me and said 'Ah, you can see them; I knew you would. That was why I brought you in.'"

At the age of about 28, Miss Dorothy Townsend saw fairies and gnomes in a little larch-wood at Coldash, Newbury, in Berkshire. She went there after tea and was not thinking about them or expecting to see them, but there they were about half a dozen of each. The fairies were playing about, and the gnomes were sawing and chopping wood. "I stood quite still," she said, "but they went in a flash. I am psychic and can, now and then, get into touch with the angels. I love the Unseen World."

Prior to the 1914-1918 war, Mrs. C. Graddol saw a fairy in Piccadilly Gardens, Manchester. Ranged along the side of a wall was a row of poppies, and near them appeared a "young girl" about twelve inches high, whose golden hair hung loosely down her back. Her dress, of a beautiful light mauve shade, reached to her feet, and its short puffed sleeves revealed her lovely arms and hands. Gently, she touched about six of the poppies and then vanished. "I can tell you, she made me very happy," said Mrs. Graddol.

When Mrs. Louise P. Jones was sixteen years old, she was basking in the May sunshine on the balcony of a convalescent home in Hertfordshire when she saw a fairy of a similar type to that seen by Mrs. Graddol. In the shrubbery, which was separated from the balcony by a long lawn, were a few poppies. The fairy appeared from behind one of the poppy plants and ran a distance of about eight feet in and out of the small shrubs, finally reaching a larger bush, from behind which she did not reappear. Her height was approximately the same as the other poppy fairy and she, too, had long fair hair, which flowed behind her as she ran. Her arms were held straight, and stretched slightly forward; her legs were bare. Unlike the other fairy, her dress was green and of a dull matt material.

"I looked out for her for the next two weeks while I was there," said Mrs. Jones, "but I never saw her again." This contributor had a further experience in the late spring of 1941, when she was sauntering in the fields in a district known as Munden, which she informed me is an Anglo-Saxon word meaning "pleasant valley." She said she had noticed the reactions of children in the happy atmosphere of the place. "But then," she added, "it supplies a stream, a very large meadow of lush grass, and always seems warm and sunny." As Mrs. Jones wandered in the fields on this particular day, she thought she saw out of the corner of her eye an elf looking over the second bar of a five-barred gate. She stood quite still, glancing sideways, and waiting for him to move. When nothing happened, she turned slowly and walked towards him, skirting a ditch to reach him, only to find that the "elf" was a young dock-plant blown against the gate, and his cap and arms were its pointed leaves. However, from a distance it had looked so much like an elf that she felt puzzled and thought: "Fairies bring luck; I must search." So she got down into the ditch and found not fairy gold, but Roman remains. Picking up fragments of tiles, she took them to Verulamium Museum for identification. This led to the discovery of a firing kiln, lots of shards, a very large pot in sections, and other treasures. After Mrs. Jones had left that district, she kept thinking of her discovery of the Roman remains and she wondered whether it really had been an elf against the dock-leaves, trying to draw her attention to that spot, and vanishing before she reached it. She had been in those fields scores of times before that day, and six months earlier the gravel ditch had been dug for drainage and was quite clean and dry.

Miss M. Vesey, when writing to me about her own experiences, made the following interesting remarks, which seem very applicable to Mrs. Jones' account of the dock-plant: "Particular places, seasons, weather, etc., may affect a human being in a favourable way so that such a human being can be easily aware of fairies. When this happens, the look, position, shape of a plant or tree, or of light and shadow may suggest to us (not necessarily correctly) something of the appearance of the fairy; they may serve as points to attract our attention." Since the bodies of nature spirits are composed of plastic matter, they are able to superimpose their shapes and features on flowers, and sometimes a flower fairy identifies itself so completely with its plant that it is hard to distinguish one from the other. Some of the garden and woodland fairies assume leaf-shaped hands and feet, and others could more aptly be called "fairy flowers" than "flower fairies" when they assume heads like the flowers they tend.

Here is an example contributed by Mrs. G. K. Evason of Kent: "One day I saw a very curious and amusing sight. There were two long columns of tiny beings, three or four deep, with heads like marigolds, walking rapidly toward the front garden of the house adjoining the one next door to me. This house has new tenants, and recently the garden was dug up and reconditioned. Sure enough, after my prophetic vision, marigolds were planted very thickly in a border round the lawn."

The Rev. G. Eustace Owen, M.A., sent another example. He was eleven or twelve years old at the time of the experience and was living in Lancashire. "I was lying in bed on my left side facing the door, which was ajar. I could not get to sleep and was going over in my mind the events of the day (which did not include fairies!) when suddenly I saw all around the door scores of little daisy-faces peeping at me and laughing, though I heard nothing. For a few seconds they were clearly visible, and I did not ask myself why they should be seen so easily in my dark bedroom. Then they vanished, and I felt sorry for I wanted to look carefully at them. I had seen only their heads, each framed with petals, poking round the door."

At about 8 o'clock on a spring morning in 1948, in the garden of a house in Buckinghamshire, Mrs. E. T. E. Lloyd saw what looked like a tiny female doll lying among the flowers, which bordered the long path. The little creature had transparent wings but one of them appeared to be broken, and Mrs. Lloyd stooped compassionately to pick her up. Instantly the fairy was transformed into a mauve flower-petal. "I am something amounting to a religious mystic by nature," commented Mrs. Lloyd, "and often, uncommon experiences have befallen me. During my early Elysian childhood in Wales, I was able almost to discern the Shining Ones (The Higher Devas or Angelic Beings) visually."

Miss E. Woodford-Grimes of Highcliffe-on-Sea, Hants., who at the time of writing was the local representative of The Poetry Lovers' Fellowship, related an experience that had occurred in the early spring of 1938. "I had been ill," she explained, "and no doubt was in what is called a receptive state. I was recuperating at the home of Miss Ailsie Hall, who was then living at Brockenhurst in the New Forest. She and I went walking in the clearing on a hillside towards a wood on the edge of the forest proper. Both of us were interested in poetry and drama, and I remember we were talking of the historical plays of Shakespeare and saying how clever it was to telescope the periods without obscuring the facts. On going up the slight incline, we stopped suddenly whilst staring at something. Then we looked at each other and I said, 'Do you see what I see?' Her answer was, 'Fairies, and they're dressed in blue.' They would be from 30 to 50 feet away, and we stood watching while they danced rhythmically as if to music, although we could hear nothing but a soft wind like a sigh. There were no other people or animals about, and we said afterwards that if we had attempted to go nearer or to make a sound they would have vanished quickly. As it was, we stood some moments before they faded."

When Mrs. Martha A. Smith was a child in Indiana, she would wander away and sit under a favourite cherry tree that grew in the backyard. There she would see the little people, and sometimes they would even bow to her. She watched them by the hour and hummed an accompaniment to their songs. Of course, like many another fairy seer, she was called "odd" and accused of day dreaming and "telling fibs." She never forgot the fairy-leader, who was beautiful and golden-looking and seemed to command great respect from all her followers. These little ones were about a foot high, dressed in vivid colours, and would come and go "in the wink of an eye."

"Every detail is as clear today as it was then," began Mrs. Elsie Willetts of Worcestershire, in her letter written in 1955. She then went on to relate what had happened nearly 50 years ago, when she was twelve. She was playing hide-and-seek with her friends in their favourite spot a lovely glade near the Harcourt Estate, off the Abingdon to Oxford road. She was the seeker, and when she had finished counting she turned quickly and saw two figures who seemed to be joining in the game. They were looking up at her and backing away to get out of sight. One was dressed in pink and the other in blue, and they were "just like the fairies on a Christmas tree," but were about the size of an average child of eight years old. Her friends had seen nothing, and she told me she was too enchanted to say anything to them.

Many years ago, in Galashiels, Mr. Thomas Shortreed's son and daughter-in-law were visiting him from Leicester, and on the last night of their visit he proposed that he and his son might take a walk to the top of Meigle Hill. It was "a very quiet, grey-dark September evening with no wind, cloud or mist," and after reaching the summit they had a look at the scenery and then made for home. They had just left the hill, by means of a gate leading on to a farm-track, when Mr. Shortreed was surprised to see a few yards in front of them a troop of figures crossing the road from North to South. It was hard to describe what they were like, just long, lanky figures;

all heads, arms, legs, moving up and down with a jaunty motion. There might have been about twenty of them, very happy-looking. The first was very tall, over six feet, and then a gradual sloping down to small figures of about two feet. There was a stone dyke on the right side and Mr. Shortreed stopped to see what would happen when they reached it, but the figures just seemed to melt into the dyke. He went and looked over, but there was no trace of them.

He turned to his son and asked, "Did you see that, Paul?"

"I didn't see anything," was the disappointing reply.

They continued on their way and, about 50 yards further on, another similar group crossed the road in front of them, but these figures were not quite so tall and not so lively looking. They were all of a white colour and did not hurry across but just danced up and down. Once again, only Mr. Shortreed could see them.

Miss H. M. McCarthy, of Hants, said that from early childhood she had seen fairies of every description, and Mrs. L. Dickens Yates, of Kent, had seen so many fairies, including leprechauns, that she said it would take days to tell me about them. A weekend was arranged so that we could meet, but unfortunately, owing to illness, I had to cancel my visit, and I never obtained the details of her experiences.

One summer day in 1948, Mrs. Eleanor Laing, of Essex, was walking through Epping Forest with a friend of hers, Mrs. Freda Garrard, and on entering a glorious glade they rested awhile and began to meditate upon the beauty of their surroundings. Suddenly Mrs. Laing became conscious of movement at the base of a tree quite near at hand. "Look, Freda!" she exclaimed to her friend. "Fairies!" Mrs. Garrard could not see them, but Mrs. Laing had no doubt at all that she herself was seeing them clairvoyantly. They were quite four inches high and had white wings. Their legs seemed very thin. With their arms interlocked like a daisy chain, they were dancing in a circle at terrific speed round the tree. She also noticed on this occasion two gnomes dressed in red coats, with green trousers reaching down to just below the knees. They had on their heads small, acorn-like hats. Each carried in his hand a small garden fork.

Some time later, she had an experience at Tiptree. Choosing

a quiet spot in her aunt's garden there, she seated herself upon a small hillock surrounded by almost an acre of differently coloured wallflowers, and, near at hand, large clusters of forget-me-nots. She soon fell a-meditating and presently became aware of a wee fairy, blue like the forget-me-nots, perching on the top of her shoe.

Her last experience of this kind was in 1950. Again Mrs. Freda Garrard was with her, and they were seated in the cemetery of Upshire Church, Essex. The church stands upon a hill providing a glorious panorama. It was not long before she became aware of a hovering movement over some of the flowers growing in the cemetery, quite close to her. Soon she discerned an amorphous mass of heavenly mauve with a tiny being in it. "Look, Freda!" she said. "A fairy!" But again her friend was unable to see anything unusual; and in a moment the fairy was gone.

"Some 60 or more years ago, when I was about nine years old," wrote Mr. James O'Connor of County Meath, in 1955, "I was coming home along the Cavan-Dublin road with an aunt of mine, Miss Alice Connell, who had been milking her cow. I looked over the hedge, which bordered a triangular field, the apex of which would not be more than 20 yards, and saw some men kicking a football. I took them to be local, as they wore whiskers like some of the men from the town, but their headgear seemed peculiar, though I can't say definitely in what way. My aunt did not notice them. Time rolled on, and I still could not get them out of my mind, but it was not until many years afterwards that it dawned on me who or what they really were. They had been kicking the football in the apex of the triangle, and this was bounded by the road on one side and, of course, by the field on the other. I realized that it would be impossible for any full-sized man to have kicked the ball without it going repeatedly on to the road or the field. The thought of these people haunted me so much that they seemed to have cast a glamour over me, and it lasted for over 40 years.

"I might add that at a distance of another half mile in the Cavan direction there is a hill, covered with gorse and bracken, called 'Cobblers Hill,' and I am sure it got its name through someone seeing these people mending shoes."

When the Rev. S. Henshaw was a child of about six, he was playing with his sister in the garden of a house in Ilkeston, Derbyshire, and, tiring of their games, he suggested that they should roll a log over, which had long lain lengthways by a boundary fence. When they had done this, there was disclosed a strange creature about six inches in height, standing straddle-legged across a hole in the ground, which was approximately three inches in diameter. The creature had the obvious shape of a man. He was completely naked, if one does not count the section of an onion that he wore as a cap. His beard and his hair, which protruded from the back of his "cap," were straw coloured. "The incident," said Mr. Henshaw, "struck me as an occasion for action, so I ordered my sister to fetch a pair of scissors from the house a few yards away that I might cut him in two. Losing patience because she was so long gone, I remember looking towards the door of the house, and when I returned my gaze to where I had seen the pixy he had disappeared. I believe he had gone up the pear tree beyond the boundary fence. I will not go into the clever suggestions that are supposed to explain this and similar experiences for I have read much if not all that modern psychology has to say on the matter. The fact is that my sister and I remember it as vividly as ever, though it happened so many years ago."

Early in the summer of 1956, Mrs. Agnes A. Powley, of Peterborough, Northants, was lying in bed wide-awake, and the night was so beautiful that she was tempted to rise and look at the garden by moonlight. Right in front of her bedroom window was a large lime tree, with several bushes nearby, and as soon as her eyes grew accustomed to the outside scene her attention was drawn to a number of small objects flitting from the tree to the bushes and flying around, touching each other in mid-air. She stood quite still for a few minutes and thought how very lovely it all looked by moonlight, "Although," she wrote in her letter, "it is really a very ordinary little garden."

She said she had absolutely no thought of fairies in her mind and at first believed then to be moths, though they were larger and their flight was daintier than that of a moth. She moved closer to the window to get a better view, and in a flash the garden was deserted.

Only then did it dawn upon her that they were fairies.

Writing from California in the same year, Harriet P. Foster, whose main job was the editing, typing, and preparation of authors' manuscripts, told me that when she visited Ireland the old boatman who used to row her around on Bantry Bay could see "the little paypul" plainly when he passed "the Fairy Isle." She never could do so, but she remembered a man in New York State telling her that he could see "the nicest bunch of little pixies" always around her.

An eight-year-old boy with whom she used to spend many happy hours in a small fairy-house he had built in a thicket under a lovely pine-tree in the wooded section of Balboa Park, San Diego, California, also had this faculty, and would describe for her the charming little creatures he could see around them both, especially one whom he called "Tinkle-Star" because she was "all sorts of shiny colours" and tinkled when she moved.

Delamere Forest is a well-known Cheshire beauty-spot, and at the age of nine Miss Gwyneth M. F. Tait went for a holiday there with her mother and grown-up brothers. She was very fond of slipping off alone into the fringe of the forest, and on this particular sunny morning she was playing among the trees in a glade full of sunshine and green shadows when she saw, standing beside a clump of tall grass, a white figure about two feet high, unclothed, but seeming to have transparent wings. It had pale golden hair, but of its face and expression Miss Tait had no clear recollection. She knew it must have been friendly because she was not in the least alarmed, and followed eagerly the delicate dancing feet of the fairy as it skipped from tuft to tuft of the forest grass. She was led in this way some distance into the woods where she had not been before, but when she lost sight of her guide among the bushes she was able to return to the more familiar paths without difficulty.

Miss Tait did not visit Delamere again until she was grown up, when, she said, she had no magical experiences and caught not the least glimpse of the fairy of the forest. But on two separate occasions she was there with a party of adults and children who were lost among the thousands of similar pine trees and could not find the main road, and although it was years since her childhood visit and she, too, did not know the way, she was able to lead them safely and confidently out of the wood.

I am grateful to Mrs. Ellen Jackson, whose own account of water fairies appears elsewhere in this book, for an experience related to her sister by Mr. Bruce Glaister. He had taken his father's gun (an act that was forbidden) and gone out on the moors to do some shooting. When it was time to go home, he was afraid his father would see him bring back the gun, so he hid it in the heather. Later, on going to retrieve it, he found a crowd of little folk around it, examining it with great interest. Feeling afraid, he ran home and told his mother, who was a very religious and strict person. She did not believe him and punished him for lying.

Mrs. Jackson also gave me the interesting information that the Yorkshire novelist Halliwell Sutcliffe told her brother he often saw fairies whilst stamping over the moors.

At the age of three, Miss Kinara Kestyn, of London, used to play in a large and very lovely garden, and there were many fairies there. "They were nothing extraordinary to me at that age," she said. "I was meeting new things and new experiences every day, and they were to me a normal part of a world I was just discovering. They were tiny, delightful, winged creatures, bathed in light, and not at all frightened of me. They went about their business, mostly flitting from flower to flower quite happily as I watched, and sometimes they watched me. I never spoke to them, nor they to me, yet somehow we communicated. For some reason I never thought of touching them."

Another time, when Kinara was about seven years old, she was lying in bed when she saw, quite distinctly, several chubby little cherubs hovering above her. Although she heard no sound, she knew they were talking and laughing, and she smiled back. They stayed for quite some time, inspecting her, and then they just faded away or she fell asleep; she could not remember which. "I had no reason to imagine any of these things," she declared, "and in spite of the teasing by my school fellows and the reasoning of adults, I have remained convinced that what I saw was true."

While stationed at Portobello Barracks in Dublin, Ireland, in

1919, Mr. I. Cooper was out alone one night, walking towards the town not far from the barracks, when he saw a fairy. It was flying about three feet off the ground in front of him and was like a normal-sized woman, but it had wings and was dressed all in white. Then it vanished, but Mr. Cooper was terrified, and after walking a few more yards he decided to go back to the barracks. On turning round to do so, he saw that the fairy had been following him, and it, too, turned round and flew in front of him again for some distance before it finally disappeared. Although the street was dimly lit, he had seen the fairy quite clearly, which of course is accounted for by the luminous quality of these beings.

At the time of Mr. Cooper's experience there was trouble with the people of Dublin, and he and the other soldiers had been warned not to venture away from the barracks unless someone went with them. He wondered if the fairy came to protect him from danger. Whatever the explanation, he said he had believed in fairies ever since.

Another soldier who had an unusual evening was Mr. P. O'Shea, of London. It was during the Second World War, and he was returning from leave and travelling to his depot at Trawsfynydd, North Wales, arriving at Blaenau Festining Station about 9:30 p.m. The camp was fourteen miles away, so he was disappointed to learn that he had missed the last bus, but two schoolteachers were kind enough to hire a taxi to take him over the mountains. He had still some distance to travel, and after tramping for a while he obtained a lift in another taxi as far as the road which led to the huts. He started to walk the last few miles in the moonlight, finding the stillness of the countryside at night rather eerie, and it was about midnight when he finally reached his destination.

Outside, on the grass, he saw a little man of about two feet high, wearing a greyish jacket and leggings of the same colour. Down the front of his jacket were large black buttons, and on his head was a round hat. His face was very round; his eyes, ears, and mouth were large, and he stood with his arms akimbo, laughing at Mr. O'Shea, who confessed that he lost no time in getting inside his hut.

"I know that some people might say I had been drinking, or

that I had imagined it," he said, "but I was *quite sober* and, being a grandfather with ten grandchildren, I feel I have passed the 'imagination stage' years ago."

Mrs. H. F. Still's most vivid memory was of the time when as a small child, she used to play about just before her bedtime at her home on Shirley Hills, in Surrey, and was able to see the fairies on several occasions during the summer evenings. She described them as being of a pale, almost transparent colour, with delicate pinky-mauve wings, and she said that every time she thought about them she could still see them dancing amongst the heather.

Miss Nora M. Best and Miss Agnes Robson were staying in Borrowdale, the Lake District, in August 1941, and one afternoon they walked by way of the Pony Track from Rosthwaite to Watendlath. After a cup of tea at the farm, they decided to return by a track marked on the map via Dock Tarn, but after walking for some time they realised that they had been confused by sheep tracks and had lost the trail. They made their way to the top of the ridge, and away below them was the road that would take them back to their hotel, but there was no sign of a track that would take them down.

While they discussed what they would do, suddenly they heard the shrill laughter of children, and, about a hundred yards below them, they saw what they thought were four or five children scampering about each other round two or three rather big boulders. Thinking that there must be a track near, the two companions immediately made a beeline for the spot, quite expecting to find a family party on the other side of the boulders. But when they arrived, no one was there, and although they searched around for a considerable time, calling "Coo-ee," there was nothing to be seen or heard.

They were more than a little mystified. "We realised," they said, "that it was an unlikely place for children to be in and, as we had reached the spot in two or three minutes after seeing them, there was no place to which they could have disappeared. Comparing impressions, we both had seen what we thought were small children with long hair streaming out behind them as they ran and a general look of quaintness about them. We have been puzzled ever since. Could we have disturbed the Little People at their play? We wonder!"

As a child, Mr. James Alvey of Nottingham lived in the country, and being a true nature-lover he went frequently for long walks across the moors to the various distant hills. It was on one of these walks that he came across a small glade in which were a few harebells, one or two crab-apple trees and some clusters of toadstools, and there he saw a group of tiny gnome-like men, all very intent on their work as though they had to carry it out very quickly. He stood watching them, dumbfounded, for several seconds, and then they seemed to disappear from view into the bracken, which surrounded the clearing.

In July 1958, a friend called for him to go to see another personal friend of his, whose house stood in its own grounds in a village, a rural setting, which had not changed much during the last four hundred years. After getting off the bus, they walked along the road and up the drive to the main door. His friend, who was a little way ahead of him, rang the doorbell, which was quickly answered, but he himself felt drawn away from the house and [went] further into the grounds, which contained a variety of very picturesque shrubs and trees. He was standing admiring them when his eyes turned to a laurel bush around which danced at least a dozen pixies and fairies, their faces expressing great happiness. At this point he heard the voice of his friend calling him, whereupon the little people quickly dispersed, leaving that unforgettable moment imprinted on his mind.

At the time of writing to me, Mrs. Mary Allan of Glasgow was over 70 years of age, and she declared that, although she had the second sight and saw many kinds of visions, she had never been able to forget her fairy experiences. The first occurred when she was nine and lived in the Isle of Skye. She was playing in the woods at the back of her home, making a garden of plucked flowers, and while she was sitting in the centre of this the fairies appeared. "They were lovely little creatures, about three inches high," she said

Later, in her home in Glasgow, she was peeling some potatoes when there came to her a fairy dressed in azure blue, with bright wings and a golden wand. Again one appeared when she was sitting talking to some friends, while on another occasion she saw one after she had retired to bed, and she described it as having pink wings, a green body, and a head, which looked like a small doll's.

Norway also has its Little People, and Miss Gjoa Waagen used to see them when she stayed with her grandparents, who had a very large estate in the country with lochs and rivers. She would watch the fairies dancing, or putting colours on the flowers, and there were also undines to be seen in the streams.

On a night before the full moon, Miss Amarilla Easthond, of Gloucestershire, was walking in the garden, as she felt troubled and wanted to be alone. Near the garden was a wood enclosed by a fence, and around it were big oak trees. She was just passing by when something caught her gaze: it was the sparkle of a few drops of rain left in the grass, but there was something else. A gust of shining little forms swept by, dancing in and out of the trees. "I looked towards the wood," she said, "and for a moment everything was dark, but suddenly a light shone forth and a group of gleaming fairies danced about. They floated by like a silvery cloud and then disappeared."

Everything seemed in a trance, as though the fairies had left some of their magic behind. Even the tall trees did not stir. Amarilla was beside herself with joy, and her trouble was quite forgotten. She said she seemed to be in a far-off land, but when the fairies had gone she slowly "came back." The moon was slightly covered by a cloud and all became dark again. Realising it was late, she ran to her home, still feeling full of joy.

At the age of eight or nine, Miss Carol George, of Cornwall, was following her elder sister into an adit that led from the main shaft of Sally Mine to the beach at Porthtowan, when she turned and looked behind her. In a side passage, which was blocked off with a roll of barbed wire, she saw a group of little people four to six inches high, standing in a circle. She had the impression that they were dressed in white, their clothes suggesting that some were male and others female. Just as she started to tell, her sister Jennifer to look at them, they disappeared.

But Jennifer, too, could claim to have seen a fairy in her bedroom, in the gloaming, and described her as follows: "She was in a bubble of light with no clearly defined edge to it, and about four feet from the ground. She appeared to have no bright colouring but just a yellow-white light, which did not glow nor yet shimmer around her. In height she was about six inches and seemed to have wings, although she did not use them. She floated towards the open window and disappeared."

While the fairy was near, Jennifer, who was about eleven at the time, felt "a sensation of quiet peacefulness," which she said was certainly unusual for her. I know that other fairy seers have experienced this wondrous peace, which often accompanies such visitations.

Mrs. T. George, the mother of the two girls, had never seen anything, but she said "I remember their telling me of these things at the time."

The fairies described to me by the writer Naomi Mitchison were approximately two feet high and had large heads. She said they were strange, embryonic-looking creatures "rather like huge tadpoles, which progressed by turning head over heels."

She was twelve years old when she saw the first one in the boom of a hedge in some water meadows near Oxford. "But," she said, "at that time Andrew Lang was trying to make me see fairies."

About eleven years later, while in bed nursing her baby in a house on the Isle of Wight, she observed a being of a similar type running out of one wall and into another, and once, when returning from a Labour Party Conference in 1936, she saw one on the downs above Brighton. These "very rapid visions" never alarmed her, but she was always rather surprised. "It was," she explained, "as though there were two pin-holes in two pieces of paper, and for a moment they superimposed." She told me she had also seen the house fairy of the Campbells at Carradale. She was having her bath in a light bathroom, and the fairy, like a darting flash of golden light, flew in through a closed window and out through the shut door.

While on the subject of bathrooms, there was an amusing incident concerning my own mother, Ellen Gertrude Johnson. She came downstairs one morning from the bathroom, looking very shocked and disgruntled. I asked her what was the matter, but she wouldn't tell me for some time. Then she blurted out: "There was a small, inquisitive face peeping through the window."

"Was it a bird on the window-ledge?" I asked.

"No, it wasn't," she retorted. "I know a bird when I see one. This was like a tiny human face and it was peering at me, full of curiosity." Although my Mother was rather psychic and sometimes had prophetic dreams and premonitions, she had not, until then, seen a nature spirit, and I thought she would be delighted. Instead, she strongly resented the fact that even such an ethereal creature as a fairy should have witnessed her ablutions, and she never spoke of it again!

When I went to Coventry, in Warwickshire, to visit Mrs. Clara Reed (a Christian seer whose sincerity was vouched for by the Rev. Paul Stacy), she talked to me of her many visions of fairies and angelic beings, and said she had often seen the nature spirits in Corley Woods not far from there. Some of them were very fond of the primroses and violets, and had dresses made of flower-petals. Others had tunics made from the bark of trees and appeared to favour the chestnut trees. They loved the beds of moss and hopped about, seeming very friendly with the birds. While staying at Carbis Bay, Cornwall, Mrs. Reed saw fairies many times, and one of these was a little fellow dressed in brown and green, with a coat and cap of leaves. She had also seen water-lily fairies, with their pretty sepal-led caps and dresses; and on another occasion she noticed a very strange-looking nature spirit, which was part-fairy and part-bird. It was standing upright, and its turkey-shaped body was grass green, while its beak-like mouth and its feet were bright red. Once, in Coventry Park where she had wandered feeling weary and depressed after the long illnesses of her husband and daughter, a fairy showed her his "domain" in the trunk of a tree. With her etheric (X-ray) vision she saw that he had thought-built a good imitation of a modern house in miniature, complete with a flower garden and a lawn. Stretched out on the latter was a fairy cat, and nearby was a garden seat and a small round table on which two fairy birds were perched.

The fairy himself had a very long nose almost like a beak and his clothes were made from fern leaves and the bark of the tree.

Only once, so far, have I been privileged to catch a glimpse of the interior of a fairy's house. It was beneath one of our two birch trees and the vision was a momentary one, but I noticed there were chairs, a table, and a rug, and I seem to remember some tiny pictures on the walls. It was a delightful experience, rather like gazing into a doll's house and seeing its display of miniature furniture and ornaments. Fairy furniture, however, such as a chest of drawers or a sideboard, hasn't always any inside to it if the fairy's imagination hasn't stretched as far! But apart from that, we could almost envy the fairy folk, for their thought-built decor can be changed instantaneously, according to the whim of the moment.

Mrs. Ruth Johnson of Nottingham had always believed in fairies, or "the Wee Folk" as her father used to call them, and she often saw them in the woods, by the streams, and in all Nature's background. As she grew older and came away from the country, she thought that her childhood visions must have been imagination. "I was not to keep to that idea," she told me, "because at the beginning of 1939 my husband and two small children and I went to live in a house where there was a spring at the bottom of the garden. Near the spring was a natural wild corner, and I said 'I am sure that belongs to the fairies.' My husband decided to beautify the spring by making a grotto, so we all got busy and dug down into the garden, making a six-foot-deep horseshoe-shaped hole, and there we built with rockery stone a lovely grotto with a pool in the middle and a little waterfall flowing down in a stream under a miniature stone bridge. We built steps down one side, but on the fairies' side we just could not disturb it. It had to remain in all its wild beauty. When we went down into the grotto, everything was very still. We all felt a wonderful peace and contentment; and there I was privileged to see a most delightful little fairy. She was four inches in height, with perfect features all in miniature and a pert expression on her face. Her dress was like the weaving of a spider's web and her wings seemed to be of vegetable substance. I looked away and then back again. She was still there. Then I spoke, and she disappeared. After that

I often felt the presence of the wee folk. Then came the ominous rumblings of the war, and air-raid shelters were delivered around. We received ours and it was left in pieces in the middle of the lawn. Now we had to decide where to build it. The only suitable place was in the fairies' own corner. We asked the wee folk if we could do this, and, oh dear, what agitation it caused, and a definite refusal at first was given. Later, as it became necessary to put up the shelter, we asked again and we could feel the wee folk go into council to decide. Then we were given consent to put the shelter in their corner. In this corner we were given protection, and felt a consolation against the blast of guns, etc. Towards the end of 1943, there came upon us an agitation to remove the shelter, but we took no heed of this as the war was not over and we felt we might need that protection. Following our refusal, a great uneasiness settled upon the garden, and down in our once-peaceful grotto was a seething discontent that grew into a malignant mischief. The feeling spread to the house and everything seemed to go wrong. Then I said we must take out the shelter and restore the corner back to its natural state, so we got busy and I know many tiny hands helped to make our work easier. We restored the corner and also the atmosphere of peace and love, and finally I saw again the wee fairy, and she gave a smile with a deep sigh of contentment. They are indeed living beings with untold energy and force, and although at times we do things that incur their hostility, they will always reward good with goodness."

Mrs. B. Leeson, of Malvern, Worcestershire, wrote: "I have had second sight all my life, and in spite of very many experiences of the intangible world, which closely interpenetrated our material existence, to my great disappointment I had never seen a fairy, although I was pretty sure they were the souls or spirits of flowers and occasionally visible to those with the gift of 'sight.' One day in the autumn of 1949, my husband and I stood beside a holly tree in our small garden and discussed whether it should be cut down or not, for it was growing large and awkwardly encroaching on the opening between the rockery and rose pergola. Also it caused much work in chopping, for, being male and having no berries, it was cut square with a ball on top. We decided to cut it down the next day. I always wake very early, and as I did so on that next morning I saw beside my bed a small figure of a pale, transparent green colour. I could only see it as far as its waist because it was close to my bed. Much astonished, I said 'Who are you?' The reply came like a sigh or a very soft breath of wind... 'Holly'; and the little figure faded and was not there anymore.

"I told my husband at breakfast, and he said immediately, 'Well, that settles it; we can't kill the only fairy you have ever seen.' So the holly tree remained as it was, and the rockery was moved further back instead."

Mrs. Daphne Charters, whose book *A True Fairy Tale* (The Greater World Association, London) deals with the origin, life, and evolution of fairies, told me of a similar experience connected with a laurel bush, which grew up against a wire fence and was getting very straggly. She thought that if the front of it, which was taking up an unnecessary amount of the flowerbed, was cut back, it would spread sideways and make a better screen from the garden next door. When her once-a-week gardener arrived, she told him what she wanted done and went to write letters in the sitting room, which had French windows leading into the garden. Suddenly she had an idea that something was terribly wrong, but she didn't know what it was. She then heard mentally a kind of screaming and went to the window to find that the gardener was hacking the bush and had cut off its top. She rushed out and stopped him immediately, and sent him off to do something else while she tried to pacify the screaming fairy-guardian by assuring her that everything would be all right and that the bush was very strong and would grow again. The fairy eventually calmed down, and Mrs. Charters visited the laurel bush frequently until it looked more normal.

A further example of the fairy folk's dismay when bushes and trees are interfered with was given by Mrs. Claudia F. Renton of Chipping Campden, Gloucestershire. She had a number of flowering shrubs planted at the top of her garden and, never having been pruned, they grew vigorously until they resembled a tiny forest. When her old gardener said, "Now, ma'am, if them there bushes were dug out, we could do something with that land," she unfortunately agreed, and he dug them all up and left them lying on their sides. It had been Mrs. Renton's custom for years to take a camp chair up there and have her afternoon rest, so on the following day she went as usual. It was such a sad sight to see all the shrubs up-rooted, and she regretted it keenly. However, she stayed about an hour and slept for a while. When she opened her eyes, she was astonished to see many little forms floating in the air. "I had never seen anything of the kind before," she confessed, "and I could not understand it at all. There they were floating in all directions and all around me, dozens of them. I could follow their flight with my eyes. Some would make a circle and land on my shoulder, my arm, my hand. I knew by instinct they were fairies and had been disturbed by the uprooting of the shrubs. I could see their little airy-fairy wings with the veins (or whatever they were) running through them as fine as a hair, and their tiny round heads just like black dots. In all they would be an inch long, some smaller." Mrs. Renton stayed watching them for a long time, then so excited was she that she got into her car and went to tell her grandchildren in Gloucester and also some in Sutton Coldfield, who came back with her. The next day they sat in the same spot in the garden, and Mrs. Renton saw the fairies but not in such numbers. To her surprise, the children could not see them, even when she pointed to one and said, "Now watch this. It is floating round my arm and has come on to my shoulder." The tiny beings disappeared after a few days, though occasionally she saw one or two of them afterwards.

When Mrs. Dorothy J. Hancock, of Walthamstow, London, was in her twenties, the family moved to a new house, which, among others, had been built on an ancient estate where an orchard used to be. Her father had made a nice lawn with a rockery, and on a day of brilliant sunshine she was sunbathing when she became conscious of movement among the flowers in the border near her head. Keeping still and only moving her eyes, she was thrilled to see some little people from two to three inches in height and of different types. They were singing, and she could hear the same musical laughter that she had heard in her bedroom as a child. They seemed to be playing some sort of game, and the flowers they liked particularly were the foxgloves. She could not resist raising herself on her elbows to get a closer look, but this startled them and they all vanished. Ten years went by, and she had married and moved some two or three miles away to a house with a smaller garden and lawn, where her husband built a rockery and made a pond. One very hot, sunny day he thought he would alter the rockery, and was doing so when Mrs. Hancock saw a little old fellow exactly like her conception of a gnome. He was four and a half to five inches high, very wrinkled, and apparently of a great age. His clothing was green in colour and seemed to be made of the same substance as the plants, for it was moist as though covered with most or dew. He was looking very angry and resentful, and was muttering to himself. She felt that her husband had upset some arrangement of the little folks and told him what she had seen. He knew of her other experiences with fairies, so he decided to replace everything as it was, merely commenting: "If they want it like that, well it's theirs." The gnome watched the work of replacement and then vanished into the undergrowth of the rockery, and Mrs. Hancock said she felt "a great calm, as though all was well." She told me that many wild birds come to her garden, which is full of old-fashioned flowers such as musk, pansies, columbine, etc., while the small rockery is composed mostly of plants given to her by her friends. An apple tree, which was grown from a pip, produces two quarts of apples a year, and a double white lilac has sprung from a branch, which had been thrown away. In the little pond dwell frogs, newts, and an old toad. "So, as you can see," said Mrs. Hancock, "it is all centred on the fairies."

The following account sent by Mr. John Pettman, of Monmouthshire, strikes a macabre note among the others in this book, yet I feel it should be included because it was a genuine experience. Recalling the time he was twelve or fourteen years old, he wrote: "When I had grown tired of the long August holiday, I decided to spend one day on a long walk, taking with me a bag containing a few things to eat. With no definite objective, I just chose north, and followed a road in that direction. I later found out I had got as far as Dowlais. The countryside turned into moorland, and houses and people became few and far between. As I was passing through a derelict brickyard, for some reason I looked over my shoulder, and about a minute's walk away I saw in broad daylight a man about a foot high, dressed in red, running along the path after me, waving his arms in what I took to be a threatening manner. But the impression that has remained with me most clearly over the 23 or so years between then and now is that he looked demented, and his face was shiny and so suffused with colour that it was redder than his clothing. Being a timid child, I started running, and after a minute or so when I looked back again there was no sign of him. Arriving at the next house, I asked if I could stay inside for a while. When they asked the reason and I gave them the story, they looked at me with the same combination of wondering pity and apprehension that has been its reception ever since. I enquired if they knew of any midgets thereabouts, but they shook their heads and I think were rather glad to get rid of me." It is unusual to hear of such extreme anger in a nature spirit, and we shall never know the reason, but it may be that the boy John had unknowingly trampled on some tiny creature or plant that had been greatly treasured and loved by the dwarf to whom such a loss through human carelessness would indeed seem a tragedy.

Mr. Gordon Harte was once a bus driver in Ireland, and one day in a lonely part of the country his bus would not start. He had dropped all his passengers and was quite alone, his conductor having gone to ring up the garage to ask them to send a mechanic. While he waited near the bus, he heard voices, and thought they were far off until out from behind some bushes no further than fifteen feet away came two little men of about two feet in height. One of them told him straight away that a battery-lead was loose, and he found this was so. They talked together about a lot of things, but "It would sound plenty crazy if I told you," he said in his letter to me. His conductor shared the next experience with him. They were coming back from a run with the bus in a very lonely place in County Sligo, Eire. As they were rather early and didn't want to leave before 7 p.m., Mr. Harte was standing waiting beside the cab door of the bus. Just then, two rabbits dashed out of a bush, and immediately after them came the smallest girl he had ever seen in his life. She was nine or ten inches tall, and he could hardly believe his eyes. When he could speak, he called to his conductor who was sitting in the back of the bus making up his waybill, and he came out and searched the bushes. Then both of them saw her just for a second on a small grass bank about 25 feet away, but when they got there she was gone. Mr. Harte's grandfather, when a young man, broke his leg while trying to jump over a river in that part of the country, and he claimed up to the time of his death that the fairies helped him from the river-edge and saved him from drowning. Meanwhile his wife was "told," though she could never really say how she knew, that he was in some sort of difficulty, so she left the house at 4:30 a.m. and went to the river, and there she found him in great pain. Neighbours helped to get him to the house, which was half a mile from the river. "In this part of Ireland many strange things have happened," said Mr. Harte, "and my Mother still tells us some queer stories regarding fairies."

When Capt. Sir Quentin Craufurd conducted some experiments with the fairies in his own garden, they caused several nonproductive plants to bloom by request. They were also able to bring into the house the scent of fresh flowers, apparently as a joke. Several of my contributors, and I think many other people, have experienced these flower scents, and some think they are brought to them by their loved ones who have passed on. This is true in some cases, but I think the nature spirits play an essential part in producing the aroma.

Regarding these flower scents, I have a touching story to tell concerning my Mother, who was just recovering from a serious illness and had come downstairs for the first time. My sister and I didn't want to leave her alone, but she insisted that we visit a friend of hers, Mrs. S., who lived on the next road and had been ill like herself. When we arrived at the house, I admired a large bunch of tulips which were in a bowl on the table. "Yes, they are nice," said Mrs. S. "I want you to take them to your Mother, but unfortunately they haven't any scent, have they?" I went to smell them and had to agree with her. If I could discern anything, it was only a faint, bitter tang when my nose was pressed right inside one of the vari-coloured flowers, which was wide open. We took them home, but it made us sad to think that Mother would not be able to see much of their beauty, for she had glaucoma and her sight had almost gone. I knew that the flower fairies always stay with their charges until they fade, whether in the garden or the house, and as I arranged the tulips in a vase I wished fervently that their fairy attendants could give them a lovely perfume for Mother's sake. I carried them into the room where she was sitting and described to her their beautiful colours, adding that it was a pity they had no scent. My sister and I sat down beside her, and we were talking quietly when we became aware of the most exquisite fragrance, and it came from the tulips. Mother sniffed, and then exclaimed delightedly: "Why, you said they had no scent, but it's glorious. Can't you smell it?" We could, indeed, and I can only describe it as being like the scent of wall-flowers, honeysuckles, and lime flowers blended into one. We all became silent, breathing it in, and I sent my thoughts of gratitude to the fairies for making Mother so happy.

Mrs. Elsie Innes wrote a book called *The Elfin Oak of Kensing-ton Gardens* (Frederick Warne & Co. Ltd., 1930) in which she told how her husband, Mr. Ivor Innes, used to see the elfin folk playing in the oak tree there. With chisel and colour, he tried to define their shapes, and that is how his well-known "Griglan" art originated. In the Fitzroy Gardens, Melbourne, Australia, is another such tree, which once was burnt in a fire and later had fairies and animals carved on its dead trunk by the famous sculptress, Miss Ola Cohn, ARCA (London), who was a firm believer in fairies after having had, during her student days, a dream-vision of what she called "a fairy elf."

It was on a Sunday evening in September 1944, when living near the Snaefell mountain, that Mr. Thomas Wignall caught a glimpse of the fairies. He had decided to walk up to the moun-tain summit by way of the old lead-mines and to return along the old tramway track back to Laxey village. "I had not been on the beer," he assured me in his letter. "The pubs are closed in the is-land on Sundays, so I could not put my experience down to having too many pints." The light was fading, and he was just over halfway down when he heard music rising from a few feet below him in the valley. It was always just ahead of him till he reached the last wind of the tram track, which brought the lights of the village in full view. Then he saw what he called "the queer ones" dancing and tumbling in the clearings or fairy rings that abounded there in the gorse and heather. "I was very scared," he continued, "and I hurried on my way to the end of the track and to the friendly lights of Laxey. I told my good landlady what I had seen, and she said I was lucky to get away from them, as mostly they are not at all friendly. From the glimpse I got of them there must have been a hundred or more, about a foot high or maybe less, dressed in light clothes that showed up plainly enough in the gathering dusk."

Major W. Tudor-Pole, O.B.E. was a servant of the Archangel Michael and was in close and conscious touch with the higher planes of being and those forces of light and power working for humanity. As many people know, it was he who launched the Big Ben Observance, and in 1958 he purchased the Chalice Well and spring at Glastonbury, together with the surrounding gardens and orchards. With the help of friends, he created the Chalice Well Trust, and the following is an extract from a letter he wrote to me in 1961. "Our Chalice Well gardens have been full of fairies and air and water elementals this summer—I only wish they could have been photographed. We intend to make our Centre there a real oasis of peace and inspiration for all our nature friends as well as for the human pilgrims who find their way there from the ends of the earth." In an earlier letter he said: "Man must not only learn how to make peace with his fellow men if true vision is to become possible, but to make peace also with the three so-called 'lower' kingdoms if he wishes to secure the friendly cooperation of fairies, elementals, and the little people. Vivisection and the horrors of our abattoirs have raised a tragic barrier between man and the fairies and the little people of the animal, vegetable, and mineral kingdoms. When will we begin to mend our ways? Until we have learnt how to behave ourselves better, we must expect to be cold-shouldered by the inner worlds of Nature and their denizens, and this point should be strongly emphasized in any writings on the subject."

Mrs. Iris W. Ratsey, who was formerly Hon. Sec. of Universal World Harmony at St. Annes-on-Seal, Lancs., has seen fairies at odd times ever since she was a child. For a few years she shared the house of a friend at Cox's Mill, near Heathfield in Sussex, which unfortunately has seen many changes since that time. "This house," she said, "possessed a real fairy wood, and on summer evenings it was quite possible to watch the little people lighting up the hollows in certain treetrunks, and to catch glimpses of them as they flew among the trees. Undines, too, used to be in the streams and small lake." Mrs. Ratsey's book *Pioneering* (Regency Press, London) contains a description of a complete cycle of fairy life.

The Rt. Rev. C. W. Leadbeater used to tell of a little wooded island on the river at the Theosophical Headquarters at Adyar, which, he said, was a special haunt of nature spirits, and many a time when he and Krishnamurti were on their way back from their daily swim in the sea, they would stand for several minutes to watch the fairies at their play.

Another Theosophist was Miss Clara Codd, formerly General Secretary of the Theosophical Society in Australia and Southern Africa, and an international lecturer. She used to broadcast a great deal in Australia, and one of her talks was called "Do you believe in Fairies?" She received two letters in reply. One was from a lady who saw flower fairies in her garden, and she said they had gossamer wings of the same colour as the flowers they tended. The other lady wrote that she had a stream at the bottom of her garden, and one day she went to pick some maidenhair ferns growing by this stream, but desisted when she saw a wizened old gnome with a red cap who looked very angry with her for touching them. Some weeks after this, she was sitting by her drawing-room window darning stockings, when she saw the same little gnome on her lawn, beckoning to her. She went out and he led her to the stream, and with a gesture indicated to her that now she could pick the ferns.

Miss Ivy Powell of Surrey conversed with and saw etheric beings "in the mental sense only," and was surprised at the intelligence of a gnome "connected with grass growing."

Seeing Fairies

The BBC has its seers, too, for when Frank Delaney was discussing books on folklore with Dr. Katherine M. Briggs in a "Bookshelf" programme in December 1979, he was courageous enough to confess that during his boyhood in Ireland he had seen fairies dancing under a tree.

Some readers of this book may remember the first BBC disc jockey in 1927, Christopher Stone. His sister was Mrs. Faith Compton Mackenzie, and in her autobiography *As Much as I Dare* (Collins, London, 1938), she recalled how she and her brother Christopher used to see the little people "without surprise" in their grandmother's garden at Walditch in Dorset. "Christopher supports me in this," she said.

Apart from the fire spirit and the wood elf described in other chapters, Mrs. Gwen Cripps has seen "delicate little creatures with colours like the rainbow, very ethereal. They spin round and round at a tremendous speed, and then vanish at the peak." She often saw these little beings in the luminous states when she was working in sleep, but she noticed that not all astral dwellers (the so-called "dead") and visitors to the astral planes could see them. On one occasion she had observed the tiny humming-bird type of nature spirits, but only those that were violet-coloured. "In physical consciousness I see only the lights and not the shapes of the fairies," she told me. "On the astral planes, one has to be very careful in distinguishing the fantastic shapes of gnomes, etc., from the thought-forms of experimenters. Unfortunately, while working astrally, one cannot always work in beauty. One has to be of service and forget one's own feelings, and I do rescue work among sex addicts and drug addicts, etc. One never finds nature spirits in these unhappy states of existence (the lower astral plane)." She never ceased to marvel at her astral experiences, and said: "It makes me very humble and deeply grateful for the absolute certainty it has given me of survival."

From Mrs. Jean Dart of Devon came the following lovely account of a procession of fairies seen by her, and of a message she received: "I had been staying at the home of my friends, Burnham and Mac. They had an old aunt living with them, and as they needed to go to London, I had offered to Aunty-sit for them. It was just after lunch whilst Aunt Lil was taking a nap that I decided to go for a stroll in the garden. Whilst I stood by the stream, which runs just below the bungalow, I had to listen very carefully, as I could hear church bells. It reminded me of Sunday mornings from my childhood. Then I heard a deep 'humm-m-m' very similar to the earth sound. This was followed by a slightly higher-pitched hum. It continued for a few minutes, getting louder all the time, when into my vision came a procession of Little People. The men were leading in pairs, followed by the little women folk also in pairs. They were not as I had imagined fairies, all gossamer and wings. These were dressed like working country folk all in rustic colours but with beautiful faces. The leading male was holding in his two hands a chalice from which was popping rainbow-coloured bubbles, just like champagne. They completed a circle around me, and I hardly dared to breathe for fear that they would disappear. He raised his hands so that I could look into the chalice. Inside I could see our world, complete and perfect. From him came the unspoken words: 'This is how your world could look and should look. Hold your hearts and minds true and strong and it will be so. It will take many years. So many now are on the right path, searching, eager to put right the wrongs of the past, that it will be so.' With these words the Little People left me. However, they assured me that we would meet again."

The next account is an extract from Nesta of the Forest's little book, *Charmed Magic Casements* (Bournemouth Times, 1939), which she kindly sent to me with her permission to quote: "My lonely childhood was spent in the Wye Valley. I was a timid, queer child, brought up by very strict, elderly relatives, and far away from my brothers and sisters. I never spoke to another child from one week's end to another, and my only pleasure was to be allowed to go into the garden and the woods nearby.

"I came to love the woods and forests—hence my name. Loneliness had no terrors for me amongst the leaves and trees. 'Pictures' of things that would happen tomorrow (the beginning of clairvoyance) were always to be seen if I looked into the pools and streams. There the Little People used to come and play with me—at least, not as ordinary children play. They just used to talk with me. I always sat on one particular stone that looked over a hill. While gazing deeply before me into the misty blue sky, I had to count seven, like playing hide-and-seek, but with my eyes wide open; and then when I had counted seven the Little People were beside me. One of the most vivid memories of my childhood is of sitting on a doorstep in Chepstow, watching most beautifully dressed Little Ladies dance up the cobbled street. It was raining in torrents, but their dresses were crisp and dry, of all hues, and their big, gauzy wings seemed to stock all the rainbow colours. I ran in and told my aunt to come and see, but they had gone. Often since then I have thought of this strange glimpse, right in the heart of a town. I have tried to find explanations, but nothing will really explain things away. Since I came to live near the New Forest, I have seen fairies on two occasions. Once in the afternoon, walking through the glades near Lyndhurst, what I saw was not a butterfly, flower, or any mortal thing. I went close to it. The tiny creature stayed quite still, as a robin or sparrow accustomed to passersby will stay, and then it fluttered away into nothingness. It was the same type of little creature that I used to see in my childhood—my lovely ladies with glowing wings; but whereas they then seemed large to me, they now seemed much smaller.

"The next time I saw a fairy was in Dorset. We were walking down a charming little lane with a profusion of flowers and herbs, which I knew by their old-fashioned folk-names. Suddenly I stopped. Right in front of my eyes, my hand partly stretched because I thought it was a flower, was a quaint little creature, which I had never seen the like of before. It appeared male rather than female—a Pwca or Gwblyn, as we call them in Wales, and such as I had heard of often in childhood but not met. I have never seen anything like it since, but it was there, and I did not dream it. Later, in the bus, I asked an old Dorset woman the name of the place. To my great joy she said in her broad Dorset accent that I must be meaning 'ower towards Puncknole.' That sounds very much to me like a derivation of 'Puck Hole.' Had other Dorset folk before my time seen the Puck there?"

In October 1955, Mrs. Winifred Spilsbury, of Sheffield, whose account of ice fairies is elsewhere in this book, had been planting along the side of the house some crocus bulbs that she had bought, and that were clearly labelled "Golden." Later, fully awake and busy inside the house, she became aware of a dark-haired girl draped in a lavender-blue robe, which was luminous and shaped over her form like crocus petals. She carried a wand that had no star on top but was like a very bright silver willow-cane. With her was a tiny cupid-like boy with flesh-pink wings, and he seemed to be dabbling in a stream of deep blue water and standing on red-gold sand. The female figure took no notice of Mrs. Spilsbury and, after a few moments, faded away. "Now," wrote Mrs. Spilsbury, "if those crocuses come up lavender-blue instead of gold I shall feel she is the fairy who is going to guard their growth." At the beginning of February 1956, the bulbs were under deep snow, but on St. David's Day the first crocus bloomed, and another at the side of it was in bud. Yes! Both of these, and those which followed, were lavender-blue like the dress of the fairy, and Mrs. Spilsbury sent me a petal that had fallen from one of the full-blown flowers. It is possible that the bulbs were wrongly labelled, but that does not matter; the important part of the story is that the fairy gave foreknowledge of the mauve colour before the crocuses came into bloom, and no golden ones cropped up elsewhere in Mrs. Spilsbury's garden.

My sister had a similar experience, but in her case a nature spirit in the appropriate colour appeared after the flowers opened. She had seen some yellow crocuses in bloom in a friend's garden in Nottingham, and later in the year she was present when her friend dug up some of the bulbs for her to bring home and plant in our own garden. In the following spring of 1956, when the crocuses came out, there were no yellow ones anywhere; all of them were white, and my sister saw a gnome, dressed in white, running at the back of them. She had a further glimpse of him on the last day of March, and again he was running near the white flowers. In January 1957, he became visible to her again, and in March she caught sight of him flying from one side of the garden to the other, and she noticed that his wings were approximately six inches long. One day in June of the same year, my sister was wandering in the garden, and I was watching her through the window when I saw a little white, semi-transparent figure (presumably the same gnome) floating near her. He certainly seemed to take a great interest in her, and on one occasion even came into the house, for I saw him standing on the landing watching her as she walked down the stairs! He was not visible again to either of us until a Sunday morning in May 1959. My sister was showing me something on a plant in our garden when we surprised him, and he gave a graceful dive through the leaves of a Michaelmas daisy plant and disappeared.

While holding in my hand an "oak apple," which I'd found under an oak tree in Newstead Abbey Park, I saw a chubby-faced little elf standing in front of me, grinning broadly, as much as to say, "I belong to the oak tree where that came from!" Another day I was looking at some pussy-willow catkins in a vase, when a little fairy appeared, wearing on her head a downy catkin shaped like a cosy bonnet.

In August 1995, Mrs. Pauline Young, of Lancashire, and her family were all enjoying "one of those lovely, hot summer days." A few years ago her husband, Bill, had built her a wooden conservatory, and the doors are so placed that when the dining room, patio, and conservatory doors are all open you can see right through the house. "On this particular day," she said, "all the doors were thrown open to let in the breeze. There wasn't anything special happening in my life or in my thoughts at this time to bring on this experience that I am going to recount. It was just a beautiful day.

"At lunchtime we sat in the conservatory to have a meal. I looked out at the garden and my little pond with the small waterfall. I love the sound of water in a garden. After a while I got up and went to do my work in the house. As the afternoon wore on, I kept feeling as though I had to go back to look at the garden; something was drawing me there. I found myself looking, really looking at things. I began to tingle, I was so happy. I remember saying to myself, 'this won't get the work done,' and I went back into the house, but I kept being drawn into the garden again. I was looking, but I didn't know why, except that everything was so beautiful to look at. I called to my husband: 'Bill, just come and look at this garden.' He came and looked. 'Yes, it does look nice,' he said, and went back in. Suddenly the whole garden had taken on a new atmosphere. I just wanted to soak it all up, so I went and got a chair from the conservatory and sat by the doors. The sun was very warm, and I just sat there looking and looking, as though I was compelled to look. It was as if someone was saying, 'Keep on looking, you'll see.' Just to the left of my little pond, I had a fennel herb growing about three feet tall, and underneath that was a flatcap hydrangea. As I sat there, looking in the direction of the fennel, I got a big surprise. There was a cheeky little face looking at me and smiling, just the head and right shoulder peeping from behind the fennel. I just sat there, feeling very calm. The garden didn't seem to be as it was. I felt I was in a different world, yet I could still hear the birds singing, and the sound of my little waterfall. I felt the breeze on my face, yet there was a kind of silence. I smiled at the little person, and its smile broadened even more. 'Come out and let me see more of you,' I said. The small creature jumped out very obediently and stood by the fennel, hands on hips, with a big cheeky but friendly smile. I looked, but really could not tell what sex it was. When I thought it was a boy, it became very girlish, and when I thought it was a girl, it became very boyish. It was very strange; my mind just couldn't decide its real gender, but I'll call it a girl. She was dressed in different tones of green, with a little hat, just like 'Peter Pan.' She had sandy, short-cropped hair, and seemed about the age of a seven-year-old, but looked very wise. I felt completely at home with her. 'Hello,' I said. 'Hello,' she replied, not moving her mouth. I realised I must be hearing this telepathically. 'Do you like my garden?' I asked, not aloud. 'Oh yes,' she said, looking about the garden. 'It's lovely.' I just kept looking at her. She was so beautiful to me. The Godman I follow came into my mind. 'I wonder if she knows him,' I thought. 'Do you know Sai Baba?' I said. At the next moment, her head went down, and she clasped her hands together in a prayerful way. There was so much love on her face. I was so happy I couldn't contain my joy any longer. I wanted to share my experience with someone else, so I called to my husband, 'Bill, come quick!' It was a big mistake. The little one began to disappear, not from my senses, but from view. I could still see her, but the greens in her clothes and the pink

111

colour of her skin and her sandy hair all faded from my view. I just sat there, telling Bill what I had seen. I was tingling all over and so happy. Bill went in after a while, and it took me ages to come back to myself. Since that day I'm very aware or her presence around me. She is always watching me, and she walks over to wherever I am and stands by me. I see her leaning on her arms, just looking and listening to what's going on. She's a beautiful soul: that I am sure of. I've never had anything like this happen before. She's a dear little friend to me, and I can see the green of her clothes in my mind's eye very strongly. She gives off such a warm glow, and I know she is real. She walks about ever so softly as though she doesn't want to disturb me. There's a very endearing familiarity about her. I can't understand why this has happened to me, as I'm certainly not lonely, so why should I see her now? It's a mystery, but she's a love."

Some people always use the "oblique glance" when seeing fairies, and in a book called *The Psychic Sense* (Faber & Faber, London, 1943) by Phoebe D. Payne and Lawrence J. Bandit, we are told that the outer edge of the retina of the eye is more sensitive to half-light than the central part, and so can see things that disappear if we look straight at them.

During one very hot, tranquil summer, my sister and I saw, out of the corners of our eyes, several winged creatures flying around some white hollyhocks. They resembled butterflies but were much larger, their wingspan being as wide as standard-sized notepaper turned lengthwise. I have checked the colours from my old diary and see that two had white wings and one had wings of creamy-yellow or pale orange. We could not count how many others there were, nor could we see them in detail, because when we looked directly at them they vanished instantly from our sight. An experience, which I treasure in my memory, was that which occurred when I was holding a stem of lavender given to me by a friend. I was admiring the scent and loveliness of its tiny flowers when I felt myself merging into one of them until I seemed to be in the very heart of the flower, enfolded in its petals and bathed in its colour and fragrance and its healing peace. It was a wonderful experience and helped me to realise more deeply our spiritual Oneness with all other forms of life.

Mrs. Leopold, of London, had a similar experience. "When I was little," she said, "and again when I was aged about thirteen, I used to go into our garden and sit and look at the flowers and pretend they could see me and liked me, and as I sat there I would feel as though I was sinking into the flowers until I experienced a kind of powerful fellowship with them and with all the garden."

Many readers may know of the Bach Centre at Mount Vernon, Sotwell, Wallingford, Oxon., where the late Dr. Edward Bach's work is still carried on by a very dedicated staff. Dr. Bach must have been greatly loved and helped by the fairies, for he had such empathy with the flowers and trees of the countryside that he was able to "feel" the emotional states of mind that certain plants would heal, and his 38 Flower Remedies, including the Rescue Remedy, are now used successfully throughout the world.

Henry Thomas Hamblin wrote a beautiful little booklet called *Message of a Flower or the Divine Immanence in Nature* (Science of Thought Press, Bosham House, Chichester, Sussex) in which he said that it is by contemplating and spiritually understanding the beauties of Nature that we can enter into the mind and thought and creative imagination of the Divine. "Let us have constantly before us a few flowers," he said. "Just a few simple blooms on our worktable or office desk, to keep us in touch with the Infinite... Life need not be the unlovely thing that it is to so many. Its cruelty and ugliness and selfishness are foreign to the Divine Idea. Let us get to our flowers, and seeing them, learn something of the Mind of God, something of the beauty, something of its serenity and calm and unruffled peace. Let us gaze into the face of a flower and see in it the countenance of God."

In an article called "The Being of a Flower" in the April 1954 number of the *Science of Thought Review* (Science of Thought Press) founded by the before-named Henry Thomas Hamblin, Dereck Neville asked his readers, "Have you ever known the being of a flower? Have you ever crept in, until the petals close upon you and you are in the flower world, with all the noise and clamour of the sense-life shut away? I do not mean merely thinking about a flower... No, I mean have you ever looked at a flower in such utter stillness of spirit that you enter into communion with its very being?... I have been into a flower and know. I have ceased to be separate, a mere observer, cut off from knowledge by a mental separation. I have moved within my heart and I have become aware of my own roots!"

Tennyson knew something of the divine immanence in Nature when he wrote those well-known lines:

Flower in the crannied wall,
I pluck you out of the crannies.
Hold you here, root and all, in my hand,
Little flower, but if I could understand
What you are, root and all, and all in all,
I should know what God and man is.

Chapter 2: The Case of the Green Wood Elves

I am grateful to "L. Verdoye," M. A., F.R.G.S., a graduate of two universities, who, in November 1955, set down for me the facts regarding the existence of what he called "mobile, semi-vegetable forms assuming human shape," which were seen by "Mr. X" and his family in some woods in Lincolnshire. The details were first communicated by Mr. X's son—a pupil in his class—who went to him and told him "in mystified consternation" the following story.

One bright afternoon in the late summer holidays, he went picnicking in the woods with his mother, father, brother, and aunt. Feeling bored at sitting, they rose and walked about together until, they found themselves in a clearing, and there they all saw some green shapes dancing in a circle, hand-in-hand. As far as L. Verdoye's pupil could estimate, they were not more than nine or nine-and-a-half-inches high. No expression or features could be seen on them but all had pointed green hats, long legs and arms, "and there was," recounted the boy, "a sort of 'king' in the centre of the ring, with a light in his hand." While the family stood petrified with fright, the ring of shapes opened and the "king" went out and sat under a large dock-leaf. He curled his legs up like a human being and fanned himself with a little leaf. Mr. X, the boy's father, could stand it no longer. He moved forward, and the figures all ran with incredible swiftness over towards a bank and vanished. The family searched frantically for some time then, but nothing remained.

The physical reaction was that Mr. X's wife was so completely unnerved as to be almost hysterical, and the aunt had to look after her. The boy said he felt "weird." They didn't know what to do, and Mr. X had to gather his family together and gradually recall them to normal, as they had "seen something nobody would believe." They went home feeling as if they had all unwittingly participated in "some awful act," but the aunt had taken a camera with her and had managed to obtain a photograph of one of the little green men, which she had surprised leaning against a tree. She kept the photograph hidden away, and nothing would induce her to part with it, but L. Verdoye's pupil saw it and drew it from memory. Like the others, it had long legs, pointed cap, green body, and lightning movement. When the photograph was taken, the shape had its back to the camera, and its hand was resting lightly against the tree trunk. It went round the bole of the tree (elm or beech) and vanished without trace when the boy's aunt moved forward.

L. Verdoye then spoke of this family's strange adventures to a trustworthy colleague, who, at the end of the tale, confessed that on Midsummer Day in 1943 he had been bird watching in the same woods alone at night, and he, too, had seen figures that seemed identical to those described by L. Verdoye's pupil. Like Mr. X and his family, he could not see any facial delineaments on these elves, which were sitting at various places under the woodland weeds and bushes, and in one place there were two or three together. After his conversation with L. Verdoye, he went again to the woods, and found they were teeming with the little creatures, which crawled away from the trees at dusk and went to and fro underneath the high leaves of dock, bogweed, hazel, etc., and then back again. He said he was "stunned" by the sight and on one occasion had gone into a kind of "swoon," for how long he did not know, but he awoke to find himself "all wet." L. Verdoye said that when he met him shortly afterwards, he seemed partially "fairy-struck."

Later, L. Verdoye himself spent two whole nights with a witness in the woods. He visited the spot where the X family had their picnic and examined every inch of the ditch up the bank of which the green shapes had vanished, but it did not reveal anything unusual, "nor," he said, "the existence of mounds that an Elizabethan manuscript said are the fairies' closed houses." He noticed however, that in the clearing where Mr. X and his family had innocently surprised the elves, there were eight or nine trees with curious holes round their roots, and on examination he found that every hole had been neatly carpeted with brown, dry, un-rotted leaves laid regularly down. At the back of the hole in each case were tiny tracks leading into the ground. He conjectured that these carpets of leaves could have been the work of (a) small children, but if so they must have spent hours on it; (b) animals such as squirrels; or (c) the elves. He believed that it was the work of the last.

The woods were closed to the public for some years after that but had since been reopened, and one day L. Verdoye overheard a remark made by an elderly woman who had been on an organized bus-trip to the woods, and she was saying to her friend: "All the time I was there, I felt that I was being watched, and the trees are such odd shapes, and the roots look all so snakey. I felt things were looking at me. What funny bare patches there are here and there. I was relieved to get into the bus. I could never go there alone. I never felt easy the whole time I was there."

After my correspondence with L. Verdoye about the wood elves, he decided to visit the woods alone on 25 June 1956. He again noticed the unique way in which the dried branches of the previous year's growth were neatly stacked between the young tree trunks, and firmly believed that this was done by the elves who had been "tidying up." He was convinced that children could not have done it because he had to burst through hawthorn and hazel bushes to see the spectacle. Again and again, in the most secluded parts of the wood, he came upon this "stacking," and he said, "As a botanist, I know that twigs do not fall naturally in this way." Where young ash trees were springing from numerous suckers, some twigs had been piled neatly between the interstices, and in the case of a lime, which had germinated from two seeds in juxtaposition, some twigs had been bent and laid across the trunks just above the join.

By this time, my sister and I were getting anxious to see the woods for ourselves at the earliest opportunity, and that same year, at Whitsuntide, we journeyed by bus to Lincolnshire, and then had to take another bus, which put us off near the woods. Unfortunately, although L. Verdoye had drawn a small plan indicating where the wood elves had been seen, the exact spot could not be found as the men from the Forestry Commission had felled many of the old trees and were making a new plantation on the other side of the road. We discovered when it was too late that we had entered the wrong part. Nevertheless, both of us saw something that confirmed the existence of fairy life there.

The plantation consisted of conifers with glades in between, and, on the way down one of these lanes, I saw what can only be described as a green, shapeless, ectoplasm mass, which may have been an embryo elf, hovering above and then flying in and out of some bushes on the left-hand side of the lane. Unfortunately my sister was some distance behind me, and by the time she reached me it had disappeared. We then went a few yards further up the lane to eat our luncheon sandwiches, and we sat down near the beginning of another lane, which lay crosswise. I had my back to it, but my sister, who was facing it, caught sight of a little figure crossing a little way down it, and in one place it vanished just as she was telling me to look at it. When we went to investigate, we found a neat little hole in the ground at that spot, and we heard later that L. Verdoye's colleague had seen one of the elves disappear into a similar crevice.

During our walk through the plantation, I came upon a small mound, which had one tiny opening and was beautifully decorated with several shades and varieties of moss and some perfect miniature plants and trees. It was so delightful that I took a photograph of it, but when the film was developed the negative of that particular photo was quite blank!

My sister and I wished we could have stayed for a much longer period, though during most of the time we were there some of the foresters were still at work in another part, and consequently the peace of the woodlands was rather disturbed. We had rested under various trees several times during the day, and on each occasion the branches immediately above us had been so vigorously and loudly shaken that we had glanced quickly upwards to see if any animal or bird were there, but there was nothing to account for it and we could only conclude that some of the elves were behaving like mischievous children. At no time did we find the atmosphere hostile, as it seemed to be to some of the other visitors to the woods, but these elves were at a very rudimentary stage of development and it must have been a great shock to the witnesses who came upon them unawares, without having any previous belief in their existence. One wonders whether any of the foresters were startled by a sudden glimpse of the little green men!

Later on I was taken by my friend and her husband in their car to visit the original fairy wood on the other side of the road and to meet L. Verdoye there, but unfortunately we missed him. It was a rainy day, and owing to the length of time taken by the journey we could not stay very long and did not see any of the little creatures although we sensed their presence and knew they were aware of us. Bert Heason stayed outside the wood, but his wife Phyllis went in with me. She thought she saw some movement at the foot of a tree, and then, being of a practical nature, decided she must have imagined it, though I do not think she had. I had left her for a moment to look more closely at a ditch, which I could see through some bushes. As I was passing under a very large old tree to reach it, the tree-branches were shaken violently and deliberately, and I was heavily drenched with showers of raindrops.

In some of his articles and books on folklore, Alasdair Alpin MacGregor mentioned the spectral Black Dog of Lincolnshire, whose counterpart in Scotland is known as the "Fairy Dog," a goblin in animal guise. The Lincolnshire Dog is known to be more benevolent than the Black Shuck, which haunts other parts of the country, and I think my friend Phyllis and I were privileged to see it. Years ago a brother and sister who were in the habit of taking a shortcut home after dark had told how they were invariably escorted by the Black Dog as far as a hand-gate at the corner of these particular woods, and on the day Phyllis and I were there we were walking towards the hand-gate, which led into the woods at the top corner, when we saw an enormous black dog standing motionless near the gate, with its eyes fixed on us intently. Both of us exclaimed at the huge size of the dog and hoped it was friendly. We wondered where it had come from, as it was alone. Just as we reached the gate, the animal passed in front of us from left to right and then turned and loped off down the field to the boundary, where it just seemed to vanish, but, strangely enough, neither of us thought of the Fairy Dog story at the time.

Over ten years went by, during that time I continued to feel regretful that I'd had no opportunity to go again to the Lincolnshire woodland. I could not stop wondering how the little elves were faring, and longed to see how they had settled down in the new plantation. The Guardian Angel of that area must have taken pity on me, for one morning, while at home and fully conscious, I was shown a clear vision of the elves in their own surroundings and was able to watch swarms of them climbing up the stems of plants and sliding down again, then darting over and through the undergrowth with astonishing rapidity. Though I knew I was at home, I seemed to be no more than a yard away from them in the woodland and could even sense their strong, magnetic quality. It was good to see them so happy and my mind was set completely at rest.

Mrs. Gwen Cripps, of Cheshire, gave me an interesting description of a green elf that she encountered during an astral projection experience, and she sent me a painting of it. "My attention," she wrote, "was attracted to a narrow ditch dividing two fields, beyond which was a high bank of long grass, and, in that high bank, standing erect and facing me, was the most weirdly beautiful little creature I had ever seen. It was apparently sexless, roughly about ten to twelve inches in height, completely green as the grass it was standing among, and holding what looked like a little cup. It appeared to be gazing at me intently, and I, with great astonishment, gazed back. When I recovered from my surprise I made to approach it from a distance of five or six yards away. I called 'Come here, little thing, come here.' A twitch passed over its very expressionless little face; it took fright and made one bounding leap across the ditch towards me and then jerked sideways away from me into some undergrowth, which proved a natural protection for it."

In her picture, Mrs. Cripps had not given the elf fingers, nose, ears, mouth, toes, or hair, as she could not see any signs of such. The eyes she had noticed carefully. There were two apertures and the iris was green, but if there was a pupil it couldn't be distinguished. "I have since wondered," she said, "how the elf obtained its nourishment; maybe from the air. The little creature certainly displayed awareness and fear of me. The twitching of its face suggests some nervous reaction. I was struck by the appearance of its not having any bone structure. Rather did its body look as if made of green spongy rubber. It was very agile and perfectly proportioned. In no way did it resemble any preconceived ideas of mine regarding fauns, leprechauns, elves, or pixies. One wonders if this little thing might be a link in evolutionary development."

In December 1956, Major G. H. Tristram, of Sussex, lent me a book called *Letters from Lancelot*, which consisted of letters received through automatic writing by his wife from their son, who had passed on at the age of eight. This book included some interesting drawings of wood elves, and the following description is obviously of a variety of elves very similar to the previous examples: "His head goes up in a point, and he is all green. It all goes pointy like a bird, but he has arms and legs like a man. He is whistling through his beaky point... He's hopping away... He went in a hole in a tree over there, and he is down below in the roots of the tree digging with his hands."

In the case of the creature last described, we are given a fascinating hint of the manner of development in the early stages of transition from bird life into fairy life. This alliance between the bird kingdom and the fairy evolution is stressed in many of the occult teachings, including the works of C. W. Leadbeater, Geoffrey Hodson, Alice A. Bailey, Flower A. Newhouse, Peter Richelieu, and White Eagle.

Apart from the small green wood-elves, there are larger types of green beings, and these seem to be connected with hedges and bushes. While looking out of the window on a fine, sunny morning, I saw one such creature gazing at me from the privet hedge, which bordered our garden. He was slender, with a pointed chin and narrow, slanting eyes, and his green naked body would be about three feet in height.

The novelist Miss Margery Lawrence told me about a "green boy" who sounds very similar to my gentleman-of-the-hedge. She saw him when she and her husband were staying at a hotel, which was a charming old manor-house set in a beautiful garden in Stratford-on-Avon. The boy's body was olive green, naked, and slender, and his head was covered with small, tight curls, also as green as an olive. He had very long toes and fingers, slit-like eyes and a narrow, foxy type of face that ended in a sharply pointed chin. He was about the height of a seven-year-old boy, but in build was more like an adolescent of some fifteen years.

I am grateful to a lady named Mrs. Hughes for an account of other green beings of similar type seen in the Wye Valley by Mrs. J. S. Mackenzie, an invalid. She was looking through her window when she saw behind one of the bushes a green face with blue eyes. She thought the creature saw her before it disappeared. Then two more figures showed for a moment and were gone. They were about the size of human beings, but slightly built.

Mrs. Carley Dawson, a writer of children's books in West Virginia, wrote: "I wish Edith Olivier were still alive. During my many years in England, she told me often of having seen 'the green men' running in the hedges, but unfortunately their size was not mentioned. She was also able to move in time and saw many things, later proved, which exist no longer. It was she who saw an avenue of monoliths on Salisbury Plain. These monoliths were then six feet underground, but later were uncovered."

Miss Olivier had other interesting psychic experiences, but she will be known to many readers through her preface to the 1934 reprint of the fourth edition of *An Adventure* (Faber & Faber, London), that fascinating book by the two cultured ladies, Miss Moberly and Miss Jourdain, who, when visiting the Trianon in 1901, experienced a "time-slip" and witnessed scenes from the past that, like all the events in our lives, are indelibly imprinted on the electrical ethers in the true Memory of Nature—known in the East as the Akashic Records.

Chapter 3: Water Fairies, Fire Fairies, Tree Spirits, and Banshees

In her childhood, Mrs. Ellen Jackson lived near Bradford, Yorkshire, in a house with a large garden, part of which was wild and heather-covered. There was a good stream of water, which, after flowing into a pond, trickled over some rocks in the manner of a waterfall, and thence to a glade of over-hanging willow trees. Indeed, she and her playmates always called this place "The Willows," and they were quite sure it was the haunt of fairies. Constantly they looked for them and would sit and sing little fairy songs to tempt them out, but their efforts were in vain. One evening, however, before answering the bedtime call, the six-year-old child Ellen and her sister, who was three years her senior, decided once again to "look for fairies." It was a lovely evening—one of those long twilights that one gets in the North—not fully light but not yet dark. They ran together down the garden, skirted the pond, which, they remarked, was looking "very sparkling," and stood above the waterfall, gazing down into "The Willows." To their amazement they saw three small, nude, female figures sitting upon a rock a few yards below them. Beautifully formed, and of a milky-white colour, they seemed between eighteen inches and two feet in height, but as they were seated it was not easy to be more definite. On the rock beside them lay some white, gauzy drapery. Mrs. Jackson said, "We stood breathlessly watching them for a few moments, then one of them looked up and saw us. She raised her arm and pointed to draw the others' attention to us, and they all slipped off the rock into the water. Just before disappearing, one of them reached back to retrieve the drapery they had left. Then they were gone." My contributor pointed out that, as she and her sister were firm believers in fairies, one would be justified in thinking they had imagined them, even though they both saw the identical figures and actions, but the kind of fairies they had thought of were always those with wings and wands and brightly coloured clothes, whereas these water sprites were wingless and colourless, and of a kind unimagined by them.

Here is a statement from Mr. Richard Ingham, who was a post-master in Suffolk: "The early years of my life were spent living in a small farmhouse on the outskirts of Halifax, Yorkshire. The house was on the edge of a stretch of moorland, and some of my happiest memories are of wandering about the moors alone, quietly watching the wildlife. One spot that always attracted me was where a stream of water coursed from the moor down a small gully of rocks, forming small pools here and there. A certain pool held a deep fascination for me, and I would lie face downward and wait patiently for the pool life to move about. I remember—and it is a scene that remains very clearly in my mind—one sunny afternoon in this sheltered place, when, slowly raising my eyes, I saw four or five small, almost transparent little people in a group on the rock and nearby grass across the pool, only a few feet away. For a moment I felt frightened, and then, without moving, I smiled, and I feel sure I saw a look on their faces of what I might describe as recognition, as they slowly disappeared."

Mr. A. J. Coster, of Middlesex, told me he'd had "many and varied psychic experiences during his life." As a boy aged between ten and twelve, he used to roam over some lovely fields in Potter's Bar, and he still remembers the wonderful feeling he had when alone, for it was then that everything took on a different aspect so that even the twigs on the hedges had "a fringe of shimmering light." There were four ponds in these fields, and in three of them the boy used to bathe and fish. The other pond was so small that he seldom visited it, but one hot summer's day he felt drowsy and went to rest on its grassy bank, though he declares he did not fall asleep. While he sat there, several small beings with wings came from "nowhere." They were smiling as they dabbled their hands in the water, and he saw quite distinctly their figures, which were like medium-sized dolls, and their colouring, which was pearl white. They did not run away but just vanished. Mr. Coster said: "I had no surprised feeling. I knew they were fairies. I saw them just that once, and although I am an old man now I have never forgotten it."

Miss Sheila Bryant, of Northumberland, also saw pearl-coloured fairies. She was six or seven years old at the time and was staying at a farm near Troutbeck, in Cumberland. The stream where she saw them was shallow, flowing gently over large stones, and there were lots of bushes over-hanging the water. These "pearly-looking beings" were about six-to-eight-inches tall, with gauzy wings and iridescent garments. "They were in constant movement, flying here and there and occasionally settling or rather poising… It was a very hot, still day."

In his notes on water elementals, Mr. Tom Charman said: "Several years ago I had an unusual and striking experience that made a great impression on me. I had retired early, and immediately on getting into bed I felt as though I were being transported through space. Suddenly I found myself under water, crawling round some huge rocks. After about five minutes of this it occurred to me I ought to be breathing, and I became frightened. But an invisible companion reassured me that this was not necessary. I mention this to show how real my experience was. So real, in fact, that I did not realize I was not on the physical plane! I seemed to remain under water for about half an hour. During this time I saw some most weird and wonderful elemental creatures, little and half-human with large heads and frog-like bodies, and others like huge tadpoles. These uncanny elementals did not take the slightest notice of me, but sailed past with the many fishes, intent on their own business. One little creature, more shapely than the others, was amusing itself with a huge and most terrifying fish. This elemental had not the slightest fear and kept pushing a sort of sponge-like substance into the fish's mouth. This time I did not see any of the higher water elementals, but on other occasions I have seen some magnificent water-ladies dressed in wonderful garments, seemingly made from seaweed and the like."

While staying at Looe, Cornwall, in 1943, Mrs. Clara Reed of Coventry saw one of these "water ladies," or sea fairies. The fairy was wearing a skirt of seashells and a bodice of seaweed, and she had a row of shells round her neck and a large shell on her head. "I was standing gazing sadly out to sea when I first noticed her," explained Mrs. Reed, "for I had received the bad news that my husband in the army had been taken ill. She said to me, 'Don't look so sad,' and her voice was so musical it echoed like bells. I told her my trouble, and she patted my cheek with her tiny hand and smiled at me. 'He will get better,' she assured me. 'Don't worry anymore; he's not going to die.' Immediately I felt happier, as though a great load had been taken from me, and later on her words came true, for my husband recovered." Mrs. Reed mentioned that she had also seen water-lily fairies, with their pretty petalled caps and dresses. The Rev. Paul Stacy, formerly vicar of St. Peter's, Coventry, who told me she was one of the heroines in the Coventry blitz, vouched for her sincerity as a Christian seer.

Mr. Frederick Leveaux, of Leicestershire, told me that many years ago when on board ship either in the Indian or Pacific Ocean (he could not remember which, since he made no note of the incident at the time), he saw something that he was convinced was not fantasy. "It was a figure like a small Neptune," he wrote. "It had a trident in its hand and was swimming in the sea at considerable speed, but I cannot recall with certainty whether or not its body ended like a fish, comparable to the traditional mermaid."

A correspondent in Wiltshire told me that he had seen the foam-crested rollers off the coast of Cornwall look, for an instant, like something more than met the eye, "I have never forgotten that strange impression," he said, "A glimpse, as it seemed, of living forms in the waves."

The following brief experience with sea-creatures took place in February 1929, when Miss A. J. Visser and her mother were sailing on a Dutch boat from Rotterdam to New York. After a few days at sea, a hurricane arose. One night was particularly bad, and the ship went over from right to left and from left to right, taking so long to steady itself again that they felt they would soon be plunging with the ship and all into the cold water. Lying awake, Miss Visser became scared, and then, deep down on the floor of the ocean, as it were, she saw two very little creatures who laughed at her fear and cheered her up. One was a bit larger than the other and had a round head. She did not see such creatures again, but she said she would never forget the experience.

The folklorist Miss Lucy H. M. Bruce, of Iona, contacted some freshwater spirits in a Highland loch. She said their intelligence might have been akin to that of animals, and in stature they were much smaller than human beings. They were sitting on stones, and formed a kind of semicircle at the bottom of the loch. Their long, straight hair was of a muddy brown colour, and their faces were pallid and freckled. They sat with their elbows on their knees and their chins in their hands, and when she came upon them they just stared at her. "They were not friendly," she said, "but neither were they exactly hostile. The look in their eyes was much the same as one would see in those of a Highland calf if one came upon it unawares."

One evening in August 1922, at Burnham-on-Sea, Somerset, Miss P. M. Clarke was walking on the seashore with two friends when the three of them observed a light shining on the horizon. As they watched, two of them saw that it was approaching the shore. Then it disappeared, and its place was taken by a shadowy ring of dancing figures about two-and-a-half feet in height. After a few minutes they faded away. It is interesting to note that while two of the party were able to see the shadowy forms of the fairies, the third person saw only the light that heralded their approach. It happens every so often that where there are several people present there is usually one who cannot see any, or all, of the phenomena.

At the age of 31, Miss Dorothy M. McIntyre saw on a grass-covered cliff-top at Whiting Bay, Isle of Arran, a transparent lime-green being, eight-to-ten-inches tall and wearing vague, flowing garments. It was speeding along and vanished over the edge of the cliff, so she had only a glimpse of it. This experience occurred on a perfect summer day. She remembers that at the time she had just been laughing with sheer happiness and well being, and wonders whether that had anything to do with it. Certainly sunshine and a blissful heart are conducive to fairy seeing.

"I once saw a rather ethereal little creature about eighteen inches high, playing round a pond we used to have at our house at Hangleton, Hove," wrote Mrs. Eleanor Upton, who was one of the principals of The Aquarian Age School of Spiritual Advancement, and also co-founder with Mr. Joseph Busby of the international newspaper *The Voice*. "I wondered if I was daydreaming," she said, "as it only lasted for a few minutes. Although so small, it looked rather stern, and seemed to be poised in the air."

From Storrington, Sussex, in 1955, Mrs. Janet Kay, describing herself as "a very practical Yorkshire-woman," sent an account of some tiny creatures of the water-fairy type. Her experience had nearly always been dismissed by others as a childish dream, but she herself commented: "All I can say is that it is as clear and real to me now as it was 70 years ago." In the 1880s she, the youngest member of a large family, was walking with her mother in Kew Gardens on a very hot and "shimmering" day. Suddenly she saw, hanging on branches and sitting on water-lily leaves, from which they flew from time to time, some tiny, baby-like creatures probably three or four score of them. They were an inch or an inch-and-a-half in size and were semi-transparent like wax, with tiny wings but no clothes. "They were certainly more than a daydream," she said, "for when they landed on a branch the branch swayed a little so they must have had some body to give weight. I don't think a child of seven would have reasoned this out. They were very sweet, and please mark this. I loved them, though as a child I could not stand babies because my sister and brother always referred to me rather contemptuously as being 'only a baby.' Therefore it was odd that I was so delighted at seeing what I firmly believed were fairies. I drew my mother's attention to them, but she could not see them, although she admitted that 'probably they were there,' and was willing to stay while I took my fill and until Victorian papa commanded that we should follow the rest of the family."

Mrs. Elsie M. Shilleto, of Kent, said that her late sister used to have a fish pond in her garden and had often seen hovering around it a dainty white fairy with small wings.

There are several different kinds of dreams, but this "dream," recalled by Mrs. McKay, of Glasgow, is one of the "true" types in which the ego, while the physical body sleeps, is shown some aspect of life and receives information concerning it from a more advanced soul, in the hope that the knowledge may be remembered in waking consciousness. "My dream took place in the spring," said Mrs. McKay. "I was walking near an expanse of water. The sky was very colourful, though, in darkish shades. In the distance was a patch of turquoise, and a rainbow hung over the water. There were creatures, which made me think of the illustrations one sees in fairy-tale books of mermaids and mermen, long flowing hair, bodies resembling humans as far as the waists, and fish-like tails; and they were floating in the water. Now this is the strange part: near them, also floating on the water, was some transparent jelly-like substance bearing half-formed creatures resembling the mermaids and mermen. My companion (I have no idea who it was) explained that these little half-formed beings were freshwater-sprite life in the process of creation."

Mrs. McKay's last sentences about the little creatures of transparent, jelly-like substance are of special interest in view of the next account from Surrey. Miss Stella Watson, an artist and modeller in clay, told me that when she was 50 years old she actually handled a water fairy. She made a note of her experience at the time, and here it is: "Yesterday (October 25, 1948) I was sitting on an old wooden bench in my garden, enjoying the lovely blue sky, the sunshine, and my tea. Near me lay my two dear dogs, and in front of me was a small pond with lilies and goldfish in it. As I was feeding the fish with a few crumbs, I noticed lying on the water face downwards a little creature like a man in shape. I bent over and carefully lifted him out. He seemed very light and lay as though dead on my warm hand. I put him down on the bench and had a good look at him. He was about nine inches in size, with very long, thin legs. His dragonfly-shaped wings were like a fish's scales in colouring, and they seemed to join on at the back of his neck. His face (to our ideas) was ugly; he had very large, round, prominent eyes and no nose to speak of, but a big mouth, a very round head, and no neck as we know it. The creature's body seemed to be made of clear jelly, like a jellyfish, but looked at from some angles it appeared to be striped yellow and green and a bluish tint. His eyes were this clear colour, too, and had no black pupil. The texture was rather like a shrimp, hard yet very fragile."

Miss Watson went on to say that her dogs took no interest in him, but she was so excited over finding him that she dashed into the house to phone for her nearest friend to come and see him. When she came back, he had vanished, and only a little wet cross on the bench showed where he had been. This strange creature may have been there for a definite purpose. He was probably in a state of transition to a higher form of life, and the powerful vibrations from Miss Watson's hand could have been instrumental in helping him on his way. Miss Watson also saw some fairies playing in a well at Talsarnau, in Merioneth; and she knew a little grotto on the old Roman Road near Tan-y-Bwlch, where she had often seen fairies swinging about on the overhanging fern-fronds, though she said that at times the entire grotto seemed to disappear.

Not all sea spirits adopt the human shape. Some are bird-like in formation, and when holidaying on the Lincolnshire coast in June 1955, I saw a number of these silver-white beings flashing swiftly over and through the waves. They resembled the sea spirit portrayed in Geoffrey Hodson's book *The Kingdom of the Gods* (Theosophical Publishing House, London).

While my sister and I were walking along a lonely stretch of shore at the Seacroft end of Skegness, Lincs., I caught sight of a very beautiful and unusual shell half-hidden among the pebbles. My sister was some distance away, so I called to her and drew her attention to it. I was just walking closer to it to pick it up when I received an unmistakable thump in the back and a push that sent me flying into a sea pool, where I was drenched up to my knees. My sister, who had just reached the spot, looked on in amazement, as there was no other person in sight and she could see me being propelled forward. After that incident, I decided to leave the shell alone, as I felt that some little sea-sprite must covet it more than I did!

The sisters Jane and Marie Elfram, whose articles on nature spirits appeared in some of the old issues of a paper called *Light*, used to have wonderful experiences with garden fairies and sea fairies, and I remember that one of them, while picking up a crab to show to her sister, slipped on a rock, cutting and bruising herself. At the same moment a sea spirit appeared before them and said "Put that crab down!" She admitted causing the accident but seemed to think the chastisement was well deserved. Meanwhile the crab had sidled behind her and remained there the whole time.

This sea spirit was dark-haired, fair-skinned, and green-eyed. She had a tail that glinted in beautiful colours, and two large and two small opalescent wings. For the sisters' benefit she raised herself and flew round some six feet above them. On the shore they saw many little entities dressed in a greenish brown seaweed colour, with tails instead of feet, and they noticed that when the tide was up these tiny creatures played and rode on the tops of the smaller waves. They could fly and swim, and their work seemed to be in helping baby crabs, which were stranded. Sometimes they allowed the sisters to see their pretty seashell treasures.

"In 1949," Miss Dawn E. Mooney recounted, "I was staying with the late Mairi T. Sawyer in her marvellous sub-tropical garden of Inverewe, Wester Ross, and as the midges were too bad to allow me to work outside I went off by myself to visit the Fionn Loch at the back of Beinn Airidh Gharr, which in those days belonged to 'Aunt Mairi,' as I called her. There is a rough road along the river Ewe from opposite Pool House Hotel, past Inveran and the little MacKenzie shooting-box called Kernsary, and then the track climbs up through some of Osgood MacKenzie's tree plantations and out on to the plateau where the Fionn Loch lies, I think about 1,000 feet up. It is nine miles from Inverewe by the road, and there are several gates, one of which Mairi Sawyer kept locked. It was a hot July day, calm and clear, and I saw no one once I had left the Inveran gates behind. I was tired and thirsty by the time I got to the boathouse at the road-end, so I sat down on a rock beside the loch and started to eat an apple. The water was rippling on the loose stones of the shore near my feet with a pleasant tinkling sound, but clearly and distinctly above the water sounds I heard children laughing gaily and in a high trilling key. It sounded so infectiously light-hearted that I thought it worth putting my hot and tired limbs to work again, and I clambered over a high boulder to spy where the picnic party was in progress—for such I assumed it to be, though it surprised me greatly

131

because there was no car parked at the road-end by the boathouse.

"My investigations led to nothing, for there was no sign of any beings within sight and no more sounds were audible. I resumed my seat and continued eating my apple, thinking that I might have dozed off without realising it, when at still closer range I heard the laughter again. Deciding that there must be some ventriloquism going on, and that I should find the children in the opposite direction from which there laughter sounded, I explored the shores to the north, walking towards the An Teallach hills of Dundonnell. But a thorough search convinced me that there were no human beings within miles of me. I went back to my place and lay down flat on my back, and the laughter seemed to flash about from rock to rock all round me as I lay, but I saw nothing whatever.

"That evening, when I told of this occurrence over the peats and eucalyptus log fire at Inverewe, Mairi Sawyer was so interested, and so convinced by my telling, that she had inquiries made by her men to discover if any cars or parties had passed up the Kernsary track, but she was assured that I had been the only person to go that way on the day mentioned. Nobody had asked for the key of the locked gate and no car had passed along the track, which, although it could be driven over, was little more than a pony track. To walk from Letterewe or Dundonnell would tax the legs of most adults and be impossible for children young enough to have such high-pitched laughter. Old 'Teeny' MacGillwray, childhood companion to Aunt Mairi and later housekeeper at Inverewe, said that it was not human voices I had heard and that 'some other people' in the past had heard things by the Fionn Loch. But more she would not say. Aunt Mairi herself seemed a little apprehensive, saying that she felt like avoiding the place because she did not care to be in the power of the little people, but I assured her that these were entirely friendly and that there was nothing bad in it at all.

"I should perhaps add that my mother is half a MacLeod and that she and I and also Theresa MacLeod, her mother, sometimes see, hear, or feel things not readily accounted for by normal methods of human reasoning."

The waterfall in Mrs. Ella Jackson's garden in her childhood recalls the fairy horses in a waterfall in some pages contributed in 1932 by Mrs. Iris Strick of Devon to the *Atlantis Quarterly*, edited by her cousin Charles Richard Cammell and Lewis Spence. This experience is quoted from the publication referred to: "Some years ago," in the 1920s, "I went for a long walk in the Pentland Hills, near Edinburgh. A niece, aged about thirteen, came with me, and we planned to be out all day and see if this time we could manage to thrust our way a bit further 'through.' We avoided explanations as to the exact meaning of this expression. In those days we were very closely in touch with each other, and my young companion seemed to have a strange kinship with Nature. We had been for some remarkable walks with a very special atmosphere of their own, but invariably, just as we appeared to be on the verge of some great discovery and the Gates of Faerie were about to open, all would change, the barriers closed down, and we were left with only a haunting longing for what might have been. Actually we never saw anything on these walks that could not be easily explained, but always we felt there was something that we had only just missed, and that another time we might slip through and see. All went well with our Pentland expedition, and about midday we stopped to rest on a hillside ablaze with bell heather. It had been rather a dour kind of grey day, but now the sun came out between the clouds, and we lay face downwards in the heather, lost in an ecstasy of beauty both of colour and scent. All sense of time passed. In Fiona MacLeod's immortal story, *The Anointed Man*, [the hero] lays face downwards in the ling [heather], and we had often talked of that story and quoted passages from it; but with our lesser experience it was the bell heather that worked some ancient magic and opened our eyes to 'something that came down the Rainbow Arches of Cathair-Sith.' However that may be, we started up with one accord and, leaving the path, ran upwards into the hills. No doubt for the time being we were fey, and there was a delightful feeling that something unusual was about to happen, only it delayed its action, for nothing happened then.

"We went up a glen, climbed a steep bank, then downward again, and presently came to a stream, which had carved its way deep into the living rock. Very strange and eerie was that valley, with the stone sculptured by Nature into weird forms over-arching the burn, so that it became a dark, mysterious water. We became obsessed with the idea that wild fruit must be found, and after much difficulty a solitary strawberry was discovered. How any strawberry had managed to ripen in such a position was a mystery, but there it was, and we divided it—probably with a sharp splinter of stone—and consumed it with fitting solemnity. Somehow this curious action seemed to be of real importance at the time, and perhaps it was. The sound of falling water attracted us to the edge of a precipice. Our stream slid over the edge, and changed into a shining waterfall. My niece lay down on a flat stone and gazed at the water as it leapt into the depths below. The sunshine had gone, and the sky was greying with hurrying clouds. A mist of spray blew back on to us from the crest of the fall.

"Suddenly the child cried, 'Oh! Quick, quick, quick, look at the horses!'

"'Where?' I shouted against the roar of the water.

"'In the waterfall!'

"I flung myself down on the stone in her place and watched intently. For some moments nothing was to be seen in the flying spray, and then I saw them. How can one ever describe the entrancing beauty and gaiety of that sight? Passing down the waterfall, at the same speed as the falling water, was a procession of small horses and riders transparent as the water itself. The horses, with their shining quarters and flying manes and tails, were more clearly defined than the riders. The latter waved their arms above their heads as though encouraging one another in the wild game they appeared to be playing. Then they were gone, and one had time to breathe, but only for a few moments. They (or others of the same type) appeared again and again at the top of the fall, repeated the same actions, and so it went on for, perhaps, half an hour. The sky had darkened, and it had been raining hard for some time, but we took no notice, drenched as we were already with the spray. It was all such tremendous fun. The joyous abandon of the water-beings made one long to plunge over the precipice and join them in their headlong rush, but that is not the way of escape for those still caged in an earthly body. At length it dawned upon us that it was getting late; that we had, perhaps, seven miles still to walk, a train to catch, and that it was pouring with rain. One last look at the nature spirits, and we climbed down through the soaking bracken and ferns to rejoin the public path. We said little at the time; the experience had been too overwhelming for immediate discussion. On that dark and dripping walk home we felt an aching longing and nostalgia for that bright world of which we had been permitted this one glimpse.

"Later we discussed the incident at great length, comparing notes as to what each had seen, and wondering whether the little horsemen had galloped back up through the rocks for the sport of plunging down the fall anew, or whether each group was a separate unit making for some unknown destination. One solitary American has put on record a slightly similar experience, but in his case the small horses were seen in the foam of breaking waves. My own belief is that, all unknowingly, we had stumbled on some ancient Celtic ritual in which the sun, the bell heather, and, above all, the wild fruit, each played their part, and that in consequence our eyes were opened."

As well as water spirits, there are fairies of the snow and ice, and in her childhood Miss Sylvia Birchfield, of Chicago, saw what she called "snow fairies," which she said were "sparkly" in their long, white and silver robes.

Miss Z. of Surrey told me that she, too, had seen snow fairies. They were about three feet tall, gleaming like shining angels in raiment white and sparkling as snow in sunshine, and their large, powerful wings resembled white feathers. Many came and danced with graceful, tranquil movements, weaving about in the manner of ballet-dancers, their flowing robes wafting in the sunlight as they floated just above the level of the ground.

Mrs. Winifred Spilsbury of Sheffield, Yorkshire, saw a long procession of beings similar in appearance but that she called "ice fairies," all going in one direction. In their semi-transparent white robes and silvery crystal headbands, they looked as if made of moonbeams. They seemed to be of different ages, and the older ones each carried a sort of wand or crystal-and-silver staff. She received the impression that this staff was a symbol of office and gave them authority to transmit psychic power and cast a protective aura over the creatures they desired to help. She spoke to them by thought, and was told: "We are gathering together to collect the spirit-forms of birds and animals, which will die in the frost soon to come. Some are changed in form, and some come back to keep the instinct of the species alive for all." This was before the arrival of the heavy falls of snow that were to drift and cause such havoc to wildlife in April 1954, and when they actually came a week later and Mrs. Spilsbury read about the large numbers of wild ponies and other animals and birds, which were dying on the moors, she said she knew that the fairies would be there, ready to take them to a new and happier experience.

On the morning of 27 December 1961, my sister called me into the garden to look at the small, white enamel water-bowl, which we kept there for the wild birds. The water in it was frozen, and clearly engraved on the ice was the picture of a small summer-house near some trees; a figure holding what appeared to be a fishing rod; and a little sailing-boat on some water, with birds flying overhead. Around the edge of the ice picture were small close lines pointing towards the centre and forming a sort of decoration to set off the design, which must have been executed overnight, as the water bowl was re-filled every day. My sister laid some tracing paper on top of the dish and traced all the lines on it. One explanation of this particular design is that at that time we had a tea service, table linen, vases, curtains, etc., all in the conventional Willow-pattern, and we could only surmise that as the fairy folk are wonderful imitators, they may have taken a fancy to the design seen in our house and attempted to reproduce it on the solid surface of the ice, though in a simplified form and with no great accuracy of detail. After seeing this, we were better able to understand and appreciate the lovely leaf-patterns found on frozen windowpanes on bleak winter mornings. Of course, for the materialist and the sceptics there is always the scientific explanation for these "little miracles," but for those of us who have kept our sense of wonder Nature is full of exquisite examples of fairy artistry.

Salamander or Fire Fairies

When the child who became the celebrated Benevento Cellini was shown a salamander by his father—who gave him "a great box on the ear" to make him remember the unusual incident—the little fire-spirit was described as being like a lizard. One of the definitions of a "salamander" in the *Oxford Dictionary* is "Lizard-like animal supposed to live in fire," but the next definition is merely "Elemental spirit living in fire." We can assume from the testimony of some of my contributors that these beings can take different forms and, like other nature spirits, can also imitate the human shape. In his book *Unseen Forces* (Hall Publishing Co, California, 1929) Manly P. Hall described some of them as being "as large as giants of prehistoric times," and others as "small and barely visible." The latter ones, which he mentions, may be similar to the "spark fairies," which I used to see on the fire-back. They had a bluish aura and flew to and fro like flies, but they swelled to the size of wasps or bees while they were absorbing the essence of the dying sparks, which they carried back to the main fire.

Mr. Tom Charman, in his notes on salamanders, wrote: "I may go weeks without seeing any, and then suddenly one or more will appear in the middle of the flames. There they will lie down, skip about, or handle the red-hot embers with great enjoyment. Often of a winter's evening, when the fire is crackling merrily on the hearth and the sparks are flying up the chimney, these little creatures will join in the dancing fire, their limbs in quaint, closely-fitting garments, shining red in the glowing embers. On their arrival the fire becomes truly alive. They are nearly always in the fire, though at times they are outside and close to the fireplace. Towards the beginning of this year I saw a very fine salamander, whom I recognized intuitively as a Fire King. His face was very ruddy, suggesting flame, and it was strong and refined. One evening soon after this, when darkness had set in, I was sitting without a light and the fire had nearly gone out. Suddenly, my attention was roused by the sight of little salamanders running about the floor. They were throwing fire about the room. It seemed as though it came from them, because all they did was to throw forward their hands, and from these there shot out long streaks or ribbon-like lines of fire. They took a great delight in doing this, and they were running about in this fashion for some time. It seemed as though the Fire-King I had seen a few days before had brought them for me to see, though he was not visible."

When Mrs. Clara M. A. Clayton lived in Nottinghamshire after her marriage, she was alone in the house one winter's evening and was reading by the fire, which was gradually getting low. All at once, something that she realised was a salamander came out of it, and the fire immediately lost its glow. "The fire fairy had no definite shape or form," she explained. "It was like a tongue of fire, yet it seemed to have a centre from which the flames rose. It was swift in its movements, and I thought it would go up the chimney when it first darted out." She spoke to it, trying to become one with it, but it flashed back into the fire, which glowed anew with bright flames that made the room warm once more. Again she tried to communicate, and once more it darted out and all the glow went out of the fire this time for good for the salamander did not return. "The happy little life that was revelling in it and shooting out flames had left it, and had entered into the great Spirit of Fire," she concluded.

The journalist and poet, Miss Odette Tchernine, of Fleet Street, London, became acquainted with fire fairies when she was living in the Maida Vale district of London. Intermittently at the age of six or a little less, she partly saw, partly felt, some small pleasing presences dancing around her in the light of the big open nursery fire. They were pink and gold and flame-coloured; graceful, transparent entities, weaving about her in silent friendliness, and seeming to be part of a glow of secret, contented well being. "I felt in tune with them, as if we knew about one another and had a sort of private understanding," she told me. "It was fun, and all rather lovely."

While being astrally projected to receive healing for arthritis, Mrs. Gwen Cripps, of Cheshire saw a fire fairy. She sent me a painting of it, though she said it gave no idea of the depth and brilliance of the fairy's colouring. It was through the intermediary services of this little creature that she received vitality "an icy-cold, penetrating power that one feels to be galvanizing and holding together the astral body." The little thing, nine or ten inches in height, kept darting backwards and forwards from behind a screen of intense white light, as if to gather energy from that source, and each time it did so she felt the impact. She could not say that the elemental had any endearing qualities, but it was strangely fascinating and powerful. Fierce, black brows dominated its alert face, and it gazed at her intently with enormous black, protruding eyes, which had no pupils. "It struck me at the time," she said, "that here was a difference, for most nature spirits have soul-less eyes." The "skin" of the face, hands, and feet was brownish, wrinkled and leathery in texture. The little creature had not assumed any fantastic clothing; rather did the red part of its person grow with the brownish "skin" of the other parts mentioned. The texture of this red part was delicate and resembled a mass of bubbles, which looked as though they had been inflated like a pressure suit glistening in the light, as if wet. Mrs. Cripps received the name "Fire Spirit" as she looked at this creature. It occurred to her that "Salamander" might be another name for it, "but I wouldn't be too sure about this," she added, "because I have clairvoyantly seen (in normal state) a Salamander, and although both of these had the same vital quality of dancing flames of fire, the Salamander was much more fluid than this Fire Spirit, which had a robust appearance. The vision was truly breath-taking."

Tree Spirits

To a sensitive nature-lover the ruthless felling of a healthy tree is a tragedy. Most trees respond to our love and admiration. They have vital lifeforce, and many of them have healing properties. Some of the old trees have such a highly advanced vegetable consciousness that they possess a definite individuality, and they can externalize themselves in human shape, like the dryads of ancient Greece. When a tree has fallen, not only does such an act antagonize and drive out the lovely spirit of the tree, but it also deprives the little elves of their homes in the crevices of the tree boles, and alas the wild birds of a nesting place and a refuge among the leafy branches.

Mrs. G. K. Evason told me that a friend of hers had just returned from the office where she worked as a civil servant, and was busy preparing her evening meal when she became aware of a spirit form on her windowsill. It said that it was the spirit of the tree that had been outside her window, and it now had no home because the tree had recently been cut down. Fortunately, Mrs. Evason's friend had not been in any way responsible for the act, for she said how she had loved the tree and found peace in looking at it when she was resting quietly in her chair.

One of the daughters of Mrs. M. Lilley drew a picture of a tree spirit whom she saw clairvoyantly. This diva was looking very upset, and a few hours afterwards, when Mrs. Lilley entered the wood at the bottom of the garden, she found that someone had cut some branches from one of the trees.

Mrs. Iris Strick used to enjoy wandering peacefully in a thick and very beautiful wood: "Wild daffodils and hyacinths, frail anemones and tiny wood sorrel grew there in profusion, and the spotted leaves of 'lords and ladies' pushed up here and there in groups. From under the sheltering ferns and bracken, shy wildlife peeped at me, rabbits scuttled from near my feet, squirrels raced up and down the tree trunks, and bird voices of many kinds filled the air with music. Under the great rocks, foxes had entrenched themselves so deeply that no evilly disposed spade could reach their safe retreat, and there was even rumour of a badger... There was magic abroad in that wood—white magic, which gave it a personality all its own... One could feel the presence of lives that are not as our lives, beings that are wild and free, and only just beyond the limit of mortal sight. Yet they seemed friendly to those who were in harmony with them; to those who could be trusted to hurt neither bird nor beast, flower, nor tree." After a long absence Mrs. Strick revisited the wood, and found that all was "destruction and despair." Great trees lay stark and lifeless, and she stumbled over a fallen Beech, which was lying "like a mutilated statue of ancient Greece, the graceful limbs hacked away; its pride, its glory, humbled to the dust." The friendly feeling of the wood had gone, and hatred and fear were all around. It was not good to linger; the atmosphere was inimical to man, to the race that had wrought all this ruin. She heard a rending crash as one of the last of the mighty trees went down, and she said that "something invisible whizzed past like a streak of agony and was gone, leaving a trail of terror and rage behind it."

At a country house in Derbyshire, Mrs. Strick introduced me to a great Cedar tree, which she said was "very friendly." She told me to lean my back against its trunk and see if I could contact its consciousness. I can recall, even now, the tremendous power of its vibrations as they flowed through me, flooding my whole being with new life and energy. Mrs. Strick said she always experienced this feeling when she leant silently against it.

Mrs. Gwen Cripps made the acquaintance of a tree spirit, which dwelt in a very large poplar in her garden, and she felt the strength of its aura coming through to her whenever she touched the tree.

While travelling on a train that was slowly passing a tree-bordered meadow, Miss Kathleen Hinde saw the lovely snow-white nude figure of a nymph step out of one of the trees into the knee-high grass, and melt away before her eyes.

Mrs. Clare Sheridan, of Sussex, the sculptor and writer, became very "fey" during the six years of the Second World War when, as a pacifist, she lived a very secluded life on the South Coast. "I found," she said, "that I was able to talk with the spirit of a very old tree, and, of course, with other nature spirits."

In 1938, Mrs. Vera Westmoreland bought a house with a lovely old-world garden, which narrowed down at the far end to where a tall tree stood near a rockery. Her father wished to make room for a greenhouse, and during May he planned to cut down the tree. Through the wide French windows, she and her mother watched him put down his spade and walk forward with the saw. The next moment he was rubbing his chest. He went forward a second time and again rubbed his chest and moved slightly backwards. At the third attempt he fell right over on to his back, and soon he came into the house looking flushed and worried. When they asked what was the matter, he told them that twice he had felt a hard "something" push at him on his chest, and the third time it had knocked him right over. Mother and daughter went into the garden, where they watched him try once more. This time, a much harder knock made him again fall backwards. He heard a voice say, "You cannot do that to my tree!" and then he saw an elf whose face was brown and wizened, and whose clothing was tattered. That settled it! He would have nothing more to do with that tree, and it became his daughter Vera's job to collect its fruit. At rare times she saw the face of the elf, and she said it was "like that of an old man in miniature," who looked as if he had seen many years of work. He would nod his head at her, so she knew that he realised she could see him.

When the 1939 war started, arrangements had to be made for an air-raid shelter to be sunk. The men whose job it was to dig the ground and erect the shelter went to the tree to remove it. Their spades broke, and two of the men fell backwards. They became so frightened that they were told they could move the rockery instead, so the shelter was put there and the tree was left alone, unscarred. "I saw that elf grin more than once when air raids were on, and I used to pop out of the shelter to make hot drinks," said Mrs. Westmoreland. "His was the only wrinkled face I have ever seen on an elf."

Many years later, she and her husband went to live in Oldham, where their work for the crippled and the blind awaited them. They lived in a very old house where the roof bent in, and the living room window was faced and darkened by two weary and withered elm trees that were barely alive in the sour soil that was burned by many years of heavy soot from the mills. The old place became a sanctuary for many handicapped people who needed help and comfort, and one day the couple planned to move those trees when the rain stopped. On the morning of the first fine day, Mrs. Westmoreland had been cleaning the windows of the house when, to her surprise, she saw an olive-green elf staring hard at her as he moved from one branch to another, though she felt nothing, and had no idea what he was thinking. She told her husband about it, and they wondered if the elf knew their plans. Then they thought no more about it, and that evening they set to and sawed off the treetop. Mrs. Westmoreland felt a strange pushing at her back, but didn't take any notice. Then quite suddenly, while standing upright waiting for her husband to tell her what he wanted moving first, she was hit by a force and pushed down by something small and strong on to the sharp tree-stump, which pierced her leg above the knee, giving her a permanent blue mark there. They knew, then, that some force was about which did not agree with their removing the tree, but, for the sake of the house-bound inmates, they struggled on, leaving a small part still growing. They remembered Vera's seeing the elf that morning, and her father's experience when he had tried to cut down a tree, so they left the other one untouched.

In the course of one of her visits to Killagally, in County Offaly, Ireland, Mrs. Eve Gall was privileged to see a tree spirit of the dryad type, and told me of her experience. "It was a beautifully warm, sunny day; a lazy day, with that soft warmth that one only gets in Ireland. My hostess and my husband had wandered off and left me to my own devices. I strolled up through the park towards the lodge gates to a place where there was a broad stretch of greensward beside the drive, and seated myself under the shadow of a huge Beech tree. I sat for a while, quietly enjoying the lovely scene before me and allowing the peace and beauty of it all to steal into my soul. Presently I found myself in that fey state of consciousness that is so easily attained in Ireland. All was still; even the birdsong was hushed, and the silence was tense with an air of expectation, when there appeared beside me, under the great tree, a very tall figure at least ten or twelve feet high. It was a female figure dressed in green, flowing drapery, which, although there was no wind at all, seemed to wave and flutter in a breeze. The hair, which was a lustrous metallic green, was long and flowing free; the skin of the face was very pale with a luminosity hard to describe; the features were fine and delicate, with an aquiline nose, high cheekbones, and full lips. Her hands and arms were stretched sideways and her face was uplifted to the sky. The outstanding impression I received was of her tremendous vitality — she was absolutely vibrant with life, and she seemed to be radiating this life and energy into the world of Nature around her. She was visible for four or five minutes, and then gradually faded from my sight." Mrs. Gall told me that without her knowing how, this glorious creature had made her aware that she was the spirit of the great Beech-tree, and she said that for the

rest of that day she carried with her a feeling of elation and exaltation such as she had seldom experienced before.

My sister and I saw the aura, but not the actual form, of a tree
spirit in Colwick Woods, Nottingham, where my sister had the ring
of blue beads returned to her by the fairies. In our youth we had
played there with the children from the farmhouse (long since de-
molished) that was part of the Colwick Park Estate once owned by
the Chaworth-Husters, where Byron's Mary had lived. We had spent
the happiest times of our lives there, gathering blackberries, mushrooms, elderberries, and picking up acorns, which we turned into
fairies' cups or elves' caps. We would roly-poly down the hillocks or
lie on the grass among the wild flowers, listening to the grasshoppers or watching the skylarks. Sometimes we would catch a glimpse
of baby partridges, rabbits, or foxes. We pretended to be Scouts, or
Red Indians, and played hide-and-seek among the trees, which we
loved and never defaced. To us, it was Paradise. When middle aged,
we had taken our cocker spaniels there for their daily exercise, and
they would drink at a little spring near the cherry and crab-apple
trees in the valley. Now, after a long interval of many years, we were
wandering again over the familiar haunts, this time in our old age,
and (though we did not know it) for the last time together. We were
in a nostalgic mood, and we sat down to rest on a hilltop, trying to
recapture the old magic. After a while, feeling more peaceful and
relaxed, we began to retrace our steps and were walking towards a
tree, which had known us intimately in our younger days and grew
apart from the others, when to our amazement it suddenly became
illumined. This was no trick of the sunlight, for the tree shone from
within, and its radiance rayed out in a golden-white aureole, ethereal and translucent. The tree wanted us to know it had recognized
us, and we stood in silent communion under its branches, enfolded
in its welcoming vibrations. After a while we had to say goodbye,
and we continued our walk home feeling blessed and uplifted. It
was a truly wonderful and touching experience to be greeted and
remembered so lovingly by an old woodland friend.

Banshees

I cannot mention the fairies of Ireland without including the Banshee (Bean Sidhe), or "Woman Fairy," who attaches herself to certain old Irish families and gives a warning when some disaster or the death of a member is imminent. Sometimes she is observed sitting on a rock while keening, but she is more frequently heard than seen.

One such account came from Miss Rolanda Hirst, of Bedwas, Monmouthshire, who in 1927 was staying at Lissadill in Sligo as governess to the children of Sir Josslyn Gore Booth. Sir Josslyn's sister was Countess Constance Markievicz, the Sinn Feiner who played such a prominent part in the Easter Rebellion of 1916. One day, Lady Gore Booth came into the schoolroom to say that she and her husband were going to Dublin at once, as they had heard that the Countess was ill in hospital. "That afternoon," said Miss Hirst, "I took the children down to the shore for a picnic and bathe. The children went into the sea and I stayed on the shore, preparing the tea. Soon I heard a terrible and mournful wailing coming from the rocks in the sea, and it went on for some time. When the children returned from their bathe, I asked them if they had heard the wailing? Their reply was: 'No, but it might be seals.' I said no more, and we had tea and returned to the house. There a telegram awaited us saying that the Countess Markievicz was dead, and would I take the children up to Dublin? She was born at Lissadill, and I think it can be inferred that what I heard was the Banshee, said to wail when any famous member of an old house died."

Mrs. Elizbeth Niven, a schoolteacher in Londonderry, Ireland, who had spent the greater part of her life in County Donegal, said, "I certainly have heard the Banshee's wail, and my husband heard it also. It followed a family who did not live far from us after we were married."

In November 1955, Mrs. Katharine Johnston, of Castlewellan, County Down, Ireland, wrote: "I cannot claim any personal visions of fairies, but my mother (Lady Coghill), as a child of eight or nine, heard the Banshee keening in the garden round her old home in Castletownshend, County Cork. This was on a June morning between 5 a.m. and 6 a.m., and she was so frightened that she sought refuge with her older sister (the late Dr. E. OE. Somerville). At breakfast-time came the news that a whole boatload of my grandfather's tenants had been drowned just outside the harbour, while returning from prolonged wedding festivities in a neighbouring harbour. This happened at the time my mother heard the Banshee keening. My mother also told me often that she had once heard the fairy music. This was long after she was grown-up. She could not describe it beyond saying it was most lovely and seemed to sweep around the house."

From Mrs. Norah de Courcy of East Grinstead, Sussex, came the following testimony with an interesting variation: "My mother had been ill for about a fortnight and was, I knew, failing fast. I had been to see her in Hampstead on Friday, August 5th, 1949. I was living near Midhurst at that time, and had to return as my daughter was under two years old and I had no one with whom I could leave her. On Sunday August 7, I was of course thinking a great deal about my mother, and at about 7 p.m. I was in the kitchen when I heard a sound, coming as if it were from the roof above me, as of a woman wailing. One can only use human terms in describing such experiences, though in reality the sound was not exactly like a woman's voice. I never heard anything so utterly sad or awesome. About a quarter of an hour later, my husband came into the room. I told him I had just heard the Banshee and then I heard it again, but he heard nothing. I could feel my hair literally standing on end. I had known for many years that a Banshee was supposed to foretell the death of members of the de Courcy family, for my mother's mother was a de Courcy (a different branch of the same family as my husband's), and she and a sister of hers had heard it when they were in Germany early in the century before an aunt of theirs died; but I had not been thinking of this at all before hearing it myself. (I may mention that although I have used the term 'hearing' I felt as though the sounds were received by other means than the physical ear.) I rang up the nurse who was looking after my mother, and she reported no change. At about midnight I heard 'bells' (the nearest equivalent to the sound) ringing above the house far up. The tone and joyful clangour were more wonderful than any earthly sound. My mother died at this moment, as far as I could discover. I have not heard of these bells in any other connection or experience, but they were a wonderful message to me as my mother and I were very close to one another until very tragically her mental powers deteriorated. Curiously enough, none of my own family heard the Banshee."

Just before the hour of midnight in the year 1905, Mrs. L. Connolly heard the loud wailing of a Banshee, and her husband did not live long afterwards. "Mother was a hard-headed English-woman," said Mrs. E. Hazlehurst, her daughter who kindly sent me the account, "but she was living in a small village in County Kildare, Ireland, when she heard the Banshee."

Mr. Willie Monks, of Lusk, County Dublin, sent this account of a Banshee heard by members of his family. "My mother, before she was married, was staying with an older married sister, Mrs. McAllister, at Staffordstown, Donabate, County Dublin. During her visit, a child got badly burned and died as a result. While he was dying, my mother claimed she heard the Banshee crying in or around the house. She said the sound was entirely different from that made by cats or other animals. This was in the 1890s. Sometime in the 1930s, at the same house, a sister of the burned boy got sick and later died. While she was ill, a sister of mine went to see her, and she heard the strange crying sound. What surprised her was that none of the other people in the house made any comment about it. Several members of the family died during the intervening years and since, but no one reported ever hearing anything unusual."

"It was during our first visit to Ireland in September 1948," recounted Mr. William C. Gall, M.P.S., of Emsworth, Hants, "that my wife Eve and I went with our hostess to spend a day or two at her brother's house at Killagally, south of Athlone. It was a big, Georgian house, almost a mansion, built on the ruins of an ancient nunnery, but being Ireland, and remoter Ireland at that, it had no modern conveniences, such as gas or electricity. Thus, it happened that in the evening we were gathered round a log fire in a huge and lofty eighteenth-century room, dimly illumined by two candles set in tall silver candlesticks, engaged in conversation such as one can enjoy only in Ireland. It was a still night, but pouring with rain; the great window shutters were closed; there was no other house within a mile; and it was half a mile to the lodge gates on the highway. We were listening to reminiscences of the past, when I heard a most unearthly howling noise from somewhere outside. I looked at my wife and she looked at me, but the others continued talking as though they had not heard it. Again there came that uncanny wailing, more prolonged this time, and still they made no remark although it was manifest that they were rather disconcerted. Our query 'Whatever was that?' passed unheeded. When for a third time there was that eerie howling, rising and falling in pitch and even more persistent and insistent than before, it was impossible to ignore it, but our host's only reaction was to rise abruptly and say, 'I think we're stirring them up too much. We had all better go to bed.' Without more ado, he bade us 'Goodnight' and left the room. There was nothing more to be said, so each of us lighted our candles and went to our rooms.

"Once we were in our bedroom, by force of habit I looked at my watch, which showed a little after ten o'clock. My wife, Eve, said to me, 'Whatever was that weird howling; one would think it was a Banshee.' I replied: 'Well, it was certainly not a dog, or a fox, or an owl.' (It was quite unlike any of these and the persistent, mournful rising and falling wail sent cold shivers down the spine.) 'I believe it was a Banshee, and if so it is a bad omen for someone here tonight.' It was with subdued and apprehensive feelings that we eventually settled down for the night. The next day our friends absolutely ignored any attempt to refer to the matter, and in the course of a really delightful holiday we soon forgot our fears and forebodings and the whole affair sank into the background of our minds. The sequel came when our holiday was over and we returned to our little cottage at Waterlooville in Hampshire, where we were living at the time. There we learnt, to our distress, that a very dear friend and neighbour had been terribly injured by two burglars and was critically ill in hospital. He was the owner of a laundry situated at the rear of our cottage, and he lived in a house at the end of the road, so he had to pass our cottage on his journeys between his home and the laundry. On the very night on which we heard the Banshee, our friend had occasion to visit the laundry office, which was situated upstairs, on the first floor. He entered the building, using an electric torch to see his way, and as he went to mount the stairs to the office he was attacked by the two men concealed there, who struck him down and then hurled a large cash-box at his head, which gave him a dreadful injury. He lost consciousness but regained it again some time later and then attempted to reach his home. It must have been a nightmare journey as he crawled along, weak with loss of blood and with spells of unconsciousness. At last he reached the door of our cottage and he has a distinct recollection of sitting on the doorstep, fervently wishing that we were at home and could come to his aid. Eventually he did manage to reach his home just as his son was about to go in search of him. For a long time his life was despaired of, but brilliant surgery and careful nursing restored him to health once more. Checking over the details with him when he was well enough to discuss them, we discovered that he was sitting on our doorstep mentally calling us in his distress, at the very same time that we were listening to that wailing Banshee in Ireland."

Chapter 4: Fairies in Houses, Fairy Glamour

Some people think that fairies are associated only with woods and gardens, but this is not so. They frequent buildings also, as the following accounts will show. In September 1952, Mr. and Mrs. Gall, of Hampshire, had spent a long, happy day making a new garden, and having finished it, they went indoors and relaxed in armchairs before the fire. They were sitting there in the twilight, talking over the day's work, when they saw a tiny fairy flying round the room. It circled twice and then disappeared through the wall as suddenly as it had come. The little figure, some nine or ten inches in height and human in shape, shone with a brilliant silvery radiance and had transparent and faintly luminous wings. It was visible for about fifteen seconds, and its disappearance left Mr. and Mrs. Gall looking at each other in amazement, asking "Did you see what I saw?" This was not the only experience that occurred to Mr. and Mrs. Gall, as will be seen in other parts of the book.

Mr. and Mrs. Sinnett, of Oxford, had a similar surprise. After the evening meal, Mr. Sinnett was resting comfortably in front of the fire, talking over the affairs of the day with his wife, when he saw a little fellow about seven inches high running around on the table and finally vanishing behind a jam pot. The small creature was dressed in what seemed to be a complete suit and hat, tight fitting throughout, and the colour was best described as neutral, or greeny-brown. Mr. Sinnett asked his wife what she saw, so that no words of his would conjure up a mental picture for her, and her description tallied exactly with what he had seen. "So," he said, "I maintain that this rules out hallucination. I have told lots of people about this, most of whom have either smiled tolerantly or openly scoffed. However, it was a very lovely experience and we hope to have more. I would swear to the truth of this before anyone."

During her stay in a house in Devonshire in 1925, Mrs. G. K. Evason walked to the lounge and as she opened the door she saw, to her astonishment, a circle of exquisite fairy creatures of female type—about a dozen of them—engaged in a dance on the hearth rug. There was no fire alight in the grate at the time, and the open French windows led on to a beautiful lawn and flower garden. All the little beings had wings and were from ten to twelve inches in height. They were ethereal, and their apparel was iridescent and diaphanous. "It was an entrancing sight," she said, "and I watched them for a period long enough to take in details of their dainty forms and features. Then a lady, who also was staying in the house, came to the door of the room to borrow a book from the bookcase, and all the fairies vanished. I recounted my experience to her and she was delighted. She said that fairies were supposed to live in the garden there, but she herself had never seen them and had not heard of any coming into the house. I had known nothing of this. One day in 1931, I visited the owner of a house in Herne Bay, Kent, and we sat in a room that overlooked a lovely garden. While we were talking, I saw a radiant blue fairy perched on the shelf of the gentleman's desk, where he was seated. She looked like a 'Queen,' for she had a tiny sparkling crown and a wand. My host could not see her but was very pleased to hear my account of her. I have had many similar experiences, and all were entirely spontaneous and unsought."

The scene of this next experience was an old military barracks in County Kilkenny, Eire, which had been converted into flats. The time was 5:45 p.m., on a day in mid-September in the year 1911, and Mrs. Isa V. Cooke had just finished laying the table in readiness for her husband's 6 o'clock meal. Drawing her armchair nearer the fire, she took her six-week-old baby girl out of her cradle and lifted her on to her knee. Resting her child's head in the hollow of her right arm, she talked to her and played with her fingers until she fell asleep. The "very happy experience" that followed is best described in Mrs. Cooke's own words: "As I was gazing at her beautiful little face and wondering what the future held in store for her, I thought I saw something like a large white butterfly flutter on to my left foot, which was resting on the fender. On taking a better look, I saw it was a lovely little doll-like creature about eight inches high. She ran up my skirt and jumped off my knee on to the arm of my chair, then round the back and on to my right shoulder, down my arm, and finished standing just at the baby's head. She was dressed in shimmering white, and held in her hand what looked like a darning needle about two inches long. My eyes were dazzled by her brilliance. Then I suddenly realised I was looking at a 'Fairy Queen.' I kept quite still as she stood gazing down at my baby. In a matter of seconds she jumped down on the arm of my chair, gave her wand a twist, and lo! Immediately the whole room was full of fairies, all dressed in the most magnificent hues imaginable. They danced all over the floor, caught the ends of the tablecloth, ran up on to the table, danced in and out through the dishes, swarmed up the curtains, and danced along the rail and the picture-frames. Everywhere I looked, in fact, there were dancing fairies. I watched them, entranced, for eight or ten minutes, and wished my husband would hurry so that he could see them too. Presently I heard him coming up the stone stairs and walking down the corridor. I was ready to say, 'Hush! Look at all the lovely fairies,' as soon as he opened the door, but alas! The moment the latch clicked, they vanished as quickly as they had come. I can see his face now, as I related my tale. He told me not to be so silly; that it was all imagination, etc. Imagination, my foot! I only know the whole scene was enchantingly lovely until my husband opened the door and broke the spell."

Mrs. Cooke hoped the little people would return the next evening, but she never saw them again, and twelve months later she and her husband left the flat. She states as a possible explanation of the fairies' visit that there was an old ruin across the road, which must have been a very large residence in days gone by, and the squire of the parish had sold some beautiful old trees that surrounded it. From the window of her flat she used to watch the lumbermen uprooting them with a big engine and chains, and she thought what a pity it was to destroy beauty that was centuries old. "So perhaps the fairies sensed my sympathy," she conjectured, "and when the evening shadows were beginning to fall and the bright glow from my fire shone out through the open window, it may have enticed them to pay me a visit." And she added, "Although I am now elderly, I often think back longingly to that enchanted evening years ago, when the little people came to entertain me and my baby daughter."

It was in the autumn of 1919 that Mrs. Edith F. Ellis went with her husband and her three children and their nanny to live in Ramsgate in a small, modern-built detached house on the Montifiore Estate, beneath which land she believed there were natural caves and underground passages. "What I am about to relate," she said, "happened two weeks before Christmas 1919. I had taken my afternoon nap and was coming down the stairs in the gathering dusk, when I saw coming towards me up the stairs on my right a small fairy, flying as if she were in a great hurry. She was about five inches in length; her arms were moving as if she were swimming the crawl stroke, and her legs were keeping time with them. Her little limbs were waxen in appearance; her small head was covered with fair, close-curling hair; her wings were like silver gossamer and she wore a small skirt of the same material. Everything about her looked beautiful in the dim light. She became visible about four feet in front of me and passed me at approximately two feet six inches from the stair tread. I turned to look after her, and at another four feet behind me she disappeared into thin air. "Well," I said to myself, "If I were a child I should say I had seen a fairy. But I did not tell anyone.

"A few days later, I was sitting in the dining room by the fire, knitting a jumper with wool of a green heather-mixture, when, from out the side of the fireplace on my right, came the same little fairy figure. I followed her flight for about the same distance as previously, when she again disappeared into thin air. I was 41 years old at the time. It was only in that house that I ever saw a fairy, and I have often wondered why she appeared, and to me only, and why she was in such a terrible hurry, as if she were late."

Writing from Worthing, Sussex, to tell me of her "one and only fairy experience," Mrs. K. Allensby, a kinswoman of the late Sir Edward German, mentioned that she had Scottish blood, and that her mother was naturally clairvoyant and clairaudient. It is not surprising, then, to know that about the year 1947, at 6 o'clock on a summer's evening, Mrs. Allensby saw a small figure, approximately two feet high, appear in the hearth of her home at Whitchurch,

Shropshire. The little creature had rosy cheeks and curly golden hair, and was clad in a bright blue dress that matched her eyes. She smiled sweetly at Mrs. Allensby, and "was gone immediately."

Around Christmas 1955, Mrs. Violet I. Larkworthy, of Slough, Bucks, was lying relaxed on her divan when she noticed that a bowl of tulips on a chest of drawers was whirling round, and balanced on the rim were some tiny fairy figures, holding hands. Everything else in the room was still, and when she glanced back at the bowl that, too, was motionless, but in a few seconds it was twirling round again. Another time she saw a small figure similar to those she had watched on the tulip bowl. It was in a kind of blue gauze and was pirouetting on the top of a settee that she had then. "But the little people I saw when sitting in the sunshine at Hedgerley were different," she said. On that occasion her son had driven her and his wife to the Buckinghamshire village, where he pulled the car on to the grass verge of the road on a hill facing some grazing fields. They all alighted, and while her son tinkered with his car she and her daughter-in-law sat down to read, but the morning was so lovely she was soon looking around her and listening dreamily to a lark, which was soaring upwards in the sunshine. It was then that she noticed some tiny figures floating down in front of her. She watched them moving about in the grass, but did not say anything about them, as she knew her son and his wife would have laughed at her.

Miss Rosalie K. Fry lived at one time in a large house in Glydach-on-Tawe, about a mile from Swansea. It was situated in lovely grounds, surrounded by trees, and backed by a wild mountain and a bluebell-carpeted dingle complete with a little stream. One day she and her sister, aged seven and nine respectively, were standing in their nursery gazing out across a small hall to a larger hall beyond the two halls being joined by an archway. As they looked, something they could only describe as being like a piece of the finest white chiffon, about eighteen inches square, floated very slowly down into view beyond the archway, moving in an extraordinarily graceful, flowing manner, and then, as slowly, wafted away up out of sight. Neither of the sisters spoke a word; they simply dashed together into the further hall. Whatever they had seen had vanished completely, although it was moving so very slowly that they knew it should still have been floating about the hall in the fraction of time it took them to run from the nursery. They searched every inch of the stairs and also the upper landing, which was absolutely bare of furniture or pictures, but they found nothing. There was no one else about at the time. Miss Fry mentioned that it was a bright, sunny morning, but there was no question of their vision being a trick of the light. Both of them had exactly the same vivid recollection of the incident. At the time they were convinced they had seen a fairy, and although they have recalled their experience frequently in the many years since it happened, they have never been able to find any other possible explanation.

"My mother and her two sisters were sitting on a large old sofa," recounted Mrs. Louisa Nicholas of Bethesda, Caerns, North Wales, "when they all saw quite a regiment of fairies, dressed in bright red and brown, coming from a space in the wall. I used to take this story with a pinch of salt," she added, "but my mother, who is nearly 80, had such a vivid memory of it that nothing will convince her that fairies do not exist. Her two sisters (now deceased) were also certain they had seen them."

Mrs. Nicholas told me that according to legend there are fairies in Cororion Lake, Tregarth, about two miles away, and her daughter-in-law, who came from that district, affirmed that she had seen them.

A wee female fairy, dancing on an old oak table, was observed one evening by Miss Bessie Gill in her home at Wadeford Chard, Somerset. The little creature stood five or six inches in height and was attired in green. Miss Gill said that at the time of her appearance she was still mourning the loss of her parents, who had died a couple of years earlier, and she felt that the fairy had come to comfort her. She wished her tiny visitor would return, for she had never forgotten her. "It was like seeing beyond this world," she wrote. "She was so perfect in form, the sweetest thing I have ever seen."

Mrs. Ethel N. Gardner, of Ipswich, told me that her father was "a man of no imagination; a spade was a spade, to him." What a source of irritation it must have been, then, when he, of all people, saw what he called "the little men," not once, but frequently! There they were—gnome-like creatures, often with hats on, always busy in the same corner of the room and seemingly unaware that anyone was looking at them. They were on a quick vibration, and their world was entirely apart from the material conditions of that room. Try as he might, the reluctant seer could never find out what they were doing. They worried him—not in themselves, but because he just did not understand them and, as his daughter said, he was far from the type who harbours thoughts of fairies or little men. Surely this account will help to dispel the idea that fairies are produced by wishful thinking!

Each week, Mr. Frederick G. E. Wakefield joined a study group in the house of Mrs. E. M. Shilleto, of Kent, and saw there, quite frequently, a little creature about six inches high, who sat on a shelf in one corner. He wore a dark slouch hat, dark jacket, and green trousers, and his face was very brown and wrinkled, yet it had an expression of great humour. Mrs. Lilley, who also attended the group, told me that another member, Mrs. Ridge, had often seen the gnome, and so had Mrs. Shilleto's late sister, as well as a visitor to the house.

A little creature named Peto lived on the canopy over Miss Hannah Jackson's dining-room fireplace at her house in Manchester. She was a retired astrologer, and she told me in 1955 that for 30 years Peto had given her messages and warnings to pass on to the clients whose horoscopes she was engaged upon, and she affirmed that anyone in the room could see him. In 1957, I heard from this lady—then over 80 years old—that she was bedridden and no longer able to see Peto, who apparently did not wish to leave his familiar quarters above the fireplace downstairs for the atmosphere of the sickroom! A friend of hers, Mr. J. Broderick, wrote confirming the existence of the elf, or gnome, as follows: "I can verify all that Miss Jackson says about Peto. I have seen him scores of times."

During her childhood Mrs. Clara M. A. Clayton lived in North Wales, and "One afternoon," she said, "I was alone in a room, playing with my doll, when I heard laughter. On looking up, I saw a little gnome with a white beard, bushy eyebrows, and sparkling eyes. He was dressed in red from his pointed cap and belted coat to the leggings, which covered his rather long, pointed feet. He smiled and beckoned to me, so I got up from the mat and went towards him. Immediately he ran along the passage and disappeared through the closed front door, and being unable to follow him I thumped and thumped on it and called for my mother, who came running in to see what all the noise was about. 'Open it quickly!' I pleaded, 'I want to catch my little red man.' I told her about him, and she drew me away from the door. 'It must have been one of the Tylwyth Teg,' she said, for both she and my father had come from the Isle of Anglesey, and their belief in the Little People was strong.

Mrs. Iris Strick, of Devon, said: "The following incident happened to me in one of the last places in the world that one would expect to make contact with nature spirits. At that time I was living in the centre of a large town, in an old house built on the site of an ancient fortress. There was no garden, only a small lawn, rough grass, and an outcrop of rock; otherwise it was surrounded by stone paving and buildings. My husband used to go fishing to a river about thirty miles away, and one day he brought home a great bough of yellow broom that he had picked on the way back. On a subsequent evening when he was away again on a fishing expedition, I was sitting alone in the drawing room after dinner and had not drawn the curtains; the room was dimly lit by the afterglow from the sunset. There seemed to be a strange tremor in the air near the branch of golden broom where it stood in its deep blue vase. I wondered if it could be caused by a bee or large fly, but the curious thing was that no flies or bees or wasps ever entered that house, as the barren height on which it stood did not attract them, so I was interested at once and watched closely to see what it could be. Again that quiver or vibration of the air near the flowers, a little higher up this time, and then something that was not quite visible flickered across the room to a beautiful pink rhododendron that was growing in a pot near the door. The rhododendron was as near perfection as anything can been be on this plane, and the little elemental—for such I imagined it to be—flew round and round the plant as if entranced with its loveliness. There were still movements round the broom, however; it looked as if two or three small beings were attending to it in some way. I am sure they were troubled about it, knowing that it was slowly dying; but the Pink Pearl rhododendron was sheer rapture to them. They did not seem to be aware of me, only of the flowers and plants. The most thrilling moment of all was when something passed swiftly across the room close to my face; a tiny puff of vapour it seemed to be, perhaps four inches across either way. I felt the wind of its passing and observed the slightly increased density of the air somewhat resembling steam, but could make out no actual form. How long the experience lasted it is difficult to say, but the end was sudden, for my husband returned and turned on the light."

Mrs. Nancy Norris, a natural psychic who has had many strange experiences, recounted a disturbing one that she had at the age of two. She was playing by herself after tea one evening in the corridor outside her nursery, in a house at Sevenoaks, Kent, when suddenly she saw a small brown man of about her own size sitting at the top of the stairs looking at her. She was terrified, and at the time of writing to me she could still recall the awful panic she felt. She rushed into the nursery, screaming that there was a man on the stairs. Her mother was out, but the nurse called for a housemaid and, each armed with a poker, they went to look for the "man" while she sat huddled in the nursery. When her mother returned home, she was most sympathetic and talked to her about the fairy folk, and although she was no longer frightened she would not go along that corridor alone again for a long while. Nevertheless, she hoped she might catch another glimpse of the little man, but she never did.

"When I was about eight years old," wrote Miss Doris King, of Nottingham, I rose early one morning and was attracted by a shuffling noise that came from beneath the table in the living room. I lifted the tablecloth to see what it was, and was amazed to see a merry little gnome. He was dressed in a blue tunic trimmed with black buttons, blue trousers, long pointed-toe shoes, and pointed cap. He was about fifteen inches high, and with him were two other sprites, which I believe were fairies, of about half the size. I stepped back afraid, but all three made friendly advances and held out their hands as if imploring me to stay. I made for the stairs quickly, and when I reached the top I turned round to see all three below, frantically beckoning and looking very disappointed at my running away. I felt at the time that they intended to take me away with them, probably to the inner parts of the earth where they are supposed to dwell. Whether this was so or not, I do not know, for I ran into my mother's bedroom, afraid at what I had just encountered."

A rather dark and dusty corn-shop in a building 100 years old surrounded by factories in the heart of the Black Country is hardly the place where one would expect to see a fairy, but when Mrs. Joan Barnett was a child of five or six years old she was amusing herself on the floor of her father's shop when she saw a beautiful little creature approximately six inches high with lovely multi-coloured wings. She played with her for a few minutes, and while doing so she experienced "a wonderful feeling of happiness." She never saw the fairy again, although she used to look for her.

Mrs. Eleanor Thaxter, of Norfolk, recalled the time when, at the age of four, she lived with her parents and small brother in a little wooden house in Englefield Green, Surrey. One memorable day, she was standing outside on a side path when a little fairy man about two feet high ran down the main path, which led from the gate to the bottom of the garden. She called to him: "Oh, please stay and play with me!" but he was too busy talking to himself to hear her, and continued on his way to the coal shed, where he seemed to disappear behind some large lumps of coal. The child rushed to fetch her daddy to help her to move them, but he didn't believe her story and said she was dreaming. "I'm not, daddy," she sobbed. "I'm wide awake. He has gone into the coal shed." To pacify her, her father went with her to search for the little man, but they did not find him. As far as Mrs. Thaxter can remember, he was wearing a red hat and green tunic, and small turned-up shoes.

The previous account reminds me of a day many years ago when I opened the door of our coke shed and saw a small, female-type figure jump lightly down from the coke and hurry in front of my feet towards a cluster of the yellow "pan-pipe" flowers of a Corydalis plant, which was growing at the base of a concrete step. What possible attraction can fairies find in corn shops, and coal-

and coke-sheds? Can these four-dimensional beings see the arche-type within the corn and the coal? But after all, if Muriel Stuart, in her lovely poem "The Seed Shop," could visualize "a dale of hawthorn" dreaming in a brown husk, perhaps the fairies could see in the corn-shop fields of golden corn; and if John Oxenham, in his poem "The Sacrament of Fire," could speak of "coal, where forests lie entombed," maybe the fairies could see the ancient tree-ferns, which existed long before we human beings came to defile the living earth.

Mrs. Winifred Kirby, of Nottinghamshire, told me of an unusual experience she had some years ago after a friend had taken her some mushrooms, which he had gathered that morning. In the afternoon she felt impressed to do some automatic writing, in which she was interested, and she was astounded when the pencil wrote: "Can I be of service to you, lady?"

"Who are you?" she asked, and the pencil wrote again: "I am a gnome. That nasty man brought me with the mushrooms." She could not remember all the conversation, but she said the gnome wasn't very pleased to have been disturbed by her friend, though he seemed very friendly towards her, and he asked again if he could be of service. She felt his presence with her for quite a while, and wished she could have seen him.

It seems from this that mushrooms, as well as the traditional toadstools, are used as perching-places by the fairies!

"I've believed in fairies," said Mr. Ernest Rogers, Senr., of Bulwell, Nottingham, "ever since the time when, as a small child, I was awakened one night by the sounds of tinkling laughter. I went downstairs and peeped round the living-room door, and saw a group of fairies playing in the fireplace. We looked at each other for several seconds, then they seemed to flit away. Though it was night or early morning, the room was filled with light—or rather, light emanated from them and the fire grate. Now I am much older, I often remember and wish I could see them again."

The Theosophist Miss Clara Codd knew a lady doctor in Donegal who, along with all her children, could see fairies. These children had a pet leprechaun in the house, and one of their favourite games was to try to catch him, but they never succeeded. She asked them what he looked like, and they told her he was speckled black and white, and that he jumped like a rabbit. She remembered a great seer telling her that some of the fairies of Northern Ireland were speckled black and white. Another family known to her used to spend every winter in Egypt, and the children told her that always on their first night there, the green fairies would come and run up and down the window curtains.

A little man seemed to have attached himself to Mrs. Martha C. Smith, of the USA, as one of the family, and while writing to me she said: "My office is dark, and across the room from me, sitting on a desk with his hands over his mouth, laughing and muttering to himself, is my little man. He is about a foot high, rather hunched, with a very old expression on his face, and he always wears a tiny hat. He is so ugly that he looks really cute. One night he seemed to make a point of tipping his funny little hat before he disappeared from my sight... I must tell you of my latest experiences with my little man. He came to me one day and told me that if I would follow his instructions he would help me with a business venture that would prove to be very profitable. I did follow his advice, and the venture turned out as he said it would. He has helped me now many times and has made only one condition: I am to keep a journal of the times he comes to me; our conversations; the help he gives me; and how it turns out."

Later, Mrs. Smith wrote: "I have started my journal as directed by my little friend, and find it very enlightening, for as I write in it I get more out of what has transpired than in just thinking about it. I went up to see my sister, who lives in the country, and when ready to leave for home again I saw the little man leaning against the tree that I had to pass. I looked at him and he winked and nodded to me, so after I got away from the folks and could stop the car, I called to him and he was in the back seat with me. He was wearing a little coat of many shades, and it was as if he had drawn the colours from the leaves and shrubbery around him. He was very anxious that I remember to set down that the fairies can show me how they send their thoughts to mankind. It was then I realized that he and the other fairies have never spoken aloud to me, but seem to transplant their thoughts into my consciousness, and that is the way I can commune with them."

When Mrs. Martha C. Smith was ordained, the altar was beautiful with flowers, including one large bouquet of white gladioli. Just as she rose to go to the altar to take her vows, she saw a nature spirit sitting on one of the white flowers. The lady standing beside her, when asked if she had noticed anything, replied that all she saw was a movement among the flowers, as though a large insect was crawling on them. When Mrs. Smith told the Rev. B., her teacher, about the fairy, he said he wasn't surprised as he, too, had been conscious of something there. "The little creature was truly beautiful with her tiny wings and lovely colouring," wrote Mrs. Smith. "I couldn't see clearly what she was holding in her hand, but it looked like a small wand with a light shining from it, and the fairy herself was surrounded by a bluish-white aura. The vision lasted for about one minute, but oh what a minute!"

Mrs. Ellen Edgar, a Theosophist living at Rhos-on-Sea, Colwyn Bay, said, "I am convinced of the existence of these Fairy People... I'm sure they go before us, smoothing life here and there. At times I think they are playful, and mischievous and tease us a bit. Nevertheless, I love to feel them around. I have seen them, but the incident was long ago. When I was at a Holy Communion service, I saw two sweet little faces in the flowers on the altar. Thinking perhaps I was imagining it, I looked away for a while, but they were still there when I looked again. I have only to think about them and I see them as clearly as that first time."

It is not an uncommon occurrence to see fairies in churches, and Mrs. M. Lilley, of Kent, said that during a Harvest Festival service one of her daughters saw two little men in green in the pew in front of her.

Mrs. Emma S. King of Australia said that while attending a liberal Catholic Church service in 1938 she observed a number of nature sprites dancing on the floor and weaving patterns before the altar. They were in the charge of one of the Angels of Our Lady, and as the organ sounded forth the form of Our Lord began to glow radiantly.

In his book *Fairies At Work And At Play* (Theosophical Publishing House, London), Geoffrey Hodson said: "During the celebration of Mass I became aware that nature spirits of many kinds approached and hovered in a great radiant cloud in the air immediately within reach of the vibrations of the ceremony. The smaller creatures—fairies, tree spirits, and some manikins—bathed in the atmosphere of power with continuous and graceful motion. The higher and more evolved members of our hidden congregation remained relatively motionless, watching, and absorbing the force poured out, and adding enormously to the purity and beauty of the service. From the very beginning to the final blessing they shared the ceremony with us, and at its conclusion slowly melted away as they returned to their homes—in the trees, the cornfields, hedges, and flowers— taking with them, each according to his capacity, something of the blessing we had received.

"In addition to these fairy people who came to Church with us, there were also present those orders of ceremonial angels who are definitely connected with the Mass."

At a Spiritualist Church service, one of its members mentioned the Little People when giving the final prayer, and as he did so Mrs. R. Daniels, of London, caught just a glimpse of a little flower-fairy smiling at her and clapping its hands. She described its face as "kind of pointed," and its hat was shaped like an elf-cap fungus.

A correspondent in Perth, Tasmania, said that many times when giving clairvoyant flower-messages from a public platform she had seen little elfin nature-spirits, particularly on the carnations.

At a Subud meeting attended by Mrs. Margaretta Rowell, of Sunderland, a lady who was a medium saw a number of fairies in the room, and said that one of them had come up to her and told her he was a pixie. He had elongated ears and wore a little hat, which was turned up at the brim. The lady was very puzzled about all this and couldn't understand why the fairies had appeared, whereupon Mrs. Rowell told them all that she believed in fairies and happened to have with her a book, which related solely to the Little People. Had the fairies known about this and shown themselves to the only person in the room who was able to see them?

Mrs. Lucy Banner, who radiated good cheer and vitality, used to have a colour-healing sanctuary at her home in Hucknall, near Nottingham, and she said that she and the members of her centre were very conscious of the fairies' help during their healing work. Frequently, when she was lecturing on the seven rays at the house of one of her students at Nuthall, where she had another branch of her work, she was aware of the nature spirits enjoying themselves in the beautiful garden and orchard there. In 1959 she wrote to me: "This summer I have been out in the country quite a lot, and through the sun's rays have seen the Little People dancing, with all the colours blending into what seemed like a large rainbow. It is a wonderful sight."

Speaking of her mother, who was of an old Quaker family, Miss Hilda R. Taylor, A. Mus. TCL., of Nottingham, a teacher of the piano and violin, said: "She was an extraordinary soul, of great calm and sweetness, in spite of many difficulties and sorrows. She told me often how the fairies helped her, and she always called them 'the good fairies' or her 'good angels.'" Miss Taylor herself was fully conscious of the fairies' presence, and both she and I could see their etheric lights dancing around her as she spoke. She said the atmosphere they brought to aid her in the interpretation of music was wonderful.

About the year 1928, Mrs. Edith Warburton, of Stockport, Cheshire, saw in the sunlight four or five fairies dancing on the soil under the lower fronds of some ferns in a pot on the window. Their white gossamer gowns flowed out as they went round and round, and on their heads were bands of flowers. "I was really transfixed. They were so very lovely," she said.

"I well remember," wrote Mrs. Ann Spiers, from Surrey, "when I was in the infants' class at Christ Church School in Folkestone, Kent, during 1924-25, our teacher, a Miss Rowe, told us that if we were very quiet and still when a shaft of sunlight came through our classroom window, maybe we would see the fairies at their work on the flowers. Well, for us children this was indeed something to look forward to, and one day we were rewarded by seeing a dainty little creature about four inches high, very slender, with wings that were two inches long and very transparent, perched on a leaf of one of the many plants that stood on the windowsill." Mrs. Spiers could not recall whether the fairy was working on hyacinths, bluebells or crocuses, but she knew that the children named her "Fairy Blue-bell" because she attended to the blue flowers only. She was clad in a very fine, pale blue, ballet-length dress, and wore a small bell-shaped hat, and sang very softly to herself as she dusted the petals of the flowers. She then climbed the "Fairy Staircase," which was the children's name for the ray of sunshine, and Mrs. Spiers remembers the children saying that the particles of dust "came from the fair-ies' mops and dusters when they [the fairies] did their work." There were 30 children in the class, which consisted of more girls than boys, and the fairy was seen by about twenty of the scholars and the teacher. In her letter, Mrs. Spiers said that she had been married for many years now and had a grown-up son of her own, but the forego-ing incident in her school life was still as fresh as ever in her mind.

When Mrs. Anne W. Metcalf was living in Leamington Spa, she had on her kitchen table a plant in a pot. On a certain summer's day about twelve noon, the sun was shining through the window on to the plant, and she was sitting looking at it without really concen-trating on it or thinking of anything in particular, when she noticed on a leaf near the top of the plant, something very tiny, about two inches long, and of a gossamer appearance. It vanished as suddenly as it came, but she told her husband about it afterwards. That was the only time she had seen anything resembling a fairy, but it had remained in her memory.

On Boxing Day in 1965, when I was sitting in front of the fire listening to the wireless, the sun made a glowing rainbow across the upright tiles beneath the oak mantelpiece, and on one of the tiles an elf superimposed his face. I could not see the rest of his body, but from the size of his head he must have been not less than one foot high. He was smiling and looking straight at me. His eyes were shining, and his expression was one of such radiant joy that I, too, felt a great happiness surging through me. He stayed for about a minute, and then the shaft of light moved away from the tile and he vanished, but my feeling of happiness remained. On another occasion I had been admiring some glorious golden-yellow chrysanthemums, which were in a vase on the table, and then I went to sit in my usual armchair facing the fire, with my back to the table. Presently, to my surprise and delight, a little fairy appeared in front of me, holding a replica of one of the chrysanthemums, which she showed me with great pride. Her hair, wings, and flowing gown were the same colour as the flower, and her face was glowing with joy.

One evening, I was relaxing in the same armchair in front of the fire when a small, grey-brown gnome in a smart, russet-coloured cloak, glided slowly past me towards the right-hand corner of the room. My eyes were closed, but when I opened them I could still see him. He turned his head to gaze at me intently, as though appraising me, and I saw quite clearly his quaint little face with its pointed chin and ears, and his eyes, which were wise and kindly. His arms were gracefully outstretched, and although he was airborne I did not notice any wings. I christened him "my homing gnome," and no sooner had I thought this than my attention was drawn to his little russet cloak, which had softly detached itself and was floating away from him in the manner of an autumn leaf. Cloud-like in texture, it drifted for a while in front of my face and then slowly disintegrated. As might be expected, when I turned again to look at the gnome, he had disappeared.

In 1954, one of my contributors, Mrs. Clara Clayton, invited me to accompany her on the 11 October to the Nottingham Theosophical Lodge, where her blind husband was giving a talk on "The Unseen Ministry." While he was speaking, a glorious sapphire-blue nature-spirit flashed across the hall in front of us, and it was so unexpected that we gave a gasp of surprise and looked at each other. It was such a clear, bright vision that we thought it must have been seen by other members of the audience, but of course we were unable to question anyone during the lecture, and afterwards Mr. and Mrs. Clayton had to rush to catch a bus back to Stapleford, where they then lived, and I went out with them.

When I was a schoolgirl, an elderly, very serious-minded gentleman paid us a friendly visit, and during a lull in the conversation we saw his eyes following something, which we could not see. My mother gazed enquiringly at him, and he said in matter-of-fact tones that he was watching a host of tiny winged creatures "like little angels" floating about the room.

In 1996, when Maureen, my kind, practical home-help at that time, was working in my sitting room, I walked in later and found her standing looking bemused but very happy. She told me that "a little shining thing" had flown under the table on a beam of sunlight towards her and had risen into the air in front of her. She saw that it was about three inches in length and was sparkling all over as though speckled with stardust. It was so bright that she could not see its face, and as she watched, it flew down again and disappeared. "It was so wonderful, and so lovely," she said. "I've never seen anything like it in my life before. I wish I could see it again."

Fairies in Bedrooms

When Miss Vicky Burt, of Cornwall, was between eight and ten years old, she was going to bed one night when she saw some very beautiful fairies dancing in front of the curtains. They were about six inches tall, and ten or twelve in number. Their clothes were very bright: "fantastic" she described them—in mainly blues, greens, and reds, and they were accompanied by some form of beautiful bell-music. Some of the fairies had wings, but the others had not. All her family knew about her fairies, which appeared every evening for a week or two, and, as far as she can remember, stayed for fifteen or twenty minutes. As each night came, she was anxious to go to bed to be able to see her fairies again, but then one night they did not appear, and although for the rest of her life she had longed to see them again, she has not, alas, done so.

Mrs. P. Leopold, wrote from London to tell me that when she was a small child she saw a fairy in her bedroom, and although many years had passed the picture was still vivid in her mind's eye. When I had time, I asked for details. But she had moved in the meantime and I was unable to trace her.

Among the fairies inhabiting Sussex is one that a teacher named

Mr. George Edward Randell spoke of occasionally to his more intimate friends. He saw it from his bed when he and his parents lived in Hove. One lovely dawn in the spring of 1907, when George was just twelve, he awoke to see a figure enter by the open bedroom door. He immediately sat up in bed, and there by the bedside stood a little man about two feet in stature. The manikin had a brown, wrinkled face and wore a brown jerkin belted at the waist, and long brown hose. As George stared at him in amazement, he doffed his broad-brimmed hat and gave an enormous grin — a grin that seemed too wide for his size. Then he disappeared. The startled boy rubbed his eyes and sought to shake himself completely awake, wondering whether he had been dreaming. But no: he felt certain that he had been fully conscious when the manikin entered. All that day the incident puzzled him. The following morning exactly the same thing happened. The manikin came to his bedside, doffed his hat, and grinned broadly before disappearing. These visits continued every dawn-time for about a week, always following the same routine, and then they ceased entirely.

From another teacher, Mrs. Enid H. Paul, came the following: "This is a perfectly accurate account of what happened on the only occasion I ever saw a fairy. I do not often speak of it for fear of ridicule. It was in 1930, when I was nine years old. I had just gone to bed, but had not yet lain down. I sat with my knees drawn up and my chin resting on them, looking towards my open bedroom door, when a small man appeared in the doorway. He was dressed in dark green, with a brown buckled belt, and short brown boots. His trousers were the breeches type, buttoned down the sides. I was filled with terror and dived under the bedclothes, hardly believing my eyes. After several minutes I plucked up courage and looked out. He then stood at the foot of my bed with arms akimbo leaning on the bedrail. More scared than ever, I plunged under the bedclothes again and stayed there for a long, long time. When I finally looked out he had disappeared, and I never saw him again. I have often wished that I'd had the courage to speak to him. The incident had, however, no significance for me then, or since, so far as I know."

In 1951, Dr. Victor Purcell, C.M.G., Litt.D., PH.D, then a lecturer at Cambridge on Far Eastern affairs, sent the following vivid description of fairy soldiers: "In the year 1900-1901, during the South African War, when I was about five years of age, I lived in Gillingham, Kent. Every night for some months, after my mother had kissed me goodnight and shut my bedroom door, there was a short interval, and then I would begin to hear distant, massed Lilliputian bands playing. The music grew louder and louder as it came nearer and nearer. There was a night light burning on the mantelpiece, and by the light of this I saw column after column of tiny soldiers marching up from the right of my bed over my eider-down (I remember its pattern and colour clearly) and across to the other side where they disappeared over the bedside. Each soldier was about nine inches high and wore a red coat. There was battalion after battalion of them, and each was headed by a brass band. As these passed, they played minute martial music, far more exciting than any music I had ever heard in the daytime. The march-past lasted for a few minutes, and then I fell asleep. The direction was always from right to left. I never tried to touch the soldiers, but they were completely real. I actually did see them, and I should be prepared to state this on oath, if necessary, in any Court of Law."

When Madame Paula Forné, of Dieppe, was a child of nine, she was sleeping in a bed between her mother's and her Eurasian nurse's bed in a dak bungalow at Allahabad in India, when she was awakened at late dawn by a faint squeals—barely audible, yet high and piercing—and was very surprised and not at all frightened to see on the punkah above the beds, and also on the end of the beds, hundreds of little figures running and jumping, and playing leap-frog. Their colouring was beige or sepia against the whitewashed wall of the bungalow. She was very interested,and even sat up and watched them for a long time, till the sun came through the window and they seemed to run away. "The next day," wrote Madame Forné, "the local doctor, who was an old friend, came to see us and asked my mother if the dak bungalow ghosts had prevented her sleeping. This intrigued me, and I asked her what 'ghosts' were, and she replied that Dr. Sutcliffe was joking and meant the noises from the trains at the station nearby. I told them about my experience and they thought it was a dream, but it was so real and so amusing that, as we stayed on for another week, I awoke each morning hoping to see them again. They came only once more, and this time they were even more friendly, as they ran over my bed quite near to me. I saw the like years later in England, when someone gave me my first copy of *Punch*. The figures I had seen were exactly like the figures on the front page."

Mrs. Betty Lambert, a classical dancer, actress, and pianist who used to run concert parties such as "The Black and White," "The Blue Moths," and "The Westcliff Miles," told me she saw a fairy many years ago at a house in a tree-lined road at Westcliff-on-Sea, Essex. She was sharing with her friend, the landlady, a large front bedroom and, owing to the heat of that particular September night, the door, which led to a balcony, had been left open. She had been in bed about ten minutes when she heard a loud buzzing in the room, and, peeping over the sheets, she saw a lovely pair of wings like mother-o'-pearl, fourteen to sixteen inches across, in the middle of which was a little being like a gnome about nine inches long. It floated across the room to the square bay-window, and then into an alcove by the mantel shelf. Mrs. Lambert confessed she was rather frightened, but she felt excited, too. Rousing her companion, who was nearly asleep, she begged her to shut the balcony door as she wanted to keep the fairy in the room, but her friend, whom she described as "a very-matter-of-fact person," refused to do this, saying "it wouldn't be right." She did, however, sit up in bed to watch the fairy, whose outstretched wings seemed motionless as it floated out into the night, never to be seen again. "Of course, people wouldn't believe me when I told them about it," said Mrs. Lambert, "but my companion had to acknowledge that it was true."

"I have had many sudden and vivid visions of gnomes," recounted Mrs. Georgina K. Evason of Tunbridge Wells, Kent. "The first time was in the early hours of the morning. I was then living in a house near Queen's Park, in Brondesbury, London, and my room overlooked a very nice garden. On opening my eyes, I was thrilled and very surprised to see on the top of my bed-covers a group of gnomes, all of the same height and proportions. They wore tight-fitting suits of various woodland shades, shoes that turned up at the toes, and tasselled stocking-style caps. All of them had long, grey beards, and faces like little old men. There were six or seven of them, between fifteen and eighteen inches high, and with hands clasped to form a circle they were dancing merrily in perfect rhythm. I watched, entranced, for a few minutes, and then they disappeared. One of these gnomes has often appeared to me, quite alone, since then, and he always stands at the foot of my bed looking at me very intently, in a friendly way."

Mrs. Dorothea Eastwood of London sent a description of an experience that she had when she was nine years old. Her home was then on Vancouver Island, British Columbia, and stood in a clearing in some pine woods. At about 8 o'clock, one summer evening, she was lying in bed on the ground floor of the house, in a room that was quite light as it had only thin curtains across the windows, when she saw "three tiny men run across the floor and disappear, apparently into a chest that stood under the window at the end of the room. They were about three inches high, looked brown in colour, had bandy little legs and wore peaked caps. In fact, they looked exactly like the traditional gnomes of the fairy stories. I had only a few minutes to take them in but I have no doubt that I was wide awake and actually saw them." Some years later Mrs. Eastwood happened to describe these gnomes to a Welsh lady, Mrs. Philip Carnons-Williams, who told her that she herself had quite often seen the same type of beings on trees and around toadstools when she was a child in Monmouthshire. There seemed to be males and females, and although the prevailing colour was brown, it varied with the tree or toadstool that they frequented. After the age of eleven, the faculty for seeing them left her. Mrs. Eastwood declared that she could vouch for this lady's absolute sincerity.

The Rev. Chas. A. Hall of Storrington, Sussex, a minister of the New Church founded on the doctrines given through the agency of Emanuel Swedenborg, told me that often he had a sense of unseen presences as the shadows lengthened in his woodland garden, and when he was very young he had an experience, the memory of which was still vivid. A coal fire was burning brightly in his bedroom, and on a table nearby was a nightlight (a squat cylinder of wax surrounded with stiff paper) in a saucer of water. There seemed to be infinite mystery in its feeble flame, and while he was gazing at it there appeared a dozen or more daintily clad fairies, none of them more than three inches tall. Forming a circle with joined hands, they danced in brilliant splendour around the light.

Mr. Hall mentioned this among his other experiences in a BBC programme called "Indian Summer," in 1961. "The vision was brief," he said, "but so deeply impressive that although I am now in my ninetieth year, I am still able to recall it in minute detail. Prosaic education is fast destroying many picturesque beliefs, but it will never rob me of my one glorious experience in fairyland."

When Mrs. Clara M. A. Clayton's eider son was very small, she went up to his bedroom and he was pointing to something and saying in his baby language "'ickle fairies, 'ickle fairies-pink-blue…" and then he asked her to open the window because the fairies had gone out that way and he wanted to follow them.

This next experience occurred early one morning in a country vicarage in Berkshire. Ursula—later to become Mrs. Turner, of Oxford—was a child of seven at the time, and she had just awakened and was lying alone in the nursery, staring at the top of the high wardrobe on which was a big box. "Brilliant sunbeams pointed to one corner of the room," she said, "and gradually there formed, as if drawn from Fairyland by this compelling light, a tiny black man with an enormous, perfectly round head of a rich red colour with silvery sparkles all over it. He had no eyes, nose, mouth, ears, or hair, but, as this engaging creature danced a jig, his great head wobbled and shimmered and he appeared to beam at me, for the sparkling of his silvery 'frosting' gave a complete illusion of a broad grin and twinkling eyes. Time was not, while I watched, fascinated. Then he dissolved into the sunbeam, slowly, as he had come."

Mrs. P. M. Teage, of Devon, had a Welsh father and an English mother, and spent a happy childhood in a large house three miles out of Cardiff. It had a good-sized garden, parts of which were semi-wild, with large trees and sloping banks of daffodils in spring. She loved every stick and stone of the place with an intense passion. One summer evening, when she was between nine and eleven years old, she was in her bedroom in the front of the house and remembers sitting up in bed, not in the least ready for sleep. There were green hanging blinds over the windows, but they let in beams of sunlight, and she saw an elf sliding down a sunbeam into the room. Her memory suggests it had very small wings and a pointed cap, and it was in a sitting position with knees drawn up. She can't recall its expression at all, but she does remember feeling full of joy and excitement. It was only in later years that she began to doubt the reality of the little creature—especially as it had been seen indoors and not in the garden.

"It was summertime, and our house is very near the fields," explained Mrs. Mary Findley, of Derbyshire. "My daughter was then only a baby, and I awoke in the night and lay for a while listening to a kind of rustling on her cot, which was at the side of my bed. I felt puzzled, as I could hear her peaceful breathing and knew she was still asleep, so I felt very quietly for some matches and lit a candle at the side of the bed. I had to wait, of course, for the candle to burn up, but when it had done so I leaned towards the cot and saw a little shape dart towards the curtains. It was a tiny man with a pointed beard, a tunic with a belt, and a little hat turned over on one side. He wore tiny boots and striped stockings—the stripes going round his legs. He appeared startled as he grasped the curtains, and he turned his bright little eyes and looked at me, then scrambled up the curtains and out of the window like quicksilver. I wanted to call to him: 'Come back; I won't hurt you,' but he was gone, I have always remembered him."

In 1956, Mrs. Barbara Logan, of Forest Hall, Newcastle-on-Tyne, awoke in the dense blankness of her bedroom at three in the morning and saw a wonderful silver form, about six inches high, on her bed rail. Feeling rather fearful, she closed her eyes, and when she opened them again the figure had vanished, leaving behind it the lovely perfume of scented geraniums. She recalled her childhood in the country, when she often sensed light beings dancing on her dress as she sat in the fields among the stocks of hay. "Even now," she said, "I am aware of their presence in my home and can feel their movements as they dance in my hair, and their gentle kisses on my cheeks."

"When I was a child of seven," said Mrs. Mary E. Burt, "I lived at Swanage, in Dorset, near a wood that had so much undergrowth that no one could really walk in it under the trees. I slept in a bedroom with my baby brother, who was just being trained to sleep in a small bed on his own instead of a cot. My mother used to light a little night lamp and leave it on the mantelpiece, but it was always turned very low and gave only a dim light in the room. One night, I was trying to go to sleep when to my horror (I say horror as I was terrified at the time) I saw seven little men in red clothing (just as one sees them in children's books) dancing in circles in and around the leg of my little brother's bed. I hid under the bedclothes, but every time I looked out they were still there, weaving circles and patterns and all the time dancing. They stayed some little while, then went out of the door, which was always left ajar. I never told a soul of this, but I dreaded the thought of bedtime for they came constantly for about two weeks, and then came no more. I was not asleep when I saw them, and I know I did not imagine it. I can still picture the red of their clothes. They could not have been more than four inches high."

Mrs. Jane K. Jacob, of County Wexford, wrote that on a winter's night in 1933, when she was nine years old, she was sharing a bedroom with her mother. The bed was drawn across the fireplace directly opposite the door, which was partly open, and the light of a lamp illumined the bedroom floor. She had been awake for some time and was aware of everything about her, when suddenly she saw "a little figure, roughly twelve inches high, enter the room through the doorway, wearing what appeared to be twisted rags of different colours around its body and head." She could see its face distinctly as, looking very young and piquant, it walked with downcast eyes towards the bed.

"Holding in its hand a smallish piece of newspaper," recounted Mrs. Jacob, "it walked under my bed, and I heard the rustling of paper for a few moments. Then there was silence, and out from under the bed came the little person without the newspaper. It walked towards the door, and when halfway there, turned and looked back to where it had been. Then it continued on its way, passed through the doorway, and was gone. I remained still, hoping it might return, but it did not. The next morning, on investigation, I found many small pieces of newspaper in the fireplace. My father said someone had told him that the house (in which we no longer live) was built on a Fairy Pass."

At the time of the following experience, Miss Lattice M. Mathias was living in Somerset. She was almost six years of age, and didn't really believe in fairies any more than she did in Father Christmas. At dawn on a lovely June morning, she awoke to find sunbeams right across the "mountains" formed by her knees in the fluffy white blankets. She remembered noting clearly that various colours seemed to glisten through the woolly surface, and then, to her amazement, she was caught up in which seemed like a great adventure. The spectrum of light on the miniature mountain suddenly came to life, transformed into tiny people dressed like elves, each in his own distinctive colouring. "So it is true," she thought at this juncture, and she watched them as in groups they caught hands and raced up and down the slopes. She was filled with joyful awe and held her breath for fear she might blow them away. She recalled how wonderfully happy they seemed: "Their laughter was like music, so that neither could be separated—their happiness and those silver, bell-like sounds were one and the same thing. Maybe the whole spell lasted but a few moments."

About a year later, again at dawn, Miss Mathias had the same vision of little people, but she felt that it was gone so quickly, with no time to hear any music. She was never able to conjure it up again, and as she grew older she often found herself trying to "go back to something," as though in infancy she had possessed some faculty that, just by growing up, she had lost. "My mother was of lowland Scots parentage," she said, "and she saw a little green man in a Devon wood when she was six years old. He was lying contently on the branch of a tree, in a shaft of sunlight."

During the 1914-1918 war, Miss Alison M. Oliver was living on the second storey of an Edinburgh tenement. "When I was nine or ten," she said, "I dreamt that I woke up, went to the window, and saw a fairy standing on the windowsill. I say I 'dreamt,' because I have since thought that the experience must have been a dream, but at the time I believed I was awake. Before I could speak, a streak of red showed in the eastern sky, and the fairy vanished. What struck me very forcibly then, and has remained in my mind ever since, was that this fairy was completely unlike my then conception of a fairy, and that is why I thought it worthwhile to tell you of the experience. My idea of a fairy then would have been one with flowing gauzy robes much in the Noel Paton tradition, and long golden hair. What I saw was a tiny creature in a vivid green ballet-type dress, with short black hair, and I doubt if at that time I had ever seen bobbed hair. Perhaps I should add that the tenement was in the section of Montgomery Street known as Brunton Gardens, with a bowling green opposite, surrounded by trees. Montgomery Street runs parallel to London Road, which is one of the loveliest avenues of lime trees in the city; and Hillside Crescent Gardens, which divide the Crescent from London Road, boast two of the largest horse-chestnut trees I have ever seen, and which must be very old. London Road Gardens stretch right up to Royal Terrace, behind which are more well-wooded gardens reaching up to the Calton Hill. All this greenery might have some relevance!"

Miss Dawn E. Mooney (late of the Gate Lodge, Inverewe) recalled an experience she had at the age of about four, when she was living at Beddington, in Surrey. On this particular morning she woke earlier than the rest of the household. (From her recollection of the bright light outside and the birdsong in the garden, she thinks it was early summer.) Her sleepy eyes opened gradually and took in the accustomed nursery furniture, pictures, ornaments on the mantelpiece, and the rose-patterned, curtains. She also saw a small creature, about ten inches high, sitting in a relaxed attitude on the end rail of her white enamelled bedstead. He was dressed in green with a pointed cap. She remembered vividly his kindly, apple-cheeked face, with bright, humorous eyes contemplating her, and the way his legs seemed to be wrapped round the rail, as though his bones were flexible. At first glance she took him as much for granted as the other objects she saw, but something "gave a click" in her brain as though a new way of thinking had come into action suddenly, and then she found it extremely queer that a strange little man should be sitting there uninvited on her bed. She shouted loudly for her nurse, and immediately the figure vanished, leaving no trace. While she tried to explain what had happened and the nurse prattled about her having been dreaming, she realised that she had until then seen these little people many times before and taken them for granted. "And," she said, "I wondered why I had now made such a fuss about it, but, with my newly-awakened sense of what was or was not considered to be 'normal,' I persisted in thinking the manikin 'queer,' and from that day to this, I have not seen another." Miss Mooney had, however, heard fairies since then, and her account is in the appropriate section.

A few years after the First World War, Mrs. Zelma Bramley-Moore, of London, author and film-story writer, went to stay for the winter at a hotel in Malaga, Spain. It was her custom to breakfast in bed, and one morning the maid brought her tray in at about 8 o'clock. There were two letters for her. "I sipped my tea," she said, "reading snatches from one of the letters between sips. It was a beautiful, sunny morning, and I glanced at the window facing me, which looked out on to the courtyard. To my surprise I noticed that the curtain on the right-hand side was shaking, and as the window was closed this was astonishing. As I watched, two fairies 'faded in.' (I do not know how else to describe it.) They were about twelve inches high, quite naked, and exquisitely lovely. The little lady had long fair hair, which hung below her waist; the little man's hair was slightly darker, cut to ear-length, and bound with gold-coloured ribbon. They both had large wings the colour of tobacco, and these were slowly opening and shutting, or fluttering when the fairies lost their balance—for they were clinging to the edge of the curtain, playing together and trying to pull each other off. They made an audible sound, and if they were aware of my presence they gave no sign of it. Their colouring was entrancing; I can best describe it as colours seen in technicolor on a film. I lay watching them for several minutes, then they gradually faded out. They did not leave; my eyes had lost the faculty of seeing them."

The second time Mrs. Bramley-Moore saw fairies was a year or two before the Second World War, when she was living at her cottage at Prestwood, in Buckinghamshire. Her bedroom faced east, and she used to lie in bed and watch the sun rise. Beside the window was an old apple-tree. It was dead, but she refused to have it cut down because she found its shape so beautiful. One morning she awoke in the pale light of dawn. The birds had not started to call, and the sun was still below the horizon. She rose from her bed and stood looking out of the window. It was then she noticed five grey "lumps" on the old apple-tree. They looked most peculiar, and she peered at them closely. They appeared to be shrouded in some pale grey material, a thin, cobwebby kind of chiffon. She still had not the slightest idea of what she was seeing until suddenly one moved and straightened up. It was some kind of fairy that had been sitting on a branch in a crouching position, its head covered by its arms, which were resting on its knees. It gave a weird little cry, like the sound of a tiny bell, then it suddenly launched itself forward and flew off due north, travelling at a tremendous rate, its garment fluttering behind it. It was followed almost immediately by its companions. One after another they sat up and launched themselves head first into the air. "These five had no visible wings. They flew through the air still in a crouching position—they might almost have been riding invisible broomsticks." It was then rapidly becoming light; the first birdcall was heard, and Mrs. Bramley-Moore returned thoughtfully to her bed.

The third occasion when she saw fairies was during the Second World War. She was then staying at a hotel in Prestwood, and sometimes at night she had been roused out of sleep by laughing voices and the sound of a trumpet, as if a crowd of happy people was passing from west to east through her room. She saw nothing, for she woke too late, but she could hear the sounds fading away in the distance. One night she was reading late because a number of bombs had been dropped in the neighbourhood and she found herself unable to sleep. She glanced at the clock and saw that it was just 2 a.m. Then she heard the laughing voices and the sound of a trumpet approaching. A moment or two later, a crowd of fairies flew through the room, travelling at great speed. They came in through one wall and passed out of the other, their little cries and laughing voices fading away in the distance. In the brief glimpse she had of them, she said it appeared as if they had their Fairy Queen in their midst.

A correspondent in the Golders Green district of London still remembered vividly an experience she had in her youth. It was day-break and she was lying in bed, wide-awake. In the middle of the bedroom was a rather old-fashioned light hanging from the ceiling, the supporting arms being of brass. She glanced at this and was surprised to see lots of little figures turning somersaults round the brass rods, and, with arms outstretched, balancing along the rods like wire-walkers, whilst others slid down from the top of the upright rod like firemen sliding down a pole. Most of them had curly hair; all had small wings, and were about twelve inches tall. She watched them for some time, until one of them seemed to see her and, coming over to the foot of the bed, walked slowly towards her. Suddenly she grew scared and hid under the bedclothes. When she looked again, all the little creatures had disappeared.

Mrs. Jean Finlayson Holmes, of San Francisco, recounted an experience she had at the age of nine. It was on a moonlit night in 1925 when she saw two little fellows sitting on the crossbar of the frame of her bedroom window. They were inside, leaning against the glass, and were very busy concentrating on some work or object, which she could not see, but she noticed they seemed to be talking and nodding to one another very alertly. Their bodies were round and podgy, although their movements were agile. Mrs. Holmes described them as having "something diabolical about them, but quite without malice — like two busy, intelligent little monkeys, they were." She did not know whether they wore any clothes or not, and declared she had never seen a drawing of gnome, gremlin, troll, or elf that quite conveyed the character of these strange little people.

"I watched them for a long time," she said, "until the dawning of my own fear at observing such a phenomenon gave the alert, and one of them turned his head and looked at me. I think he was as frightened as I was. I didn't wait to watch where or how they went but rushed to tell the grown-ups in another room just what I had seen. Of course, the whole thing was treated as 'imagination.'" Throughout the many years that had elapsed since then, Mrs. Jean Finlayson Holmes remained convinced that the little people were as real as she was in the sphere to which they belonged.

A pixie perching on a clock was seen by Mrs. Joan Georgina Cheeseman when she was fourteen years old and lived in a house on the Pitsea Marshes, in Essex. She had just entered her bedroom when she noticed the little creature. It was four or five inches high, dressed in green, and wearing a small, round hat. It jumped off the clock, came to the edge of the mantelpiece, looked at me, and then vanished. "And," added Mrs. Cheeseman, "I don't think until then I had believed in fairies, but even though I am now married, with two children, I can never forget, or ever again disbelieve."

One morning in 1950, when Mrs. Mary Johnson of Stanishaw, Portsmouth, Hants, was lying in bed after her husband had gone to work, she had a very strong feeling that she was being watched. She turned her eyes to the fireplace, and there on the big old-fashioned mantelpiece stood a little man wearing a green cap and suit. His face was quite brown, and he appeared to be very old. She experienced no surprise at seeing him, but what did surprise her was his height of two feet, for he was much taller than she had imagined a gnome to be. He gave her a really wide grin, and she said "Hello" to him; then he vanished. "At least," she explained, "I could see him no longer, but felt sure he was still there. He had been visible for perhaps three to four seconds." As in the case of some of the other contributors, Mrs. Johnson said she was at that time feeling "extremely happy," and she thinks that is why she saw him.

A fairy on a pillow was seen by Mrs. B. M. Grimwood, of Suffolk, when she was middle-aged. The time was about 7:30 a.m., and she had just woken. The little visitor was between nine or twelve inches in height, wingless, with fair, tufted hair, and pale blue eyes which opened and shut mechanically. Mrs. Grimwood fixed her gaze on it, trying to retain it, but gradually it vanished.

When Mrs. C. V. Burrow was a child of about seven, she lived in a fairly old terraced house at Portsmouth. Her mother believed in sending her early to bed, but she was nervous, and sometimes could not get to sleep, despite the fact that a nightlight was left burning on the landing outside her bedroom and the door was left open so that her room was not in complete darkness. "My fear of the dark," she confessed, "used to reach an awful peak, and then I would see 'little people' moving about my room, talking to each other, dusting the walls, and being very busy." She was always so greatly intrigued by this, that she no longer felt afraid and used to glide peacefully to sleep. Approximately four inches tall, and very slender, the fairies flitted noiselessly and rapidly from place to place, and appeared to be luminous. They passed without difficulty through the plaster walls, but never seemed to go through the skirting board. "I am sure I was awake," wrote Mrs. Burrow, "because I remember one night hearing the clock ticking in my mother's bedroom and thinking how awful it would be if that ticking had been the clock inside the crocodile in Barrie's play *Peter Pan*."

In a cottage near the centre of the town in Southport, Miss Kathleen O'Shea, then aged about five, had elfin visitors on two or three nights when she lay in bed. They had no wings but seemed to dive through the air at a good speed. They were dressed in red and were in a golden haze that enabled her to see them in the dark. There was one, four to five inches long, which she saw exceptionally plainly. The rest of them seemed smaller but were further away and kept together, diving in and out about each other. "I know I was not dreaming," she told me, "because I was afraid, and used to creep closer to my mother, with whom I was sleeping." She admitted, nevertheless, that it was a lovely experience, and one that she had never forgotten.

Another contributor who saw fairies in her bedroom when she was about five is Mrs. Doris Poole, of Gloucester. "They came in," she said, "through the window—six or seven of them—all dressed in white, and very pretty they looked, floating about the room. They didn't flutter their wings quickly like butterflies, but moved with the grace of ballet dancers. One came down and sat on the rail at the foot of the bed. Outside the window was a very large French currant tree in full bloom, and I have always connected the fairies with its flowering, although the blossoms were pink."

Mrs. Edna E. Murray, of West Perth, Western Australia, was ten years old when she saw a flower fairy about five inches high in her bedroom at a house in Mt. Lawley, but she could not give a full description because her attention was mainly centred on what the fairy was doing. It appeared to be carrying a basket and was throwing all over the room small posies of violets, which shone in the darkness like diamonds. The whole area above the bed was studded with them.

"A little chap dressed in green and dull red" was seen by Mrs. Hilda Scott, of Bucks, when she was a small child living in Essex. The house was one of six in a row behind a busy shopping street. It faced a steep railway bank and the station building was just opposite the house. As far as she could remember, the time of year was Midsummer, and just before the 1914-1918 war. Her father was late, and she was waiting anxiously for him to come home. Her mother had died the year before, so she was alone. She sat on the edge of her father's bed, which was in a downstairs front room. Two of the Venetian blinds were drawn, and the narrow side of the bay window was clear to the street. A lamp shone from outside right into the room, so she didn't bother about a light, but just sat there waiting and wondering. The time was between 12 and 1 o'clock, and the last train had come in. She felt numb with prolonged unhappiness. "I hadn't looked out of the window for some minutes," she said, "when quite suddenly I was conscious of movement. Looking at the window, I distinctly saw a little man jumping in a dancing fashion and waving his arms as if to draw my attention. I was so surprised that I got up to have a closer look, but as I neared the window he scampered round the wall. I pulled up the other blinds, but he had disappeared." Mrs. Scott described him as being roughly a foot high, with a sturdy little body, and a round jolly face of brownish-red. His clothes were a dark chutney green, and there was a dash of red somewhere about him that she couldn't quite place. He wore a close-fitting cap, but not of the stocking type. She said she was thrilled at seeing him but was disappointed that he had gone so soon. She lay down on the bed without undressing, hoping he would come again, but of course she went to sleep, and the next day brought rapid events, which put the episode out of her mind for many years.

Miss Mildred C. E. Richardson of Berkshire told me that in her younger days she lived in Lincoln and spent much time in and around a small village named Canwick. As her governess was fond of walking, Mildred was allowed plenty of freedom out of doors, and when very young she felt and saw things that her sister and brothers thought childish and fantastic. One night in particular was still very clear to her, although it was so long ago. She was awakened suddenly by a feeling that someone was near her, and she sat up in bed and looked at the others, who were sleeping silently. There was a mist near her, and as she watched and wondered, not feeling at all afraid, she saw a little fairy, tall enough to reach to her pillow. It was like a harebell, but with the form of a very small man, and it had a sweet, childish face, which looked at her as it spoke. She couldn't remember the words that were said, but she recalled that after the little figure faded away she could hardly wait for her nurse to come so that she could relate her wonderful and joyful experience. Deep was her distress when nurse calmly said, "Oh, you've been dreaming." Throughout her life, Miss Richardson maintained that it was not a dream. "I was wide awake," she declared, "and to those who would understand, I have many times told the story."

Further testimony came from Mrs. H. Spelman, of Cheshire, who could still remember the little green man who came to the foot of her bed over 30 years ago. She saw him quite clearly and was not asleep because she had only just retired for the night.

The following, which is described as "a true, unvarnished account," came from "Sincere" of Gloucester, who wrote: "I will on no account give you my name and address, as, on the only occasion I related this experience, the ridicule I endured for months afterwards was unbearable.

"One morning, in the spring of 1950, I awoke at my usual hour, 7:30, and lay quietly thinking over the problems of the day ahead, when I became aware of a slight movement by the fireplace. As I stared in that direction, I realised I could see through the polished wood at the foot of the bed and found myself gazing at two little men about a foot high in the recognized garb of gnomes. They were deep in conversation at the left side of the fireplace, although I could hear no words. Suddenly, without raising his head, one of them sensed I was watching and looked at me from under his eyebrows in a speculative manner. Bending his head still closer to his companion, they both turned and simply disappeared through the tiles of the fireplace. This was in the Cotswolds, where we then lived." In a postscript to her statement, "Sincere" wrote: "As I am a married woman with five children, you may guess I am not given to whimsical fancies!" This contributor lives up to her pseudonym, for the "throughness" which she experienced is part of etheric sight, and stamps her account as genuine.

The following reports of fairies were written in 1996 by my good friend "Lena," who has been helping me to finish the typing of the manuscript of this book. "Before meeting Marjorie," she stated, "I had not believed in fairies, and after meeting and speaking with her I was still very sceptical, probably because I had never experienced seeing them personally. However, several things have happened to me that have since made me more convinced of the reality of fairy-life.

"My first experience occurred while lying in bed wide awake one morning, when I found myself walking down a lane, to the right of which was a border of flowers. As I drew near, I was aware of three small, green-clothed figures, about two feet in height. Two of these were tending the flowers and the third raised his head, looked straight at me, and then carried on with his work. On the next occasion, I had a vision of some wonderful, vividly hued flowers, from which flowed a cascade of luminous colours and the appearance of a single tiny, winged fairy. A further happening occurred during a period of emotional upheaval in my life. I was feeling rather depressed, very tearful, and quite sorry for myself. I was lying in bed wide awake my bedroom overlooking the lawned garden—when I became aware of a small figure, approximately one foot in height and wearing a dark cloak, coming scurrying across the lawn. At this point I turned over on my side, then with such clarity I heard a tiny voice near me saying 'Please don't cry; we'll look after you,' and at the same time a strange earthy smell seemed to come from my pillow. I felt no fear and had felt a part of this experience, but the smell made me sit up in bed, my depression lifted, and in amazement I realised something quite extraordinary had taken place. I repeatedly sniffed my pillow, but the smell had now completely gone."

Mr. John Winfield, of Nottingham, recounted to me the experience he had at the age of five. He had entered the room where his baby sister lay sleeping peacefully in her cot, and around her he saw a ring of dancing fairies. There were many of them, all dressed in pretty colours, and he says he will never forget the lovely sight.

On a beautiful spring morning in 1939, Mrs. Shirley Eshelby, of Carbis Bay, Cornwall, was awakened at six o'clock by the soft perfume that emanated from a vase of leaves and blossom standing on a table by the side of her bed. These blooms had been gathered in a lovely, haunted dell-garden in the heart of Sussex, and had been untouched by any hands but her own. "The room was flooded with a rosy glow caused by the sun shining through rose-coloured curtains," she explained. "The leaves in the vase changed colour as I watched them, and the blossom moved a little, shedding some of its petals. I wondered if a spider were weaving its web about them, and as I mused in this way I heard a strange, sweet sound of tinkling bells and pipe music, which I can only describe as 'tiny,' and soft, quick, and light—the kind of music that makes one want to smile without knowing why. It was most stimulating and I actually felt that I could dance with joy. "As I listened to the prelude a cloud filled with crystal drops began to spin slowly in the centre of the room, and as it gained in velocity it grew smaller and smaller until there was only a little something left that looked like a bunch of shimmering leaves and blossom but did in fact form the dress of a lovely little creature that vibrated with life. I watched this small being dancing a delightful staccato caprice that lasted for a few seconds and although she appeared to me to be dancing in space, she was evidently stepping on something that was solid to her feet, because she never danced below a certain level. When departing she skipped away in high jumps, touching the invisible line with her tiny, naked feet. Although the window was open, she avoided it and passed through the wall.

"The question in my mind was 'What was that?' And a voice inside my head replied: 'A playful little nature-spirit, a flower fairy. There are lots of them about in the springtime.'"

As I have no other accounts of trolls, I am glad to be allowed to quote the following passages from A *Woman of Spirit*, written by Doris Collins, the well-known Spiritualist and healer, with the kind permission of the publishers, Grafton Books (London): "In 1980 I went to Finland to fulfil a series of public and private engagements, which had been arranged for me and which took me all over the country, from Helsinki to Lapland and the border with the Soviet Union. I would have cancelled the trip on the advice of my doctor, but extensive plans had already been made, because I had developed an ulcer on my right leg, which was in plaster, and I was walking at the time with the aid of two sticks. I explained the problem to my hosts and told them that they would have to look after me, which they agreed to do. It was in Rovaniemi on the Arctic Circle, that I had a very extraordinary experience. We flew there in the early morning—there being only one flight a day from the capital—and the snow was four foot thick on the ground. I was met by the man who was to be interpreter and with whom I was to stay. We drove by car to his lovely modern flat, where I was introduced to the lady of the house, who did not speak a word of English....

"I had risen early to catch the plane and was not of course in the best of health, so I told my host that I wanted a good rest before the evening, when I had a public meeting to deal with. My room was a double one with a large bed. I removed my dress, lay on the bed, and covered myself with a blanket. I thought that if I actually got into bed, I might not want to get up later. I shut my eyes to rest them. I had hardly made myself comfortable, and I was certainly not asleep or even dozing, when I heard chattering all around me, there were people in the room. Perhaps, thinking I was asleep, they had come to inspect the strange creature in their midst from England. Cautiously, out of politeness rather than fear, I opened one eye slightly and I was right: there were people in the room, but they were little people, no higher than the bed. They climbed up and pushed pillows behind my back, tucking me inside the blanket like a child. I felt like Gulliver, but I knew their intention was to look after me. Could they have been Lapps, I wondered? I had heard that Lapps were not very tall but these people were tiny, like midgets. As suddenly as they had come, they went. The chattering ceased and there was total silence. I drifted off to sleep. I woke up at about three o'clock in the afternoon. Only the lady was in the house but I could not question her. I washed, dressed, and started preparing for the evening meeting while I awaited the return of my interpreter. When I told him what had happened and asked him who the little people were, he looked at me nonplussed. He spoke to my hostess and then said quite simply that she had told him that nobody had been in the flat. There was something strange in his expression and I decided not to pursue the matter because they obviously did not seem to know what I was talking about. The evening was a great success, and the following day I travelled to Tampere, where I met the man who was to return with me to Helsinki and act as interpreter for three days. He had taught at London University and spoke impeccable English, but he said he thought he might find his job difficult since he knew nothing about my work. I told him not to worry, and to reassure him I also told him a great deal about himself, which appeared to amaze him. We went for a walk in the countryside the following day, and I related my experience in Rovaniemi. I expected him to laugh when I spoke of the little people, and his reaction surprised me. 'Yes,' he said, 'I fully understand.'"

"'You believe what I've told you,' I asked.

"'Of course I do,' was his reply. 'You are in the land of the trolls.'"

Miss M. J. Field of Somerset wrote that some of her friends had found that fairies were particularly likely to visit them when they were ill or convalescent. "Has this also been your experience?" she asked. I can answer that I have had an experience, though it differs from those of other contributors. It was very poignant one and is deeply imprinted on my memory. I had just retired to bed on the night of 24 April 1988, when I saw a fairy flying round my head. She was joined by other fairies, and they kept flying slowly in front, over, and around me, till I had a strong impression that they were preparing me and trying to strengthen me for something that was to come. It came all too soon, for the very next day my sister and I were sitting talking happily together when her words suddenly became mumbled and she had a stroke. She lingered, paralysed, for a few days, and then passed away peacefully. It was she who had shared with me some of the experiences included in this book, and the fairies loved her. They knew that they could not prevent her transition, so they had tried to strengthen me, and had it not been for their loving ministration beforehand I know that the shock would have been much greater than it was.

At the beginning of 1965, Mrs. I. Morrison of Glasgow was not well, and every time she wakened during the night she saw some fairies sitting in a circle at the foot of her bed. They were all in lovely colours and seemed to be very busy talking and making signs with their hands. Seeing fairies was to her a common occurrence, but during the times she was ill they seemed never to go away. On one occasion she awoke about two o'clock in the morning to see two lovely little people in a large circle of helio, green and blue. They came walking through it, smiling at her, and then passed right over her on to the ceiling, where they turned into two tiny lights.

Mrs. Dorothy J. Hancock, of Walthamstow, London, had her first fairy experience at the age of twelve, while she was convalescing after an illness. Just after daybreak one morning as she lay in bed, she became conscious of tiny voices and laughter. On looking around, she saw in a ray of sunlight on the other side of the room a group of at least thirty little people, each about four inches high. The men wore conical hats and had trousers and shoes "all in one," of a shiny material, which had the appearance of skin in beautiful and varied colours. The women's dresses were of a cobwebby texture in pastel shades, and "something like wings" flowed out from their shoulders. "Mere words cannot describe the beauty of it," Mrs. Hancock said, "I could not understand their language, but their laughter I shall never forget—it was like the tinkling of tiny bells." They did not seem to see her, and to her amazement they all came across the room and vanished into the wall. She saw their backs quite clearly as they went.

When Josephine, the eldest daughter of Mrs. Winifred Kirby, of Leicestershire, was six, she became ill with scarlet fever. Her mother was sitting by the bed one day when Josephine suddenly sat up laughing, and made as if to grasp something that kept eluding her. When asked what she was doing, she said, "I am trying to catch that little man." At the time, Mrs. Kirby thought the child was delirious, "but," she said, "since then I have realised that the little man came to make her laugh, also to make her well again."

Mrs. Martha C. Smith, of the USA, was just about to turn out the lights ready to go to bed, when she noticed a blue haze in the bedroom. After saying a silent prayer for faith and attunement, she stood and watched. There seemed to be about five fairies, though where she was standing she could not see all of the room. Her "little man"—a nature spirit who is often with her and about whom there is more in another section of this book—was leading a very spirited discussion of some kind, and it took a few minutes to discover they were talking about her. She had been very restless and unable to sleep for a few nights, so she had asked for help, and that is why they were in conference. When they left, the room stayed a very pale blue. She went to bed with the impression that she would sleep, and she noticed there was a faint odour of medicine or herbs. She slept soundly through a terrible storm, and although her front door had been blown open during the night, she hadn't even heard that. "When I awoke in the morning," she said, "I knew I had been somewhere during the night. I also knew that I would be over my 'nerves' and feel very much better. That is the first time I have had a healing from the fairies, and I welcome them."

Writing from Tasmania, Mrs. F. E. Cotton told me that while a relative of hers, Mr. Jackson Cotton, was convalescing after an illness, four small people two or three feet high were his constant companions, and all of them were helpful and friendly. Two males sat on one side of the bed and a male and female on the other. They were dressed in smock-like garments, and the males wore beards. To the seer, they seemed as solid as his relatives and other visitors until an approaching step was heard, and then they would vanish but reappear as soon as all was quiet again. Although he was "taking it easy" after his illness, Mr. Cotton said he was certainly not suffering from hallucinations.

Mrs. Grace Ridge, of Gillingham, Kent, who has seen the Little People since early childhood, was also visited by them in her bedroom. She had been very ill and was lying alone feeling extremely sorry for herself, for the day was dull with no sunshine to cheer her. Then, suddenly, the room was illumined with a rose-coloured light, and she saw just above the foot of the bed five lovely fairies dressed in pink flower-like dresses, which reminded her of roses. Holding hands, they danced in a ring very quickly; and when they disappeared they left behind them a healing power that uplifted her.

While giving her sister-in-law magnetic treatment in her bedroom in 1937, Mrs. Emma S. King saw that her patient's astral body was lying in a green meadow, studded with daisies and small poppies, etc. "In and out between the grasses, some brownies and tiny white etheric creatures came and went, actively and energetically binding into her the healing aroma of the grass and the flowers. They were in the charge of a fairy about eighteen inches high, mauve-coloured in both wings and drapery. She touched Coral on the forehead, and told her to 'absorb the perfume of health, human child.' It was very pretty to watch.

"On 27 April 1937," Mrs. King continued, "I went to Albert Park to bring my friend Mrs. S. to stay with me for a few days at Kew (Victoria), as she has a weak heart and has had pleurisy. We concentrated on giving her magnetic treatment before taking the little journey, and in the centre of her body I saw a whirling vortex of blue force, vibrating and glowing until it spread and enveloped her whole body… A fairy stood on her forehead—an exquisite little thing, all shimmering mauve with a lovely little light on its head and a tiny wand in its hand. On other occasions when I have been helping to treat her, I have seen brownies working on the pleurisy patch and drawing away the trouble in what looked like white threads. In fact, both of us have seen this on several occasions, Mrs. S. being much more clairvoyant than I am."

Another instance of how the Little People brought healing came from Mrs. D. Goddard, of Totton, Hants. When she was ill with quinsy, she sensed quite definitely two little men—one on the top, and the other on the end of her bed. "They were about six inches high," she said, "and had such pink little faces. Their beards were not made of hair, but something much finer in texture. They radiated happiness and love, yet gave the impression of much strength of purpose and energy. They were unlike anything physical. They seemed to be throwing a kind of gossamer thread backwards and forwards to each other, and this went on for several minutes. I recovered very quickly, although my throat had been so bad. I know now that the thread was just a materialised form of healing power." Mrs. Goddard added that she felt a sense of loss when they seemed to go away, and a feeling of regret that the ordinary person is unaware of the presence of such brings.

When Mrs. Eva Parker of Ilkeston, Derbyshire, was about four years of age, she also was confined to bed with quinsy and was just about to fall asleep when she perceived that she was in a field dotted with small hillocks, on which some tiny figures were playing. Each of these was dressed in green with a brown apron and a cone-shaped hat, and they were all jumping over each other's backs and appearing to be enjoying themselves very much. They made Mrs. Parker feel very happy and carefree, and when her sister came into the room and stood watching her with her arms resting on the bed rail, she pretended to be asleep because she did not want her to speak and spoil her lovely experience. Left alone again, she saw one of the gnomes sit down on a hillock and hold out his apron, and one after another the gnomes dived headfirst into it and disappeared. Afterwards she felt very uplifted and much better in health.

Early one morning, in the sunlit bedroom of a house at Cranleigh, in Surrey, Mrs. M. O. Weller was looking anxiously at her husband, who was ill with heart trouble, when something else attracted her attention. Eight fairies were floating gracefully round the room. With their pretty faces framed in fair hair, they were like miniature dolls five to six inches in height, and had wings. Their long dresses were each of a different hue—cerise, pale green, blue, deep pink, mauve, orange, gold, and lemon. Spellbound at the colourful picture they made, she watched them quietly for some time, but although she told her husband, he could not see them. "And," she told me ruefully, "my family won't believe it!"

Mrs. Alys Pare Flewitt, D.C., an osteopath of Kensington, London, always saw fairies and gnomes encircling one of her patients to whom she was giving treatment. "This patient possessed, to a marked degree, the natural youth, fullness that is so attractive and in her public work she was much loved," said Mrs. Flewitt, who told of another experience she had at a public meeting at Victoria, London, when she was conscious of fairies around a women a few seats ahead, and this person, too, seemed to possess "a special, innate quality."

In a letter to me in June 1959, Mrs. G. K. Evason of Kent said, "As I took up the writing pad, I seemed to be surrounded by fairies, all radiating vibrations of intense happiness. I only sensed their presence then and could not see them, but on commencing to write to you I am aware of a ring of them about my feet, led by a 'Fairy Queen.' She has wings, and her raiment is like gossamer, white, and pale blue. Her tiny wand is radiant with light and has a brilliant star on the top. Now she becomes clearer still and turns her exquisite face to me. She has lovely hair of a light corn colour, and it is rippling about her head and neck in waves and curls. She is beating time and singing, and she lifts a cluster of silver bells. The fairies in her band are dancing and singing in time to her conducting, and now I become conscious of their vibrations being directed to the left side of my throat. The Queen fairy points to the trouble spot and conveys to me that she is focusing healing power there. This is much needed, as the condition has given me considerable inconvenience for a long time."

While living in Leeds in 1926-1927, Miss Muriel M. Golding was suffering from insomnia after a severe attack of influenza, and suddenly, as she tossed on her bed longing to sleep but unable to do so, she saw on her pillow a little creature of the goblin type, not more than a foot high. He seemed to be wearing blue-and-white pantaloons and a little jacket, and he had a curious small, mischievous face. He was laughing at her, but she couldn't believe that he was really there and shut her eyes. When she opened them, there he was still, and he kicked up the bedclothes, put his face on the pillow, and winked at her. Then he vanished. "If he came to cheer me," she wrote, "he certainly succeeded."

Miss Rosemary Harrison was resting in the sick bay at the W.R.N.S. Station at Wavenden, near Bletchley, Buckinghamshire, when she saw several little people floating all around her bed for quite a considerable time. She assured me she was wide-awake and was not delirious. The tiny creatures had wings and were about four inches high.

Even a dentist's surgery is not immune from the presence of fairies. Certain drugs and gases can affect the vibrations of the human body, and when an anaesthetic is used, it causes the etheric or vital body of the patient to be partially driven out of the physical body, and this makes him or her more sensitive to superphysical vibrations. At such times, some patients have flashes of clairvoyance, and this was the case with Mrs. Gwen Morley, of Nottingham, who assured me of the vivid reality of the fairies, which she saw while having dental treatment under gas. They must have utilized some of the ectoplasmic substance from her loosened etheric body, for they were of a transparent white colour. Their dresses were of the traditional ballet type, and they carried wands, which they waved as they flew around her, no doubt in order to transmit the healing power. She was so entranced by the sight of these delightful little creatures that she wished she could have stayed longer under the anaesthetic; but then she became aware of the dentist's hand on her cheek, and all the fairies vanished abruptly. She told us she felt genuine regret that she could no longer see them.

In 1959, I read that some rescue workers were trying to release a student who was trapped 1,000 feet underground in a Derbyshire cavern, and one of the men said: "The carbon dioxide makes you extremely light-headed. You think you can see fairies… it is most eerie." Alcohol had the same effect on some people, and John De

Burgh Leaks wrote in the September 1940 issue of *Prediction* that a scientist whom he met claimed that he could see fairies dancing on his dining-room table every time he took a few glasses of whisky!

Nature spirits have a wonderful faculty of tasking strong thought-images and projecting them on walls, etc., and sometimes even physical objects in a room are "taken over" and woven into a kind of magic transformation scene. One wonders whether these visions are intended merely as entertainment for the viewers—who must unknowingly have provided the right conditions for such phenomena—or as a pleasurable experience for the nature spirits. The following accounts seem to show that both conjectures are correct.

Mrs. Maud B. G. Longuehaye and her husband, of Middlesex, occupied separate beds facing approximately north, placed together in a fair-sized front bedroom with an easterly outlook. They usually retired to bed between 11 p.m. and midnight, though sometimes a little later. Writing to me on 3 April in 1955, Mrs. Longuehaye said: "Some six months or more ago, a short while after retiring and putting out the light, I told my husband I could see a most peculiar scene and asked him whether he could see it and, if so, what it was. I was very surprised when he said he could see nothing, and I thereupon described the scene to him while I was looking at it, and I have thus described similar scenes, with variations, many times since. At the end of my bed, or a little further away, a spot of light grew into an egg-shaped, misty form, which appeared to the eye about three feet at its longest diameter. The 'material' from which it was formed was at first a white cloud-like vapour in constant motion, in the course of which it gradually built up organised forms. These were difficult at first to make out, but the most prominent eventually shaped itself into a figure less than a foot tall, which gradually became sufficiently clear to be recognised as that of a young woman dressed in some loose white drapery. This figure was in constant movement, performing a kind of dance, moving legs, arms, and shoulders with a sort of flowing motion, and constantly turning. I have, in fact, never gotten a clear view of the face, as every time I tried to do so the figure seemed to sway or turn away from me. Upon various occasions the figure has differed in size and clearness, but on the whole its characteristics have been the same, reminding me somewhat of the semi-classical figures one finds in illustrations to Victorian storybooks. The egg-shaped structure is very definitely three-dimensional and contains a scene in which the figure moves. This scene in a way resembles those landscapes contained in a glass sphere, which can be bought at toy shops. It is brightly coloured, and the colours move and change. They seem to shine with their own brightness, are very attractive and difficult to describe, as they are different from ordinary colours. The nature of the scene varies while actually under view. The impression is of the described figure dancing in a glade, or amongst coloured rocks, or upon a seashore, surrounded by colours. There is often an impression that there are other figures, too distant, small or crowded together to be clearly distinguished.

"On the night of 28 March last, a new feature appeared. Two spots of light, separated by a few feet, developed into two egg-shaped structures. One progressed more or less as described before; the other had a vaguely defined scene of its own, but did not become sufficiently clear to allow of a description. This is so far the only occasion when two of the structures have developed simultaneously. They seemed independent, not just duplications. The appearances are rather pleasant, and when they are absent for, say, a week, I am inclined to miss them. They do, however, keep me awake, and as I like to describe them to my husband, I sometimes have to deny myself this, as otherwise I keep him awake. I have no explanation of the foregoing and have been very far from seeking such visions, which have imposed themselves upon me unasked."

On 11 April 1955, Mrs. Longuehaye sent me a further experience. "The way in which the scene has manifested recently has changed. It has developed as an egg-shaped structure, but this has soon disappeared, leaving the scene unenclosed but surrounded by a kind of misty blue and gold atmosphere. On the night of April 9, there was a further development or extension, and the nature of the scene was different. Immediately [as] I put out the light, it appeared, first on the rectangle of wall above the fireplace opposite my bed, which was the largest part. It then developed at two other points, one a few feet to the left of the first, and another to my left, just above my husband's bed. These extra developments were not very distinct, but formed part of the main scene, which was a forest glade, and gave an impression of vast space, of woodlands, and it was surrounded by trees with interlaced boughs. The whole was suffused by a pale mauve light and was full of soft mauve shadows. (One shadow came right on top of me, but I had no particular sensation.) A vast concourse of people was present, and it appeared as if some ceremony was in progress. Facing me was a broad flight of steps, which led down to a kind of rail. At the top of the steps, on either side, were two pointed niches (like those found in Gothic churches intended to contain the images of saints). In each niche stood a figure, and I knew them to be alive. They shone with their own light—bright and silvery like moonlight. Descending the steps came the figure of a man, which appeared to be about a foot tall. I took him to be a priest, and as he came to the rail I thought he was going to give Communion. However, he stopped, raised his arms above his head, and brought them down straight below his waist three times. I sat up to try to get a better view of his face, but just as it was getting clear he walked back up the steps. Then he appeared to turn over and over, as if he was turning a somersault, and shot into the air."

Mrs. Longuehaye's description of the "priest's" ludicrous behaviour establishes beyond doubt that these visions were produced by nature spirits, who can keep a certain form only as long as their minds are fixed on it. The mock priest's mind evidently began to wander, and he lost his equilibrium, forgot the dignity of his role, and became once more a rollicking nature-spirit. He appeared again about a week later, this time dressed in a purple cope. He came down the steps, holding a sword straight in front of him, an end in each hand. When he reached the bottom of the steps, he held it up in the air and twisted it about three times. He turned, and Mrs. Longuehaye did not see him anymore.

On 14 April she saw a small, but quite bright, light over the bedroom fireplace. "This grew larger and then developed into an egg-shaped structure, which gradually dispersed, leaving a sort of light that slowly formed into what looked like a long pathway between trees with interlaced boughs, which were of different soft colours. People, girls, began to walk about. Stone steps then appeared, and the figures went down them until they got quite close to me. The scene then opened out into what seemed like a large hall, full of beautiful colours; first a lovely mauve, which gradually turned to pink, and then all the other colours were present, like a soft but bright rainbow. The figures moved, glided, and danced in this setting, attired in white dresses, which shone like moonlight. The principal figure was distinct enough for me to see that she was dressed in a skirt gathered tightly at the waist and, so far as I could make out, a white blouse or upper garment of some kind." On this occasion, rays of light streamed from her and formed a half-circle of light from her waist upwards, and this made a kind of umbrella over her head. "Then the scene melted away and it became like a stream or pool, and the figure seemed to dive and glide towards the left and disappeared. The scene then became broader again, and rocks formed. The figure reappeared and climbed from rock to rock. These were almost like steps, and she was gliding here and there. I then went to sleep, and when I awoke at 4 o'clock, the scene was still there.

"On 15 April the vision began by the formation on the right-hand side of the fireplace of a little ball of light, much brighter than usual, about the size of a golf-ball. This grew and became less bright in the centre, eventually forming a scene, which was, however, very indistinct. The figure appeared and glided about in the middle. It went away from time to time and then departed for good. There was one new feature in this experience, in that while the figure was present I could hear the tinkling of a bell, and it was like the sound of one of the little bells that are put on Christmas trees.

"On 16 April the scene developed on my right-hand side, nearer to me than usual. The figure was small, self-luminous, and the whole scene seemed as though it was a great distance away — rather as if I was looking at it through the wrong end of binoculars. Nothing happened; it was more like a tableau and remained so until I went to sleep. The figures in these scenes are very much alive, about a foot high, of light build, and in perfect proportion. They have beautiful hands, pink like those of a healthy human being. I have not been able to see their features as they turn away whenever I think I am about to do so, but my feeling is that they are quite normal and human-like."

The constant flowing or pulsating movements observed by Mrs. Longuehaye are typical of the astral plane. So, also, are the lovely luminous colours, which she states are "different from ordinary colours.. There are, indeed, several more shades in between those of the visible spectrum, and these additional colours have no equivalent in the physical world.

Mrs. Muriel M. Golding, who has an account elsewhere in this book, likewise had a vision in her bedroom. It was of a lovely garden full of flowers and flooded with light, and she could see it with her eyes open or shut, each flower and leaf was distinct in every detail, and out of every flower a fairy rode like an emanation. These beings were diaphanous and many-hued, and were either moving up and down or flitting here and there, never still for a moment. "It was a most entrancing picture," she said, "and this was only the beginning of other visions. Sometimes the room appeared full of flowers; they were all about me in gentle and perpetual movement. I feel I ought to be able to touch them. It is really as though a breeze were passing through them, and they are always so fresh and unblemished, never a faded flower. I imagine them to be archetypes in an etheric world. The other night I saw, for the first time, precious stones of every colour, all shining and luminous, as though lighted from within. So lovely!"

A contributor of several accounts, Mrs. Lily McKenzie had bedroom visions which were equally fascinating. In 1964 she told me she had wakened between 5 and 7 a.m. one day to find her bedroom wall lit up, and there was a lovely spray of leaves trailing from one corner. She thought she had been dreaming, but after an interval of several weeks the visions continued and she knew she was fully awake. "In fact," she said, "my daughter-in-law brings me a cup of tea, and I am already sitting up in bed looking in wonder at the beautiful decorations all over my walls."

At first she saw only the trailing leaves, and she asked the fairies if they could put roses on the walls and also show her who was the artist. The roses appeared—not in colour but in black and white—and then she saw about eight little figures of a golden hue, busily working on the wall in a circle of light. The fairies also produced visions of ferns. One night she was shown a country scene, with two large oak trees and a little cottage at the back of them. She often saw trees, and sometimes their branches spread right up to her as she lay in bed, and they were so bright that they lit up the room. Previous to these visions, a golden fairy had appeared about 2 o'clock in the morning. It was floating in the air in a circle of light, and has appeared several times since. On another morning she wakened to find the space at the side of her bed covered with golden and bronze chrysanthemums, with dainty gypsophila growing in between. They seemed to grow from the floor, and the gypsphila flowers had little lights flitting in and out among them. This lovely carpet of flowers possessed a radiance of its own, and she watched until it disappeared. In September 1965, she saw three little dwarfs in her bedroom. They were dressed in a drab brown colour with hats to match. One of them was at the foot of her bed, and the other two were standing on her dressing table, admiring themselves in the mirror.

Around 2:30 a.m., one day in November of the same year, she saw a small green tree being carried around the room by a gnome. He was looking for a place to set it down, and at last he put it on the floor and disappeared. A little later he came back through the window with a bigger tree and put it beside the first one. This went on until there were seven or eight trees of different sizes on the floor. "I felt I was sitting in my garden instead of sitting up in my bed," she said, and in a further letter she told me that the gnomes still continued to bring her these trees, especially when the leaves had fallen from those in her garden.

A few days later she was awakened by something touching her face, and saw that it was a long, trailing branch of leaves hanging from the ceiling. At the same time she saw the golden fairy flying into her room through the window. There were some plants on the table, and the fairy flew to an asparagus fern and flitted all over it. She was like a large butterfly of about four inches. In the moonlight Mrs. McKenzie could see her reflected in the mirror of the dressing table: "A very lovely sight, fragile and dainty, and like shining gold." It is interesting to note that the leaves touched the seer's face, and therefore must have been composed of substance of an ectoplasmic nature, and this is borne out by her descriptions of the decorations: "A few times it looks like white fur. I see it spreading slowly over the walls, where it remains for a little while and then gradually fades." Distance is no object to the nature spirits, and when Mrs. McKenzie went to stay with her sister who lived 370 miles away, her bedroom became decorated with flowers and trees similar to those she saw in her own home.

One evening, Mrs. R. Steer, of London, turned her head to the wall side of her bed, when suddenly the whole area became white, and golden lilies appeared there, surrounded by a massive golden frame. Then a field appeared over her bed, in which were groups of silver flowers, swaying as though in a breeze, and she seemed to be standing in the field among them, with a Christ-like presence near her left side.

Mrs. V. I. Larkworthy (see her other account in this book) told me that she, too, had seen beautiful colours and scenery on her walls, but she did not give me detailed descriptions.

Fairy Glamour

"Glamour" (otherwise known as "gramarye") is the art of illusion created by the fertile imagination of the fairies. One form of this magical art of glamour in which these nature spirits excel is their mischievous habit of leading people astray, and those who experience it are said to be "piskielated" or "pixie-led." Surroundings, which once were familiar to them, become strange. They wander about, sometimes for hours, feeling lost and bewildered, searching for the path across a moor or a gate, which seems no longer there. Sometimes they find themselves in the middle of a fairy village or market, or see houses or castles which can vanish just as suddenly as they appear. It is really a harmless deception of the senses and not at all evil, though, at the time, the victim is under a sort of spell.

Miss Kathleen Hinde, of Dorset, was pixie-led in her youth. With three cousins she went to have tea at a friend's house, and as they were coming away after the visit she remarked: "I have never gone through that field on the left. It's a way home by the moor; let us do it." Her companions agreed, but when they were all halfway across she had to admit: "It's odd, but there seems no way out." They looked back, only to discover that the gate through which they had passed was no longer there! The eldest cousin declared "Nonsense! This just can't be. Let us each take one side and work round carefully. Of course there are gates—we have seen them." The others did as she suggested, but on joining forces in the middle of the field they were much flustered because in each case they had seen nothing but a thick, unbroken hedge. By this time they were feeling rather frightened and were just deciding to make an attempt to break through the hedge, when one of the cousins caught hold of Miss Hinde's arm and pointed. There, in front of them, was a large white gate, and with one accord they rushed through it before it disappeared again. Later, when this experience was related to the friend with whom they'd had tea, she exclaimed: "Oh, I wish you had told me; I would have stopped you! It's the pixie field, and we are sick of friends coming back to our house, quite shattered, having spent ages trying to get out." Miss Hinde told me she had never seen a fairy or a pixie, but she once caught a glimpse of a tree spirit (the experience is included in the appropriate section of this book).

The greyhound breeder, Mr. Ralph Parsons, of Cornwall, had a similar experience of what he called being "pixie-laid." "It was back in the days when I had to poach a couple of rabbits or there was no meat for the family," he related in the weekly *Dog World* of 17 February 1984. "This night in particular I was out and had a whippet working, and on hearing a peculiar sound in the field I went to investigate. It was not completely dark, just enough to discern an object. I made for what I imagined was the centre of the field, but failing to find anything I started back for the gate. For some strange reason I just could not find the place where I had come in. I went around the field time after time but to no avail. Eventually I got out by putting the whippet on a lead and telling her to head for home, and she was able to lead me to the gate I had been unable to find."

I wrote to ask Mr. Parsons about the sound that he heard, and he said: "It was like the call of a bird—a low-pitched whistle, perhaps. I went in because it was so unusual. Perhaps I thought the dog had caught something. Although it was not a black night, it was some time before the dog found me. There was no moon, and it was, in fact, a perfect poaching night—a night when the rabbit did not cast a shadow. It was a field where I would have gambled on catching one, but the dog just returned to me without a thing. And on going with the dog, she pulled on the lead and I went with her, whereas at other times she would walk alongside without straining at all." Mr. Parsons tells me that since then the field has been enlarged and the hedges removed to make way for bigger machines, but each time he passes by his thoughts wander back to what happened there nearly 50 years ago.

Mr. Thomas McGreal of Airedale, Castleford, Yorkshire, wrote to tell me he had seen "fairies in dozens" and would give me details if I wished. Unfortunately he passed away shortly afterwards, but his son, Mr. F. McGreal, who had shared his father's experience, was kind enough to send me the full story, as follows: "It happened in the autumn of 1933. My father and I had been visiting friends, and dusk was falling as we set off for home around 5 p.m. We had to cross a small mountain lying between Westport and Drummin, near a village called Letterbrock, in County Mayo, Eire. To a person who was unfamiliar with the place, it would be very easy to get lost or drowned, but my father and I knew the way home blind-folded. The journey itself, under normal circumstances, would take only half an hour. We left the cart road and entered what should have been rough and marshy land, but suddenly the area changed and the ground became solid. It was very strange, and my father and I tried to get back to the cart track, but we couldn't see any familiar landmarks. Father studied his position and came to the conclusion that the fairies had got us. We carried on walking, but we hadn't a clue where we were going. Father put his fingers to his mouth and gave a sharp blast like a whistle. Immediately little brick and slate houses sprang up in all directions about a quarter of a mile away from us. Little people came out holding storm lamps and running around. I cannot recall the dress they wore, but they were approximately two feet six inches in height, and there seemed to be eight or twelve little people to each house. I remarked to father that maybe they had come to help us. We would change our direction to one of the houses, but when we thought we were almost upon it, it would disappear and spring up elsewhere. This went on for some time, and I began to get afraid, but father said they were only having fun and they would not let any harm come to us. He told me to bend and pull up turfs of grass to make sure that we were not on a lake (there are two on our normal way home), as he would stop the little people if we were not on water. I found we were still on solid ground, so my father took his coat off and turned his waistcoat inside out. As quickly as they had appeared at his whistle, they now disappeared. We looked around us and found a familiar landmark, so we knew where we were. How we had arrived at this particular spot without getting muddy, wet, or even drowned is still a mystery. Although the journey, under normal circumstances, would have taken only half an hour, on this particular night we had been walking for several hours, yet had not felt tired until the spell was broken, and I was exhausted when we arrived home about 11 p.m. My grandmother was waiting for us, and before we explained what had happened she remarked that it was 'a very strange and eerie night.' If my father had been alive, he would have corroborated the story. He was a very highly respected person in the place where he lived."

After receiving the foregoing accounts, I thought how interesting it must be to be pixilated, little dreaming that many years later, on 31 March 1979, I would have a similar experience—in a large, well-known cemetery, of all places! I had been up the same road to the chapel at the top of the hill many times before, to attend the funerals of various friends and relatives, but on this day I had gone just to look in the Memorial Book. Although it may have no relevance to the experience that followed, I had better mention that the outer door to the Memorial Chapel seemed to be locked, and I pulled and struggled for several minutes without avail. I couldn't understand it, because the door was always opened at a certain time every morning, before people arrived for funeral or cremation services. I seemed to be the only person in the cemetery and had just given up in despair when two men arrived in a car. I asked them if they could help me, and both of them struggled with the door, but with no success. Then one of them said, "Wait here, and we'll drive to the office at the entrance and ask for the key." They returned looking rather puzzled. "The people in the office told us that the door isn't locked," said one of the men. "It doesn't stick and should open easily." As he spoke he turned again to try the door, and it opened at once! The two men seemed to have come just to look at one of the graves, and by the time I came out of the Memorial Chapel they had gone. I felt strangely uneasy about the door incident; there seemed something queer about the atmosphere, and I was anxious to get away from the place as soon as I could. I started back down the hill only to find that the road had altered! It should have been straight, but was now curved. I couldn't understand it, but there seemed to be only one explanation possible. As there are several parallel roads in the cemetery, perhaps, absent-mindedly, I had taken a different one, but I knew that all of them joined a horizontal road at the bottom of the hill and that this would lead me back to the entrance gates, so I was not unduly worried. I continued walking for another few yards and then stood still in utter bewilderment. The road had become very narrow and ended in a small, purposeless loop, the inside of which could not have been more than three feet long and two feet wide. I looked around me and saw several other paths on either side, much narrower, but when I followed them I found that they, too, ended in loops. After exploring the last of them, I turned back to the road, but it had disappeared and, apart from a large old thorn-tree under which I found myself standing, only gravestones were there. I looked down to where the long, horizontal road should be, which would have led to the entrance gates. It wasn't there; the gravestones reached right to the bottom railings. I seemed to be near one end of the cemetery, but there was no way out. There were railings along the side, and beyond them there appeared to be a road, but with no signs of life on it.

Then I noticed, for the first time, two plain-looking brick houses within the railings, which seemed to have sprung up suddenly not far from where I was standing. Anyone reading this will wonder why I didn't go to one of them to ask for help. I couldn't, because I was filled with apprehension. I knew that they hadn't been there the moment before, and if they had been real houses there would have been a gate in the railings to give ingress and egress to the occupants. The air was deathly still, and by that time I had realised—especially when I thought of the paths with their nonsensical loops—that the fairies were playing tricks on me. I did not want to be offered any of their etheric food, as it has a strange effect and can make the recipient very otherworldly. So I went away from the houses and walked in the opposite direction, trying to pick my way between the gravestones, which now stretched ahead of me, seemingly for miles. I did not relish the thought of having to spend the night there, and I knew that my sister would be wondering what had become of me. Then I thought of shaking myself and twisting my body around to shatter the existing vibrations, at the same time declaring that the divine spirit within me was all-powerful. Instantly the spell was broken: I saw a straight road, and on rushing up it I found myself back at the chapel. From there I was able to see the road up which I had come originally, and that led me safely down to the entrance gates. I arrived home very late and, fortunately for me, my sister believed my story because she could see how shaken and exhausted I was. I could not get the experience out of my mind, and felt I must go again to make quite sure how much of the scenery really had been transformed on that day. I begged my sister to go with me, and we went some months later. The landscape on this occasion was back to normal, and we were able to confirm that the roads had no loops, and that they led straight down to the road, which lay horizontally along the bottom of the cemetery. There were no tiny paths with loops, and where I had seen gravestones reaching to the railings there was only a wide grass verge. As I had suspected, there were no houses where I had seen the two standing.

I must confess that I kept feeling drawn back to the place, but thought it wiser not to go there alone, though I did go again later, and this time I walked along every path and explored every part of the large cemetery, until I was able to prove to myself that under ordinary conditions it would be impossible to get lost. I looked to where I had seen the railings at the end, with the road beyond, but no road was now to be seen; only a small woodland full of tall and beautiful trees, which must have been there for many years. I searched for the large old thorn tree under which I had found myself standing on that day, but it was now no longer to be seen. According to tradition, hawthorn trees are used by the fairies as trysting places, and the fields on which this cemetery was made may once have been fairy ground, such as the grounds of Kenilworth Castle and Kensington Gardens are reputed to have been.

Chapter 5: More Fairy Experiences

Tom Charman

Mr. Tom Charman, of Godshill, near Fordingbridge, Hampshire, was intensely interested in elemental life, and I am grateful to his wife for allowing me to take some extracts from his notes.

As a child he saw only one fairy. "Well I remember," he wrote, "how I was in the middle of howling over something or other, when suddenly there appeared in the darkness a sort of animal rushing through the room, in shape and size something like a huge rat, and on his back sat a little nature spirit. It was all so quick that I cannot recollect what he was like beyond the fact that he (the nature spirit) wore a little cap. But it quite stopped my crying! It was not until many years afterwards that I became clairvoyant again. During this interval I was a sceptic and a materialist. I have always given thanks for the gift of psychic vision, which came to me and has never left me since, because it meant to me the opening of the gates to the vast invisible world around us, and made often repeated spiritual truths become living realities. The elemental or Fairy World is a vast world including all conceivable varieties of elemental beings. They differ from mankind chiefly in that they are rudimentary both in body and mind, and represent partial stages of development. Proportion or balance of form is lacking amongst most of them. For example, quite a number have very long thin necks, whilst others have scarcely a neck at all. Some appear almost all head, whilst others appear almost all body and so on. From this it looks as though they develop one part at the expense of the rest, only becoming balanced by degrees. Beauty of proportion is seen amongst the highest types of fairies, who are as symmetrical as human beings. Frequently on a stormy day when roaming through the wind-swept trees, I have seen sylphs flying with the gale, now soaring above the treetops, and now taking great swoops downwards, after the fashion of swallows. What with the flying leaves, the swaying branches, and the artistic evolution of these beautiful creatures, I have felt enthralled by this mingling of earth and fairyland… These air elementals, or sylphs, are amongst some of the most beautiful of fairies. I have already said how they love to be tossed hither and thither by a storm, and how my walks on a windy day are enlivened by these airy sprites. The most typical of them have long, thin necks, with long hair and flowing garments, which stream gracefully behind them as they float through the air. They bring with them an atmosphere of gentleness and calm, which shows itself in a grace and smoothness of movement seen amongst few other fairies.

"One of my most beautiful clairvoyant experiences was the witnessing of one of their great gatherings. I had shut my eyes and was thinking of nothing in particular, when there appeared in the darkness a little sylph clothed in a most exquisitely coloured dress. No sooner had she come than multitudes of others equally resplendent came floating in from all sides. The magnificence of the colouring and the grace of the dress took my breath away, and I could not refrain from exclaiming at the beauty of the scene. Then they floated gracefully up and down and round about, in a continuous undulating line. This continued for a long time and I had a rare feast. Their dresses resembled light and feathery clouds at sunset time, or rainbow-coloured cobwebs on bright, early autumn mornings. As the word 'fairy' has become associated with beautiful and fragile beings, it is not descriptive of many of the forms I see, so I shall often use the term Elemental, which is at times more appropriate. I can only draw then when I am, so to speak, so much in the fairy world that I am almost one with them. Whilst drawing, actually I feel I am doing with them the different activities shown in the pictures, my pencil moving almost unconsciously. An intensely vivid vision will often give me the necessary inspiration for a drawing. The unusual appeals to me, and the Fairy world is full of the comic and the grotesque. My love of this and my natural turn for the comic may have made me unconsciously exaggerate some of the figures. I have frequently seen little Red Indians elementals running along, with bows and arrows. At one time I saw them sitting on the hands and shoulders of the etheric body of an Indian, who was obviously pleased and interested in them. Once I saw a number of hairy elemental savages, and I have frequent glimpses into the regions of Chinese elementals. This makes me wonder whether the varieties of human beings on earth had first an elemental existence on the etheric plane.

"Personally I have never seen fairies with wings, but this does not in the least imply that they do not exist. Different people often see into different planes. Also, their wings may be purely decorative and, like their clothes, the product of etheric thought, which makes it as easy to have a pair of wings as a gauzy dress. I have occasionally seen fairy palaces and houses of the utmost quaintness. They often have very artistic domes and minarets. On earth most of them would be structurally impossible. There, however, that question does not arise, and so, as with clothes, they have full scope for any dwelling they fancy. Their little cottages are often made of crooked branches and any kind of rough material, so that they harmonize completely with the curve and colours of nature.

"Most of my clairvoyant experiences occur on retiring at night, which I often do at an early hour, for the darkness and quiet of my room provide just the right conditions. Then, with my eyes shut or open (it makes no difference, because I am seeing with my etheric eye), I get fascinating glimpses into the Fairy World. When I am in this psychic state, I am never in a trance, which is fortunate for me, as I am always extra-conscious and so able to enjoy my visions. But I am never able to command a vision of fairies. It comes or it does not. There are, of course, numbers of nature spirits of all kinds, including little folk in brown clothes, which some people call brownies. These seem to keep guard whilst others more beautifully dressed play about on branches of trees, or swing from bough to bough like monkeys. These are usually in green, with little caps on. The gnomes, or little old men and women, have kind faces, and appear to take great interest in the smaller elementals around them. As well as those with the special characteristics of earth elementals, there are some amongst them very similar to one or other of the groups already described, as though they were a combination of two types. I have drawn a number of pictures showing little boats riding huge waves in stormy seas, and in the boats quaint little figures. Now, it is probable that these little fishermen are an amalgamation of earth and water elementals. I have seen quite a number of dancing fairies. This is a favourite pastime amongst them, and some are especially gifted. They are on the whole slight in build, with long thin necks, and long thin arms and legs. There are those, though much fewer in number, who are beautifully proportioned, but these dancers are more angular in build and less smooth in motion than sylphs. One night I had a beautiful vision of a little dancer. As she floated into sight, she began spinning round and round, slowly at first, and then gradually gaining in speed, until I could see nothing but a blur of colour."

This spinning motion, it might be noted, has been seen by Mrs. Gwen Grippe and Mrs. Shirley Eshelby, and is mentioned in their accounts.

Mr. Tom Charman continues: "Then the speed slackened once more, and the thought crossed my mind as to whether she knew I was admiring her. At that moment she looked over her shoulder and smiled at me. This is the only time I know of a fairy responding to my thoughts. I have tried to get into mental touch with them but without success. Frequently they dance together, taking hold of each other's hands. At other times as many as a dozen may form themselves into a ring by taking hold of long, thin, gauzy drapery, which they love to see floating into the air. They have no set dances as far as I can see. My most gorgeous and fantastic visions are those of fairy processions. There is no fashion in the fairy world, so each individual wears just what takes his fancy. In these processions they are all dressed in most weird and wonderful garments, and some of them appear decidedly overdressed and bejewelled. They seem to specialize in queer hats, and their hair is often adorned and put up in the most fantastic of ways. Sometimes a hat will have on it an ornament in the shape of a turnip or a carrot. In fact, it would seem, the more weird, the more beautiful! They usually carry in the procession the most trivial things with the utmost dignity. These processions are usually very long. I cannot find out what purpose they serve. I have said that fairies inhabit the astral or etheric plans, but I have used these terms for want of a better. I wish to emphasize that all elementals seem to inhabit a plane, which is halfway between the etheric and astral world and this physical world, and that in this state, contrary to what we know of beings on the etheric or astral plane, they are able to contact objects and elements of our world in a glorified form. Thus they can enjoy the elements and natural objects of this plane, but not suffer from them. Only those human beings who are able to contact their vibrations, to a greater or lesser degree, are able to see and feel these little creatures."

Of special interest and importance to the seer Mr. Tom Charman were some curious cat-like elemental creatures, and his description of them is well-worth quoting: "The bones of the hands and feet of these animals are already divided up into fingers and toes, but are not visible, as they are enclosed in a bag-like formation of skin. Their bodies are covered with down-like hair, and they vary a lot as regards stages of development. Thus in some of the lower forms the mouth consists of a slit, whilst in the higher forms actual lips occur. All of them show varying degrees of dawning consciousness. During the summer of 1920, my wife and I spent nine weeks camping in the New Forest, and during this time we had many visits from these cat-like creatures. Frequently of a night, one would poke his head into small hands and feet, as though they were able to change themselves at will—perhaps according to the different kinds of work they were engaged upon.

Other Witnesses

Another fairy seer, Mrs. Georgina K. Evason, of Kent, said she had certainly perceived some "very comical cats, half-finished looking," as though they were in process of trying to materialize or develop. These had always been indoors, and she took them to be "subjective pictures of undeveloped creatures at a certain stage of progression."

In 1956, Mr. A. W. Smith, B.A., of Essex, wrote: "My little girl (she will be two in October) persistently insists that there are 'pussies' all over our house, and on one occasion when she was trying hard to get me to look at one I felt a distinct 'chill' and a positive

213

sense of physical 'malaise.' Incidentally, a little girl in the house opposite ours was most unwilling to sleep in her new bedroom (when the family moved in) because she said there were pussycats playing in the room. There is no question of one child influencing the other."

It may have been another creature of this type that Mrs. Martha C. Smith of Indiana saw in her large basement. "It is fairly dark there," she explained, "and only part of the floor is finished. The other part is dirt trampled down very hard. I had gone down to get a box when suddenly I was conscious of a tiny noise behind me, such as a mouse or small rat would make. I turned, and over against a wall I saw a little object about the size of a half-grown cat, which I thought it was until I realised it was standing on its two legs. It was a musty dark colour, with an animal-like face, and had what appeared to be a furry-looking coat and brownish-coloured pants. Its feet were more like an animal's than those of the other little people I have seen, and its features were pointed and coarse looking. It had no hat, but just a bunch of rough fur, and when it sped out of sight it jumped like a rabbit instead of walking upright as humans do. I was also conscious of an unpleasant odour. I have been down several times since, hoping to see it again, but all I can find is a little mark on the floor like that left by the three toes of a chicken."

In the 1950s, Mrs. Jessie Kay Scott and her husband were listening to the wireless on New Year's Eve in their home in Kent when there came from behind the grandfather clock "two furry brown little creatures," which commenced to dance in front of the radio. Both husband and wife watched them in amazement, until at last one of the tiny figures darted on to Mrs. Scott's shoulder and thence to the couch, where it disappeared. "They had such lovely brown twinkling eyes," she wrote. "We have never seen anything like this before in our lives."

Mrs. E.D., of Cheshire, had a similar experience when a pixie, like a little brown-skinned or furry animal in appearance, with ears shaped like ivy leaves, was seen by her in daylight. Its height was five or six inches, and it stood against a chair leg for a few seconds, and then vanished.

Mrs. Vera Westmoreland

During their early childhood in Runcorn, Cheshire, Mrs. Vera Westmoreland and her sister Doris saw various elves. Some were clothed in green, and their faces were slightly greenish. Others wore brown and had faces more pointed and coloured "like sunburn on pale skin." Vera saw her first fairy at the age of six, while she was ill in bed. It visited her frequently and would poise itself on the bed rail, or dart about the room. Its delicate aura varied from time to time with colours that were always of pastel shades, blended like shot silk, and glowing like a faint rainbow.

In 1912, a well-known medium, Mr. Tom Tyrell, used to visit Vera's parents. He saw fairies constantly and would describe them to the family. He told them how he was taken to a wood by some people who bandaged his eyes and tested him with trees. His task was to point out the dead trees amongst many healthy ones, and this he was able to do successfully. He explained to Vera's parents how he did it, and gave them a demonstration in the unfamiliar woods and countryside to which he was taken. In the trees, which were alive, he could hear the sap rising and falling, and he also followed out what the fairies told him. He said they showed him much of their life and work with the flowers, and he could describe, while still blindfolded, what flowers were before him.

During 1915, Vera was taken to live in the country at a place called Kingsley. There, the nine-year-old child was often lonely, and would amble round the fields and cottage garden. Gradually she became conscious of the hidden life and could sense which parts were the haunts of elves and fairies. The villagers used to avoid certain places, and she realised they were afraid, but didn't know the reason. Later, she saw the wee folk, sometimes clearly, at other times as if in a mist, and she noticed that bird life was very closely linked with them. The garden had an old, lonely plum tree, which stood a fair distance from all other trees, and it was under this tree that she always found happiness. Spirit children had always been a greater part of her childhood play, and when they sometimes brought with them one or two fairies it certainly made the hours fly too quickly for her. They would become as solid as she was and she

215

forgot all else until the time came for them to vanish from her sight.

Near the lane in which she lived, there was an old spring, which bubbled slowly, and had to be reached by a thickly hedged path. The villages said the well was haunted and they avoided it, preferring to walk the long distance to the village pump, for none of the cottages had any water supply. Vera's youthful curiosity took her many times to the lonely well, for it was quiet there and she had a feeling of peace. The water was in a square hole in a narrow setting and was not very deep. It was so clear that one could bend down to look into it. She wondered why so many grown-up people were afraid of it. Then one day she espied two elves leaning out of the greenery at the back of the well. They seemed very happy and not likely to want to frighten anyone. She told some of the village people they need not be afraid, but their fear remained so the elves were left in peace. She saw these little creatures many times, especially after rain, when they were too busy to notice her.

Years later she went to live in Liverpool. Her childhood had passed by, and only the memory of those early visions of fairy life remained. She was now married to Derrick Westmoreland, and one day in February 1936 she walked from her home to visit her parents three miles away. "They did not expect me that day," she said, "and when I arrived I found they had four visitors who, like myself, had come to see them on the spur of the moment. Two of these people were entire strangers, whose grief at the loss of their son, an only child, was the cause of their visit to see my father. They did not know any of us, nor had they ever seen us before. Their great need for solace made me long to help them, so I prayed quietly to be allowed to give these two sad souls some comfort. The seven of us sat in perfect silence, and my faithful collie dog lay near my feet. Suddenly I saw a quivering light coming towards me. It shone and sparkled very clearly, and soon the first fairy playmate of my childhood stood before me, poised on her toes and smiling. On opening my eyes, the bright sparkle remained around her, and I gazed for quite a long time until my father asked: 'Vera, what is it you see?' I replied 'I will tell you in a minute.' At this, the fairy pointed towards my collie dog, which slowly rose and walked straight to her. Everyone saw the dog wag its tail and nose something gently. The fairy touched my dog's head and pointed to the lady who was crying for the loss of her son. The dog went to her and put its nose under her hand. The fairy then pointed to me and again to the lady. This time I saw the spirit of the boy standing by his mother, and I thanked the fairy, who gradually dimmed and faded away. All said, they felt that something stood there, but couldn't see what it was, though two of them had seen the light sparkling the whole time. Proofs of his survival came from the boy, who told his father and mother many things that none knew about the boy and themselves. That fairy had cleared away most of the heaviness and left behind her a brightness that remained with the couple for a long time. The dull weather and the heavy grief of the bereaved parents must have made it difficult for the coming of so delicate a life as hers, yet she had done so."

In November 1947, Mrs. Westmoreland attended a lecture at the Psychic Truth Society, Liverpool. In front of the platform stood a huge bowl of large chrysanthemums, and one flower had a broken stalk and hung downwards. The lecture was interesting, and she had been listening carefully when a movement among the flowers caught her eye. An elf was peeping round the flowers and looking at her with a merry expression on his face. Then with a grin he pointed at a faint light, which she saw quivering over the broken flower, and this cleared to reveal a fairy of iridescent colouring, busily hovering round the broken stem. She was amazed to see the fairy take from the elf something that looked like a sticky web, and this was wound round and round the stem until the flower stayed upright. When the fairy had finished, she glanced at Mrs. Westmoreland and, with a gentle wave, rose and faded from her view. The elf seemed to stretch, and then he, too, vanished. Mrs. Westmoreland sat there feeling dazed with the wonder of it all, until the scraping of chairs and the sound of feet moving on the wooden floor of the hall disturbed her. She rushed from her chair straight to the flowers, and saw that the broken stem was held together by a firm, sticky substance. Some of the people asked her what she was looking at so eagerly, and she told them. The lady who had placed the flowers there said she had broken the stem when bringing the flowers to the hall, and when she saw it had been mended she said she would keep that flower for a long time afterwards. Two other ladies had seen not only the flower move but also some of the leaves, and when asked where, it proved to be right on the spot where the elf had been moving.

In 1950, Mrs. Westmoreland's health was so frail that she and her husband, Derrick, went to live in Swanage. They had been there a month when they found a ground-floor flat, which had spacious gardens and a lovely old church set far back on its lawns. A rippling brook flowed alongside the road and the lawns and hosts of daffodils bloomed and swayed in the sunshine. One day, Mrs. Westmoreland was looking at them when she saw several glimmering fairies moving above them. A noisy car rushed by, and the vision vanished. In vain she watched for them to return, but she was never given that joy again.

She and Derrick arrived in Taunton in 1951, and eventually made their home there, in a lovely old-world thatched house surrounded by its garden and array of trees. This house became a sanctuary for the sick and crippled, and although the town had crept its way around outside the garden, the peace and mellowness within were retained. The trees varied from tall, stately firs, copper beeches and ash, to nut trees and fruit trees. It was amongst these that occasionally she sensed the wee folk and wondered how they could stand the active life of the present day, for she thought that the years of change would affect them.

In 1954, she was resting in the lounge when she saw a tiny figure gliding towards her. It was her fairy playmate and the same fairy who had come to her in February 1936. This time the room was full of sunshine, and she saw the wee soul move in and out of the bright gleams from the window. She felt the fairy's greeting was a happy one, and watched her go through the window and out into the garden, where she vanished into the distance.

While staying in Folkestone at the home of her friend Mrs. Dickens-Yates, who had seen many nature spirits, including leprechauns in Ireland, Mrs. Westmoreland wrote to me: "The garden here is full of elfin and fairy life, and so enjoyable. Each time I visit

218

a certain spot there appears a delightful wee man, young and full of life's joy, who told me his name is Peppetoes, though I do not know if I have spelt it correctly. He moves swiftly and is the same one who kept pulling at my stockings when we were packing to come."

Her next home was near Matlock, in Derbyshire, and she was browsing amongst the heather on a hilltop when she noticed a strange impression on the grass. The depth, and the way the grass had been pressed, set her wondering, and while looking at it she saw many little faces of different types, all peering hard at her. It was a circle of Little People, and their leader was sitting cross-legged on a strange bushy plant that Mrs. Westmoreland knew had not been there before that day, because she often wandered round that part with her puppy. Some of the wee folk were in brown shades of various tones, and others were in grass colours. "I felt like Gulliver," she told me. "So huge and overwhelming; but they eyed me fearlessly, then greeted me in odd movements and faded away from my sight." She stood for a long time sending her thoughts to them. She could see the grass ring depressed and knew they were still holding their own special gathering. Then came the feeling they wanted her to leave them in friendliness, so she walked slowly away. "Sometimes in the sunny weather," she said, "I go to a special woodland here, where I see the various wee ones, who greet me in their different ways. Rock elves and tree sprites abound round here. The fairy clans are coloured in varied array, some with faint, glowing shades round them, according to the clarity of vision I am granted at times."

In the 1960s, she and her husband moved from Derbyshire to Leicestershire, from where she wrote: "On our first night here, such a lively group of elves visited us and seemed very curious about us. They had such friendly grins, and were a kind I have not met before. Their faces and ears were sharply pointed, and their eyes slanting. They wore delightful hats and green jerkins, and brought with them a fairy animal like a lioness so tame and lovable. I saw its yellow eyes with green flecks in them. Then the little fellows pointed to where they lived, and to my joy it seemed to be round the old ruined castle, which stands inside its own moat as though on a green island. Now one of the elves, whose name is Etto, comes frequently to my house, so I feel accepted."

Vera and Derrick Westmoreland were not there very long, as they decided to emigrate to Australia. Unfortunately, Derrick passed away shortly afterwards, and Vera, whose own health was deteriorating, made a new home in Queensland. I did not hear from her again until 1977, when she sent an airmail letter describing her surroundings. She said she was glad to see three wee folk appear and follow her and a friend round the garden, which consisted of flowers and of many trees bearing fruits such as bananas, cocoanuts, papaws, and mangoes. Two of the gnome-like little men were attired in strong greens and reds, and the third was in orange, and she found them very different from those in the south.

Writing generally on the subject, she said: "Many people must have experienced the seeing of wee folk but are afraid of being disbelieved. Truth can never be denied, nor should the delicate life and work of fairy and elf be spoiled by ignorance. This is not the only world they visit, for they have many journeys to do and their speed is not limited. They know and understand our language, and are conscious of our thoughts. It is a definite fact that no sphere of life is without them, and animals and birds are very aware of them. They are all part of God's spirit, and do far more for us than most people realise."

Miss V. Vesey

The following are accounts of some of the occasions when Miss M. Vesey, of Abergavenny, Monmouthshire, has been clearly aware of the presence of fairies. Her vivid descriptions of the scenery make one feel one is actually there with her.

"I was in the west of Ireland, in County Galway, in mid-August 1931. The weather had been wet and stormy, but had just changed. The day was very bright, with a light wind, and everything glittered. The fuchsia hedges were full of bees. In the early afternoon I walked inland by a road across the open country between the sea and the mountains. When the road was near to the mountains (it goes through a gap between them), it came under trees. There was a steep, high bank on the right, on which grew tall trees—some of them beeches, with moss, small plants and fallen leaves below them. On the left the ground went down steeply, covered with a tangle of trees and bushes, to a small river, which ran hidden. The trees arched over the road. The sunlight fell between the leaves in bright patches among shadows. I was aware of a tall fairy standing rather high up on the bank above the road, beside a tree. He was not looking at me but was looking out across the road towards the trees that grew down to the river. I remained there for some time. When I went on, I felt entirely happy and at peace, and extraordinarily light and untiring. I walked a long way. During the return, when I passed the same place, the later sunlight, more golden, came between the branches on the bank and on the tree's stem. It was warm and peaceful, but this time I was not aware of anyone there. All the way home, going and returning, and throughout that evening, I did not feel tired; and the happiness remained.

"Near a place in Wiltshire, where I lived for some time, a lane leads from a bridge over a small river, across low, flat ground, then curves uphill. One can turn off through a field to woods. By the lower, flat part of the lane are hedges and under them low banks covered with small plants, and in winter with fallen leaves, tall trees, chiefly ash, grow beside the lane. One day, on a cloudy, late afternoon, I was passing there, as I often did, and I became aware of several fairies, or elves, rather small, on the bank below the hedge at one side. They seemed friendly, and it was as if they smiled. On many other days or evenings during the years 1949 and 1950, I was aware of them. At first it was late summer; the trees and banks were deep green. Later, in autumn, the nearly bare hedges became dark and the leaves were fallen and brown. The presence of the elves made a secret, friendly feeling there.

"In Monmouthshire, near the Breconshire border, a path leads along the lower part of a rounded hill, and bends towards a small valley between this hill and the next. (These are foothills of a higher mountain, and from here the top of the mountain behind shows above the small valley's gap.) There are some small trees (elm, thorn, hazel) on the lower side of the path. One looks past these trees, south-westwards and west across a wide valley, and from here one can watch part of the sunset sky, or see the clouds travelling up with the southwest wind from beyond the farther mountains. Sometimes when I have passed this place, I have been strongly aware of a tall fairy standing beside these trees, which are just below the path. His back was to them and sometimes he had laid one hand on a branch. Sometimes he was looking towards me, and more often out over the slope below. When I first had this experience, it was an afternoon in late summer, but I have had it since at many different times of year: in mild, cloudy evenings in autumn, with a wind blowing along the wide valley beyond; and in very early spring, in the first mild days, with grey clouds moving slowly, the hillsides still grey, grey-brown, and the bare woods dark. The upper part of the rounded hill above the place mentioned in my previous account is partly covered by oak woods. I have sometimes felt the presence of fairies there. This was a more generalised yet a definite feeling that there were many of them. I have had this experience when looking into the wood from one side, rather high on the hill, in summer. Green bracken, not very tall, was growing under the green-leaved oaks; the afternoon sun shone gently in, here and there. Also I have felt many fairies there sometimes in autumn on a cloudy evening, when I was looking, from below, up at the edge of the wood; up the slope of bracken, which had died down, and dark gorse-bushes and grey-green turf; dry leaves clinging still to the oak-trees.

"In Monmouthshire, not very far from the scenes mentioned in the two previous accounts but in the flatter country a little way from the mountains, there is a small triangle of a wood at the point of a field. Along one side of this runs a large road; on another is a side road, which leaves the larger one at a sharp angle; at the third side spreads the field. As one walks along the large road, one sees into the wood; in some places there are very small paths leading away among the undergrowth.

"I was passing there one day and was aware of a fairy standing on one of the small paths. I had the impression he was two or three feet high. This experience was in the summer, 1952 or later, and all about where the fairy stood was green. On other days and at other seasons, I have sometimes been aware of the fairy people there, one of them being the same man fairy as at first, while some of the others seemed to be girl fairies. And once when I was sad, I felt their presence, and I became much happier, and reassured.

"In Surrey, near a London suburb, there is a brook with steep, high banks. Thorn trees grow thickly on both sides, and some larger trees, oaks, and others, in some places arching over the brook. Bushes grow all along the farther bank; on the nearer side, along which leads a path, they are in groups, with gaps between. One can see across, and can see the brook below, shadowed. When I was walking there in June, many years ago, I was aware of a fairy on the farther bank, among or behind the flowers of a hemlock-like plant that rose bright from light green sprays under the dark bushes, above the dark running brook. This was a lady fairy, and she seemed not very tall; about two feet high, I would say.

"One year I was in Switzerland, in the Canton de Vaud. It was summer, and I was walking along a zigzag road up a very steep mountain-side, above a place, which I knew well. The road in this part led between fir woods; the sunlight where it came through was very bright on the road; under the firs the shadows were very dark. During part of the way, above me on my right, there was a steep bank up to the fir trees. Some wild martagon lilies, of lilac-rose colour, grew at the edge of the trees above, partly in shadow and partly leaning out into the sunlight. I was aware of a fairy standing there, just within the trees. This was a man fairy. I think that he would have appeared to me as if slender, dark, and perhaps about four feet high."

Chapter 6: Fairies of Iona and Fairies Seen by Gypsies

Mrs. Pauline McKay, of Glasgow, described Iona as "an unforgettable little island vibrating with spiritual power and beauty." She had most of her fairy visions while visiting Iona, and any clear fairy or gnome forms which she had seen usually came when she was resting with her eyes shut. On one occasion, while in her favourite bay on the Isle, she saw the expanse of sand there and a little man sitting right in the centre with his knees drawn up to his chin. He was wearing a white, tight-fitting suit and a tall scarlet hat, which was rounded at the top like a mushroom, and all round him tiny bright lights were dancing. He was looking in the direction of the sea. Many of Mrs. McKay's experiences came to her before sleep, and the first was a vision of a tiny fairy with violet-coloured wings attached to a minute body. The effect was as though the little creature were made of violet-coloured light. I will quote the other entries as they were given to me, from her diary:

"January 3. 1953. I saw a large green and gold wing like that of an enormous butterfly. It had a pulsating and radiant quality and I felt it belonged to one of the lesser Devas.

"March 12. A cherubic face in the centre of a daffodil, with the corolla making a frame round it.

"July 6. A little elf-like figure, wearing a white suit and green cap, sitting on a toadstool and watching me intently.

"October 16. A fairy or small angelic form with very blonde hair and two small white wings.

"October 28. A large fairy form all made of light, wearing a little Juliet cap. She shone with a star-like effect.

"November 6. An elf with very large ears.

"December 9. A small fairy form in the centre of a brilliant flash of light.

"December 14. A fairy with a light band round her head, a star above her brow, and smaller stars encircling the band. Also gnomes sliding down things shaped like ? [Apparently MJ could not read the words here; she placed a question mark.] I could see their little homes, resembling apples with apertures cut in them, and tiny windows.

"January 22, 1954. I saw light whirling and cherubic forms drawn into it, shaping the mass of light into small clouds.

"April 25. A Devic-looking Being in intense coloured light—a small sweet face beneath a head-dress of shining threads of light, which vibrated continually. A halo of spring green and sunset pink all round the face and headdress.

"April 30, 1955. A pixie wearing a pointed hat, sitting on the steps outside a closed house-door. He was dressed all in green.

"November 13. A tiny man standing on the bench in our garden shed. Very large eyes. Dressed like a human. Head and face very large in comparison to body."

In August 1956, Mrs. McKay wrote to me from Iona: "The little folk abound here, no matter where one looks they flash by in great numbers." Later she told me: "If I am allowed to sit quietly, long enough to stare at one group of them, their vibration seemed [sic] to become slower and they would glide and swoop rather than flash by. They never took form though, but remained as points of intense light. Occasionally a soft pink glow would appear among them, as though a member of a higher order of beings was trying to manifest." In August 1957, the weather was wet and misty while Mrs. McKay was staying on Iona, but she said, "The mist has its compensations though, for apart from the feeling of remoteness it brings, the Little Folk seem to shine more clearly against a pearl-grey background... In no previous year have they been so abundant... Everywhere I turn my eyes I see bright little lights hovering, leaping or flying, and small clouds of soft colour, mostly pink and yellow or gold."

Another contributor, Mrs. Ellen Hilton, was also able to see the wonderful fairy lights on Iona.

Miss Margaret Tait of South Shields, County Durham, had already visited the island for a day with a party of other tourists, but their chatter "struck a discord" and, feeling strangely attracted and attuned to the sacred atmosphere of the place, she longed to return there alone on some future occasion. This she was able to do in the 1920s, and she set out across the machair to visit the Atlantic side of the island. The sky was blue, the air was warm, and there was a breeze playing around. As she sauntered along, she rejoiced in her freedom, the quietude, the beauty of the little iridescent pools of water among the green grass, the feeling of space around, and a sense of being cared for, as though a beneficent being was shower-ing blessings on her. She reached the shore—to her right, white-sanded with pulverized little white shells; to her left, rocky. She stood at the water's edge among the rocks until the fresh sea-air soaked into her and the rhythm of the waves bemused her. Then, turning, she wandered up and down the stony beach looking for anything of interest among the greenish-brown, rocky debris. After picking up a lovely specimen of a "mermaid's purse" tinted in rich olive-green, she began thinking of lunch, and stepped back on to the green sward, still looking down. She had not gone many steps when she saw gazing shyly up at her a little fairy not more than ten inches high, with a broad forehead, brown eyes, and a pointed chin. Her dress, of a soft pink silk-like substance, hung in folds to the ground, where it appeared to be caught. Miss Tait smiled at her and said softly and playfully, "What! You here?" The fairy kept her eyes on her and smiled back very demurely. Delighted with her "find," Miss Tait straightened up and looked around but could see nobody. When she directed her gaze downwards again, the fairy had vanished. Later, she bought a guidebook and discovered that the spot where she saw the fairy was only a little distance from the Sithean Mor, or Great Fairy Mound, of which she had not heard until then. This mound was formerly known as Cnoc an Angael (Hill of the Angels), the traditional site of St. Columba's tryst with the angels. The author and folklorist Alasdair Alpin MacGregor said there were natives and visitors alike who swore to having heard fairy music issuing from that mound: and the Yorkshire writer and poet Dorothy Una Ratcliffe also informed me that the Fairy Piper had been heard by many people on Iona.

I cannot mention Iona without referring to the Lordly Ones, otherwise known as the Sidhe (Shee), or Tuatha de Danann who dwell in the hills. They are a radiant, God-like race, eternally young, and Miss Lucy H. M. Bruce, a well-known folklorist on Iona, believed that they belong to an earlier world period than ours, and are not, properly speaking, sylphs, as their bodies are not formed of one element only. "How beautiful they are, the Lordly Ones," wrote Fiona MacLeod (William Sharp) in his well-known Fairy Song set to music by Rutland Boughton in *The Immortal Hour.* George Russell (AE) told in his book *The Candle of Vision* (Macmillan & Co. Ltd, London, 1920) how one of the Lordly Ones passed over him as he lay on the sand dunes by the Western sea. First he heard music, and then he saw this flowing figure pervaded with light as if sunfire ran through its limbs. Over its brows was a fiery plumage like wings of flame, and on its face was an ecstasy of beauty and immortal youth.

In 1941, there was held at the Scottish National Gallery an exhibition of paintings, including those of fairies and other little etheric creatures, by the distinguished Edinburgh artist John Duncan, R.S.A., who for nearly 40 years was a member of the Theosophical Society. Charles Richard Gammen, F.R.S.A., said in a letter in 1952: "I knew Duncan very well. He was, perhaps, the only mystic painter Scotland ever had, the Scottish Blake. He was also a poet, a scholar, a man of singularly gentle and wise spirit, and a close friend of Fiona MacLeod during that poet's last years. The faerie folk Duncan saw in the islands were not only the Little People but the Lordly Ones." Alasdair Alpin MacGregor, who also knew John Duncan, told me that the painter first went to Iona for a brief holiday but stayed for months, coming more and more under the enchantment of that sacred Isle. While walking alone one day, he had noticed two figures — tall and of strange aspect, descending a hillock in his direction. Their feet did not bend the thick heather over which they walked, and they made no sound as they passed close to him and then "faded out." From that moment he knew that he was fey. Subsequently he saw other members of the Sidhe on Iona, and always obliquely (out of the corner of his eye). "He had so much experience of Faerie and the Lordly Ones there," said Alasdair, "that he found himself losing touch entirely with the earth and his own earthly existence. So, in the end, he thought it wiser to tear himself away from that mystical, haunted Isle."

In the springtime, the Lordly Ones have been glimpsed by Mrs. Nancy Norris: in 1939, in beech-wood clearings in Chiltern Hills districts; near the Tor at Glastonbury in 1939 and 1940; in woods at Clyffe Pypard (six miles from Avebury) from 1941 at intervals until 1945; and at Holford Glen, Quantock Hills, in 1954. "I have to say 'glimpsed' when I see these Lordly Ones," she explained. "They don't remain long. To me, in appearance they are as made of shining gold-white light. They are very tall and have elongated faces, hands, and limbs. They are quite impersonal, but they bring with them a sensation of tingling excitement. In fact, for a moment one experiences a breathtaking realisation of a lifeforce lived on another plane. Even as I write these words, I have that faintly tingling sensation up and down my spine. I don't think it is very difficult for me to contact them. I'm possessed of a quite unfailing energy, the kind that one associates with the Lordly Ones—and I can go on and on without food or sleep… I'm usually surrounded by children, who seem to think I'm their age. I seem to have a magnetic power over animals. Also I have green fingers. Apart from these things, I'm an ordinary, intelligent, practical, normal person. But I must admit that at times I feel as if I had possibly strayed into a sphere of manifestation to which I do not rightly belong… My maternal great-grandfather was Capt. Marryat, R.N., of *Peter Simple* fame, and Florence Marryat was my great-aunt. Both had recognised psychic faculties, which I have no doubt inherited."

Sometimes the Lordly Ones assume strange shapes, and Mrs. Norah Hanbury-Kelk saw them in another guise in 1907, when she was picnicking with a party of friends on a hill above one of the lakes at Glendalough, County Wicklow. She was eighteen at the time, and although partly Irish she had never been in Ireland before. The party was very gay and noisy, and she said she was in anything but a mystical state of mind when she saw, moving along the road by the side of the lake, what appeared to be columns of dust about three feet in height, and in motion they seemed to take on a spiral shape. She admitted she was rather puzzled when she came on to the road and found it was not at all dusty, but even then she did not realize she had witnessed anything supernatural. Not, that is, until later, when her cousin, unknown to her, wrote about her experience to W. B. Yeats, and he was very interested and replied that she had certainly seen the Sidhe. "I knew nothing of the fairies of Ireland," she asserts, "and had never heard of the Sidhe. I think I have seen them again, in Galway, but the experience was not nearly as vivid as on the occasion at Glendalough."

Fairies Seen by Gypsies

In the old days, when the nomadic Gypsies slept in primitive tents in wild, unspoilt surroundings, their close contact with Nature and with the magnetic currents of the earth developed in them an independent form of clairvoyance. They took the Little People for granted, but were reluctant to speak of them in case it brought them ill luck. According to Smart & Crofton's *Dialect of the English Gypsies* (Asher & Co., London, 1875), the "deep Romanes contained no word for 'fairies,' so the Gypsies coined the phrase 'Mi-Dooveleski-bitta-folki' which meant 'My God's Little People.'" The old clairvoyance still lingers in some of the descendants of the true Gypsies, and here is an account of fairies, which my contributor, Miss Doris G. Stephens, of South Wales, obtained from a Romany friend. It was printed as a letter in Vol. 24 (Third Series) of *The Journal of the Gypsy Lore Society* (Liverpool University), and I received permission to quote it in full:

"Caroline Petersen (nee Price) is a South Welsh Gypsy whose mind is full of strange fancies, so that one never knows what may be lurking in it. But the two following experiences she related to me on different occasions seem worthy of record, and she herself firmly believed they actually happened.

"At the time of the first incident she was living in a wooden out in a quiet lane not far from a Roman camp, about two miles from Carmarthen. We were standing outside the hut one day, when suddenly she asked me: 'Do you see that tree, Miss?'—pointing to an old May tree full of blossom shaking eerily in the wind, with its black branches standing out against the sky. 'I have often seen the fairies swinging in it. They sway up and down in the branches. I can see them from the window when I am watching for my husband to come home from his work.' The next time I visited her, I asked if she had seen the fairies again. 'Yes indeed, I did see them only last night. They came right into our hair (house) this time and were all over our little kitchen.'

"'Do tell me about them,' I said.

"'Well, they were like tiny men and women, no bigger than dolls. The men had tiny peaked caps, little belted jackets, pointed shoes and long stockings up to their waists. The women had hats like old Welsh ones and long skirts and cloaks. The men climbed up on the mantelpiece and up and down the curtains. They sat beside my teapot and peered into everything. And most of the women sat on the floor by the fire and warmed themselves. Oh, but they were pretty! I wish you could have seen them! All colours their clothes were. I believe they were just going to begin dancing in the firelight, when I heard Petersen opening the door, and, in a flash, they all disappeared.'"

Another Welsh Gypsy who saw fairies was Rosie Griffiths, daughter of Rosaina and Theophilus Griffiths, and granddaughter of Benjamin and Caroline Wood. Her account, taken down by Miss Dora E. Yates of Liverpool University was, like Caroline Petersen's account, printed in *The Journal of the Gypsy Lore Society*. Before then, it had been published in *The Children's Microcosm* (circa 1931) edited by Dorothy Una Ratcliffe. Permission for me to use it was given in both cases.

Rosie Griffiths recounted that when she was seven or eight she was camping with her parents and brothers in an old green lane in the middle of Wales. One evening, "when the sun was getting low and slanting all golden through the grass," she was lying on her face under a big oak-tree, kicking her heels in the air and "thinking of nothing at all." The others were all up at the tents, so she was by herself and feeling very lonesome. Suddenly she began to hear the most wonderful music, which she described as being "like as if you was in Heaven." At first she could not find the source of it, but when she pressed her ear to the ground the music seemed to come out of the earth. She looked up, and there in front of her, in a ring round the old oak tree, were scores of tiny fairies dressed in cherry-red jackets and breeches, playing ball. Their heads were just peeping above the grass, and the ball, which they were tossing to one another, was no bigger than a pea. They danced around her, and she rubbed her eyes, thinking it was a dream. Her mother had often told her about the Little People, but Rosie could not believe she would ever see them with her own eyes. Then, just as suddenly as they came, they all went from her sight, and she began to weep. After a while, when she was taking a quiet rest, they were there again, but there was no music of any sort this time, and the next moment they were gone. The following morning there was a bright green ring round the oak tree, and Rosie lay there again, thinking she would have the same pleasure of seeing her little friends. "But there was no fairies and no fairy music ever again," she said, "and I was lost of my dear little joy." She kept searching around the oak tree where they had played, and "suddenly" she came upon "a tremendous large penny." (Pennies dated *circa* 1807 were very big and heavy.) Running quickly to her mother, she showed it to her.

"Wherever did you get this penny from, child," she asked.

Instead of just saying she had found it under a tree, Rosie answered in detail: "I found it under the old oak-tree where the fairies danced."

"Oh, you foolish, foolish girl to have told your luck. There was many more pennies to be had where that came from. It was your luck, and now it won't be your luck no more, 'cos you couldn't keep your silly little tongue still!"

Her mother was wild that she had talked, and sure enough when Rosie went back that night to look for the fairy ring, there was nothing to be seen. "That same night," she concluded, "one of my little brothers was took ill, and we had to break up camp and hurry off in the morning. And though we com'd back to Wales time after time with our van, search how we might, we never found that lane with that dear old oak-tree again."

In his autobiography *The Book of Boswell: The Story of a Gypsy Man* (Gollancz, London), Silvester Gordon Boswell mentioned that he and his sisters and younger brother, and also many other Gypsy children, saw and played frequently with the fairies on some sandhills at the back of the tents and wagons on South Shore, Blackpool; and always when the Boswell family returned their after their travels, the children would be off to see the fairies, and would find them in the same place.

Chapter 7: The *John O'London's Weekly* Letters

I am glad to be able to quote the following letters, which were published in 1936 and 1948 in that long-since defunct and sadly-missed literary journal *John O'London's Weekly*, as it was instrumental in starting me on my colourful quest for true accounts of fairies. At that time, I had only one other cutting, a magazine article by Alasdair Alpin MacGregor, who was to come into my life much later.

With the editor's help, I was put in touch with some of the writers of the letters, and am pleased to acknowledge the years of valuable help and friendly correspondence that I received from Mr. J. H. Graigon, Miss Doris G. Stephens, Mr. I. W. Beer and his wife, and also from Miss Edith Sparvel-Bayly who had written the original letter to the said weekly paper inviting readers to send in their fairy experiences. Mr. Struan Robertson had died the year following the publication of his letter, but his widow wrote to tell me that "he could keep an audience of 4,000 spellbound, listening to his strange experiences of 'faerie' and 'the Sight.'"

For the purpose of this book, slight revisions have been made by some of these correspondents, including myself, to clarify, delete superfluous lines, or add more details to the accounts where necessary.

Letter dated 7 March 1936: "Can any of your readers give first-hand accounts of fairies seen in this country? There seem to be many who do see them, but who are chary of relating their experiences. In this part of Wales some queer things happen occasionally. An elderly woman was walking home one moonlit night in February when she saw what she thought were big brown moths flying over the meadow by the road. She stood still, peeped through the hedge, and watched a number of small brown men settling themselves round a large stone. Seated on it was a fairy lady dressed in white, who talked to them in Welsh about many things, which they seemed glad to hear.

Then she told them that they would not be able to use the meadow much longer, for a rich man would buy it and build a house there, and keep a carriage to run the roads without horses. There was then no lead of such a thing in the village, but in the course of a year all this came to pass, for a wealthy retired milk-dealer from London had a house built in the meadow, and drove his car up and down the hills. This is a first-hand account. In the small place in which I live was a respected tradesman who confessed that he himself had seen an odd thing. He had been to a village and was returning home after dark. His way lay through a wood, but it was not until he came out on to the road near some houses that he heard a skipping noise beside him and saw a creature with a round body high up on two long legs. It went hopping in front of him into a street, and then with a leap and a bound it was off and away over some high iron gates into the grounds of a college." — E. Sparvel-Bayly, Wales.

Letter dated 23 July 1948: "A local clergyman, the Rev. Edwards, told me that his uncle, a farmer, was walking with another man beside a river one evening when they observed a strange light on the other bank. On approaching this, both of them saw a crowd of tiny people dancing, clad in gay and beautiful colours like flowers. The friend was scared and ran away, but the farmer felt entranced by the lovely scene and stood watching for some time till the light suddenly vanished with the dancing beings. His nephew, the clergyman, was interested to learn that early one morning, on the hillside above the farm, the same kind of scene had been observed by his grandmother when a young girl." — E. Sparvel-Bayly, Wales.

In a letter sent direct to me in the 1940s, Miss E. Sparvel-Bayly said that she'd had a young friend named Maureen Jones, who had always been interested in fairies and used to make feasts for them when she was a small child. One day she went with her mother to a wood and was playing round an old oak tree when suddenly she ran up to her mother, beaming with delight. "Oh Mother: I've seen a fairy," she exclaimed, and she told her that a tiny lady in white, very pretty, had come out of a hole in the base of the oak and smiled at her.

Letter dated 21 March 1936: "A few years ago, on the Cornish-

Devonian border, I was surprised to see on the cliff above me the figure of a tiny man, dressed in black, strutting round in a rather vain-looking way. So incredulous was I of the existence of the 'pisky' people that I said to myself, 'In a minute I shall see what he really is—a bird, or a shadow.' But no, he went on being a tiny man—until he changed into a quite indescribable thing (are not the piskies' Irish cousins known as the 'shape-changers'?); something with the appearance of a long, furry black roll, which gambolled about on the grass and then disappeared. A few minutes later, however, two more little shapes became visible—slightly longer and much rounder than the first pisky-man. They were sitting one on either side of a gorse bush, making movements similar to those made in sawing with a two-handled saw. Curiosity impelled closer investigation, but the shortcut I took up the cliff ended in unclimbable steepness and rubble, and I was obliged to return to the shore. By the time I had reached the gorse bush by the usual path the pisky sawers were gone. Nothing except a form of air, though, would have sat on air as the sawer on the sea side must have been doing—for the bush hung some inches over the cliff-edge." — Joyce Chadwick, London, W.1.

Letter dated 28 March 1936: "Let me briefly describe four experiences. The first fairy I met was alone upon a hillside near Aberfoyle, where Robert Kirk wrote his *Commonwealth of Fairies*. She was very friendly, beckoned me to follow her, and eventually showed me the most wonderful of sights. One afternoon in Arran, I saw ten fairies playing out and in among gorse bushes and round about the grazing sheep. The sheep were quite undisturbed except that if a fairy went too near one of them it would trot off for a few yards. Wandering in a wood in Arran one morning, I heard the silvery, plangent accents of fairies, and following the sounds I saw quite a clan of them hurrying along a green footpath. They seemed very angry about something. Observing me, they chatted loudly, scattered as one sees a flock of excited sparrows scattering, increased their speed and fled. Tramping near Loch Rannoch, I was attracted by tuneful tones coming from clumps of rhododendrons, and advancing cautiously beheld the most beautiful dancing: I was too interested to count the number of fairies, concentrating upon how close I could get. When I was within ten paces of them, one sighted me, and alarming the dancers she shepherded them in among the bushes. I shall never forget the glance she gave me as she disappeared, and the gesture: the grace of her exit, I have seen approached only by the incomparable Pavlova herself." — Struan Robertson, Stirlingshire

Letter dated 4 April 1936: "Most of the stories of 'piskies' or little people recently published seem to emanate from the South or West Country, but here is a first-hand account of one of them seen quite lately in more matter-of-fact Hertfordshire. I was driving a car through a quiet country lane, and my thoughts at the time were solely on the car's performance. Rounding a bend in the road, where the hedge and trees had been cut down to the ground, I was suddenly surprised to see a little round-faced fellow wearing a pointed cap, the peak of which fell over the side, nightcap fashion. He was sitting on a tree stump and looking straight across the road in front of him. Standing, I judged he would be nearly a foot and a half high, but he was gone in an instant, and though I slowed down at once I did not get the chance to have a closer look at him. The sight made a vivid impression on me, and is not likely to be easily forgotten." — I. W. Beer, Herts

Letter dated 11 April 1936: "During the War we lived in the heart of the Welsh countryside, four miles from a town, and one afternoon in June, at the time of the hay harvest, the following incident occurred. My mother and I were sitting in the garden with two maids. Suddenly she pointed to a neighbouring field in which the hay had only just been cut. 'How very early the farmer and his workers have started making the hay,' she said. 'It cannot have had time to dry.' I looked in the direction she indicated, and I could see lines of figures going backwards and forwards, apparently busy raking the hay. We called the two maids, who also noticed the lines of figures. That evening we met the farmer and asked him why the raking in that particular meadow had been started so early. He said we must be mistaken. He had walked past the field that afternoon, and there was no one there at all! It seemed as if we had witnessed a kind of psychic phenomenon. From the earliest times fairies have been said to show a fondness for copying the work of human beings, and quite possibly it was some of these creatures we had seen." — Doris G. Stephens, S. Wales

Letter dated 2 May 1936: "I had read with amusement the descriptions of fairies given by your various correspondents. They entertained me, but left me unconvinced. That was my reaction, until... I was sitting alone one night, writing. It was late; everybody else had gone to bed. With a flourish I turned over a page. The draught it created blew a paper (a laundry bill, incidentally) off the table to the floor. I saw it flutter down, and went on writing. (I was not going to let a laundry bill interrupt my romantic cogitations.) Some two minutes later I rattled through another page, having entirely forgotten the paltry bill at my feet. It was with mild astonishment, then, that when I turned the next page I beheld the same bill fluttering floorwards again. I concluded that my first experience was pure imagination, but when the same thing happened the third time. I bounded up and searched for the invisible person playing the trick on me. Then I went down on my hands and knees to see how many bills had conglomerated on the floor. I found only a solitary one, the laundry bill. I picked it up, secured it to the table, sat down, and tried to collect my startled wits. It was a failure, and so I went to bed in a daze. But until I fell asleep, I seemed to sense the presence of somebody else in that room. Who or what was it?" — Kenneth A. James, Sydney

This brings me to my own letter dated 28 March 1936, in which I described a green wood-elf. As there may be some readers of this book who saw those early letters and have perhaps kept the cuttings, I would like to take this opportunity to explain that I purposely omitted to mention that my elder sister, too, had seen the elf, because she was very reserved and dreaded any resulting sensational publicity and visits from reporters, etc. Later, both of us realised that by not including her as a witness, the experience was robbed of much of its authenticity, as there was no proof that it was not just a childish dream of mine, so I have amended the account accordingly:

"The house in which I was born was surrounded by a lovely garden with a small orchard, and was near fields and woods in a lonely part of Nottingham. It was there, when I was six years old, that I had an experience I shall never forget. Just beneath my bedroom window was a small lawn, and growing against the house wall was a cream rambler rose known as Alberic Barbier, which reached right up to the open window. I was lying in bed enjoying the early-morning sunshine, which streamed into the room, when suddenly I felt impelled to sit up and turn my eyes to the empty firegrate. There, on a filmy cobweb, which was stretched like a hammock across the iron bar, sat a quaint little creature from four to six inches in height. Its body was like shiny green jelly surrounded by an aura of green light, and on its head a red, pointed cap of the same protoplasmic substance. Its mouth was devoid of teeth or gums, and its eyes had no pupils. It seemed quite unafraid, and, from the broad grin on its face, appeared to enjoy my observation. At first, I just kept still and stared, and it gazed back at me with a blank expression, which showed very little intelligence, yet its eyes had a strange, mesmeric, effect on me. I nudged my sleeping sister, Dorothy, who was nine years older than I, and she sat up in bed and saw it too. Soon I had to satisfy my childish curiosity by climbing out of bed, but when I drew closer than a foot to the elf it seemed to lose its equilibrium and immediately quivered away. I clambered back into bed, and when I turned round it was perched in the same place. This developed into an exciting game, and the elf's disappearance and reappearance continued until I foolishly brushed away the cobweb to see what the little creature would do next. Needless to say, I was soon full of remorse at what I had done, for we never saw the nature sprite again."

Many years later I was to read in Geoffrey Hodson's before-mentioned book of his personal observations on *The Fairies at Work and at Play* that elves differ from other nature spirits chiefly in that they do not appear to be clothed in any reproduction of human attire, and that their bodily constitution seems to consist of one solid mass of gelatinous substance, entirely without interior organization.

The tiny elf in the bedroom of my previous house was not the first nature spirit that my sister and I had seen with physical-etheric vision. Years later, after I had started compiling this book and was discussing it with a cousin who used to play with me, she said, "You saw other fairies before the elf!" Then I met an old friend of the family, who confirmed that when I was "a toddler" I used to babble to her about the pretty colours of the fairies, which I'd seen among the flowers. Unfortunately I have not retained any memory of them and must have taken them for granted, though I do remember talking to the flowers, birds, and trees, and seeing everything through eyes of wonder. It was also not until many years later that my sister told (after she thought she was safe from the reporters who had visited me!) that a fairy had appeared in front of her in the old orchard when she was a small child and I was not yet born. It stood smiling at her—a dainty little fairy dress with silvery wings. It had a pretty coronet on its head, and in its hand was a wand with a tiny, twinkling star on top. My sister said she was so thrilled that she ran up the garden path to fetch Mother, who hurried back with her, but of course, by then, as usually happens, the little creature had disappeared. But Mother knew from Dorothy's joy and excitement that she was telling the truth. We were very lucky in having wise parents who never scoffed at us or crushed our excited outpourings, but always found time to listen understandingly to what we had to say.

The addresses of the following contributors to *John O'London's Weekly* could not be traced, as many records were lost during the bombing of London in the Second World War, but the editor kindly gave me permission to use these letters on condition that I put the correspondents' initials instead of their full names.

Letter dated 5 April 1936: "During the last summer of 1934, I stayed at the [name withheld] Hotel in Large, Ayrshire. One very hot afternoon, about 4 o'clock, I was walking in the grounds with a Kilmarnock lady, a resident, when she drew my attention to a large flowering shrub over twelve feet high. At a distance we could see small forms whirling around the blooms, and on closer inspection we saw that a host of fairy forms were at play. I was so astonished that I foolishly went to the large shrub, shook the lower branches, and stepped back to see if the forms were still there. They were, but soon disappeared among the blooms, and we did not see them again. We mentioned it to the manager who said that another resident had seen fairies in the grounds. He had suspected that his informant was 'soft in the head' and had paid no attention to the story. I consider myself hardheaded, but I did see things that afternoon. It was the first time such an experience had befallen me, and until that moment I should have laughed at anyone who maintained that fairies are real beings." — J.K.

Letter dated 11 April 1936: "When I was a boy of ten, we lived in Lanarkshire beside a large park with trees and flowers. At early dawn one morning I awoke to see on a chair, which always stood beside my bed, two small old women of about eighteen inches tall. Each wore tall, conical dark hats, and dark long gowns. They looked at me for about twenty seconds and then smiled at each other before jumping in slow motion to the carpeted floor, where they passed from my line of sight. Very gently I eased myself up into a sitting position, so as not to scare them, but they had disappeared. I got out of bed, peered under all the furniture and into the cupboard, but could find no trace of them. The moon was full, and red streaks showed in the sky. They were solid beings: I noted that their busts stood out clearly against the window across the room. It all happened 40 years ago, but it has never gone from my mind. They seemed to appraise me as a horse dealer might do a horse. There was really no affection in their eyes, and the feeling I had then was that I should have liked to catch them in my hand, like birds." — W.J.F.

Letter dated 16 May 1936: "In 1916 I was staying at a cottage in Cookham Dean, Berkshire, and one afternoon took a basket in order to gather blackberries on a common some distance away. The blackberries were fairly plentiful but small, when I suddenly noticed some particularly fine ones growing on a bush, which stood quite by itself. I was tugging at some rather out of reach, when the whole bush seemed to shiver, the sprays parted, and from out the centre of the bush parted a lean, brown man, dressed in brown with pointed cap and straggly beard. He was solid as far as the waist, but his legs were transparent and shadowy. He slid away like lightning and entirely disappeared. I regret to say that I was so surprised and startled that I dropped my basket, took to my heels, and ran all the way home. I do not doubt that he was the 'fairy' of the bush. I have never had the good luck to see another." — N. V. M.

Letter dated 23 May 1936: "I have followed with keen interest your letters from various readers who have seen fairies. Of course there are fairies, only one is rather backward in telling of them. As a little girl of six or seven, I would never tread upon daisies—because it was in a daisy field I saw my first fairies. There were usually seven or eight together, dancing in circles about three feet from the ground. They had long pointed caps, thin bodies tapering off to very pointed feet. I remember their puckish grins and seem to remember them as being dressed in brown. Then, just before I reached my teens, on many occasions I kept tryst with a lovely fairy in a bower of wild roses near my home. Looking back now it seems I was always aware of this fairy in that leafy nook. She was usually a few feet from the ground, in shining pink raiment, with long golden tresses, and always in a pink aura. The fairy never stayed long in my presence, but it seemed quite natural to me that she should be there." — I. H.

Letter dated 6 June 1936: "In August, 1931, several fairies—females without wings, wearing some sort of flimsy transparent gowns—were seen by myself and my eldest daughter on eight occasions among the flowering shrubs at the bottom of our garden in Warwickshire, which was bounded by a brook. I saw the same little lady on three separate days, as she wore a pink gown, while the others wore bluish ones. She was so shy that she only peeped at me around a bush, and disappeared when I was about ten paces off. She was not afraid, I thought, so much as anxious to avoid close intimacy with mere humans. They were about a foot-and-a-half high, and looked like 'sweet seventeens' reduced in height, but they were simply lovely in face, form, and movement. I cannot get their loveliness out of my mind." — H.G.

There was, of course, the usual letter from a sceptic, and this one, while not doubting our sincerity, suggested that we may have been "the innocent victims of a trick of the brain!" Needless to say, the writer of this letter hadn't the courage to put his or her name.

Chapter 8: The Gnomes of Wollaton Park and Fairies as Imitators

On 23 September 1979, several children between the ages of eight and ten were playing together in the grounds of Wollaton Hall—an Elizabethan Mansion in Nottingham—when out of the bushes came a number of merry-faced, bearded little men in small cars—two in each car. The children who shared this experience were Angela, her sister Julie and brother Glen; Andrew and his sister Rosie; and Patrick. They were pupils of a primary school, and their head-teacher very kindly sent me a tape of his separate interviews with three of the children, Angela, Patrick, and Andrew, which he had recorded two days after the sighting. In his covering letter he said: "I think the tape reveals the wide measure of corroboration between the children, as well as the fluency with which they were able to describe the events. I remain sceptical as to the explanation of what they saw, but I am also convinced that the children were describing a real occurrence." As these three recordings follow the same pattern of questioning, they are not here set out verbatim, but the story is as follows:

The three girls and three boys were playing near a swampy part of the grounds at dusk, when Andrew said, "Look at the little men." Julie replied, "Don't be stupid," but then about thirty cars came out of the bushes and through a little gate, one after another, and Julie said "You're right" and apologized to Andrew. The little men in the cars began to chase them, though not, as it turned out, with any intention of harming them. Naturally, the appearance of these gnome-like creatures in such large numbers created some fear and confusion. Angela said her brother Glen was crying because he was "scared," and Patrick said that Andrew fell over a log as he was running away and went head-first into the swampy ground. When asked afterwards how the cars crossed the logs, which lay over the swamp, he said they just leapt over them, and although there were at least thirty cars there was no sound of engines. They seemed to be of simple construction and of various colours. Angela saw red and white cars; Andrew saw green and blue ones, and said they had "a thing they could turn round, with a handle on it." Patrick saw them in red and other shades, and he said they had triangular lights on them, and bells in place of motor horns. While he was looking at them, ten of the little men got out and walked. Although the cars had been driven close to the children, at no time had they actually touched them. Angela mentioned that she had returned to the same spot in daylight but had found no trace of car wheels on the swampy ground.

The account of these cars may tax the credulity of some readers, but nature spirits have the power to visualize and create out of universal thought-substance a simple etheric imitation of anything that takes their fancy, and the gnomes may have seen small children trundling along in toy cars, and may also have witnessed the car rallies, which are held from time to time in Wollaton Park. To the schoolchildren, the little men's cars would seem solid (materialized), but they could have vanished like puffs of smoke if the gnomes had turned their attention to something else. Both Angela and Patrick said the long beards of the gnomes were white, with red at the tips, whereas to Andrew they looked black. There may be a simple optical explanation for this, but fairy visions are often coloured by something in the seer's own personality, and even two or more of the best seers, when sharing a psychic or occult experience, have been known to differ widely when trying to describe the details.

Angela, who thought the little men were "similar to a dwarf" in type, recorded that they were dressed in "yellow tights with blue thin tops," and each of them wore a cap with "a big bobble" at the end. Patrick, in his statement, said their hats were green "with red pom-poms," and he confirmed that their trousers were yellow and their tops blue. Andrew, when asked what he thought the little men were, replied "Gnomes, or summat," and said there was "something green" on them. When asked to describe the shape of their headgear, he said it was "like the night caps people wore in olden days when they went to bed," and he was reminded of "Noddy." He agreed their tops were blue, and he thought their trousers had yellow patches. He mentioned that he had seen other little men in the bushes within the wired fence; in holes in the tree-trunks; and also up in the trees. (Angela and Patrick omitted to confirm in their tape recording that they, also, had seen these beings up in the trees, but they had mentioned this earlier, to a reporter.) When Andrew was asked why he could see the gnomes' faces so clearly in the dusk, he said there was "a light hanging in the trees" where the gnomes were. When asked what sort of a light, he hesitated and then said: "An ordinary light because when we looked up there was a light." This seems very improbable unless it was a streetlight shining through the trees, for the children admitted that it was a fenced-off area, which they had managed to enter by crawling through a gap. When Patrick was asked a similar question about the gnomes, which he saw on the ground, he said he thought it was their bright clothing, which enabled him to see them so plainly. "I could see 'em in the dark—they showed up," he told the head-teacher. Both of these boys had tried to give a practical explanation for something they did not fully understand. Neither of them knew that the materialized bodies of nature spirits are self-luminous, and this may also account for the light in the trees, which Andrew mentioned earlier.

When the children were leaving the park, they were chased round the gate, so they started to climb over it. Then, on finding it was still unlocked, they ran through the gateway as fast as they could, and the gnomes went back in the bushes inside the wired fence. They had made no attempt to follow the children, and Angela said this was because they did not like the streetlights outside. (That being so, the gnomes would surely not have been in a tree where an "ordinary light" was hanging.)

There was some difference of opinion over the time the children had entered and left the park, but Angela and Patrick thought that during the period of their stay the gnomes had played with them for about a quarter of an hour. They said they had glimpsed them before, during the school holidays, but on that occasion the little men, on seeing them, had gone back into the bushes. Andrew had heard the sound of bells, which proved on the second occasion to be the car bells. There was complete agreement that the gnomes — which Patrick said were up to his waist in height and Angela said were half her size — had old, wrinkled faces; were very friendly and happy ("joyful" was the word Angela used); and they laughed a lot while they were playing. None of the children heard them speak, but Patrick said some of the gnomes appeared to be "shouting" to others who had gone too far, though no sounds were audible.

Needless to say, this weird occurrence attracted the attention of the press, and many people flocked to the area in the hope of catching a glimpse of the fairy men. Unfortunately such an intrusion creates the wrong atmosphere and drives nature spirits deeper into their own element. One of my contributors, Mrs. I. W. Ratsey, said in her book *Pioneering* (Universal World Harmony), that the ray of curiosity is a cold ray and therefore repelling to the little people, so they hide away from it because it makes them feel uneasy and they do not understand it.

Fantastic though the children's story must have sounded to their disbelieving parents, there are several features that stamp it as genuine and, considering the following two accounts of experiences that took place before this adventure, I think there is a large, and possibly ancient, tribe of gnomes in Wollaton Park. Perhaps, in between their valuable work with nature, they live in a world of glamour, acting-out among themselves the numerous exciting and colourful events that take place in other parts of the grounds, especially during the Nottingham Festival.

Prior to the schoolchildren's adventure, Mrs. Jean E. Dixon, then of Nottingham, had an equally unusual experience in Wollaton Park. She was walking there alone, in a pensive mood, when she became aware of the presence of gnomes, who seemed eager to show her some of the various scenes and objects that delighted them. Simple and commonplace though some of these things may seem, the gnomes helped her to see them in an entrancing new light. She knew that in order to be in tune with the nature spirits she had to keep very quiet and listen carefully "inside herself" while they told her which way to go, and when to stop and look. She said afterwards that at each stopping-place she had found a feather, as if the gnomes had laid a treasure-hunt trail for her to follow.

First of all, they took her to a lovely spot where she was bidden to look into a wood. There she saw a sea of green fern waving in the breeze, and she said it was "the greenest green" she had ever seen. The gnomes must have been very proud of this vista, for the woodland ferns and the roots of all plants are under their special care. Rudolf Steiner, the founder of the Anthroposophical Society, rightly called these little earth-folk "the spiritual midwives of plant reproduction," and the green that these gnomes wished their human friend to absorb is the basic colour of Nature—peaceful, soothing, and refreshing. Corinne Heline, in her booklet *Healing and Regeneration through Colour* (J. F. Rowny Press, Santa Barbara, California), said that in the radiations of this magic green light the fairies perform their enchantments over field and forest. Mrs. Dixon was being led onward, and this time she thought the nature spirits were teasing her. ("They are good at this!" she said.) But no, there was a slight movement and as she watched she saw a little fawn. It raised its head and stood up, showing her its beautiful body, "all pink and beigy," and then she saw another and another, and yet more, until the wood seemed full of these lovely creatures—some lying down, some sitting, others just moving around. Next, her attention was drawn to a dead tree-trunk. She wondered what they expected her to see there for it was all rotting, yet she found three silvery spiders' webs, each differing in shape from the other, and each with its own delicate beauty. She wondered what other treasures the gnomes had in store for her, and this time they took her to a live tree. Throughout her walk she had been very conscious of the sun, and now it was shining behind this tree, sending gleams of light through its branches. She was told to listen and not to let anything else intrude. And then she heard it. The tree was full of sound—a wonderful music, which seemed almost to consume it. Her next stopping-place was by a pool of water where a little pipe emptied its contents. Here she was introduced to another delightful sound, "a tinkling symphony—a real joy," and she knew that the music of both tree and water was part of the eternal harmony, which sounds through all creation and can be heard by those who are spiritually attuned. Then the gnomes drew her attention to a distant view, this time to observe a dog, which was running, and the graceful, rhythmic movement it created was almost breathtaking, for she realised that the energy that activated it was the divine life, joyously expressing itself through the canine form. "I had witnessed such a scene many, many times before," she said, "but how different when seen through the eyes of these nature spirits!" Her walk with them was almost over, but before they left her they took her to the edge of a wood and showed her a small patch of tiny white, star-shaped flowers. Even the minutest things can be doorways into the infinite, and as she gazed at them "it was as if the heavens had for a moment joined the earth." And then she saw a small white feather waving in the breeze, and knew that her little friends were bidding her farewell. She was once again walking alone, but the memory of her wonderful experience would remain with her always. It was not until later that she realized the things she had seen represented all the different kingdoms of nature, as well as the four elements of earth, water, air, and fire (sun).

Another account confirming the existence of these gnomes was given to me many years ago by Mrs. C. George, of Stapleford, Notts. As long ago as the year 1900, she was passing Wollaton Park Gates when she saw some "little men" dressed like policemen, standing just inside the lodge entrance. "They were smiling and looking very happy," she said. "They hadn't any wings, and as far as I can remember they were between two and three feet in height." She also recalled that fairies had been seen dancing around the lake in the park.

It has been shown in two of the three previous Wollaton accounts how nature spirits love to imitate the human activities and styles of dress, which appeal to them. Some of the fashions adopted by them may go back many centuries, like the medieval "two-stee-pled" headdress I saw on a fairy who was proudly tending a purple hyacinth in a pot on a friend's mantelpiece. (Incidentally, the house stood on ground which once had been the Thorny Wood part of the ancient Sherwood Forest.) When this flower fairy noticed that I was admiring her plant, she flashed me a radiant smile. The intense joy on her face as she absorbed the vital lifeforce from the atmosphere and imparted it to the hyacinth was wonderful to see, and I was able to experience some of her exaltation. My host was beginning to tell me that he, too, could "see something," but his wife pooh-poohed the idea and said it was his imagination, so he became silent!

The following is "a true account of a happy and wholly unexpected incident," which happened to L. A. Bardsley, of Cheshire, when, at the age of seven, she spent a holiday at the home of her grandmother in the summer of 1909. "The house was in the small village of Bridgemont, near Whaley Bridge in Derbyshire. It had a flagged backyard, which sloped steeply, and a long, low flat-topped stonewall about a foot wide enclosed it, separating it from the rest of the garden. This long wall formed a narrow platform, which was ideal for us children to play upon, and I frequently enjoyed running and dancing along its top. The drop from the wall on the garden side was steep and rather dangerous, but playing on it was always fascinating because of the element of risk. A false step would certainly have resulted in serious and sudden disaster. On this particular warm summer afternoon the sun was shining brilliantly, making the whole wide surroundings show up very clearly, and I had the whole wall to myself. My grandmother was inside the house, though within calling distance. Having climbed on the top of the wall, I started to dance along its smooth, well-worn surface, and somehow I became suddenly filled with an enhanced sense of well being—a state of sheer joy in being alive. I felt the sun's warmth in the stones beneath my feet, and the peace and beauty of the garden below me. I was completely suffused with a sense of heightened consciousness for I felt so fully at one with myself and all my surroundings. This stopped my game of running along the wall, and I stood still, gazing beyond the garden to the quiet, green countryside. Then suddenly, to my great surprise and delight, I saw a truly amazing sight, for there, in one of the nearby fields, was a number of miniature horses harnessed to tiny open trotting-traps racing circularly round the edge of the field—quite a dozen or more of them. In each trap a little gnome was seated, grasping the glossy reins in one hand and holding a whip upright in the other. They were all beautifully dressed, some in bright green jackets, others in scarlet, and all with hats to match, and wearing high black boots, which shone in the sunlight like patent leather. They wore gauntlet gloves, and all seemed very pleased with themselves and proud of their appearance. They continued racing excitedly round and round the field, keenly competing against each other. I could clearly see their little faces, which were perfectly formed, with rosy complexions and high cheekbones. They were so intent on the game, and so serious about winning, that they were quite unaware of my near presence. The horses were lovely, and well-groomed, with shining harnesses and equipages; some were chestnut, others darker, but all trying their hardest to win, and very responsive to the commands of their masters who were seated behind them. I could see quite plainly the golden colour and light build of the traps as they passed and re-passed each other, and even the ripple of muscles of the horses' flanks as they moved their legs and hooves to and fro. The race became increasingly fast and furious; the gnomes were filled with glee and excitement, and horses and riders alike were intent on winning. The whole field was bathed in brilliant sunlight, making it look greener than the other surrounding fields, and I stood rooted to the spot, watching and enjoying the lovely, amazing spectacle for quite some time, absolutely spellbound. At last the fascination of the whole scene became so intense that I couldn't stand the sight of it any longer by myself, so I called out to my grandmother in the kitchen to 'Come quickly, come quickly' to share my pleasure. Alas, I immediately regretted calling her and somehow realized I should not have done so, because as she came outside and moved towards me, grumbling because of her 'rheumatics' and the insistence of my voice, which had made her leave her chair, to find out what was amiss, I felt an increasing diminution of consciousness. Then, as she got nearer to me, her proximity began to blot out my vision, for she was what one would term an 'earthy-earthy' woman, and when she reached me the whole scene vanished completely and I could see nothing but the empty green field. My grandmother, of course, scolded me for disturbing her 'for no reason at all,' telling me brusquely there was 'absolutely nothing there.' At that time I had never even heard of Trotting Races, and I had no previous knowledge of fairies or little men, therefore, I certainly could not have been recollectingly thinking of such things, and there was nothing to lead up to the phenomenon. One moment there was nothing, and the next moment the vision was there, vividly and instantaneously before my eyes. Although but a child at the time, and with no knowledge of clairvoyance and such-like things, I inwardly knew that what I had witnessed was a case of second sight, and also why it was that my grandmother's aura would, and did, blot out my vision.

"After her derisive outburst, I kept the secret to myself until I was grown-up. Then, one day, I recounted the happening to my aunt (her daughter), and she, to my surprise, said: 'Why, that is the very field my father used to tell me about when I was a girl, and how they used to hold Trotting Competitions there, and all the sports-loving men came from miles around to take part in them. But those things died out many years ago and have never been revived since.' So evidently the little gnomes were imitating the old races they had seen held there year after year in times past, and on that particular afternoon I must have become *en rapport* with them owing to my enhanced state of consciousness. Even today, I can still vividly recall and relive the sudden mood of joy that I experienced as I witnessed that entrancing scene. It must have been an exact replica of a human Trotting Race, except that everything was on a diminished scale of about a quarter the normal size, with every detail standing out perfectly."

Miss G. R. Nicholson had been living in her house in Leicester for only three months when she had what to her was a unique experience. On this particular day she was feeling "very calm and happy," and was looking out of her window at her small strip of garden, thinking how fortunate she was to have a garden and a little home of her own again, after having been in rooms for several years. It was then that she saw on a primrose leaf a figure like Sir Walter Raleigh in miniature, wearing knee breeches, short brown jacket, and brown hat. She was amazed, and even more so when she saw on another primrose leaf further along the garden a tiny figure resembling Shakespeare. "I looked, and looked, in astonishment," she said, "and then they disappeared—but I felt so wonderful and light as air afterwards." It is possible that these quaintly dressed little men, who reminded Miss Nicholson of two famous characters of a bygone period, were Brownies, for, according to the seer Geoffrey Hodson, whole tribes of earth nature-spirits are to be found in England wearing an Elizabethan style of male attire.

Mrs. G. Graddol, whose account of a poppy fairy appears in an earlier section of this book, saw in a park about nine miles from Pendleton a round-faced, inquisitive-eyed creature appear between the forked branch of a tree, gaze at her quizzically for a moment, and then vanish. He seemed about four inches in height and his appearance was unusual, for he wore the peaked cap and uniform of an Admiral of the Fleet, complete with gold braid trimmings! This fairy gave her the same feeling of happiness, which she had when she saw the poppy fairy. She had gone to both places as a very sad woman and had come away feeling "on top of the world."

One of the most intriguing and hard-to-believe experiences that I had was of seeing in a rose a fairy wearing a nun's wimple in white. I am not a Roman Catholic, and at that time we had no television set and I did not always bother with the radio, so I did not know until I read about it in the newspaper that a Pope had been crowned in Rome. Even if I had known and then forgotten, I would never have conceived the idea of a rose fairy wearing a nun's headdress. Nature spirits can go anywhere in the wink of an eye, so had this fairy been to Rome and seen a nun in a white wimple in the crowd? Had she witnessed the ceremony on a neighbour's television set? Or had she seen it in the Reflecting Ether, which is not the real Memory of Nature like the Akashic Records (the "Book of Life" in the Christian Bible), but it reflects rather blurred pictures of all past and passing events, and can be viewed by the nature spirits. It is an interesting thought.

Chapter 9: Animals and Fairies, and Fairies Enlisting the Help of Human Beings

Many dogs, cats, and horses are psychic and are aware of the fairy folk, but they react to their presence in different ways, just as children do. Some animals seem really afraid of them, while others are friendly towards them. A friend of Mrs. Joan Rasmussen, of Queensland, recounted in a letter to her dated 18 September 1956, his first experience with fairies, which concerned his horse, and I am very grateful to both of them for allowing me to quote in full, as follows:

"I lived then in Queensland, and one of my favourite pastimes was to ride quietly through the bush in the moonlight. Though I owned many horses, I invariably chose a thoroughbred named Penelo on these occasions, because he somehow understood and shared my contemplative delight in the soft beauty and peace about us. One night we entered an almost circular clearing among the trees where the moonlight seemed to have a remarkable yellow-ivory brilliance. Penelo stopped, and I dismounted and sat on the ground, then decided to stretch out on it for a time in sheer enjoyment of the stillness. A while later, I noticed Penelo's ears point forward, and then he stood taut and motionless, clearly interested in something near the trees. I wondered what it was—perhaps a possum, wallaby, or snake—so I turned cautiously on to my side to look, and was intrigued to see several very diminutive elfin-like figures moving in excited conference at the edge of the moonlit circle. Then I caught the faint sound of their high-pitched, rather tinkling voices. The pitch was far too high for me to distinguish all their words, but the trend was obvious. Finally they overcame their doubts and advanced. Penelo nuzzled me and then resumed his alert stand. Silent now, they halted about four feet away to inspect me. My attire, particularly the boots, interested them intensely, and amused them. They vied with each other to point out something about me. It was at this stage I smiled. They noticed it, and their voices tinkled again in rapid exclamation. One felt my boot, then all closely examined the fabric of my clothes with their fingers. Slowly I advanced a hand, whereupon one of them—dressed as a forester might have been over a hundred years ago and thus distinctive from the others whose attire was more gossamer—felt my wrist and tried to move it. Another, with beautiful golden hair, had come round behind me. Suddenly she leaned over my shoulder, placed her head against the side of mine in a delightful, friendly way, and tried to speak to me. On a subsequent occasion I gathered that her name was Valerie, or one that sounded very like it. A noteworthy aspect was their playfulness. I saw one try to tickle Penelo's foreleg with a long piece of grass, and all that happened was the arching down of the horse's neck to watch proceedings. A few minutes later, at a signal, they left us. That was my introduction to fairies.

"I was able to go there again two nights later, and after a while they came, making me aware of their presence by tickling me about the head with grass, from behind my back. I have always wondered whether Penelo saw them just as I did; or was he merely aware of their voices, or instinctively conscious of something unusual at that spot? It was interesting that, given free rein, he invariably made for that particular place if it were a similar moonlight night, but not otherwise."

The Derbyshire poet, Miss Teresa Hooley, wrote in 1958 that her Southern Irish ancestors would cry shame on her if she said she did not believe in the Little People. "I have never seen one of them," she admitted, "but I've been very near them. There is a little patch of green woodland in an almost deserted wee lane in Somerset, and always whenever I took my terrier there he would dash madly round in circles, wildly elicited and happy—always in the same place! I am sure they were there, and that my dog was playing with them."

In 1942, Mrs. E. M. Tampin, of New Malden, Surrey, was evacuated to North Devon. With her two children—one aged five and the other a baby of eight months in a pram—she was returning one evening in May to her billet at Chilsworthy after visiting a lady at

Halsworthy with whom she had become friendly. At the bottom of a steep hill was a small river or stream, over which was a little bridge, and as she climbed down the hill to approach it she noticed a pony trap coming down a hill on the other side. When the pony reached the bridge, it stopped dead in its tracks, and although the old man in the trap tried his hardest to make the pony go on it was useless. By this time, Mrs. Tampin was nearing the bridge from the other side, but when she was about 100 yards away she, too, stopped for no reason. Darkness was falling, and on turning her face to the right she saw a line of little lights about a foot from the ground, moving slowly up the hill on the same side as the pony and trap. Then she looked down the road and saw that the end of the line was just going across it and through the hedge. There seemed to be hundreds of little lights, and it took a long time for them to go by. As soon as they had passed, the pony started off again, and Mrs. Tampin, too, felt she could go on. "The old man stopped and told me not to tell anyone what I had seen, or the little people would make things uneasy for me," she said. "I was not scared, but I didn't say anything about them all the time I was in Devon. I kept thinking of them for ages afterwards, but couldn't get myself to go down there again in the evening."

Mr. E. M. Armytage, of Ludham, Great Yarmouth, could not say that he believed in fairies or that he had ever given the subject serious thought, but he admitted that there is much that we humans do not know, and his reaction to the following experience was not one of surprise. Rather did he accept the vision as a matter of course. About 6:30 on the evening of Tuesday, 11 January 1955, he was sitting in an armchair with his dog, Bruce, at his feet. He was reading the paper, but put it down to look at whatever it was that had made Bruce sit up and watch the floor in a friendly, quizzical way. And this is what he saw: about a yard away, between him and the brick fireplace, were the shadows of several little feet moving very quickly, almost dancing, backwards and forwards in a straight line across the tiled floor. "I thought it was mice," he said, "but there were no bodies and no substance."

The "leprechaun" which Miss Bryant saw was, she declared,

"a vague and momentary thing." She was grown-up then, and was living in a house which stood on ground that had once been a very old wood. The roots of the trees had branched out again, so where it was not cultivated it was very thick, and many rare birds used to nest there. She was wandering with an old retriever when suddenly he stiffened and stopped dead. Glancing in the direction in which the dog was looking, she saw a queer little face peering at them. They all stared at each other for a matter of seconds, and then the little figure disappeared. He would be no less than a foot high and seemed to be covered in something tight, of a light green colour. She saw no wings. When the creature vanished, her dog was frightened and wouldn't move forward. Nor would he go into the wood for some time afterwards. She doesn't know why she said to herself, "Oh, I have seen a leprechaun at last," nor why she should see one in Northumberland "for," she thought, "surely they are Irish!"

Mrs. Esme Swainson, of Batheaston, Bath, once saw the fairy group who gather sun-force round the apples to help them ripen when the weather has been unfavourable. These beings appear like bright points in a ball of silvery mist. She was fortunate in having lived with a friend who had always seen fairies. "Only a few years ago," she said, "he saw them on the lawn—just beyond where we were having tea—playing what he called 'ring-a-roses.'" They were quite small and had wings. She recalled the time she lived at Harborne, Birmingham, and had musical weekends—she playing the violin and the piano. On one of these weekends, they had been playing a lot of Mozart. There were just three people left in the room and Mrs. Swainson's black cat, who they always felt was psychic. This animal started to behave in a very queer way, first watching something dancing about on the piano (a baby grand), then something flying about the room and evidently touching the cat's nose every now and then. Mrs. Swainson asked her friend to turn on his "sight," and he said there was a green nature-spirit about twelve inches high, dancing about on the piano and having a game with the cat. After this, she often saw the game going on in the garden, though she could not see the fairy.

Our first cocker spaniel, Peter—the friend and defender of wild birds and field mice—seemed to enjoy being teased and played with by the fairies. He would twist and turn in all directions as his eyes followed their flight into the air around him and down again, and his face would assume the most ludicrous expression when they tweaked one of his long ears, pulling his head down on one side. He was a very portly dog, and sometimes, when he seemed to be trying to dance with them on the lawn, it was a sight to behold.

To the fairy folk the solstices and equinoxes seem very important, and on those dates they hold various celebrations or ceremonies. I think it might have been one of the latter, which took place on the night of the winter solstice 1971. My sister was gazing out of one of our front bedroom windows when she called to me to join her. It was very late, but in the eerie glow of the streetlights I could see what seemed from above to be several white crinkled paper balls, but which, if viewed from the right angle, could have been wide, frilly dresses or tutus worn by tiny beings. My sister, who had been watching them for some time, said, "Keep on looking. They are rolling now, but I've seen them walk! They must be some kind of fairies." I gazed in astonishment as two or three of them began to trot, and after them came many more small white beings of the same size, who rolled, leapt in the air, and then literally danced towards the others. Presently a solitary one came down the road, and two of the first arrivals went to meet it and walked back one on each side of it. Then they began to come from all directions, and when the newcomers reached the main throng there seemed to be much rejoicing among them and they "larked about" just like children, though my sister and I couldn't hear any sound, and their faces were not visible to us from above, owing to the dim lighting. As they were all dressed alike, the thought came to me that they had come to take part in some kind of graduation ceremony. At this point, we felt we were being watched, and we noticed that just inside our front gate was a "sentinel." Another one was posted inside the gate, which led to the passage between our house and that of our neighbour. Then we heard footsteps on the road, and a man came along with his dog. All the little beings (with the exception of the two sentinels) had now gathered together in a large crowd on the pavement. My sister and I watched breathlessly, wondering what they would do, but when the man reached them he walked right through them, obviously quite unaware of their existence. The dog, however, saw them and paused, then walked carefully round them, lowering its head to look at them and sniffing inquisitively before following its master. A car had been parked all the afternoon and evening near the gate, and suddenly, near midnight, the small white sprites with one accord swooped beneath it and were lost to our view. With the aid of their "glamourie," they would be able to see it as a grand Assembly Hall, where they could hold their ceremony away from our prying eyes. The sentinels, however, remained at their posts, and conveyed to us a strong feeling that we must not go out to investigate, so we went reluctantly to our beds. Early the next morning I watched the car being driven away, but of course there was no sign of the wee folk.

I had in my bedroom a miniature ladder-back chair twelve and a half inches high, with a small, lavender-filled cushion on the seat, and when we had a cocker spaniel named Trina, she would run into my room every morning and stand wagging her tail vigorously at something she saw in the chair. Then the time came for my room to be painted and decorated, so all the contents were moved out and jumbled together elsewhere. As soon as the work was finished and everything put back in its place, I was able to return, and in the morning Trina came running in, looking expectantly towards the little chair. When she reached it, I noticed that she did not wag her tail but turned away looking very dejected. This kept on for several days, but when the smell of the paint had gone from the room she again started wagging her tail joyously at she approached the chair.

It is not unusual for the nature spirits to become fond of one's fairy-seeing friends, and one day the fairy of the chair showed herself to Mrs. Vera Westmoreland, whose many experiences are included in this book. Vera described her as being "lovely, delicate, and ethereal," and she said that she had told her in a clear, bell-like voice that she had left my room for a while because so much in it had been disturbed, and the smell of paint had lingered, but now she had come back to her chair and had regained the same setting and colourful rays round that particular spot. That explained the behaviour of our dog Trina, with her alternating moods of disappointment and pleasure. Vera Westmoreland's psychic gifts far exceeded my own, for up to this point I had been unable to see the chair's occupant. However, Vera and her husband had spent the afternoon with me later on that summer, and then departed in their car for Derbyshire, and some time afterwards I went upstairs to my bedroom and was surprised to see for the first time a misty little figure gliding towards the miniature chair. Within the next few days I received a "Thank you" letter from the Westmorelands, in which they said that the fairy had accompanied them for part of the way home, perching between them on the back of the car seat, so it may be supposed that when I saw the fairy going to her chair she had just returned from her joyride!

On 13 May 1961, some friends came to our house for a few hours and brought with them their two cocker-spaniel bitches, Peppy and Judy. It was a hot day, and we all sat in the drawing room with the door wide open so that the dogs could walk in and out as they pleased. Judy had fallen asleep, and I was facing the open door with Peppy lying in front of me. Suddenly she raised her head, sniffed, and craned her neck to look at something in the hall. I peeped out and saw standing there the semi-transparent figure of a gnome, or dwarf, one-and-a-half-to-two feet in height, with a large head, a beard, and a pointed cap. Although I was unable to see any colouring, he appeared to be wearing the traditional belted jacket and trousers of his kind. I think there were two more of them, but he was the clearest. He seemed to be very interested in the dog, but after a while he disappeared and Peppy settled down to sleep. I kept a watchful eye on the hall through the open door, and presently the little man returned and Peppy stirred, and again raised her head to sniff and look at him.

On 22 July of the same year, our friends paid us another visit, and this time we were sitting in the dining room and the other dog, Judy, was facing the open door. I was seated at the side of the door and could not see into the hall, but I noticed that Judy was looking out and wagging her tail. Then the wagging stopped, but it started again after a few minutes, so I gathered that what Judy had seen must have reappeared again after a short absence. As the owners of Peppy and Judy lived in a pretty cottage in a small village surrounded by fields and woods, no doubt the dogs were used to seeing fairy folk. I might add that on this and the previous occasion the other human beings in the room were much too busily engaged in conversation to notice anything!

It is certainly true that fairies try to enlist the help of human beings when an insect, bird, or animal is in trouble. Miss Sylvia Birchfield, of Chicago, described an experience she had on her parents' farm in the northern part of Illinois during the summer of 1956. While walking through an open field, she was amazed to see some fairies flying out of a wooded area towards her, barely missing the tall grass as they came. Feeling that they wished her to follow them back to the woodland, she did so, and at this they showed obvious joy. As soon as she had crossed the fence, they flew towards a fallen tree—which recently had been struck by lightning—and hovered over a particular branch. She walked around it and found there an injured bird, which she later learned was a grosbeak, a bird rather rare in that section of the country. Lifting it from the branch, she took it to her brother, who fed and tended it for a few days until it was strong enough to fly onward to join its kind. All the while she was with the fairies there seemed to be "high chatter" among them, and she explained that by "high" she meant a sound of higher frequency than we can normally understand: "like the hum of electric wires in extreme cold."

My sister and I have been "called out" (telepathically) on several occasions to re-stake plants, which have been blown down by the wind, and to rescue birds and bees in distress. One day my sister was urgently "summoned" to extricate a very angry and frustrated bee which had just become entangled in a spider's web. On one occasion when I was responding to a "call," the timing was so perfect that the bee was just falling through the air to land at my feet as I stepped out into the garden. Many bees are affected by the wretched chemicals with which man is poisoning the earth, air, and sea, and consequently all forms of life, and this bee was apparently lifeless, but a few drops of that magical antiseptic elixir, honey, placed on a leaf, slowly revived and strengthened it, and eventually it flew happily away, after circling round my head in a sort of farewell salute.

Mr. Geoffrey Hodson tells us in his book *The Coming of the Angels* (The Theosophical Publishing House, London) that the bee is developing mind, just as plants and trees are developing emotion. According to theosophical concepts of the Ancient Wisdom, bees came originally from the planet Venus. My contributor Mrs. Georgina K. Evason had a Venusian visitant one night, and was shown a vision of a bee in flight. She was told that bees travel on the humming sound vibrations just as the spaceships and flying saucers are said to do. In her book *Natives of Eternity* (L. N. Fowler & Co. Ltd., London), the Rev. Flower Newhouse described her out-of-body journey to Venus with one of the great Masters. They visited a beautiful garden, and she wrote: "In that same garden we saw a form that resembled a mammoth bee, for it was as large as a small dog; and I sensed that it was a Venusian household pet." It is interesting to note that these three foregoing references to the bee and the planet Venus come from three quite separate, independent sources.

Chapter 10: Transportation of Objects by the Fairies and Fairy Apports

It is well known among many of my contributors that the little people can cause objects to disappear and then to reappear, though not always in the same place. C. W. Leadbeater said in his before-mentioned book *The Hidden Side of Things* that as the fourth dimension is a commonplace part of the nature spirits' existence, it is quite easy for them to remove articles from a locked box, or to transport flowers into a closed room. Ella Young in her book *The Flowering Dusk* (Dennis Dobson Ltd., London, 1945) also mentioned this mischievous side of fairies, and Capt. Sir Quentin Craufurd had proof of this during his experiments with a group of wood elves. However, they have no evil intent, and I do not think they are any more mischievous than some children and young animals.

My Mother had mystifying disappearances and sudden reappearances of thimbles, scissors, and pencils often in the presence of my sister and myself, and I had a strange experience concerning an important letter containing accounts of fairies from a fairy seer. I had placed it carefully with my other papers, but when I wanted it I could not find it anywhere. I had searched in every nook and cranny, every drawer and cupboard in the house. I was sure I hadn't transferred it to my handbag because I kept only unanswered letters there, and I had acknowledged this one immediately after receiving it. I had already glanced in my bag, and such a bulging packet would have been instantly recognizable — but this was my last hope. I emptied the bag entirely of its contents and examined everything separately several times, just to satisfy myself. I also felt inside the lining, though I knew it could not be there. After that, I gave up searching, for I guessed the fairies had taken it, and I asked them to return it as soon as possible. A few weeks passed, and I was feeling desperate, because I daren't ask my correspondent to rewrite all her experiences. Then one day I went in a health food shop and made some purchases. My handbag had a safe, stiff clasp, which even I had difficulty in twisting, but when I bent down to open it for the money I saw to my horror that it was gaping wide open, and I thought I'd been robbed. Then I noticed there was something bulky sticking right up out of it, and my horror turned to delight when I discovered it was the precious letter. Why had the fairies kept me waiting so long? Had they needed special conditions before returning it, such as the atmosphere of a busy shop, where they could obtain power from other people in order to re-materialize such a bulky letter? Only the fairies themselves can answer that!

When a friend told me that Miss Edith M. van Horne, writer, traveller, and lecturer, shared her flat in Edinburgh with a gnome and a fairy, I wrote to Miss van Horne for more details. She said the fairy first appeared as a bright, glowing light moving about her study. Then she reappeared at various times and under any conditions, always bringing with her a happy atmosphere. The gnome was about a foot high, wearing a brown jerkin, red pantaloons, and brown pointed boots. He had been seen several times by Miss van Horne's friends, but often he was only visible as a shadow-like shape. Sometimes she could hear him call her name, and a friend's little boy said that "Gnomey" had told him he would always look after her. Despite his concern for her welfare, however, "Gnomey" could not resist getting up to mischief, such as moving things around the house and hiding her glasses.

Another contributor who was teased by the fairies was Mrs. Claire H. Cantlon. "The fairies help me very greatly with my garden and will make beautiful flowers come up for me," she said, "but in the house they hide my things in a most annoying way, and seem to delight in making me vexed. Hours, sometimes days, afterwards, they will put them back in the most obvious places, like my thimble in the middle of my bed or table, where it certainly was not to be seen a minute before."

Miss Kathleen Hinde, of Lyme Regis, confirmed that they played pranks on her, too. "They love taking away my things and then putting them back," she commented.

Mrs. H. Spelman, of Cheshire, referred to them as "little imps," and said: "They move things, and then you find them."

In July 1963, my contributor "H" wrote to tell me that he had started doing a fairy picture for me, in oil pastels, but he added: "One thing is annoying me. Every time I lay a pastel down, it just disappears! I have plenty of whites, but if it happens with the colours I shall have to buy some more. I have lost four whites already—actually I lost five, but found one in my bed! You know what's happening, don't you? It's those darned, mischievous little fairies who keep pinching them, because normally I am most careful to put crayons, etc., down where I can put my hand on them easily. I do wish they would put them back... Ever since I first started, I have also been aware (without actually hearing anything) of rustlings and flutterings around the room—especially while sketching the fairy who couldn't fly. Isn't it strange how one can sense sounds very strongly and yet not actually hear anything physically?"

In April or May 1943, Mr. G. H. Allen and a lady friend were in Yorkshire on one of their cycle outings. The weather was clear, with bright spring sunshine lighting up the Pennine Fells. Nevertheless, there was a strong wind blowing, so that high up in the hills it was rather cold.

After mounting almost to the top of Kidstone Pass, they decided to leave their cycles in the shelter of a limestone wall while they climbed over to have a clearer view of the mountain stream, which tumbles steeply down the almost sheer slope of the fells to the right side of the roadway. They reached a place about a quarter of a mile away from their cycles and watched the lively stream leaping down over many boulders on its way to reach Cray Gill and eventually to empty itself into the river below. The grass and herbage were just beginning to take on a fresh green appearance, and forget-me-nots, violets, and the yellow wild pansy were growing in profusion. Mr. Allen remarked to his companion, "This is, I believe, a place to find fairies." He felt sure that it was one of their haunts, for it was wild and remote. After some fifteen minutes, they slowly returned to their cycles, but before continuing their ride his lady friend opened her handbag for her cosmetics and discovered that her lipstick in its container was missing. Earlier in the morning she had proudly shown him this new lipstick in its expensive container of pale green and ivory encircled with gold bands, before returning it safely to her handbag. They searched her handbag and then their saddlebags, their clothes and pockets, the ground and the drystone wall, but there was no sign of the missing article.

"The fairies have taken it," said Mr. Allen, and reluctantly they remounted their machines and continued their journey, and they were soon travelling at twenty miles per hour down Cray Gill towards Buckden. After passing through this lovely Dales village side by side, some four to five feet apart, they reached the small hamlet of Starbotton and were riding through it when Mr. Allen heard the sound of something striking his friend's cycle. It hit it in three places before falling on to the road, and he called to her to stop, thinking it might be a nut from the machine. They both turned round, and there, some 60 feet behind them, they found the container with the lipstick safely inside. His friend said she had distinctly felt something strike her on the chest before she heard the tinkling sound it made as it struck the cycle. She assured him that the new lipstick in its case would not come out again. It would be preserved and treasured always.

The most disconcerting experience in this connection was recalled by Adam Campbell Hunter, of Skelmorlie, Ayrshire. "When," he said, "the Brownies stole the philibeg off me, along with sark, jacket, and vest, and left me naked except for hose and brogan. It happened in Glen Oykel in 1938. I had been told I'd get a grand view from the top of a certain low hill on the Sutherland side of the river, so one Sunday afternoon in October I set off alone to climb this hill and see the view. The day was sunny and very warm, especially for someone in a kilt, and as I crossed the heather I started to peel off my clothes. I was within 50 yards of the top when I sat down on a big boulder, which made a natural chair, and I laid my clothes down beside the stone and put another stone on top of them to keep them from being blown away, as there was a strong breeze. I sunbathed for a while and then decided to walk up to the top, but first I put a stone on top of my boulder seat to mark it. After going up to admire the view, I came down again to my boulder seat and my clothes were gone—vanished! There were only four or five other large boulders on the hillside and I ran to each in turn and looked, but there were no clothes and no one was hiding; there was not a man, deer, sheep, or bird in sight. I ran the 50 yards to the top of the hill again and viewed the landscape—empty! I circled the hilltop; I quartered the hill; then I searched it haphazardly. I jumped on every stone, but there was not a soul to be seen. After two hours search I was forced into accepting the fact that my clothes had vanished for keeps. I was hungry and it was time I was getting home, so, naked except for hose and brogan I set off across the muir. When I passed MacLeod's peat stack, I saw an old torn waterproof coat, so I put it on. It covered me to near the waist, but the lower portions were torn away. Thus attired I scrambled down to the Glen road and went along it and over the swing bridge to the croft house where I was staying with Alex MacLachlan. I got right through the house and in at my own door without a soul seeing me. I went up to the attic and changed into some clothes, and then came down to my very late tea. Alex and his wife were already at theirs, and when I told them the yarn they laughed fit to kill themselves. While I was having my meal, Alex ran out to rouse the crofters, then he and the brothers Seumas and Duncan MacLeod, Alex Ross, and Jack Fleming went with me back to the spot to find my kilt and clothes. They were all quite confident they would find them right away.

"It was a lovely evening, and a glorious red sun was slowly setting over Ben More Assynt. I showed the crofters the boulder on which I rested (the small stone was still on top of it to mark it) and also the spot where I'd laid down my philibeg and jacket and shirt, etc. They spread out and quartered the hill—first east and west and then north and south; then they circled it, and finally concluded that I had taken them to the wrong hill. I must have been up Ben Buie, they said, and they would climb it tomorrow. I was most emphatic we were at the right place, and told them I was no townie to mistake one hill for another. They then split up and combed the hilltop haphazardly, jumping on top of the half-dozen big boulders to look around. One lad came down off my boulder seat just as the sun set, and I immediately replaced him and watched the last rays disappear. The crofters were already starting down the brae for home, leaving me there on my own. I gave a last look to the spot where I had laid my clothes, and there they were! With a yell I jumped and pounced on them. The other men ran back and just wouldn't believe it. They had all searched that spot a dozen times, and there was no great growth on that hilltop—only one or two tufts of heather. We experimented then in the fast-fading light, and could see the clothes from 200 yards away, yet none of us had seen them before. Why? We couldn't explain it one way or the other, except that it was the work of the Brownies. Anyway, I kept a fast grip on my philibeg and we lost no time in getting down off the Brownies' hill. It was a most astounding experience."

Mr. Hunter concluded by giving the names of the men who could corroborate his story. Alex MacLachlan, the MacLeods, and Ross were still in Glen Oykel as far as he knew; but Jack Fleming, who belonged to Gourock was in Abadan, Persian Gulf, the last time he had heard of him.

However, the brownies or fairies cannot always be accused of having dematerialized or hidden the various objects before returning them. They can be very helpful in finding articles that have been lost or mislaid by the owners. For instance, when my older sister Dorothy was a child, she possessed a ring that was made of blue beads, and while playing in Colwick Woods (then a private estate), in Nottingham, with the children from the farmhouse nearby, the ring slipped off her finger and was lost in the thick grass. "We all searched for it without success," she said, "and finally we had to go home to tea. I was still very upset about my treasured ring, and silently I asked the fairies to find it and give it back to me. I told them I would go up to the woods at twilight—alone—to receive it. I was full of faith and had no doubts at all about getting the ring back. At the appointed time, without saying anything to the other children or my parents, I slipped out of the house. Just before I reached the woodland, I was able to discern in the dim light the ring moving towards me about a foot above the ground, as if floating on air or being carried by some invisible being, and, as I watched, it dropped at my feet." On recalling this experience many years later, my sister admitted that it sounded utterly fantastic, but she said that at the time she took it all for granted and did not feel any undue surprise.

Lost objects were restored in similar fashion to the novelist Mr. Shaw Desmond, of Middlesex, who had a lifetime's experience of the supernatural. He said he could not see the fairies who waited on him, but he would ask them to find mislaid articles such as manuscripts, or studs, and they would oblige him by flinging them down at his feet. Incidentally, he told me that his Danish wife saw a little troll man walk around the edge of her table in daylight.

A South Kensington correspondent wrote that at an early age after the death of his twin brother, he used to see and talk to the fairies in the garden of his home in County Armagh, Ireland. When he grew a bit older, he became more conscious of these little friends, and he saw them again later, when his parents moved to County Down, but none of them seemed to have "wings." Very often, from 1902 until he was nearly fourteen years old, he heard fairy music at two blackthorn trees. When he was five years of age, he would find money left for him close to his bed, on a table or window ledge. This was always in silver three penny-bits—two, three, or four at a time. Later, there were sometimes sixpenny pieces, but the money never exceeded two shillings in value, no matter what coins were left. His parents laughed about it and called him a lucky boy, and his father blamed his mother until it was brought to light that when she was away from home the money still arrived. Then his parents could not understand where it came from, for they did not believe in fairies. This good luck followed him regularly until he reached manhood, "and even now," he said in his letter, "I find small money in the strangest ways and places. There must be many beings outside our range of vision, so why not fairies? I think we can only see and sense according to our own vibrations. All I have said here is very true to me, and I believe in fairies."

The most remarkable account of fairy "apports" came from Mr. William Fell, of Llandudno, but first I will describe his introduction to the little people. He was living in a lovely house in Colwyn Bay, surrounded by five acres of garden and pleasure grounds, and on the east side of the estate a mountain stream flowed through a wooded ravine down to the sea. After retiring one evening, he was surprised to see a perfect little lady about two inches in height, carrying a small drum, which she placed on the window ledge. She then commenced to dance and sing. He had a long chat with her afterwards, and she told him her name was Veronica, and that she would live forever. She also taught him how to make a sound that would bring the fairies to him whenever he wanted them. Several weeks later, when a doctor and his wife and three-and-a-half-year-old son went to stay at the house, the little boy was very excited one morning. "Mummy," he cried, "the fairies were dancing on my bed last night," and he gave a perfect description of Mr. Fell's fairy friends, who were never more than three inches in height and looked like dragonflies. Each of them had two large and four small wings, and when these were folded a perfect, human-like form was revealed.

Years later when Mr. Fell moved to another house, he was joined by a band of fairies together with their leader—whom he called "Princess Goldilocks"—and these were the smallest he had seen so far; they were barely half an inch in size, and were green like grasshoppers. He watched some of them running up and down on the back of the couch in front of the television set. One day he had been grumbling about rates and taxes, and happened to mention, "I must ask Princess Goldilocks about it." Then remarkable things started to happen. He, along with two or three friends, began to find silver sixpences in all kinds of places. For the first three weeks he never missed a day without picking one up. One evening, near midnight, he said "The fairies have let me down today," but there on the rug at the side of his bed lay a sixpence.

He had three Pyrenean Mountain dogs that thoroughly enjoyed playing with the little people. Once, he placed the dogs' rug on the lawn to give it an airing, and when he went to fetch it in he found a sixpence in the middle of it. On another occasion he stopped his car on the promenade to give his dogs a run, and as he stepped out he saw a sixpence lying on the ground at his feet.

Later, he was constantly finding silver three-penny bits, shillings, two-shilling pieces, and half-crowns, and these turned up on floors, chairs, mantelpiece, television set, billiard-table, ironing board, pillow, tray, doors, an electric point, a plant on the table; on top of door in passage; on the garden path and the putting green; on a tall daisy; inside a golden rosebud, which Mr. Fell was cutting, and also in a bunch of Michaelmas daisies; in a "fairy ring" in the long grass; in moss near the summer house; in a packet of dog biscuits, a cigarette packet, the bristles of a hand brush; in slippers and shoes; on Mr. Fell's knee; on carpets and rugs, and inside the car; in or under the dogs' bowls, and other places too numerous to mention. One day Mr. Fell was writing a letter to me, and his first wife Dorothy was sitting in the same room with a friend, Miss W., when they heard a "plop," and Miss W. picked up a shilling, which had fallen on the carpet. She offered it to Mr. Fell, but he said "Keep it, and if they meant it for me they will bring me another." In less than a minute a second shilling arrived. On another occasion the fairies told him beforehand that they were giving a coin to his guest, Miss Q. This lady was busy with her knitting, and Mr. Fell was sitting chatting to her about the little people, when a sixpenny piece dropped out of her ball of wool. I was given a detailed list of the amounts and the dates on which they were found, but it is too long for inclusion in this book.

Mrs. Margery S. Sellors, of Belper, Derbyshire, wrote to me in 1956 about two small jugs, which she found in her garden. These jugs are seven to eight inches high, and are replicas of ordinary stoneware jugs, being stone colour at the bottom and brown-glazed at the top. She explained that her husband had dug the garden twice a year and, of course, planted out and hoed, yet one day she found the first jug amongst the pansies, and a few months later a second jug amongst a different lot of pansies. She added in her letter: "It is possible, I suppose, that the first jug was thrown up by my husband's spade, but the second one is a different matter. You see, after the first find I used to look over the pansy beds about every week, and this jug appeared in February or March this year. I think it would be about August of last year when I found the first one. They both looked fairly fresh. The pansies were planted only two years ago, and I love them very much because they always remind me of fairies or butterflies." One of the jugs had its handle broken, and Mrs. Sellors sent it for me to see, together with a sketch she had made of the perfect one. I suggested that the little jugs might have fallen out of a doll's house, which some child had been playing with in the garden, for I'd had similar jugs in my childhood, but she said that apart from her daughter, who was sixteen, there had been no children there for 40 years. "In the house we were in before this one," she said, "we firmly believed we had 'little men' living with us. There was the incident of my rubber hot water bottle, which I always brought down with me in the mornings. One evening I could not find it anywhere. I indignantly denied leaving it upstairs, as I distinctly remembered bringing it down. We finally ran it to earth lying slap in the middle of my bed, which, of course, was made earlier by myself. Once I found my sewing machine needle had been threaded in the short time I had been out of the room." Mrs. Sellars told me some other very interesting experiences not germane to this subject, which prove beyond doubt that she is psychic, so perhaps one day she will see the fairy donors of those tiny jugs, which she found in the pansy beds.

The next experience occurred to my sister and me, and I have left it until the last because it is slightly different from the others. One day we found the body of a beautiful blackbird in our garden, and we buried it with due solemnity. A few days later we found the corpse of another poor bird, and buried that, too. For the next few days the weather was too cold and wet for us to go into the garden, and one afternoon I went up to my bedroom for a book and was greeted by an awful stench, which seemed to come from underneath the bed. I pulled up the bedclothes and there, on the floor underneath, was the body of a bird in an advanced state of putrefaction. I called my sister, and when she saw it she cried out in amazement, "How could it have got there; I vacuumed all the bedrooms this morning, and you know I always vacuum under the beds. Besides that, I would have smelt it at once." We kept the outer doors shut, so no cat could have got in, and at that time we were without a dog. Owing to the weather, the only window open in my bedroom was a small high one, and it was open no more than two inches

274

because the rain had been coming in. I removed the dead body and hurriedly buried it in the wet garden, glad to be rid of the offensive odour. The next day my sister called me upstairs. She was standing in her bedroom, and the same nauseating smell greeted me before I walked in. "Look" she said, and there under the bed lay the decomposing body of another bird! And the windows were closed! We stared at each other, and the same thought was in both our minds. The fairies must have seen us burying the first bird in the garden and approved of our action. The second bird in the garden may have been left there by a cat, or the fairies had already decided to make use of us. When the weather was too bad for us to go out, they thought they'd attract our attention by bringing the corpses inside. The next time it might be a dead mouse or a rat; a frog, hedgehog or squirrel, or anything else they thought fit to transport, and as time and space are no objects to the fairies they could start bringing us dead birds and animals from far and wide so that we could give them a decent burial. It was too much, and I said aloud to them: "I know your intentions are good, but please stop this at once. We are not going to be your official gravediggers, and if you bring any more in we shan't bury them." The fairies must have heard me, for that was the end of our macabre findings!

Chapter 11: The Vesting of Psychic Power, Fairy Playmates, and Fairy Photographs

Sometimes it is possible for a seer to vest his power temporarily on a non-seer when in proximity or by means of touch. I am grateful to Col. K. Chodkiewicz, the writer and lecturer who delivered the Blavatsky Lecture on "Physical Forces and Spiritual Intelligences" at the annual convention of the Theosophical Society in 1958, for sending me the following translation of a letter he received from a Polish friend of his, who did not wish his name to be mentioned. "I got acquainted with a farming family, with whom I spent a few days. The farmer, scientifically minded like myself, nevertheless believed that gnomes, fairies, etc., really exist. Asked how he can believe in such fables, he answered that these are not fairy tales.

"Next day he took me to the river for fishing, and we went with our angling rods and sat on the bank of the river. After a while he turned towards me and said, 'Here they come.'

"'Who?' I asked.

"'Fairies,' was the answer. I gaped at the spot but I did not see anything. At this moment my friend grasped my hand firmly, and at once I saw two female figures floating above the ground and approaching us. I wanted to touch them to have proof that it was an illusion, and I moved towards them, releasing my hand, but when I lost contact with the hand of my friend I could not see them anymore. My friend took hold of my hand again, and once more I saw both figures. Next day my friend showed me the home elemental in his house, with whom he spoke as with a man, and who, disappearing, left a small, shining cloud, lasting for hours. I thought later about the whole problem, and considered the fact how I, a serious student of science, could fall under such spell or illusion. I must either change completely my whole scientific attitude, or I must think that it was an illusion indeed."

Two weeks later, the Colonel received another letter from his

Polish friend, who had been unable to alter his scientific attitude and had convinced himself that it was an illusion, and that his host had "put the picture of the fairies telepathically" into his mind. As Col. Chodkewicz said in his covering letter to me: "One can never convince anybody who does not want to be convinced. Such people would rather deny the facts when they cannot explain them in their own way." How true! And if the visions had been solely due to telepathy, the link-up would have been purely mental, and no physical contact would have been necessary! A more uncomfortable method than the mere holding of hands is described in the Rev. Robert Kirk's book *The Secret Commonwealth of Elves, Fauna and Fairies*: "For a curious person to get a transient sight," the "Inquirer" was told to put his left foot under the seer's right foot, and while, the seer's hand was laid on his head he looked over the seer's right shoulder. Another way consisted of laying ones head on the seer's knee!

Col. Chodkiewioz informed me that the children in Poland often see fairies, play with them, and give them various names. "Unfortunately," he said, "the power to see them generally vanishes when the youngsters grow up, for the etheric retina is then fully coordinated with the physical eye, and the 'etheric' sight is lost." Many children at one time or another have had fairy playmates, which are by no means all imaginary.

J.R.D., of Notts., used to have four fairy playmates, and he would play games with them regularly at one end of the bedroom while his mother bathed his baby sister in front of the fire at the other end. He called these sprites—which were quite visible to him—Bobbert, Diddett, Foggy, and Jewels.

Mrs. Ada Amiley West, who for many years had a herbalist's shop in Nottingham, knew a little boy at Newton Abbot, Devon, who could see fairies. He had some playmates and was very fond of them. She said he would walk along, chattering away, and one day she heard a boy ask him whom he was speaking to, and he replied: "Ssh! I'm talking to the pixies."

Mrs. West herself used to see elves and fairies in the house and garden when she was younger. She said they were about six inches high, some with wings and some without. She had had beautiful visions of angels, too.

Her friend, Mrs. Syvia [sic] Woods, saw the fairy folk regularly when she was a child and lived in London. As soon as she was alone in her bedroom at night, they would come and play with her in the bed, and she had such wonderful times with them. She was always impatient for her mother to kiss her goodnight. "Hurry up and leave me, Mummy," she would say. "The fairies won't come till you've gone."

Mrs. Isobel Grant Whittle was "negatively clairvoyant and clairaudient" when, at the age of three, she lived in Liverpool. Being an only child, she played "alone" with two fairy companions named Puck and Parry. She was not sure whether they were pixies, elves, or gnomes, but they were dressed in green and reached almost to the height of her shoulder. She gathered they came from Cornwall, and they told her much about it. She talked with them "time on end" in a language that her mother could not follow. Her parents knew nothing of Cornwall and had never mentioned that part of the country to her. She was therefore delighted when, at the age of twenty-five, she visited Cornwall for the first time and found it was exactly as the fairies had described it. "How much of this memory is subjective and how much objective I cannot say," she concluded, "but at that time they (the fairies) were as real as any physical person I met."

Fairy Photographs

Unfortunately, photographs of fairies are not sufficient evidence in themselves, as we know only too well after the disclosure of the hoax over the ones taken at Cottingley by the then girls Elsie Wright and Frances Griffiths, and I must apologize to the many contributors and other correspondents for assuring them, through all the years I have been doing this fairy work, that the photographs were genuine.

I had been "taken in" not only by Mr. Geoffrey Hodson's faith in the girls' integrity, but also by a statement I had received in 1950 from a Mr. Granville Kendall, a commercial photographer in Blackpool, who said he had asked one of the girls to take some photographs in his presence, with slides which he had loaded in his own darkroom, and when he developed them he was surprised to see on them "the dainty figures of fairy folk."

Unfortunately, his friend at Bristol, through whom he had sent the statement, had enclosed with it a note saying: "I have now received from my friend Mr. Kendall his account of the taking of the photographs in E. L. Gardner's book *Fairies*." I had no reason to doubt the writer's words, and assumed the photos were among those that were already published, so as I was very busy at the time I did not see any reason to investigate the matter further. After all, how was I to know that there would be such doubt and controversy over the Cottingley photos in the future? I had even been told that both Elsie and Frances had died abroad!

I must also apologize to the kind lady in Birmingham, who in 1955 wrote to tell me that in her schooldays a special friend of hers had unfolded to her the hoax behind the Cottingley photographs, and said that Elsie Wright had shown her how it was done. I regret that in reply I assured her that the photos were genuine, and I told her about the statement made by Mr. Kendall and said that Mr. Geoffrey Hodson also was convinced of the *bona fides* of Elsie Wright and her cousin Frances Griffiths. Perhaps I should also have listened to my sister Dorothy, who *never* believed the photographs were genuine.

Later, when I discovered that no mention was made of Mr. Kendall in Mr. Gardner's book, and that the years did not tally, I wrote to Mr. Kendall for further particulars, thinking the photos must have been additional ones, but my letter was returned "Gone Away," and I was unable to trace him. I had heard by then that Elsie and Frances were still living, and that Elsie had become Mrs. Hill and resided in a Nottinghamshire village. I spoke to her over the telephone, but she said she knew nothing about Mr. Kendall, and when I asked her for her cousin Frances' address she refused to give it to me.

I remember that another of Mr. Kendall's friends (now deceased) had told me Kendall had been involved in an altercation with Mr. E.L. Gardner, who wanted any fairy photographs taken at Cottingley to be kept within the confines of the Theosophical Society. If that were so, why didn't Mr. Kendall tell me about it in his statement? I would have believed it, because Mr. E. L. Gardner had told me in a letter that he was not too keen on anyone other than himself showing the lantern slides of the Cottingley photographs.

On hearing that Mr. Kendall had died, I wrote to his son Leslie, but he, too, had passed away, and my letter was answered by his granddaughter, who said that apart from the ones that were published in the book there were no other Cottingley photographs in existence, and Mr. Kendall's name did not appear in any of the records. Unfortunately that did not prove anything, because if the story of the dispute were true, Mr. Kendall's name would for obvious reasons have been kept out.

By then, the friend who had sent me Mr. Kendall's statement had died, so I wrote to the editor of the *British Journal of Photography*, asking if he knew anything about Mr. Kendall and his fairy photographs. I received the following reply from the editor, who had been looking through the documents, which he had amassed from his series of articles on the Cottingley affair: "...There is no substance whatsoever to his claims. It was all sorted out at the time..."

A further problem arose when in 1983 I received a telephone message from Mrs. Elsie Hill via a man from Cheshire who had been interviewing at her home in Bunny. He said she wanted me to know that she had never seen any fairies and never believed in them, and that Mr. Geoffrey Hodson was a liar because he had only tested them for three days, and she and Frances had only pretended to see the fairies and had made up the descriptions.

First of all, Geoffrey Hodson was certainly not a liar. He had a worldwide reputation for being trustworthy and meticulous in all his clairvoyant investigations, so surely he would have been equally meticulous at Cottingley. It is unfortunate that right from the beginning Elsie seemed to take a dislike to him and had perhaps chosen that way of "paying him out." In Joe Cooper's book *The Case of the Cottingley Fairies* (Robert Hale, London, 1990), the author assumed that Mr. Hodson was a "medium," and he said that often such folk, when genuine psychic phenomena do not come along when expected, will slip into prevarication or lies, through he did add that he found it very difficult to believe that Mr. Hodson was the faker that Elsie and Frances declared him to be when they were on the Yorkshire TV programme.

I must stress here that Geoffrey Hodson was not a medium. And he said in one of his books that the methods of training taught by Theosophy have nothing in common with those of mediumship and trance. In his obituary in the *Theosophical Journal* of May/June, 1983, Vol. 24 No. 3, it said that "his aim was to lift the faculty of clairvoyance out of the atmosphere of charlatanry, mediumship, and fortune-telling which has surrounded it and made it repellent to the scientific mind, and secondly to show that it has a place in the evolution of human consciousness, and is of value as an instrument of scientific research."

It also stated in the *Journal* that right from childhood Mr. Hodson had had psychic experiences, chiefly consisting of visions of nature spirits, ghosts, and also symbolic dreams. He was not only a Theosophist but also a co-Mason, a priest of the Liberal Catholic Church (founded in Holland), and a keen worker for societies against cruelty to animals. He was also a prolific writer, one of his works being *The Hidden Wisdom of the Holy Bible* in four volumes.

He had trained himself through meditation, prayer, etc., to tune in at will to other states of consciousness, without lessening ordinary consciousness, and after the First World War his clairvoyant powers had enabled him to work with medical and scientific men in London and on the continent of Europe, and his powers had been accepted and tested by them. He went on lecture tours in most countries of the world, and gave his last public lecture in May 1982, only eight months before his "death" on 23 January 1983, at the age of 96.

His contact with the angels produced an intensification of awareness and he was able to see their glorious colour-language and also to receive their teachings, which he published in his books *The Coming of the Angels, The Brotherhood of Angels and of Men, The Angelic Hosts*, etc.

According to Elsie's message to me, Mr. Hodson had stayed at Cottingley only three days. This was not true, for the published notes showed that Mr. Hodson arrived with his wife, Jane, on 6 August 1921 and they were in the glen, field, wood, or at the beck with the girls on the 8, 9, 10, 11, 12, 14, 15, 16, and 18 August. (Mrs. Hodson predeceased Mr. Hodson, long before these accusations were made.) In his book *The Fairies at Work and at Play*, and also in a letter to me, he said he had spent some weeks there, and during his travels he must have had to keep an engagements diary, so surely he would know!

Mr. E. L. Gardner had said that Mr. Hodson pointed out the various fairies and asked the girls to describe them, but when Mr. Hodson was interviewed in New Zealand by Frank Wilson he told him that he would see fairies and gnomes coming near them but would remain silent, and quite often soon afterwards one or other of the girls would say she could see a fairy and would point to and correctly describe it.

We shall never know what actually happened, but if the girls had only pretended to see, yet "correctly described" the fairies, then the explanation seems often to be similar to what I have written at the beginning of this chapter about the transmitting of psychic power, and Mr. Hodson's greater degree of clairvoyance may have stimulated the girls' own limited vision, so that they weren't, as they thought, imagining or making up the descriptions but were really seeing what Mr. Hodson saw.

They were obviously doing their best to foil his attempts to test them, and it may be that they took advantage of him when his attention was turned to something in another direction, and as some fairy visions are only momentary ones they could say they had just seen such-and-such a nature spirit and he would not in that case be able to contradict them. However, he would certainly have known when they were exaggerating or giving silly descriptions, and perhaps then, instead of rebuking them, he would prefer to ignore them, and they might have taken his silence for confirmation of their descriptions, which would give them the excuse to call him a "phoney." He was certainly not that, as he would know only too well what the karmic consequences would be if he misused his powers of seership.

It was unkind of them to try to trick him, for the task set him by Mr. E. L. Gardner was an unenviable one. It must be very difficult to judge others' clairvoyant powers, for in any description the personal element is strong, and psychic people have their own modes of seeing, according to their "make-up." If some of the girls' descriptions seemed inadequate, Mr. Hodson would have to make allowances for the fact that their clairvoyance was more limited than his own, and in one of the notes he had used his higher astral vision to complete a description.

Some readers might think that if he possessed such powers he should have known the truth about the Cottingley photographs, but I do not think he can be blamed for believing in the girls' integrity, for he said in one of his early letters to me that when he questioned them they had assured him many times that they had taken the photographs. Of course, they could say that without feeling guilty, for they had "taken the photographs," but not of real fairies!

Mr. Hodson would never dream that they would need to use cut-out figures since both of them had simple clairvoyant faculties (Elsie had seen ghosts if not fairies), and Frances had told him that she had often seen and played with the fairies at the beck.

He had also heard from Mr. E. L. Gardener that an "expert" on faked photography had examined the quarter-plate negatives of the first two photographs and had declared that the dancing figures were not made of paper or of any fabric, and were not painted on a photographic background. Indeed, he said that the figures had moved during exposure!

Furthermore, Mr. Hodson told me that Cottingley Glen was swarming with elves, gnomes, fairies, etc, and that while he and his wife Jane were there they lived in a veritable Fairyland.

Could Elsie see, or could she not see fairies? In her message to me, she said she had never seen any, yet she said in an interview for the *Woman* magazine that she had seen fairies but only when Frances was with her, in which case her close proximity to Frances may have enabled her to see them—but she made so many conflicting statements that it is difficult to know the truth.

Frances became Mrs. Way, and her daughter said that to her mother's dying day she insisted that she had seen and played with real fairies at Cottingley, and that the "Fairies and their Sunbath" photograph was genuine.

When I wrote to Mr. Geoffrey Crawley, the editor of the *British Journal of Photography*, about Mr. Kendall, he said in his letter: "The question of fairy and spirit photography is a red herring, and if one is acquainted with how the image is formed in a photographic material, then even if there are spirits and fairies, they would not be recorded. The fact that a photograph purports to show them is proof that it is a fake."

I do not agree, as I have seen several photographs of real fairies, but the ectoplasmic figures have not been clear enough for reproduction.

The following accounts are about fairy photographs, which were shown to me, or taken by some of my contributors, whose sincerity I can really vouch for.

Miss Helen Fraser Morrison, of Rome, wrote to me of an unusual photograph taken in Tuscany between the two world wars: "At the time of the vintage, I was among the vines with the peasants who were gathering the grapes. I was not working, but only looking on, and occasionally picking a few grapes to eat. Under my arm I carried my little black Pekinese. An Italian friend who was with me had a Kodak camera and was taking many photos, one of which was of myself and my dog. When this was developed and printed, it revealed a figure standing close to me among the vines, as clear as the photo of myself and my little dog. The creature's face resembled my own, but was younger. Her skirt was of vine leaves, from under which two very human-like legs appeared! Under one arm she carried a little white dog that stretched out towards the black dog in my own arms, and my dog appeared to be reaching out towards the white one, so it was evident they could see each other. The female figure was not looking at me. In the photo she was full face, while I was slightly turned to one side. My friend, who had developed and printed the photo himself, had not noticed this important detail, clear as it was, and that I saw at first glance. Then he saw it too, and so did everyone else to whom it was shown. It was therefore not merely a shadowy effect; it was a clear and unmistakable photo of a separate being from another realm, though invisible to the human eye.

"We had the photo enlarged, and the figure was clearer than ever. We thought to send it to some society interested in such subjects, but unfortunately never did, though I sent prints of it to many friends. Then the Second World War broke out, and I had to go into exile hurriedly, leaving all my possessions behind. In the interval my beautiful home in Florence was blown up, and I lost all my treasures, including that precious photo, of which I had no copy with me. I have tried to remember to whom I sent prints but have not been able to trace anybody who possesses one; and my friend, the young Italian artist who took the photograph, was killed in the war."

Mrs. Doris Seccombe, of Cornwall, saw two small grey figures about a foot tall, with round heads, come out of an old stone of Cornish granite. After playing around for a while, they went back into it. On another occasion she saw in a friend's garden a little gnome, clad in a red jacket and green trousers. He smiled at her and then vanished. She told me that on moonlit nights she could see hundreds of fairy lights flickering in her own garden; and that a friend (now deceased) was walking in the vicinity when she heard a strange bussing sound in a gorse bush and, on going to investigate, saw that it was full of fairies. She went quietly to pick up her camera, which she had left on the ground, whereupon the fairies disappeared with the exception of two, which she managed to photograph very clearly while they were in the act of flying away from the bush. Although Mrs. Seccombe had been given a print, her son Mr. Ronald Seccombe could not find it after her death, but later he managed to trace an old "re-print" of the photograph, and I am grateful for his help and also for the kindness of the owner, Mrs. Violet M. Gresswell, for allowing me to see it with a view to having a copy made for reproduction in this book. The tiny winged figures seemed quite plain to me because I knew what they were, but when I took the print round to the chief photographic centres in Nottingham, none of them wanted to copy it. I was told that another negative would have to be made from it, and that in the finished picture the figures would appear merely as two indistinguishable whitish blobs.

A sample of a poor reproduction was contained in a book of reminiscences, *My Times and Other Times* (Donegal Democrat Ltd) by Capt. John S. Hamilton J.P., D.L., of Brownhall, Ballintra, County Donegal, of Ireland. The photograph was of one of his trees, which he told me was "full of fairies," but although I thought I could see a semblance of a tiny face here and there, it was impossible to distinguish any definite figures owing to the blurred background.

In a letter dated 25 January 1953, Mrs. Pamela M. Gott, of Hampshire, wrote: "Lady Rawlinson told me of a snapshot taken on the moors of Scotland that, when developed, showed a little gnome gazing up at the tall human beside him, as though saying: What on earth are you doing here?"

When Miss Clara Dodd, formerly General Secretary of the Theosophical Society in Australia and Southern Africa, came to lecture in Nottingham many years ago, she told me she had seen in New Zealand a friend's photograph of a little gnome at the foot of a tree.

Another contributor, Mrs. Iris Ratsey, said in 1984: "Nora and Anita Bruce (both now deceased), who used to live in Ireland and were great believers in fairy life, once showed me a photograph taken in a large garden in Ireland just before (or after) a luncheon party. Everyone was in position for the picture taking except the small daughter of the house. When called, she said she must wait because the fairies weren't ready. The family became impatient because they thought she was playing, but when, eventually, the picture was taken, there around the kneeling figure of the girl were the fairies! It was quite distinct.

"In their house on the outskirts of Cheltenham, the two sisters had a lovely bowl of roses, which they wanted to photograph. They fixed their camera for a time exposure and went away from the room. When the picture was developed, that, too, showed fairy life."

Seeing Fairies

During a holiday in Sheringham, Norfolk, my sister and I went by bus to Castle Rising to see the ancient castle. Nearby was a little wood, and as I strongly sensed the presence of fairies there, I went and knelt among the trees and played on my homemade bamboo pipe, while my sister photographed me. Fairies are attracted to music, and I knew that one or more fairy figures were building-up out of the ectoplasm from my aura. The print showed this, and it was admired by all my psychic friends, but the sceptics said, "What a pity the light got into the camera!" One cannot win!

As the writer Leslie Shepard said in one of his letters to me: "Nobody can be sure of anything with photographs or sound recordings. But even if found later to be untrue, they stimulate the imagination. I don't mean that fairies are imaginary, but only that perception of them is in that area of experience reached through imagination, as opposed to hard, matter-of-fact 'commonsense.'"

Chapter 12: A Fairy Sanctuary

The contributor of the following experiences is certainly not afraid of revealing his identity, but we both feel it is wiser not to divulge his name or the location of this wonderful Fairyland, as he wishes to protect it from publicity and hordes of pseudo-investigators. I have met "H" and have been corresponding with him for many years. During the long period of these occurrences, I found myself in touch with the Devic Guardian of the area, and had some curious experiences of my own, which I am unable to divulge but that linked up with those of "H," so I can vouch for the truth of his statements and his absolute sincerity. Although he may sound otherworldly, he is also very practical and has always busily engaged himself in public affairs.

At the beginning of his experiences, "H" was residing in Nottingham but was in the habit of spending his summer holidays in a village near London in the latter part of June. In 1960, on the second Saturday of his vacation, he went for an afternoon stroll, taking a neighbour's dog with him for exercise. About a mile outside the village, his walk took him by the site of a moated grange, which, three centuries before, had been sacked and burned by Cromwell's soldiers. As it was not badly damaged, it was made habitable again and restored to its former glory until some time in the nineteenth century, when it was again damaged by fire and abandoned. Finally it fell into decay, and "H" remembers seeing, in his early days, some parts of the masonry. He walked on for perhaps another quarter of a mile. Then, not wishing to tire the dog, which was stolid and getting lazy in its old age, he turned for home. As they passed the site of the ancient building for the second time, the dog suddenly became rigid and stood looking towards it. "H" called to the animal to "Come on," but it seemed terrified and, before he could see what it was looking at, it gave a howl, snatched the lead from his hand, and set off for home faster than he had ever seen it travel before.

He tried to call it back, but without avail. Feeling very puzzled, he looked to see what had frightened it, expecting to see another dog or some other animal. Then he saw a movement, but as the ground was far from level at that point it was a few seconds before he could be sure what was there.

"I was astounded," he told me, "to see what appeared to be three immense butterflies—two of them hovering in the air above one that was fluttering in the grass. They were many yards away, and their wings—the span of which was larger than an opened sheet of foolscap paper—obscured their bodies and made identification difficult. As regards colour, the two in the air appeared to be blue blended with chestnut-brown, the one on the ground being primrose or daffodil-yellow. The ground remained comparatively static for a few seconds, then moved away—the two still flying above the primrose one, which was travelling either on, or very close to, the grass. I noticed that its wings were fluttering much more rapidly than those of the other two, as if it was trying unsuccessfully to rise in flight. The wings of all three appeared indescribably rich, shimmering far more than the richest satin, and in shape closely resembling those of butterflies. They continued across the grass until the primrose one stopped on a raised hummock of ground, which may have been a large molehill, and began to beat its wings harder than ever, while the other two fluttered agitatedly round and round above it. Faster and faster beat its wings until their shape was lost in a blur of colour, and it left the hump of ground and began to move very quickly across the grass. I became acutely aware of a strained atmosphere as it went shimmering along. Then suddenly it left the ground and soared up, and the feeling of tension vanished as it fluttered delicately and lightly in the air. The three went flying towards the trees and then were no longer there. They had simply disappeared. I waited possibly half an hour but saw nothing else. A brief examination of the ground revealed nothing, and neither did several subsequent visits. The dog had arrived home on its own, very tired but none the worse for its fright. I explained away its behaviour by saying that it had been startled by a car backfiring. When I first saw the creatures, the time would be around 3 o'clock, and I reached home at about ten minutes to four, so I would assume that the experience and subsequent wait lasted approximately half an hour. There may be nothing significant in the fact that previously there had been a heavy downpour of rain."

In a footnote to his statement, "H" added that as a child he had spent many hours in the vicinity and had developed an affection for the place and its history, so that there was possibly an affinity with its atmosphere, which provided a common meeting-ground between himself and the nature spirits.

On 6 April 1962, I had a telephone call from "H," who had just returned to Nottingham from another holiday—an earlier one than usual owing to the illness of his mother. I learned that he had paid several visits to the site of the moated grange in the hope that he might see another fairy, but nothing had transpired until the penultimate day of his holiday while he was sitting on an old fallen log smoking his pipe and waiting as before. The shadows were lengthening but it was not quite dusk.

"Then," he related, "I heard a soft, fluttering, rustling sound. I looked round and there, not ten yards from me, was a fairy about as tall as my knee and apparently solid. She resembled a lovely girl and was wearing a ball gown of the eighteenth century, made of rich, deep crimson 'satin,' and where she held it up in front I could see a foamy puff of petticoats. Her wings were just ceasing to flutter; they were shaped precisely like those of a butterfly, but were far, far lovelier—plum-coloured patterned with deep crimson, shimmering, patiny petals of glowing fluorescent colour. They were large—the upper tips reaching well above her head to the height perhaps of my thigh, the lower tips almost brushing the grass. Her hair was powdered and dressed high, but not exaggeratedly so, in the eighteenth-century style. As I gaped in astonishment, I heard other rustling sounds and, turning round, saw other fairies (in size about 30 inches to the uppermost wing-tips) fluttering down, looking like lovely be-winged roses in their billowy, frothy-petticoated gowns of deep reds and primrose, and shimmering blues and greens. They seemed to glow all over, as if with an inner light, and their gleaming wings—breathtakingly beautiful—were patterned

like those of tropical butterflies. They leaned back on them, their
knees bent, their feet—in delicate 'satin' slippers—held high, and
as each fairy neared the ground she straightened up and landed
with a little bounce and a flurry of frills. They gathered together
in a little crowd and strolled around like a group of fashionable
ladies of centuries ago, except that these beauties had wings. They
continued in this manner for several minutes, maybe five or even
longer. I was too much engrossed to look at my watch, so can only
guess. Then the one I first saw turned away from the others and
picked up her gown, holding it high. She stood for several seconds
with wings full-spread, then began to flutter and to trip daintily forward on tip-toe. Faster and faster she fluttered, then bending at the
knees and with an extra-strong flutter, she leapt lightly into the air
and soared upwards. One by one the others followed her, and I
watched them drifting around perhaps twelve feet high. Then I suddenly realised that one—in a particularly billowy deep lilac gown,
with lilac-and-blue wings—was not with them but was still on the
ground, fluttering desperately hard! She was holding a double armful of her oceans of skirts high, but so voluminous were they that
her legs were still hidden by the foamy clouds of frills. Her wings
were whirring as she billowed frantically along. Bending again at
the knees, she leapt into the air but fell back. Again she tried, and
again. Her movements attracted the others, who swooped over her,
and at last she redoubled her efforts. The astonishing thing is that I
could hear her—the stiff, rustling 'frou-frou-frou-frou' of her gown
and the whirr of her wings. At last she threw up both her arms, releasing her skirts, and soared high into the air. Then all the fairies
flocked together and, joining hands, began an aerial dance, whirling round in a circle. This soon ended and they flew round and
round in ones and twos until, one after another they began to fade,
eventually dissolving into a shimmering, coloured mist. For a few
seconds I could still hear their rustling, then a clear, girlish laugh,
followed by silence. It was almost dark. I felt absolutely worn out,
and very sick. I went straight home to bed, where I stayed for twelve
hours before I fully recovered."

From the depleted condition of "H" after his experience, it

would seem that he has a loosely-knit etheric body, from which the fairies must have drawn lavish amounts of ectoplasm to enable them to densify their own bodies and to indulge more freely and objectively in their glamorous imitations of eighteenth-century costumes. The seated grange that once stood on that fairy-haunted ground must have been a fine house in the eighteenth century, and no doubt many grand balls were held there, attended by all the gentry from roundabout. The fabulous ball-gowns and hairstyles of that period must have left a deep impression on the fairies—hence their desire to adopt them.

After this experience, "H" recalled something that had held no significance for him at the time. When he was in the junior class at school, he was taught by a teacher who must have been very "fey."

"She used to tell us fairy stories when we should have been doing lessons," "H" said, "and of course we encouraged her! Nobody took much notice of what she said, as she was thought to be rather 'queer,' but I wish now that I had been old enough to understand and had paid more attention to her tales. We thought they were just imaginary, but they were centred around the area of the house site. 'In the fields, up ___ road,' or 'Along ___ road,' she would say, and the house-site stretches between those roads. She told us the fairies were dressed *like great ladies of hundreds of years ago, and they had butterfly wings, yet couldn't fly.* I know she was wrong about the fairies being unable to fly, but she'd probably seen them trying and failing over and over again, as I had done. So it seems I am not the first to see them. I am sure she did, and I wish I could speak to her now."

In June 1963, "H" went again to the village. He travelled on the Friday night, and the next morning (15 June), being unable to sleep, he rose at about 5 a.m. and went for a walk. Of course he felt drawn towards the scene of his previous fairy experiences, but the site of the old house was deserted and there was a feeling as though nothing was likely to happen there, so he went round a little wood nearby—another scene of many happy childhood hours. For a time nothing occurred, then he realised that about ten yards away, near some bushes, he could see a pair of wings!

"They were perhaps a foot in height, of an indescribable blend of dark and light blues and silver, shaped precisely like those of a butterfly and of the same rich, satiny texture, but incredibly sumptuous, putting the loveliest satin quite to shame. I could see no sign of a body; just those gorgeous wings fluttering daintily near the bushes, some three or more feet from the grass. I watched with breathless excitement until some few seconds later, they flew out of sight behind the foliage. I went after them, but, as I expected, there was no sign of them. Then, about twenty yards farther on, I saw them again. They flew from behind a tree, hovered for a few seconds, then went back behind the tree again. I waited for them to re-appear, which they did very shortly. They fluttered a little way towards me, then retreated to the tree, turned again, and hesitated. Suddenly I realised that I was being invited to follow them! As soon as I started forward, they flew behind the tree. I hurried on and, as I rounded the tree, I could see them crossing a little glade. I followed through the bushes into another glade, and then I suddenly realised that, as far as I knew, there never was another glade! I also realised that I could now see the body of the fairy who had led me—that of a lovely girl, dressed in a costume that was just like a short ballet tutu, with a wide, foamy, dark blue skirt. In that strange, dreamland atmosphere, I was unable to assess size and, for all I could tell, she might have been as large as me. That doesn't mean that she was, of course, but normal, everyday standards of size and place seemed to have disappeared. She was so slim and beautiful in her frothy costume, with her long hair, soft and thick and black, reaching below her waist, as she fluttered with those oh-so-lovely wings only just off the ground, her long legs raised in front, her arms held like those of a ballerina. It was a vision of such bewitching loveliness that I shall never forget it. I followed the shimmering vision across the glade—then I realised with a thrill of wonder and awe that we were not alone. The whole glade was filled with fairies! They were all like lovely girls, but with such indescribably glorious wings. I can't explain it, but if I tell you that they made butterflies' wings look like those of moths by comparison, you will perhaps realise a tenth of their loveliness. Even the most expensive satin used for gala ball gowns would have looked like rags compared with their beauty.

Some of the fairies wore what looked like inverted roses for skirts, others were in daffodils and primroses, and others in foamy frillies. They were laughing and dancing like happy children, playing with each other. One landed and immediately started to rise again, but two others took hold of her wings just as she made her little leap, and held her, laughing as children do. They played a sort of leap-frog, one bending over, wings upright and skirt foaming out stiffly, while several others fluttered up and over her, landing in their turn and bending over. Others joined hands and skipped in a circle, wings beating lightly. Because they were so close to each other their wings fluttered against their neighbours', and one fairy broke away from the circle and looked over her shoulders, examining her wings as if to make sure they were undamaged. Then she tried to re-enter the circle but wasn't allowed to, so she flew up and landed in the middle, dancing round and round on her own. One bewitching creature was all in black and silver, complete with black-and-silver wings. Round her hips was a foam of black frills, and her black bodice was decorated with silver. She did not join in the games but spent her time frothing out her frillies with her hands, spreading, folding, and re-spreading her wings, and posing and re-posing, occasionally making little fluttering flights, obviously very vain. All of them seemed able to fly with the utmost ease, floating around like thistle-down, as lightly as butterflies but without the erratic darting of that insect, and with none of the desperate whirring beating of sings like the other fairies I saw. The whole glade was alive with fluttering wings and rustling frills and shimmering 'satin' and rich colours, and the atmosphere seemed filled with a magic, gauzy light such as I cannot describe. Then, all too soon, they were gone, and all I could see was the original tiny (by comparison) pair of blue-and-silver wings. They fluttered away and I followed back to the other glade, then they, too, were gone. I looked and looked, but all I could find were the trees and bushes and tangled undergrowth. The magic glade had quite disappeared, and I know in my heart that it never really existed in the world in which we live. Now, at long last, I know what they meant in those old books by 'Fairyland.' A few other things occur to me. First, the grass was saturated with dew—except in the glade of the fairies. Second, although I could hear them, it was more that I could sense the sounds. There was a strange, all-pervading perfume—sweet and slightly piercing, yet flower-like and very delightful. The skin of the fairies was silky, yet with exactly the texture of a rose-petal, creamy-pink and white, and their eyes were limpid and shining. They seemed to shimmer slightly all over; they were like magic flower-butterflies in human form, and their frills were not just frills, as humans' are, but frothy puffs of rustling foam. I should explain that these fairies in the magic glade gave no indication of having any knowledge that I was there. They never came nearer than a few yards, and I was far too spellbound even to think of trying to touch or speak to them."

On 23 June 1963, "H" wrote me a further letter: "I have had yet another fairy experience! This time it was different from the other three. I returned to the wood in the evening to endeavour to contact the fairies. It was about 9:45 p.m. I went to the first glade and waited. Presently I realised that I felt very tired, so I sat down on the grass, thinking that my weariness might be the result of so much walking about after the train journey and rushing around in the morning. Soon, however, I was fighting off a heavy fatigue that was so strong that I could hardly keep my eyes open. Suddenly I became very dizzy and I felt myself falling through a void, as if I were 'going under' gas at the dentist's surgery. Then, in an instant I was all right; I felt not only perfectly fit and energetic but also exhilarated and very happy and carefree. The glade was no longer drowsy in the approaching dusk but bathed in light—not sunlight, but a shimmering, cobwebby sort of radiance, as if I were looking through a very fine film of delicate gauze, which made it seem unreal and without substance; soft and without the hard brilliance of daylight. All around were fairies, lovely creatures with gleaming wings, dressed similarly to those I told you of last time. On this occasion, however, there were no games and dancing. Instead, they all seemed to be concerned with trying to make themselves as pretty as possible, as if they were preparing for a party or a ball… There was an air of great excitement, bustle and hurry, which transferred itself to me so that I felt 'tingly' and stimulated. Incidentally, once again all the fairies seemed of full human size, and there was that strange perfume all the time. At length, one of them, in a very rich blue ballet tutu, began to beat her elaborately patterned, multi-coloured wings very rapidly, but without rising or moving... She just stood there, poised like a ballet dancer, then she began to trip forward, running (but very delicately, with no effort such as it would be to a human) round the perimeter of the glade. The others joined in behind, until they were a fluttering queue of fairies. Then they rose in the air and with legs raised and arms uplifted in front, went rushing round and round, spiralling upwards with a sound like the soughing of the wind. The excitement rose to a terrific pitch—then I became very dizzy and suddenly felt that I was falling again through a void, but this time falling forwards, as if returning to where I had come from—and then it was all over. I was in the glade and it was pitch dark. It was raining slightly and everything was real and ordinary. As I blundered out of the wood I felt very shaken and 'trembly' as a result of the intense excitement. In the darkness my hand was pricked several times by thorns—one of which pulled a thread out of my jacket. Other things occur to me as I think. These fairies seemed to be more richly dressed than the others in the magic glade, for their costumes had gold and silver threads in them and were scattered with flowers, and I seem to remember that whereas the satiny-winged fairies had little gold, silver, etc., slippers, the gauzy-winged ones were barefoot—but I am not certain of this."

In a later letter "H" enlarged on the fairies "very great—indeed, exaggerated—elegance of gesture, pose and movement, so much like that of a ballerina, or the exaggerated elegance of the eighteenth century. They fluttered their fingers in emphasis of the use of their arms, and have an exquisite grace to the point of a toe or the twirl of a frill."

Other contributors (especially Struan Robertson) have noticed this perfection of form and grace of movement.

"Nature spirits, like children, can be very mischievous, and here is a good example," wrote "H". "Last Friday night (23 August 1963), I saw one of the gauzy-winged fairies standing in a corner of the room. She was holding her face in her hands and seemed to be 'crying her eyes out.' I was, of course, greatly concerned, and then, just as I thought: 'Poor thing, what on earth's the matter?' she looked straight at me with such mirth and cheeky wickedness on her face that it was quite obvious she was only pulling my leg! I felt like slapping her, as you may guess. She immediately put out her arms sideways, went up on tiptoes with a little jerk, as if launching herself and then fluttered straight up through the wall."

On the night of 9 October 1965, "H" had been reading and didn't notice the time, so when he eventually got to bed at 1 a.m. he couldn't sleep through being over-tired. He lay there for perhaps an hour or longer, becoming more and more irritable and as a result becoming less able to sleep. All at once, however, he felt the familiar "swimming" sensation, which lasted perhaps a second or two, and when he recovered he seemed to be standing (or lying—he wasn't sure which) in a little, very overgrown lane at home—one that leads to the house-site and that was perhaps a back drive for the use of wagons. Although the light was of the same gauzy, unreal quality previously described, it seemed to be broad daylight, and the considerable vegetation—flowers, very long grass, bushes, etc., the great profusion of which is a feature of this lane—seemed to be in the full flush of high summer.

"Then," wrote "H" in the letter that he sent to me the next day, "I noticed a movement in the grass and, to my surprise, saw that it was caused by a fairy in the shape of a little gnarled, wrinkled and very cantankerous-looking old man with grey hair, a long, straggling beard, and startlingly bright blue eyes. He wore a long brown coat, rusty-red pantaloons, and a hat like a brown sock pulled low over his brow and dangling down his neck. He was hobbling along with the aid of a short, bent stick, and his lips were moving as if he was muttering to himself. On his back was a pair of long, dragon-shaped, pale green wings, gauzy and veined, quite unlike the rich satiny sails of the girl fairies. He continued to hobble along, and then I noticed that hiding behind the vegetation, parting the leaves to peer anxiously out, were the house-site fairies, glamorous in their dazzling ball gowns, foaming frillier and shimmering, lovely wings. They appeared to be watching the 'old man' but were intent on not letting him see them. I recognized the one in crimson 'satin,' with crimson and plum-coloured wings, as the 'leader' in my earlier vision. There were several others whom I recognized, and, yes, the one in lilac, who couldn't fly. She still wore the vast, billowing gown she wore on that occasion, and I was able to examine it fairly clearly, since she was near me. It was (in human, descriptive terms) made of innumerable tiny frills of lilac 'chiffon,' banded with very harrow velvet ribbons, off the shoulder, with large cobwebby 'chiffon' sleeves. It was worn over a tremendous cloud of gauzy frills, and it spread over them in a sweep far wider than the fairy's height, except where it flattened somewhat behind to allow her to use her wings. Her hair was high and powdered, and she wore jewels in it. I confess that I was so interested in her that for a moment I forgot the old man. Imagine my amazement when I saw that, still hobbling along, he was vanishing in parts! First his arms and stick, then his legs and his body, until finally only his head—still nodding, and muttering—and his wings, were visible. The latter parted and began to beat with a harsh, jerky rustle; then, before the old man could rise, he was all gone."

Some of the old gnomes do fade away in parts. He was probably ready to pass into another form of life.

"H" continued: "At once the fairies came out of hiding, looking very relieved, and smiling, skipping about and clapping their hands as if in self-congratulation at escaping notice. They appeared to be telling each other about it, all talking at once (but no words were audible), each seemingly convinced that she had been the most clever. Then the one in lilac frills pretended to hide behind a slim nettle (as if it could conceal such a billow of foam!), while another, in red 'velvet,' pretended to be the old man, stumping along in parody, her vast skirt dragging behind her. Then they all burst out laughing and clapped their hands, and several others wanted to play the same game, but the one in crimson wouldn't let them. She called them together and—once more the sophisticated ladies of high fashion—they began to stroll sedately along the lane, round the bend and out of sight. Suddenly it grew dark as night again, and I seemed to be rushing through space. Dizziness and slight nausea followed—and I was back in bed! It was a strange vision, but it seems to shed a little more light on the natures of the house-site fairies. They appear to be a curious blend of mature, beautifully mannered ladies and very happy, mischievous children. But I believe fairies are apt to be like that."

It seemed that "H" was to be drawn yet again into the glamour of the fairy world, for on 14 August 1968 he wrote to say that during the night he had had the most incredible vision of all. Being unable to sleep, as the air was warm and humid, he had risen from his bed and gone out for a walk. He did not note the time, but it was fairly dark, with enough starlight to show him the way, especially as he knew the area so well, having been born there. He went along a lonely and pleasant little road, which served only two or three farms in its total length of over a mile. It ran near the site of the old moated grange, and halfway across it was a small grassy lane, which actually led to the house-site and had doubtless served as a rear entrance to the house. Just past this lane was a field of corn, and on the other side of the road was a small, oddly shaped field that contained a few calves and was the haunt of hares, which seemed quite bold and almost tame. "H" was overcome with a sudden strong desire to go into the field, so he went through the gate and began to walk across the grass. Within moments he noticed that it was mysteriously getting lighter. He thought it was dawn at first, then realised that it was a strange, cold, pale bight, almost like moonlight, but becoming quickly as light as day. And suddenly he seemed to find himself in a village! There were houses all around, and he was walking along a road, which, although flat enough, seemed made of beaten earth and stones, rather like the roads must have been centuries ago. The houses, too, were very old-fashioned, with the tops larger than the ground storeys, diamond-paned windows, wide eaves and thatched roofs; moreover, they seemed oddly shaped warped, leaning at strange angles, almost as if seen through a cheap bottle-glass window or a distorting mirror. Then he noticed that also around him were numbers of fairies. They seemed as naturally at home as any human being in a real-life village. Some were rose fairies, in costumes just like beautiful upturned pink roses glistening as though the dew were on them. Their wings were exactly like rose petals in shape, colour, and texture—a soft, rich pink, and their delicate slippers were green. Other fairies were bindweed sprites, in costumes exactly like the little pink bindweed, which trailed all over the verges around that district, and they had wings of creamy pink. They tripped lightly and very delicately around and often rose in tremulous, fluttery flight. There were others that "H" called plum fairies because they were clad in calf-length, bell-shaped dresses the colour of ripe purple plums, their wings being exactly the texture of that fruit. They walked around much more gravely, and when they wanted to fly they needed to poise, flutter, then run forward a few steps in the way other fairies had done in "H"'s earlier visions. He wandered through the village, while fairies of all sorts—some dressed like flowers, some in ballet tutus, and others in gauzy, trailing draperies—fluttered softly as a sigh round about him. Some drifted on lightly-fanning wings over the roof-tops of the houses, (which seemed as large as humans' cottages; the fairies being as tall—or so it seemed—as children of, perhaps, twelve), and some would be walking along when all at once, with a little flutter and a skip, they would take to the air. There were also several gnarled old gnomes, little elves in doublets and hose, with long, slim dragonfly-type wings, and one rather odd creature—a very old but pleasant-faced gnome in long coat and pantaloons.

"H" witnessed many things, and eventually it dawned on him that all the fairies were going in the same direction as he was, and were, moreover, all going somewhere in particular. Then he found out where, for, in a field between the houses, he came upon a fairy market! The field was very small and apparently triangular, for he saw only three hedges—one very neatly trimmed like a garden hedge, and the other two of what looked like hawthorn in full May-blossom: this was in August, but why not, in a fairy village? The market was composed of many stalls, all put higgledy-piggledy anyhow, and heaped up with a large variety of commodities. All this passed like a few moments of flickering visions, yet looking back it seemed to "H" to have passed many hours. All he has described happened like so many little scenes, each crowding upon the other. Then he said it began to grow very misty, and suddenly the air seemed full of fairies in flight. The last vision he had was of a fairy from the house-site in a deep rose-red gown, bending forward so that she faced the ground, putting her hands high behind her and sweeping up an immense armful of petticoats towards the front of her. With wings beating, she ran forward on tiny, pointed, satin-shod toes, her cumulous-cloud of frills still dragging behind, despite the mass of them, which she already held, but "H" did not see whether she managed to fly. A little fairy in a tutu, looking more like a ballerina than any human dancer, fluttered near enough to him to be touched had he thought of it. Then, with a shock, he found himself once more standing out in the road in the darkness. He thought at first that he'd had a quick dream or hallucination while leaning on the gate, but then he saw that it was open as though he had been through. He turned and ran back into the field, but it was just ordinary and normal. All the magic and the beauty, the lovely colours and otherworldly life were gone. Sadly he went home.

"Here is the strange thing," he concluded in his letter. "I couldn't have been in the field more than a few seconds during that experience, for my feet were dry although the grass was wet, and the shoes I happened to have on would have let the water in. Yet, after going back into the field for a couple of minutes for the second time, my feet were really wet!"

This brings to mind "H"'s experience dated 15 June 1963, when he found that the grass was saturated with dew—except in the glade of the fairies! It seems from this that, at the point when he walked through the gate into the field for the first time, and also at the moment when he entered the fairy glade, which was non-existent on the physical plane, he must have been in his astral body, while his physical body remained at the gate. It is possible that the fairies put on that show especially for him.

On 25 June 1970, "H" attended a ball at a large house not very far from the site of the moated grange. He sat for a while, watching the people dancing on the lawn. Then, as the shadows lengthened and the sun dipped behind the hedges, he made his way home, got out of his dinner jacket and went into sport coat and slacks, and wandered up to the old house-site via the back lane, getting there a little before 10 p.m. Back at the ball, a tiny spark of light showed where the rigged-up lights were turned on. He leaned on the fence, smoking, and after a while he thought he could hear the band in the distance.

"I decided," he said, "that the band was playing oriental music. This was very odd, but then I realised that although what I could hear was music of some sort, it hadn't really got an actual tune. All very mysterious but 'Oh,' I thought, 'It's just the distance playing tricks,' and I tried to listen harder to catch the tune in the reedy thread of music as I stared idly up the field. Then I saw the fairies. They seemed miles away, yet close at hand, as if I was watching a television picture. They were strolling towards me yet advancing at a terrific rate as if coming from miles away at a hundred miles per hour. Suddenly they were before me, standing as calmly as if they had been there for some time. When I say 'before me' I mean they were perhaps ten to fifteen yards away and slightly to my left, but somehow they seemed so insubstantial and unreal that, although they were apparently of full human size, I couldn't possibly have pin-pointed where they really were. They were delicate, slightly shimmering all over like a colour film, and they wore the same breathtakingly lovely gowns as always —'satins' and 'brocades,' 'lace' and 'chiffon,' 'tulle' and combinations of all of them such as 'lace' over 'satin' over clouds of frilly 'tulle,' or heavy 'silk brocade' over layers of 'chiffon' and 'tulle.' I use the human equivalent to describe the gowns, but of course such equivalents are only very approximate. How can one describe fairy materials properly? Like cobwebs; and flames of red and blue and amber; like nets of sea-foam and summer clouds; like evening shades; dawn and sunset, and flowers in a mist. Their wings were equally lovely—perfectly poised butterfly creations almost skimming the ground behind with their lower tips, and reaching high above their heads with the upper ones, like butterflies standing erect. One fairy, in billowing amber 'satin' over foams of frills, began idly to dance. The others soon joined in and they went circling and posing round, threading through the throng, a quick ballet-pose and back around, pose and circle, pose and thread through, pose and back. Their skirts billowed and frothed; clouds of frills foamed and were hidden again by the sinking gown-skirts froth and shimmer, billow and flutter, pose and off again. And all the time the distant thread of tuneless music, like a strange violin, continued. Perhaps there were fifteen fairies, perhaps twenty; I couldn't think to count. Some held their skirts up; some ignored the apparently cumbersome layers of material. But nothing had any weight or solidity; it was like the lovely dancing of flower-butterflies in a dream, or like winged moonbeams a-flutter in an enchanted flower garden. I then realised that more of them had begun to flutter their wings, and soon all were doing so, lightly, delicately, not with the frantic, whirring thrashing I'd seen before. They danced on, billowing and rustling their frillies — obviously deliberately, since they used their hands to froth out their petticoats, and often I saw a fairy stretch out her hand to toss a neighbour's petticoats up to make them foam out to add to the effect. Or is that correct? It seemed they had only to stretch out a hand and the skirts spread without being touched. They also used their arms as extra wings, beating them as wings beat, all seemingly part of the effect. Then, without any effort at all, they rose into the air and formed a ball like a many-coloured dandelion clock, dancing in the air as they had on the ground, in three dimensions instead of two. Constantly fairies sank to the earth, then just stretched their arms high, fluttered, and rose back to the aerial dance. One ran on the air as if on the ground, round and round, laughing and beating her wings rapidly but soundlessly. Some soared and darted, dived and circled, like birds. Then they formed a great rainbow of 'satins' and rich fabrics, frillies and fluttering wings. After a minute or so, they receded at a tremendous speed until they were a tiny glittering horseshoe, and were gone. I waited some time, then, as it was practically dark, I went back home, feeling very dazed."

"H" did not write again until July 1973, when he said that apart from brief, nebulous corner-of-the-eye glimpses of fairies he'd had just one proper "sighting." "This was a wood fairy, half-flying, half-dancing on tip-toe, with butterfly wings and a foamy, gauzy, frilly tutu the colour of a cornflower. She was laughing and very merry, revelling in her loveliness, the sunshine and riot of flowers. Smelling a blossom, then throwing back her head and lifting her arms like a ballerina, she fluttered —her toes barely touching the ground—to another flower, and another. She danced and posed, light as thistledown, as if a tiny puff of breeze or the slightest quickening of her wing-beats would send her floating into the air. Yet she didn't fly, but eventually disappeared out of the clearing amid the trees."

On returning to the house-site on the 28th of the following month, "H" had no real hope of seeing any fairies as it had been raining heavily and the grass was wet. Contrary to expectations, they appeared immediately, and he wrote to me on the following day: "There were seven of them, and some were fairies I had seen before—those with gowns and wings of lilac, daffodil-yellow, and plum and crimson. One wore a gown of pink and cove-grey, and had silver and pink wings; another was all in green. I can't remember the other two. They prepared for flight in the usual way, lifting their gowns, rising on tiptoe and standing poised for ten to fifteen seconds until their wings were beating very quickly, then running forward. The one in lilac became so light that she was all but flying. Her toes barely touched the grass, and as she was unable to direct her steps properly she tottered haphazardly here and there, hanging from her desperately buzzing wings and trying frantically to lift her hems from the grass. The others were even less successful. They billowed about in a rustling froufrou of frills and wings in a tremendous effort to rise, and the sound was like wind in the leafy branches of the woodland. The low sun sparkled on them, and it was an entrancing spectacle—a sort of butterfly ball in competition dancing gowns! They kept rushing on to any high points—molehills or anthills—and attempting to launch themselves, only to fall back in a confusion of frills and vainly fluttering wings."

It was at this point that "H" recalled that I had asked him to try standing further away from the fairies in order to reduce the amount of ectoplasm that they drew from him to build up their gowns and petticoats. So he began to walk away from them, and "almost at once they seemed to grow lighter, insubstantial, and more like a cinema film." When he retreated still further, "they floated into the air as lightly as thistledown" and vanished. But as he pointed out to me, he could not always keep his distance, as his escape was limited by the high hedges in the lane or field wherever he might happen to be, and if he moved along the lane to increase the distance between himself and them, he lost sight of them. Also, in their take-off attempts, he said the fairies were as likely to run towards him as away from him. So, in subsequent accounts, they still seem hampered by their many layers of etheric garments.

"H" has no photographs of the fairies, because he says that while he is seeing them he is completely unaware of himself. "I get so wrapped up in watching them that I forget myself entirely, and don't know what I should do," he explained.

On 9 June 1974, "H" wrote to say that on the previous night he had seen the house fairies again for a few minutes. They were fluttering and dancing happily on tiptoe gowned as before like eighteenth-century ballroom dancers, with flowers and sparkling "stones" in their hair. Every now and then, one gathered up her billowing skirts and petticoats and buzzed her wings in an obvious attempt to fly, but although she tried repeatedly to launch herself up, she could not leave the ground. One in daffodil-yellow "satin" with matching wings tried very hard indeed, again and again, but failed. "H" felt the usual sickness and depletion, but less than in the early days.

He had a different type of experience in 1976, and wrote on 7 February: "Having seen no fairies at the house-site, I was returning down the lane when, rounding a corner, there they were! The party seemed to consist of a 'queen' with a retinue of six 'ladies-in-waiting' and about a dozen 'guards' round them. The latter wore jackets of stiff cloth or skin, in dark green, with matching tights of shiny material. They carried long rods, staves, or perhaps spears. Their jackets were something like the present-day Norfolk shooting-jackets but longer, mid-thigh, and had no collars or lapels. I don't know for certain, but they were what I'd imagine gamekeepers or huntsmen wore in the eighteenth century. Their wings were a russet colour and were much smaller than those of the ladies, which were the rich scarlet of October hawthorn leaves and were butterfly-shaped, with the lower tips brushing the grass. The gowns of the ladies were of stiff, cobwebby 'net,' with 'velvet' bodices and long, slim, puff-shouldered sleeves of a soft woodland green. The 'Queen' was a splendid creature; her colour scheme was totally different. Her huge wings were a glowing crimson like her 'satin' gown, which, over frothy, matching frills, streamed behind her on the ground. Her hair was shining silver, flowing down her back almost to the ground, in a gleaming waterfall, and on her head she wore a circlet of green leaves and red berries. She was a head higher than the others, her gown more billowing, her wings larger. She glowed all over, like a lamp, and beside her the others looked as dull as moths. They walked steadily forward for some way, looking neither left nor right, and then seemed to go through an invisible door! You know how a person going through a door or round a corner disappears progressively, not just vanishing but going out of sight? Well, the fairies did that in the middle of the open lane. It was quite weird. One by one they went through this invisible door and were gone!"

In a letter dated 29 January 1977, "H" said: "I saw a fairy again today—the first for a long period. I went up the lane behind the house-site field to get a fallen bough for firewood. It had come from an elm tree overhanging the lane, not from the site-field hedge. I looked for fairies in the site-field for a start and leaned on the fence by the oak-trees in the corner. Seeing nothing, I went on almost to the gate at the end of the lane to get the bough. On my return, I had just passed the fence, which was about level with the hedge dividing the site-field from the next, when I put the bough down to change the position on my shoulder. I turned round to pick it up again and, on glancing into the site-field, I saw a fox. I wasn't very surprised, as they are not unusual here, but I paused to watch it. It was moving at a slow trot, with its head down, and then I realised that it was following something. It came through the fence and turned away from me, and I saw that just in front of it was a fairy! She was around fourteen inches high to her top wing tips, and wore a frilly, petticoated gown of soft, dull, dark green material resembling tulle. Her wings were a satiny, pale green, large and butterfly-shaped. She was obviously trying to fly but unable to do so, weighed down as she was by her gown, and impeded by her dragging petticoats, and she could find nowhere higher enough from which to launch herself. The fox seemed interested and puzzled as she fluttered vainly along, and the two of them continued into the field, which had an old, half-dead orchard in it. They went into this, and I followed them as soon as I'd shaken off the sort of dream-like paralysis, which always affects me when I see the fairies. As the orchard had not been pruned for over 30 years and was dense with undergrowth, I could not progress as easily as the fox and the fairy, and lost sight of them. There were countless ways they could have gone, and I didn't see them again. Perhaps the fairy vanished; perhaps she flew. I can't think the fox would harm her; it seemed in a sort of bemused, trance-like state, as though under a 'fairy spell.'"

"H"'s next sighting was in September 1978. He was gathering hazelnuts when he saw a fairy carefully picking her way along inside the hedge, which was very overgrown and must have been about nine feet high and six feet wide. She was having great difficulty in getting along, because her voluminous green gown and layers of pale green frilly petticoats, and her huge nut-brown and gold butterfly wings impeded her considerably. Eventually she tired of it, climbed a yard or so up the trunk of half-fallen, sloping crab-apple tree and tried to fly off it. She was unable to spread her wings fully, however, and despite fluttering hard she could not rise, so she jumped down, breaking her fall with her wings as well as she was able. She then set off across the field but this was the flat part, lacking the big molehills or ant heaps from which she might have launched herself, and she was obviously quite unable to rise at all. Then, after she had fluttered quite desperately hard for some 25-30 yards, she disappeared.

"I have seen another fairy," "H" told me in a letter in August 1979. "I had been waiting for a long time without success and was just about to give up when a fairy appeared, actually in flight, fluttering from left to right some five yards in front of me, about eighteen inches from the ground. She was dressed in a foamy pink tulle-like gown with many frilly petticoats and she had darker pink wings. Suddenly she began to gyrate very quickly in a tiny circle, her wings beating very rapidly, and I saw that she had caught her gown on a thistle. She was very soon free, however, and soared high into the air and disappeared. A gown that can catch on a thistle must be solidified and have some weight. No wonder these fairies have difficulty in rising from the ground!"

In March 1983, "H" had an experience which made him realise that the lavish amount of ectoplasm from his etheric body, on which the fairies had been depending for their very solid-looking materializations, was now diminishing as he grew older. He had noticed that a number of fresh molehills had appeared in the site-field and the vicinity of the lane so, as nobody was about he settled down to wait and see what would happen. Eventually he saw something about five or six yards away. At first he couldn't make out what it was, then he saw that it was a portion of a butterfly-shaped wing, "like the little bits you sometimes see in old spiders' webs, but much bigger." Then the whole of the wing began slowly to appear, but tremulously and uncertainly, finally resolving into a pair of wings. Suddenly they vanished, then instantly reappeared, but translucently, because he could see through them. They kept flickering into momentary solidity, then he could see the whole fairy, but the vision was vague and still flickering, like the picture on a worn-out television set. She seemed to be trying to appear, but was not quite able to do so. Then suddenly she appeared completely and solidly, holding up the skirts of her gleaming "satin" "lace" covered gown. After standing quite still for about one second, she spread her wings wide, but they vanished in an instant. A look of utter stupefaction came on her face. There she was, poised for flight, but without wings to fly with. She became hazy and tremulous, and just disappeared completely. "The whole episode lasted no more than 30 seconds, perhaps less, and it seemed to come as a surprise to the fairy as well as to me," "H" said. One is left wondering why the wings of these fairies seem so necessary to them for, according to Geoffrey Hodson, wings in general are really streaming forces from the nature spirits' own astro-etheric auras.

Edward L. Gardner said they have no articulation or venation and are not used for flying, but I know that there are many fairy seers who have seen wings as delicately veined as those of insects, and have watched them opening and shutting during flight. On the other hand, some apparently wingless fairies can soar through the air quite effortlessly.

In the case of "H"'s fairies, it is possible they have evolved from butterflies, since they attach so much importance to the use of their wings, and "H" himself says: "I am firmly of the opinion that fairies, which are fully materialized, fly like butterflies by the power of their densified wings. At least, these do. Otherwise, why this lifting of their gowns to balance themselves; leaping off high places to launch themselves, and avoiding sheltered places out of the wind because they need a breeze to catch their wings and increase the power of their beating? They stand upright in order to balance as perfectly as possible, and in the air lean back a little on their wings, their feet lifted in front and their knees bent. They remind me vividly of swans—excellent when actually on the wing but very poor when it comes to rising from the ground."

It seems to me that some sort of experiment was being conducted, and that "H" had been deliberately chosen by the Deva-Guardian of the area as a suitable person to help in the evolution of that particular band of fairies. He may have had a special link with the Fairy Kingdom in a previous existence. As Geoffrey Hodson said: "We do not know how far back our relationship to the nature spirit world may not be traced."

Chapter 13: Mediums and Fairies, and Fairies in Dreams

When I visited Mr. and Mrs. Taylor, known as "Mildred and Bunnie," in part of a charming old house in Kent, the corridor had on its walls exquisite miniatures of children, painted in watercolour by Bunnie, who was a very gentle and unassuming man in delicate health. After his passing, Mildred was in communication with him, and in a letter to me she wrote: "Bunnie (in the Spirit World) has been to see the fairies dance. He said it really was a wonderful sight. He and his Guide came to a large field, in the middle of which was a little cone-shaped house, and sitting on the top of the house was a little old man—a gnome who was in charge. Suddenly the door opened and out trooped the fairies—fairies in every colour of the rainbow, and directly their feet touched the grass up sprang a tiny toadstool and became the stage property for the dance. They did many different dances, each one lovelier than the last. Bunnie was enchanted. He is having a most wonderful time exploring the heaven worlds, and growing young again!"

Mrs. Lily McKenzie was a member of Glasgow Psychic College, of which Mr. David Smith was then the principal, and in March 1962 she wrote to me with the following news: "One evening while we were sitting concentrating, I got the feeling there was a fairy beside me. I don't see, but sense, things. I said to myself that when Mr. Smith asks us if we experienced anything, I will not say, and just see if he saw the fairy. Well, the first thing he said to me was: 'Mrs. McKenzie, there was the loveliest fairy sitting on your shoulder, nine inches high.' I said 'Yes.' It was a beautiful golden colour, and Mr. Smith said it had its hands outstretched towards me and was looking so lovely and so very pleased."

A month later I had another letter from Mrs. McKenzie. It was full of excitement. "I want to tell you," she said, "I have seen the golden fairy in my own bedroom—have seen it twice in the last three weeks. It's so dainty, and it appeared floating in the air in a lovely circle of light, about 2 o'clock in the morning." After that, Mrs. McKenzie started having other fairy experiences, many of which are in this book.

In a letter to me dated 9 July 1950, Mrs. W. Marjorie Robinson, of Swanmore, near Southampton, said: "Miss Lucy Bruce of Iona was sitting alone in my sitting room while I was busy, when some little elves clustered round her and said they would like her to ask me if they might make their home here. I am in touch with my husband, who was killed in the First World War, and he has often spoken to me of the Little People. I had a very beloved horse and often, when I was riding on the downs, he would suddenly look intently at what seemed to me to be nothing, and then take a flying jump either sideways or backwards. I used to laugh at him and tell him he was silly to shy at nothing. Then one day at a sitting with Mrs. Osborne Leonard, the well-known spiritualist medium, my husband said: 'By the way, don't tell Sherry he is silly when he behaves so strangely on the downs and in the woods. He is not shying at nothing; he can see more than you can and he often sees the Little People and is startled. I have often been with you when it has happened.'

"I asked him if he knew anything about the colony of elves Miss Bruce had spoken to. He said 'Yes, they are all about you in the cottage and garden, helping you. They only go to live where their true condition is set up by human adjustment, and they have made their home with you and they love working in your garden. A garden in which the Little People are welcome, where there is a conscious invitation extended to them, will be beautiful. It may be weedy or untidy even, but there will be points of beauty in it that will be missing in even more well kept gardens. They put vitality into the soil and help things to grow. We can see them though you can't. They are always around you and they bring happy life into your home. They are very pretty and have beautiful spirit colours around them. They only come where they are loved and welcomed.' That was several years ago. Quite recently he told me that the colony had greatly increased and that there are large numbers of the Little People here now and they are very happy and try to help and cheer me if I feel tired. I am conscious of their presence, and I talk to them although I cannot see them."

When the novelist and spiritualist, Miss Margery Lawrence, was living in Spain in 1955-1956, she was in close touch, via a medium, with an interesting group of hill fairies of the gnome or earth-folk type. She was staying with friends in a house with a charming garden outside Torremolinos, and several of these little people evidently liked the garden and used to come and play around in it. One of the ancient, gnome-like entities said he was almost 300 years old, and that all his folk lived to be at least 200. They dwelt in the hills far behind the town, and worked among the minerals—mainly in crystals, a few of which were grudgingly allowed to be found now and then by men. "My friends and I went up to the hills several times," said Miss Lawrence, "and we used to see quantities of small lights—which were too big for glow worms—flitting about. A friend who stayed with us saw a few of these little folk, but only at a distance. She said that some of them were bearded, and that they looked humped, clumsy creatures with big feet, and wore peaked hoods and tunics."

I heard from Miss Doreen Hutchinson, of South Harrow, Middlesex, that in 1956 her mother was giving spiritual healing to a certain Mr. Glasson when she saw a fairy clothed in blue and gold. The little thing, according to Mrs. Hutchinson, was waving her wand, as if to grant a wish. She immediately mentioned her vision to Mr. Glasson, who made no comment until the healing session was at an end. It then transpired that at the moment she had described the fairy, he had been granted his dearest wish—that he should again see his mother, who had passed into the spirit world several years ago. Four or five days later, Miss Hutchinson and her mother had a sitting with Mrs. Coral Polge, a psychic artist residing in Kenton Lane, Harrow Weald. "When it came to my turn," said Miss Hutchinson, "Mrs. Polge was considerably startled because she had been shown some fairies, and she said she did not believe in them. However, we expressed delight at this proof, and I have in my possession her original sketch and two very pretty-coloured portraits

313

of two wee fairy folk."

When Mrs. Frances Pinter, of Leeds, attended a private séance, she had the following experiences: "First, there was a lovely fragrance, and exquisite flowers appeared. Secondly, at least twenty elves dressed in grass green circled in a joyous dance round a bowl of flowers. Then they flew across to a cage of birds and flitted all over it before they went back again to the flowers, round which they gave a final dance before disappearing."

Another contributor, Mrs. Minnie Griffiths, attended a séance conducted by the Preston medium Mr. James Gordence and saw fairies there on four occasions. "I felt their little dresses touch my hands," she said. "They are very lively and friendly little souls, and seem to like the tune of 'Jingle Bells.'"

In 1952, Miss Katie Richardson, a spiritualist in London, was being used as the medium for a small group who met for absent healing, and they had been sent the name of a small boy aged three or four, for whom the doctors could do nothing. The moment the child's name was given out, the woman guide said, "Oh, but this little one belongs to the Little People," and even before she had finished speaking these words we were shown a vision of the fairies carrying the child away and placing him on a small couch, which just fitted his body. "The fussing and petting, and the feeling of happiness that came from them was unbelievable. They patted the coverlet, and his hair and face, and moved in a constant stream around him." Miss Richardson, whose mediumship took the form of conscious control, remembered thinking what a fuss they were making as though he were a long-lost brother, and the controlling guide told the group that the little one had already been gathered up by his own kind. Afterwards, they heard that the boy had passed over between his name reaching them and the day of the healing circle, so the guide's words were corroborated. This experience intrigued Miss Richardson so much that she asked her guides during a period of meditation if they could offer any more information regarding the remarks at the healing circle, and they said "Oh yes, this little one was caught up in the wrong stream of life. Doctors could never have been able to affect a cure."

Fairies in Dreams

Nerys Dee says in her book *Your Dreams and What They Mean* (Aquarian Press, Northants., 1984) that physiologists refer to the non-dreaming sleep state as NREM (non-rapid eye-movement), and the dreaming sleep state as REM (rapid eye-movement). The NREM sleep decreases nearer morning, and the REM sleep increases. It is in this latter state that many of us have psychic dreams that we remember on waking—dreams that are real experiences on the astral plane, which is the fairies' true home. Through all the years up to the time I started work on this book, I had frequent vivid dreams about fairies. I would be with them in fields, woods and gardens, and sometimes my sister, or an unknown companion, was with me.

I started collecting cuttings of true experiences in 1936, and several people tried to persuade me to compile a book of them. One day in the 1940s, I was thinking seriously about doing so, but was a bit apprehensive as to whether the fairies themselves would like it, and I wished I could obtain their consent. That night I went to bed thinking about it, and early the next morning I had a wonderful true dream. Standing in front of me was one of the higher devas, or "Shining Ones," and I had never before seen such a vision of loveliness. She glowed with light; her hair was long and golden; her gown was flowing and opalescent; and the aura, which surrounded her, coruscated with all the colours of the rainbow, I christened her "Iris," and felt she was a Guardian of the Fairy Borderland. She was standing on front of a symbolic filmy curtain of gauze, which she drew aside and beckoned me through, so I knew I had been accepted. She was showing me some interesting things when something—perhaps a sudden noise—made me waken, but not before she had impressed on me that whenever I saw the rainbow-flash of her aura I was to ask the person who might be next to me in a street, shop, or other building, etc., if he or she had, or knew someone who'd had, any fairy experiences.

I know that must sound incredible, and I had to take the risk of being thought crazy, but I wanted to collect as many accounts as I could, so I plucked up my courage to do it, knowing that the lovely deva was guiding me. Fortunately, on each occasion I received a serious answer and had a long and interesting conversation about fairies with the person concerned. One was a man in a printer's shop; another a lady concert-pianist; another a clairvoyant house-wife; another I met at a meeting, who invited me to her house; and another a tourist in the porch of Coventry Cathedral, etc! When, in 1955, Alasdair Alpin MacGregor, the Scottish author and folk-lorist, started collaborating with me in collecting more accounts, I stopped seeing the rainbow-flash, but I know that subsequently the deva often led me into certain interesting experiences (such as when I was pixielated in a cemetery!) in order to give me more insight into the ways of the fairy folk.

I like to call this next experience "The Fairy's Gift," and it came about in the following way.

On Sunday morning, 21 October 1956, I had a vivid dream in which I was in the garden and it was rather dark. Then I saw a light glowing on a plant, and as I looked at it, it became a tiny, silvery fairy about one and a half inches high, with silver wings. When she knew I had seen her, she cried in a clear, tinkling voice: "Help! Oh, please help!" I was just walking towards the plant when I was awakened by my mother, who was calling to me from her bedroom. I had not had time to recognize the plant in my dream, so I silently asked the fairy to lead me to it, and when I went downstairs and into the garden I was led straight to an antirrhinum (commonly known as "snapdragon") plant. The night had been stormy, with gale-force winds, and although it was a dark morning I could see that a stake, which my sister must have put there some days earlier, had come loose, and the plant and its flowers were lying dejectedly on the ground. After I had replaced the stake and raised and re-tied the drooping stems, the plant looked much happier and I felt the fairy was pleased.

On the following morning I went to the solicitors' office, where I worked as a shorthand typist, and a few minutes later my colleague arrived and presented me with a large bunch of linaria flowers, which she felt I would like. They were in lovely rainbow colours, and as gardeners well know, they are similar to snapdragons but in a miniature form, and are of the same family (Scrophulariaceae). Hilda M. Coley, in her delightful book *The Romance of Garden Flowers* (W.H. & L. Collingridge Ltd., London, 1948), wrote that "Our garden snapdragons are related to the wild Linarias and the yellow toadflax." My friend tossed me the empty seed-packet to show me the variety in case I wanted to grow some, and I saw that the seed merchants called that mixture of seeds FAIRY BOUQUET!

There was a surprising sequel in eight days' time. My sister was standing near the snapdragon plant in our garden when she saw a movement on it, and a tiny fairy flew out and settled on her arm for an instant, perhaps trying to show her gratitude to my sister for putting the stake there in the first place. When I asked for a description, my sister said she didn't look more than one and a half inches high and was "silvery, with small silver wings"—just like the fairy in my so-called dreams! Was it a mere coincidence that I received those dainty antirrhinum–like flowers the day after I'd had the dream? Or was it the snapdragon fairy's way of thanking me by sending, through my friend, a Fairy Bouquet?

The great antivivisectionist and mystic Anna Kingsford said her fairy experiences took place on the fairies' own plane during sleep, and she considered the nature spirits her kith and kin because she knew she had come from their kingdom.

In the early part of the morning, when Mrs. Clara Reed, of Coventry, was half-awake and half-asleep, she could feel a gentle pulling at her nightdress and heard the sound of merriment. This went on for quite a while, and then she found herself being lifted and carried away, and knew, from the delighted voices, that she was with the fairies. She felt a rush of air as she was taken out of the house to a strange little garden where there were beautiful rainbow-coloured stones. On one of these sat a "fairy king" under some lovely trees, surrounded by many of the little people. This was all Mrs. Reed could tell me, but eventually she must have found herself safely back in her own bed.

"I am interested in Nature and in all things spiritual and mystical," said Mrs. Winifred Kirby, a contributor of several other accounts. "In my dream I seemed to be standing with an unseen companion, in front of a small hill at the bottom of which was a tiny door. Then, somehow, I was through the door and standing at the top of a flight of six steps, which led down into a charming little sitting room. I can see the tiny room now, and I remember I felt just like Alice in Wonderland and wondered how I could get into such a small space. The room was beautiful. On my left I could see a tiny window, and by the side of the hearth was an easy chair covered with a material that looked like flowered cretonne. Poised in mid-air, and looking towards us with a welcoming smile, was a lovely little fairy. I can't remember if she had a wand, but I certainly saw her wings."

Mrs. Kirby mentions an unseen companion, and several other contributors have mentioned unseen or unknown companions in their experiences. It is probable these are spirit guides, or fairy or angelic-guardians.

Miss Helen Fraser Morrison, of Rome, had an experience that is not exactly in the "dream" category, but she says she went to sleep. One hot afternoon between the two world wars, she was sitting peacefully reading under a tree in a wood on a hillside in Tuscany, when a strange sound distracted her, and it seemed to come from a tree facing her, a very ancient one with a hollow trunk. "There was one straight branch that stretched out higher up, above the hollow," she said. "I thought the sound was made by some small animal, for it did not sound exactly like a bird, a kind of tapping and squeaking was the only way I would describe it. It went on and on while I was wide awake and alert and interested. Then suddenly I became drowsy and must have slept, but the sound continued, and on the straight branch three little objects about a foot high appeared and looked down on me. Two were like little humans, the other half-animal and slightly smaller. They continued the strange 'chant' and looked friendly. I felt friendly, too, and no longer surprised. It all seemed so natural, but when I awoke realised it had not been a dream. I had been on another dimension, though not actually on the astral, as I have sometimes been. This was different, a most pleasant and enlightening experience. I knew something first-hand, which I had not known before."

Chapter 14: Fairies' Attachment to Certain Objects

Mr. Wm. C. Gall, M.P.S., of Emsworth, Hants., sent me the following uncanny account of some kind of elemental, which could not be seen but that certainly made its presence known. "The first event happened in June, four years ago. I was typing out some notes for a lecture; my wife Eve, who had been crippled by a stroke and had only very recently returned home from hospital, was resting in an easy chair; her sister was in another chair near her; and Rufus, the dark grey Archangel cat, was lying on another chair near the fireplace. Suddenly he roused himself, started sniffing the air, and then, in a state of nervous excitement, began to stalk something invisible to us across the floor. Whatever it was, he followed it about the room for a while, watched it apparently climb up the side of the chair on which my wife was sitting, cross over her lap, and climb down the other side of the chair. By then I had left the table—which was at the other side of the room where I had been working—in order to watch the queer behaviour of Rufus. The cat continued to stalk the thing across the floor (from the direction of the cat's gaze we judged its height to be about twelve inches), then round behind the dining table where it was concealed from his sight owing to the unusual construction of the table legs. Rufus appeared to be using his sense of smell as well as that of sight, and was continually sniffing the air. He began to creep out to a position from which he could see behind the table legs, and then refused to approach nearer. I went up to him, speaking gently, as he was very disturbed. He was a picture of nervousness and curiosity, fascinated by what he saw and afraid of it at the same time. Then I tried to coax him nearer to where the creature seemed to be, but he resisted strongly, and as I thrust him closer he suddenly spat and struck out with his paws at something just in front of his face. At the same time, his fur stood up on end, his tail bushed out, and his whole body tensed for action. This was most unusual, for a gentler and less belligerent cat never existed. Nothing would induce him to go nearer, so we left him alone. After a while, the creature appeared to cross back down the room, followed by Rufus at a respectful distance, to a position under a low coffee table at the far end of the lounge. When I tried once again to get Rufus nearer the creature, he spat as before, leapt high into the air right across the coffee table, and rushed out of the room, which we could not get him to enter again that evening. Of course, we discussed this strange happening between ourselves, but, being unable to account for it, we christened the little creature 'our gnome' and left it at that.

"For a long time afterwards, Rufus was reluctant to use the room. In fact, he refused to go in for a week and never entered it without a preliminary survey. He would stand in the doorway, sniffing the air and peering cautiously in all directions until he was satisfied that the creature was not present before he would come into the room. However, no further happenings took place, and with the passing of time he seemed to forget all about it; but very recently there have been similar episodes. My wife is now confined to bed with severe paralysis caused by a second stroke, which occurred shortly after the events of which I have just written. In the circumstances, I naturally spend nearly all my spare time in her bedroom, doing all my work there whenever possible, and I decided to use again my very much-neglected typewriter. As well as Rufus, we now have another cat—a little snow-white one rejoicing in the name of 'Pinkie' because of the pink tips to her ears and nose. Both cats are fond of sleeping on the carpet at the foot of my wife's bed, enjoying the warmth of the electric fire, and they were there when I commenced typing. After a while, Rufus began to sniff the air and, with the same mixture of nervous excitement and curiosity as before, watched something go across the room close to the table where I was working, rise into the air to the top of the dressing table, and then float across the intervening space on to the bed where my wife was lying. I went to pick Rufus up and place him on the bed, but at the touch of my hand he leapt into the air and ran out of the open door on to the landing, where he hid behind a chair. Here he stayed, sniffing the air and watching the open doorway most intently. Presently the creature apparently moved out of the room and towards Rufus. He watched it approaching slowly closer and closer and then he spat out and gave a prodigious leap, which carried him over the chair and landed him about four steps down from the head of the stairs, from where he looked apprehensively about him. I went out, picked him up and tried to soothe him. He quietened down, so I carried him into the room and put him on the bed beside Eve so that she could continue to stroke and soothe him. He remained quiet for a little while, and then he became alert and appeared to be looking at something climbing up over the end of the divan bed. It approached nearer and nearer to him when, without warning, he gave a great leap into the air right over my wife, to land on the floor on the far side of the bed, from where he watched the creature pass across the room to a waste-paper basket beside the dressing table. I tried to get him to approach the basket but he resisted strongly and, when forced near it, he again struck out wildly with his claws at something apparently just in front of him, at which he was spitting and growling in an obvious state of fear. My sister-in-law came in just then, and she also tried to coax him to go nearer the waste-paper basket, but without success. Violently he attacked something there that was quite invisible to us, and he seemed only too glad to get out of the room. Pinkie, the white cat, who in all her ways is quite a common little thing compared with the aristocratic and lordly Rufus, looked on in amazement at these strange goings-on and did not appear to be able to see the creature causing the trouble. However, a parrot, Polyanthus by name, who lives in a cage in the bedroom (she is an African Grey, an intelligent bird and great company for my wife), was an interested spectator of the incident. She obviously saw the creature, watched its comings and goings, and showed fear when it approached the neighbourhood of her cage.

"It was the best part of a week before Rufus would come into the room and settle down. He was in the room in his usual place when I next brought the typewriter upstairs. At the time he was fast asleep, but after I had been working for some time, he suddenly woke up and evinced all the signs of fear and excitement once again. This time there seemed to be something under the table at which I was working, and at the first opportunity Rufus made his escape from the room. It was only at this third episode that I realised that, whatever the creature was, it seemed to be connected with the typewriter. I do not use it very often, and it is only when the machine is in use that the creature seems to move abroad and disturb the cat. The origin and history of the typewriter I do not know. I purchased it second-hand about ten or eleven years ago from some acquaintances of a friend."

Mr. Gall's supposition is quite feasible, for his machine was not the only one that attracted the attention of a small creature. Many years ago a reporter in Bournemouth said that several times he had seen a little fellow dressed in shades of brown and green, perched on the top of his typewriter. Sewing machines and stoves also seem to hold some fascination for nature spirits, as the following accounts will show.

"I am 50, sane, healthy, and have never suffered from mental blackouts, aberration, hallucination, or hypnotic trance," wrote Mrs. Edya Edwards, of London, in a letter to *Woman* in 1950. She then told of the day she was using a hand sewing-machine, the wooden lid of which lay beside it on the kitchen table. As she turned the handle at full speed, she saw out of the corner of her eye a little man sitting on the machine cover. He could have been no more than eighteen inches high, and wore a tight-fitting green coat, black tights, and tiny boots of soft, dull black–something like suede." The needle holder seemed to fascinate him as it bobbed up and down, and as he stared at it his head was nodding, too. Mrs. Edwards didn't know why she wasn't paralysed with astonishment, but she slowed the machine down very gently, at the same time turning her head towards the manikin. As the machine stopped, the little man also turned his head and looked straight at her. Their gaze met, and he instantly disappeared, but not before she had seen that his eyes were tawny gold. "To my dying day I shall know that the little people exist," she concluded, and in a letter to me some time later she said she would always regard that incident "as one of the most vivid experiences of her life."

Miss M. Gentle, of Watford Way, Hendon, was amazed to hear of a similar experience to her own, for she, too, had seen a gnome on her sewing machine, intently watching the needle going up and down. "Personally," she said, "I was too ashamed to tell anyone, except my lifelong friend, about the little gnome, as they would promptly ask me 'How many did you have?' I am a perfectly practical-minded business woman, not given to seeing things in any shape or form."

Another account came from Mrs. Dora Dunn of Bradley, Derbyshire, who saw an elf sitting cross-legged on an old sewing machine that she had been using at the rectory where she used to live. The little creature, she estimated, would be about six inches high if standing, and as far as she could remember it was dressed in red and green.

And here is yet another account, this time from Mrs. Lily McKenzie, of Glasgow, who awoke about 5 o'clock one November morning to see two pixies about 24 inches high, sitting cross-legged on top of a sewing machine that stood near the window of her bedroom. "I could not believe my eyes," she said, "for they were dressed in what looked like an imitation of the same brown fur fabric out of which I was making a coat at the time, and some of which was lying on a chair in the room. They were also wearing hats of it and seemed very pleased with themselves."

In 1952, Miss Avril Walford-Headen, of Liverpool, sent a letter to *Woman* describing how her mother, on going into the kitchen one night to fetch their pet dog, saw a quaint little creature of "the tubby sort" sitting "cross-legged in a perky fashion" on the stove. "He was dressed in a yellow suit with three little black buttons down the front, and he had an orange collar and a yellow cap with orange piping." Her mother blinked in surprise, and when she looked again he had disappeared, but afterwards she saw him several times when she was alone, on the stairs or the landing.

In the kitchen of her previous house in Fleet, Hampshire, about the year 1927, Mrs. Esme Fielding was leaning against a table facing an old-fashioned range four feet away. It was the kind that had an oven each side, one of which she kept hot for cooking, while the other was always cool, with its door generally open about eight inches because the gardener used to put in it some wood to dry, which he had picked up in a copse behind the house and chopped up for kindling. A few hundred yards from the house was some rough land, part of which consisted of trees and wild rhododendrons; the other part was used as a golf course. Mrs. Fielding said that the last thing she was thinking about was pixies, when partly out through the open door of the "wood oven" came a little brown man about a foot high, and then, on seeing her, back he went into it. "That's the only way I can describe him," she said, "and that was the end of it! Could he really have been a brownie who had come in with the wood?"

Mrs. Evelyn Paxton used to have in her house in Washington, USA, a little fellow named Isadore, who wore a yellow shirt and green tights, and lived on a shelf where some Quimper dishes rested, behind the sugar bowl. "His shoes and his nose turned up," she said, "and his hair was black. He was small, but his size seemed to change with his interests. He loved machinery—sewing machines, washing machines, dishwashers, and automobile motors. He deserted us to go with a railroad engineer who came to the house one day, and he's probably riding the rails at this moment. There were also small groups of fairies, some blue-toned, some gossamy-white. They loved the barns, the garden, the children, and the cat, and swooped everywhere, riding in the cart and on hummingbirds' backs. They also played tricks, like snatching a needle and thread, making it invisible, then dangling it in the air in front of one's nose. They left when the children were grown. "Sometimes I can feel fairies around my place now, and sense their singing; but they play no tricks, and are different from the earlier fairy folk."

Miss Upton, of Nottingham, told me of an unusual experience that she had when engaged as private secretary to the female director of a local firm. Her employer was in the middle of dictating letters when she was called away for a few minutes and, to pass the time until her return, Miss Upton sat gazing idly at a picture that hung on the wall. It was a painting of a country scene, and depicted quaint cottages against which some of the village folk were standing. As she looked at it, she was amazed to see tiny figures dressed like the villagers, step out of the picture and walk along the frame — some balancing like tightrope walkers, and others executing a series of delightful gymnastics. She watched breathlessly, and she told me she kept blinking her eyes to make sure she wasn't dreaming and that it was not an optical illusion. Then, much to her disappointment, the office door opened abruptly and her employer hurried back into the room, whereupon all the figures vanished instantly.

On being asked what was the matter, as she looked so shaken, Miss Upton described what had happened and ended lamely: "I don't suppose you'll believe me."

"Oh, but I do," came the unexpected reply, "because I myself have had a similar experience!"

In the case of an artist, one sometimes hears the expression "He put his whole soul into his work," and this is very apt, for much of his creative energy goes into and remains with his paintings, and the nature spirits are able to utilize this astral and mental matter for their own enjoyment. Miss Upton, being in a subjective state, had apparently "tuned in" to the pictures radiations, in the same way as her employer must have done. Maybe this explains a strange thing which occurred when a visitor came to our house with an Afghan hound. When it entered the room, it caught sight of a picture that hangs on the wall above the settee. It is an original oil painting of a river with a path at the side, on which a fisherman and his dog are walking. The dog is no more than half an inch in height, but the keen-sighted Afghan had apparently seen it. He dashed to the settee, stood on his hind legs and, resting his paws on the settee-back, gazed intently at the picture for several minutes, as though fascinated. Was he seeing the life in that dog as the artist must have seen it?

On many occasions when they were being interviewed on the radio, novelists and playwrights have admitted that their characters have somehow "got out of hand" and seem to develop wills of their own and behave in ways that are quite different from those that were originally intended. The Rt. Rev. Bishop Leadbeater said in his before-mentioned book *The Hidden Side of Things* that nature spirits can ensoul the strong thought-forms created by an author and enact scenes of their own; and in the second volume of *Spiritual Unfoldment* (The White Eagle Publishing Trust, Hampshire, UK) White Eagle wrote: "I would add that fairies love to work with an author, and will often stimulate his imagination with fantastic ideas and plots."

It is well-known that Robert Louis Stevenson, while in the dream state, received constant help with the plots of his stories from what he called his "Brownies" and his "Little People"—though perhaps he gave them these appellations without being aware of their true nature, for he asked: "Who are the Little People?" It is certainly true that we leave something of ourselves wherever we go, with whomever we meet, and on whatever we gaze, and there is constant reaction and interaction between these elemental beings and us.

Chapter 15: Fairy Music and Fairies Dancing to Music

It is said that the elusive strains of fairy and elfin music are fragmentary echoes of the Celestial Song, and Byron had a similar thought in his *Don Juan*, XV when he wrote:

> There's music in the sighing of a reed;
> There's music in the gushing of a rill;
> There's music in, all things if men had ears;
> Their earth is but an echo of spheres.

In her lovely book *Rediscovering the Angels*, Flower A. Newhouse said "The tiniest elemental moving among the grasses in the fields, or lowly wild flowers, sends out a miniature 'lariat' which circles the grass blades or plant shoot he concentrates upon, filling it with two or three tones of pulsating colour. Moreover, all the while this display of colour-changing continues, a soft humming of the Song of Creation attends the workers."

In the summer of 1936, while holidaying at Sheringham, Norfolk, I had a vivid "dream" in which I walked through some woods with my sister and saw a brown pixie peeping at me from a tree branch. The next day my sister and I went to Pretty Corner, where I sat playing for a while on a homemade bamboo pipe—there being no one else about at the time. We walked home through the woods at twilight, and just as we passed a group of trees I heard music coming from one of them. The tune was repeated many times, like the pealing of tiny bells, or notes played on a miniature harp. I went right up to the tree and peered through its branches, for, although the light was fading, I could still see clearly enough to convince myself that no human being was hiding there. Neither could I see the fairy musician, probably the pixie of my "dream." Although the music seemed at first to come from the tree, it did not stay there, but rose and fell and swayed over the treetops. It continued for some time, but my sister, who was usually able to share these experiences, could not hear it. I tried to remember the notes by writing them down there and then, in Tonic Sol Fah, and later I sent the fragment to Dr. Thomas Wood, Mus.D., who had heard fairy music on Dartmoor, and he put it in correct musical notation for me. Of course, it would be impossible to say it is exactly the same as the original, but it is as near as anyone could get from memory. Just before the Second World War, I went for a weekend to Lunds in Wensleydale, Yorkshire, and it was there I heard the wild, haunting singing of the undines in a waterfall. The notes were high and plaintive, and rose in scale beyond my range of hearing. The sound was so alluring that I was filled with a strange longing.

Miss Stella Watson often heard minute, bell-like notes in her lakeside garden in Surrey, and also near the house. She described the music as being like that played on tiny handbells, or which might result from striking fine wineglasses with a glass rod—very clear and sweet. "The sounds come in groups," she said, "and seem to be now ahead of me, then to the side, and then behind, and so on, as if it was a tiny band going in circles."

When the husband of Mrs. A.R. Hastings was a young man, he lived for a while with a family in Cork. One day, when lying in a peaceful field in the sunshine, he heard the most delightful tinkling music "like tiny bells." On his return he asked the family what it could have been, and they were greatly thrilled that he, they stated, had undoubtedly been singled out to be able to tune in to the music of the Little People.

This type of music seems popular with the fairies, for at break of day on a summer morning in the year 1905, Miss Edith Hudson, of Warwick, was awakened by "the dulcet sound of tiny bells." She looked at her watch and said to herself, "Bells at 3 o'clock in the morning?" She arose and went to her window, which was about fifteen feet above ground level, and the music sounded louder as she drew nearer to the open air. For as long as ten minutes it continued, and during that time the bells seemed to pass and repass close to her face. Then gradually the sound receded into the distance as though minute hands were ringing the bells as the ringers continued their journey through space. Miss Hudson was living at that time in a house in the Market Square, Warwick, with a friend to whom she related her experience. "My friend promptly declared I was dreaming," said Miss Hudson, "but I told her that was impossible as I'd walked to the window and the music had continued. Then she asked me, 'Could it have been a wind-harp?' and she described that instrument, but I replied 'No, these were definitely bells,' so she had to admit: 'They must have been fairy bells that you were privileged to hear.' Both of us taught music, so we were all the more interested in the experience. The sound of those tiny bells ringing out their sweet music will never be effaced from my memory."

The well-known writer Mr. S. P. B. Mais also heard fairy bells, very sweet and low, at the furthest point of Dig, above the Atlantic; and Dr. Walter Starkie, C.B.E., Litt. D., who, at the time of writing to me was the British Council's Representative in Spain, said he had heard fairy music in Kerry, where his mother came from, and also in West Cork.

I was told by Mrs. Iris Ratsey that on one occasion she and her (then) small son listened on Midsummer Eve to fairy music at a ford, which led to the house where Rudyard Kipling wrote his *Puck of Pook's Hill*, and the ford is mentioned in that book.

Miss Edith M. Atkinson gave me the interesting information that her Welsh grandfather, the late James Bilsland Hughes (Iago Bencerdd), the harpist whose history is to be found in Robert Griffith's book *Llyfr Cerdd Dannau*, once stated that he had heard and written down some fairy music.

Another music lover was Mrs. Marguerite Connelly, who received inspiration from some fairy music that she heard. Many years before her marriage, she was a student in a class for Music, Art and Drama in Harrogate, and at the end of term she was chosen for the part of Melisanda in Maeterlinck's "Polleas and Melisanda," which was to be acted to a select audience. The book she studied had words but no music, and in the mornings she used to walk alone in a beautiful valley to learn her part. It was there that the music for the verses that she had to sing came to her "out of the blue," and received much appreciation when subsequently rendered by her, but unfortunately no recording was made. She asserted that she was not a clever musician, had never composed anything, and knew of no music for the part at the time.

Fairy music, "like tiny flutes being played," was heard by Mr. Wm. Spiers in the woods between Farnham and Lion Lane when, at the age of twelve, he was lying there "feeling at peace with all the world.. He said it sounded in the air all around him, and although he never saw the fairies he felt their presence very strongly.

The folklorist, Miss Lucy H.M. Bruce, of Iona, told me that an artist, walking along the north shore of the island, heard fairy music and said it was like a miniature orchestra in which he could distinguish several different instruments. Miss Bruce also met a woman who had heard fairy music in a hill in Ireland and said that it was far more beautiful than any earthly music.

In the 1930s, when living in Edinburgh where he was studying science, Valentine Rippon, M.A. Oxf., went on a coach tour through the Highlands. At the halt for the midday meal he escaped from the crowd and went alone up a hillside to eat his sandwiches and fruit. The air was very still, and he was sitting enjoying the sunshine and the countryside when suddenly he heard music. It sounded sweet and happy, but lasted only a few moments, stopping as suddenly as it had started. At that time, when science was all in all to him, he tried to explain away the occurrence by thinking that a puff of wind had brought the music, though he had to confess to himself that he hadn't noticed any breeze, and that he had, during those few minutes, "sensed a presence." The music had also brought a feeling of joy, which persisted for the rest of the homeward journey, and since then, whenever he thinks of it, he experiences the same feeling of happiness. Perhaps it is as well to remind young readers that in the 1930s the sound would not have come from a transistor radio.

The same applies to this account, for it was in 1933 that Miss Lucy Walpole and her sister had a little house built at Ufford, in Suffolk. At that time Ufford was a lovely village in a setting of tall trees and green water-meadows, with a stream running through. The house stood on a hill overlooking this valley, and part of the

330

hill was called on old maps "Fiery Mount" which, Miss Walpole was told, was probably a corruption of "Fairy Mount." The whole place had an almost magical feeling of peace and quiet. One summer soon after they came to live there, Miss Walpole's sister heard on several occasions the sound, as if in the far distance, of a simple little tune being played, and it was she said, like the plucking of the strings of a tiny harp or other stringed instrument. As it was always very early in the morning when this occurred, Miss Walpole told her sister to come to her bedroom and waken her the next time she heard it, so that she could go back with her and listen at the open window which faced the "Fiery Mount." This she did, and both of them heard the little tune of about six notes, repeated many times. The two sisters were never able to think of any sound like it that human beings would make in such rural surroundings at such a time—about dawn—and they always spoke of it to each other as "the fairy music," for after that one summer they never heard it again.

About the year 1938, Mrs. T. Hanley and her husband were being driven in a car over the Denbigh moors by a friend to have supper with him and his wife, who was a Welsh novelist. The friend stopped the car on a high bit of the moorland road so that they could look back at the magnificent sunset, and they all got out to stretch their legs. The evening was deathly still, without a breath of wind, and to Mrs. Hanley's surprise she could distinctly hear music, although there was nothing in sight to cause it. She thought at first it might be a wireless from somebody's house, but one could literally see for miles in all directions and there was certainly no house in sight. Then she wondered if it might be an unusually musical telegraph wire but there was none, and her husband and friend, when questioned, said they couldn't hear anything like music. Indeed, both of them remarked on the extraordinary silence of the moor. She asked the friend, who knew the place well, if there were any houses near, though she hadn't seen any and he said he didn't think there was one within a radius of five or six miles. The music was "lovely and mysterious," consisting of long, dreamy chords—a sort of singing, but not vocal. It was a composite sound like an orchestra, and might have had flutes, violins, and horns, though it would be difficult to say what the instruments were, or to make out any particular tune or air, and when she tried consciously to concentrate on the music it faded slowly until she could hear it no more. They continued on their journey and eventually arrived at the friend's house, where they met his wife, and told her that Mrs. Hanley had heard music on the moors. They described whereabouts they had stopped the car, whereupon his wife exclaimed, "Oh, that's odd. There is a field there, where, tradition has it, the shepherds used to go to listen to music. It was fairy music, they said."

In 1927 Mrs. M.K.F. Thornley and her clergyman husband were spending a few days in Cornwall at a cottage situated in a strange and lovely valley close to a rocky cove. To her, the place, though very beautiful, seemed sinister. She sensed a great melancholy brooding over its stream, its woods, and its old disused quarries. While with her husband, she felt safe, but when alone she almost feared the place. Only once was she away from him, when she went to post a letter a quarter of a mile off. The sad whispers of the trees and mourning of the brook seemed full of meaning, and she returned walking rather fast, anxious to get back. As she crossed the low plank bridge over the stream, she unmistakably heard the sound of harps, and sad, sweet, alluring voices floating upward from the water—and they were not good to hear. She knew she must not linger nor listen. Husband and wife, glad to quit the scene the following day, were afterwards to hear others speak of strange influences sensed in that sad valley.

When, later on, they decided to live in Cornwall, they made friends with a lovely young sculptress belonging to an old, established Cornish family. She was a singularly pure-hearted, sensitive creature, rather retiring, with uncommon tastes in poetry and music, and a great tenderness so towards all plants and animals. "One autumn afternoon," said Mrs. Thornley, "she proposed to take us to a 'fairy wood' she had loved since childhood, where she said we might 'hear something.' We set out across the moor, and when we drew near the wood my husband became engrossed with the observation of some insects at work, so the girl and I left him and went into the wood together. After a few minutes, she whispered: 'Do you hear?' I think her presence helped my perceptions, for in a few moments I heard lovely sounds like a murmured cradle-song, voices of surpassing sweetness and contentment gently singing an endless, ageless melody—a melody of such character that it imprinted itself on my memory there and then. It seemed to me to be nothing less than the brooding over their charges of those beings who foster the seed-life of the trees and the gentle plants around them, bringing their generations to life out of the unseen mysteries of sap and seed, the voice of creation at work among the primal simplicities. On reaching home I was able to put the melodious chant into form and have it for solo violin among my secret treasures, as 'The Song of the Woods.'"

Miss Lorna Heath, also of Cornwall, was comparing notes of strange experiences with two other playwrights at St. Ives Arts Club, and one of them said she had actually seen a little man about three-feet high, with a sack over his back, near Chanctonbury Ring in Sussex. Her dogs, who usually barked at strangers, took no notice of him, and he completely disappeared into a patch of scrub and low bushes. The other friend said that when she was seventeen she heard strange, unearthly music at night, and Miss Heath was able to say that she'd had a similar experience at the same age. "With me," she explained, "this took the form of what sounded like a violin playing outside my bedroom window, very late one rather stormy night in Wales. I felt compelled to run downstairs and find out what it was, but when returning I was caught by my terrified parents, who thought that I was sleepwalking. I think that I may have been in a trance-like condition, but I was not unconscious of my surround-ings." Evidently Miss Heath found no ordinary explanation for the music she heard on that occasion, but she is quite frank about a further experience she had, which proves that things are not al-ways what they seem to be. She was walking along a country road in Cornwall one windy day, when she heard the most wonderful music like wind bells and organ pipes combined, but on going to investigate she found that a new field opposite a builder's house had a fence with a top rail made of disused rain-water pipes!

Iain Dahl, the author and painter who was then living in St. John's Wood, London, contributed the following material, which I quote in full: "From about 1923 onwards and until the outbreak of the Second World War, I spent much of the summer and an occasional spring in the Island of Barra, then one of the most unspoilt fragments of the British Isles, and indeed of Europe. In the early 1920s, at least, it could be said that no place had changed less in the last five hundred years: there were no telephones, no wireless, no motorcars. Small droves of horses dozed or loitered in a half-wild state in the hills, and, if a mare were harnessed to a plough or go-cart, as likely as not a foal might be seen ambling or trotting at her side. In 1929, with the help of a cropper and a couple of old men 'great at cutting the stone,' I continued to build a cottage of the old pattern, oval in shape, with thatch set back deep within the thickness of the stone walls, the stems held down with boulders and tied with leather ropes against the fierce Atlantic gales. The site was striking, as the cottage stood on a small spur of Ben Mhartuinn above Allasdale, one of the quietest corners of the island, looking westward to America, with wild headlands to north and south, while, from the kitchen window, the turf rose a thousand feet to the skyline. (Incidentally, as I later discovered, 'Allasdale' is the anglicised form of an older name, which Carl Hjalmar Borgstrom—the Norwegian etymologist who has made a study of Norse place-names in the Western Isles—traces to the old Norse 'Alfa-stodhull,' which means 'the Fairies' milking-place.' *Alfa* is a fairy and as such it might well be accepted, for between the few dwellings and the sea, there lies a wide sandy plain or machair, which in springtime glows with wild flowers, and at any season of the year has green feeding for fairy cattle.) I found the people rather shy of speaking about fairies or fairy experiences, for already they had been laughed at; but it was not hard to see that a belief was there, held in check, perhaps, by a layer or two of prudence or religious teaching. Stories at second-hand were to be heard, but I was wondering if I might not come upon some small personal experience of faery, which to me would be worth all the elaborate tales of another.

"I felt drawn to the wild mountainous centre of the island, and one still, warm August day I followed the rough track that leads from Upper Borve over heather and bog through a mountain pass to Skallary on the east side. With me was Miss X., a friend who has come in contact with the fairy world herself, and has heard chords and musical sounds in lonely places. As we climbed, we spoke little, but listened, and once or twice it seemed to me that there was an undercurrent of music in the air, but this I put down to eddies of air in the heather, wild bees, or the small water-music of unseen burns. At the point where the pass is narrowest, a great rock overhangs the approach, and here we both stopped dead, halted by a tiny, stinging note like a silver trumpet. Music seemed to be coming from some- where inside the rock—a short, repetitive phrase, rather like the tenor voice of a cello or the lower notes of a clarinet. We listened, and Miss X. quickly drew out a notebook lined for musical nota- tion, and began to jot down what she heard. This was made possible by the fact that the phrase was repeated more than once, returning on itself, so that I, who do not write music but have 'a good ear for picking up tunes,' was able to memorise it; it was almost as though the rock were announcing a 'signature-tune.' We continued to lis- ten at different parts of its surface, putting our ears to the stone and moss, but now its mineral body seemed quite inanimate and the air itself deprived of vitality. We went slowly on our way, alert for any further echoes of the music, but heard nothing that could not be put down to the rustle of water in the peat-hags, the drip of a burn, or the whine of wind in heather. I had kept the tune well in my head, and, without seeing what she had written, I hummed it over to my companion. We were delighted to find that our two versions were almost identical. A little later, a neighbour related, to our great amusement, how Jonathan Maclean—a giant of a fellow with farms both here and on Mingulay—had heard music coming from a rock in a cleft of the hills, and 'had taken his soles out of it, runnin' as though the Black Chase was after him!'

"A year or so later I had two further experiences in the same region. On a clear day with small wind-currents that seemed to be coming from all directions, I was climbing through heather near the pass, when I heard a voice in the air just above my head. It was the kind of small, girning voice one might expect to hear from a gnome or a manikin and it continued to skirl and complain like a bagpipe, as if some creature were trying to express a happiness to which it was unaccustomed. For a couple of minutes it continued to grind away in this fashion, and then, as suddenly as it had begun, the voice ceased. There was no human being anywhere within sight, and it must have been several miles to the nearest dwelling. On the second occasion, the day was exceptionally still and almost sultry. I was approaching the pass and was perhaps a quarter of a mile from its mouth on a broad sweep of soggy turf, when I heard a rushing sound, such as might be made by some creatures in flight. I looked up and was surprised to see no sign of any birds that could conceivably have caused it; but while I was staring about me, the rushing returned, and it seemed as if two or more creatures were weaving about in the air, diving and swooping up again quite close to my shoulders. As they did so, there came a sound: 'Hoo-oosh!' just by my right ear, then, almost immediately, 'Hoo-oosh' a little to my left. Something or things were playing, perhaps trying to frighten me, in the way that swallows will sometimes play and dive above sheep. There was a final 'Hoo!' from overhead, and the sounds withdrew. Everything was now very still. I was somewhat startled, and as the sun was about to set, thought it wise to return home.

"My next experience began in a remote little valley or fold of the hills to south and east of the fairy pass. Again the day was still and sultry, and I sat down on a clump of turf by a burn to drink and meditate. As I rested, I grew conscious of a sound in the air that was somehow persuading me to hear it—a three-note call, I agreed, and, perhaps, not entirely unfamiliar. In a minute or two I knew what it was—it was the fairy call in answer to which Mary Rose disappeared in J. M. Barrie's play—the same curious interval, drawing away indefinitely on the third note, continuing in an almost irritating fashion. I got up and shook off the impression. It seemed to me altogether too easy, too whimsical a notion that the valley should be impressing upon me the call from a fairy play; nobody would believe a thing like that.

"I decided to say nothing at all about it, but a week or two later

I happened to be at a ceilidh in a house near Castlebay. There, among my friends, was an artist—Miss Anna Maclean. We talked a little about painting, and all at once she said: 'You know, I've found a lovely little spot I call it the 'Mary Rose Valley.'

"'Oh?' I said, 'Where exactly does it lie?'

"As accurately as possible, she described the position of the valley I was thinking of. 'But why do you call it the 'Mary Rose Valley,' I asked.

"'Well,' she replied, 'I was rather tired carrying my sketching things when I came to it, so I sat down there a while to rest. Then I kept on hearing the call—I'm sure it was the same call that is in the Mary Rose play—have you seen the play? You remember when Mary Rose gets drawn away –'

"'I remember,' I said. The music for the play was written by the late Norman O'Neil. I have been wondering if and how the 'Mary Rose Valley' continued to enter his ear."

Most of the nature spirits delight in music because they are able to bathe in the sound waves. A fairy seen by Mrs. Martha C. Smith, of the USA, was dancing on the top of her television set to the music of the "Scarf Dance" that was being played by an orchestra. The little creature was about twelve inches high with tiny iridescent wings. She was dressed in sheerest gossamer, and around her was a light that scintillated like the facets of a diamond.

In May 1957, Mrs. G. K. Evason, of Tunbridge Wells, wrote to me: "I had been thinking this evening that there were no fairy experiences to relate at present. Then, catching the fragrance from some lilies-of-the-valley which were in a vase on my table, I looked towards them and became aware of a little white Fairy Queen with a diadem of flowers in her hair, and carrying a wand with a bright star on it. She was dancing by the table, just beneath the flowers."

In a further letter Mrs. Evason said: "The little white fairy appeared again in the dawn hours, right in the aperture that I had left between my bedroom curtains, which are of a golden colour. She sparkled with the usual radiance, and a little in front of her appeared a group of fairies dancing to the tune and singing the words of a song entitled 'The Little People.' It is a charming song, and I often used to feel impelled to play it and would experience a wonderfully happy upliftment whenever I did so, but I did not know who was giving me the impression until I saw these fairies so vividly around. Now, whenever the name, words, and music of any of the Fairy Songs suddenly flash upon me, I realize the fairies' sweet presence and know it is their way of requesting a certain tune to be played."

Later she wrote; "The snow-white fairy frequently appears to me, sparkling and iridescent. Last night after I had retired to bed and lain awake for some time, I suddenly felt the atmosphere alive and vibrant with moving figures in beautiful swirling clouds of colour, and the words 'The dancing fairies' were plainly audible. There were little elves and sprites and the usual band of fairies and gnomes enjoying a very happy dance in the atmosphere halfway between floor and ceiling. It was such a joyous experience, and then I went peacefully to sleep."

In December 1957, Mrs. Evason wrote again; "A group of dancing fairies has appeared a number of times during the Christmas season. They come in the usual lovely colour vibrations, singing the fairy songs that I play for them sometimes, and the elves play on little panpipes. One has a tiny silver trumpet, and I feel he uses it also to summon the group to the fairy ring for their joyous revels. It is so very wonderful, and one cannot doubt their existence."

While penning another letter to me, Mrs. Evason said, "I am conscious of a little elf beside me. He is dressed in a pure white tight-fitting garment, and his white cap is shaped like an inverted tulip flower with a short stalk at the top. He appears to be greatly interested in a small 'Belling' electric heater, which gives out a gentle warmth but no light. In his hand he holds what appears to be a tiny imitation of a conductor's baton, and now and again he beats time to the music of a symphony concert, which is coming through the radio. He gives me such a joyful feeling."

A few weeks later, Mrs. Evason wrote that she was listening to music on the radio when the little fellow again appeared, dancing gaily and evidently enjoying himself immensely. "He seems to prefer to come alone, and disappears quite suddenly." On another occasion Mrs. Evason saw quite a number of fairies dancing in a ring round the radio.

The Hon. E. C. F. Collier said that his first wife, who died in 1952, had remarkable powers of second sight but was very reticent on the subject and seldom spoke about it except to him. He related that whenever Tchaikovsky's "Valse des fleurs" came over the radio the fairies used to come and dance in front of her. He could not see them, but she used to describe what happened and what they looked like. She said they were wonderful little creatures between nine inches and a foot high. They looked very happy and were beautifully dressed. Usually they brought along with them garlands of flowers and performed delightful evolutions of dancing together. "If I remember rightly," Mrs. Collier said "they all seemed to be of female form, and there was always the very obvious Queen with them. They were well aware of my wife's presence and always finished up with an obeisance to her. Although so perfectly formed, there was something about them that my wife found hard to define beyond the fact that they were not human. They used sometimes to bring a pet rabbit along, and once, I think, a small white poodle. As soon as the 'Valse des fleurs' stopped, they gathered together to give the farewell obeisance and then all scampered away and vanished."

In his book *The Hidden Side of Things* (Theosophical Publishing House, Adya and London, 1948) the Rt. Rev. C. W. Leadbeater told of an elf in Italy who was so fascinated by a certain piece of music that when it was being played on the piano he would leave his wood and come into the room to bathe in its sound waves and pulsate and sway in harmony with them. The author wrote that more than once he had seen a shepherd boy in Sicily playing on his homemade double panpipe with an appreciative audience of fairies frisking round him.

A concert pianist recounted to me in 1951 that once, when she and her friend were rehearsing on two pianos, her friend stopped suddenly and said that while they had been playing she had distinctly seen several fairies at the side of her piano, dancing in time to the music.

Many composers have been inspired consciously or subconsciously by the fairies and the higher Devas. Cyril Scott, in his book *Music: Its Secret Influence Throughout the Ages* (Rider and Co.), said that Grieg was the musical interpreter, the intermediary between the little nature-spirits and humanity, and one can well believe it. Wagner certainly captured the weird, exultant cries of the air spirits in his "Ride of the Valkyries," and there are magical fairy passages in Mendelsohn's Overture to *A Midsummer Night's Dream.* Mr. S. Jackson Coleman, F.R.G.S., F.R.A.I., etc., who was the Hon. Administrator of the Folklore Fellowship, told me that the airs of a number of Manx songs, including "Arrane y Ferrishyn" (Song of the Fairies), "Tappaghyn Jiargey" (The Red Topknots), and the "Arrane Ghelby" (The Dalby Song), are regarded as fairy tunes.

Chapter 16: Angels and Angel Music

The seer Geoffrey Hodson, author of *The Brotherhood of Angels and of Men, The Angelic Hosts,* and *The Coming of the Angels* (Theosophical Publishing House, London), described these beings as "Nature spirits that have attained to self-conscious individual existence" and "Mind-born Emanations from the Absolute." The Greeks and Romans called them "gods," while in the ancient Sanskrit language they were "Devas" (pronounced "Day-vahs"), meaning "Shining One," for their bodies are self-luminous. The various dictionaries define them as "Divine attendants," "Messengers from God," and "Ministering Spirits," etc. Included in their ranks are Angels of Healing; of Music; of Beauty and Art; of Maternity and Birth; Guardian Angels; Ceremonial Angels; Nature Angels; and the Building Angels, who embody the Archetypal ideas.

Mrs. Flower A. Newhouse, founder of the Christward Ministry at Questhaven Retreat, California, USA, said that the Christian Bible refers to the activity and reality of these radiant beings 295 times. She truly sees into the realm of angels, and her beautifully illustrated books, *The Kingdom of the Shining One, Natives of Eternity,* and *Re-Discovering the Angels* (L.N.Fowler and Co.Ltd., London), are authentic records of her experiences. The angels are as fully a part of her consciousness as are her family and friends, and she said "This faculty of extended vision, which permits me to see the Radiant Ones, becomes useful only when I share its perceptions with others."

Just as the lesser nature-spirits help the garden end woodland flowers to unfold, so do the angels help us to unfold what is known in the East as the "thousand-petalled lotus" (the Crown Chakra, or spiritual centre in every human being).

When communicating with each other, the angels use a colour language, but when communicating with human beings it is usually by telepathic means. However, some seers of fairies and angels receive a strong impression of real vocal sounds, which come through in the seer's own language. Swedenborg said that the speech of an angel is heard as sonorously as the speech of one man with another, yet it is not heard by others who stand near because it flows first into the man's thought, and, by an internal way, into his organ of hearing, and thus actuates it from within.

An angel told Geoffrey Hodson, "The First essential on your side is a belief in our existence," so they want us all to open our hearts and minds and become receptive to their benign influence and eternal presence. Then the dense clouds of materialisation can be pierced and the necessary channels be formed, through which they can send greater outpourings of healing power to the hospitals, and fresh hope and guidance to our sick and war-scarred world, for it is true that the strife in the world is the outward manifestation of the inner conflict of the individual, and that the cause is within ourselves, since everything begins with the power of thought.

Many years ago I was able to catch a glimpse of a great golden Healing Angel at a Divine Healing Service held by Brother Mundus of The World Healing Crusade, Blackpool, in a Nottingham Chapel. Presiding over the service, the angel seemed to be helping to distribute and focus the strong flow of healing power to the patients, and while those with rheumatoid arthritis were being attended to, glorious rays of rose-coloured light flashed down from the great Being's aura, so that some of the patients could walk better, and their hands were straightened. Two colour-healers who were sent at an earlier service told me that they had seen streams of blue light pouring from the Angel to the patients who had cataracts, and that in several cases the eyes became perfectly clear.

Once, at a service of Holy Communion, I was privileged to see the "Angel of the Presence" at the altar. This Angel has a face of supernal beauty, and represents the Christ.

Late one night, in November 1977, when an exceptionally fierce gale was blowing and a warning had been given over the radio that there might be structural damage, I stood in the bedroom, hesitating about going to bed. There were moments of sinister silence, and then the full force of the gale came again in great moaning gusts. I could hear things clattering and falling outside, and I felt terrified. I prayed for protection for my sister and myself, and for all the neighbours, and although I decided to climb into bed and switch off the light, I remained sitting up.

It was then I saw a shining form of pure light at the side of the bed, and all my fear left me. I felt calmed and strengthened, and waited for the Being to speak, but after a few minutes it vanished, leaving an inward request for me to open my Bible and receive its message. I had an "Olive Pell" Bible on my bedside cupboard, so I switched on my torch and opened the book at random. The pages fell open at the Psalms, and my eyes were instantly drawn to Psalm 4, verse 8. The words were: "I will lay me down in peace, and sleep; for Thou, Lord, makest me dwell in safety."

A pilgrim to Hereford Cathedral saw two of these radiant Beings, one on either side of the altar, just after the celebration of Holy Eucharist; and a few weeks before the Battle of Britain about eighteen of them were seen in St. Paul's Cathedral focusing all their forces above the altar.

The late Ivah Bergh Whitten, Colour Healer and Founder of A.M.I.C.A. (Aquarian Metaphysical Institute of Colour Awareness), was full of gratitude for the co-operation of these Angelic Beings, who were so clearly objective to her sight, and in a book called *Light of Ivah Bergh Whitten* by Dorothy Agnes Bailey, Mrs. Whitten is quoted as saying, "These Deva friends have ever been so much closer to me than even my best beloved friends on the earth planet. They seem always to understand my motives and to anticipate my wishes, surrounding us with deepest love and devotion."

She described them as being slight and exquisitely proportioned, and moving with a rhythm born of a gracious consciousness. "Some of them," she said, "have a vehicle of pale violet, others of green, all emit some degree of luminosity. The largest and most beautiful ones have an effulgence resembling mother-o-pearl."

In Dr. Roland T. Hunt's book, *Fragrant and Radiant Symphony* (C.W. Daniel Co, Ltd., 1937), he quotes the following extract from a letter written by Mrs. Ivah Bergh Whitten: "When I am ill (or in trouble) She (the Deva, or Guardian Angel) seems to cover me with the soft-rosy mantle of her loving consciousness, which appears to act as a sort of stethoscope, enabling her to detect my every vibration. If I am in pain, she sends a pale clear apple-green light, with a violet diffusion, something I have never seen with my ordinary healing lamp; it is more like a green light with a violet aura than anything I can describe. About it and through its radiance, there are soft notes of musical rhythm—the tempo seems to increase as the centre of the pain is reached; then, slowly, it fades to a dreamy softness of vibration, like the humming of the angels. I have no awareness of perfume until the pain has ceased; then, as the force withdraws, leaving only the faint rhythm of colour and sound, I am conscious of a most delicate violet odour."

Miss Josephine Burton, of Nottingham, who was in charge of some Girl Guides at Elton Camp, near Nottingham, felt her responsibility and earnestly prayed for their safety. During the night, while sleeping under canvas, she suddenly awoke to see a very bright and beautiful angel, with large wings, and it told her have faith that the girls would come to no harm while in her care. Then it disappeared.

The late Douglas Hunt, M.A., of Hertfordshire, a part-time journalist and author of *Exploring the Occult*, told me that he had never seen fairies or angels, but when in the Chair of a Masonic Lodge (international Co-Freemasonry), he had been acutely conscious of the presence and help of the great Angelic Being that presides over the Chair, and he said there were also lesser Beings attached to the other offices in the Lodge.

Miss Mary Evans had rhythmic movement classes in many parts of the country and overseas. She had been a pupil of the late Isadora Duncan, and was a member of the Order of the Cross. This radiant, joyous soul, who "lit up" a room when she entered it, told me that she was always aware of the Angelic Beings while she was dancing.

Mrs. Ellen Hilton, who had a healing sanctuary in Lancashire, once lived in what was known as a Pilgrim House, the doors and windows of which were never locked day or night—a fact that was known for miles around. There lived in the village a boy who in these days would be called a "problem child." Brought into court for a serious offence, he was asked by the magistrate why, although he had broken into every other house, he had never attempted to steal from the Pilgrim House. "I couldna, sir," he replied. "There wus allus angels at t'door."

A hush fell upon the court, then the magistrate said gently, "You know, Tom, that the doors and windows of that house are never locked?"

"Aye, sir. That made no difference. I couldna geet in noways 'cos o' t'leets (lights)."

I was told by Mrs. Elsie Fairful, of Brisbane, Australia, that every night before she went to sleep she saw a very beautiful angel standing high up on the right-hand side of what appeared to be a wide stairway of black and silver to which the Angelic Being always pointed.

Mrs. Irene Bradshaw, wife of the Rev. Arnold Bradshaw, of Cambs., wrote in 1956: "I wish I could believe in fairies. But I'll tell you what I have seen—I've seen angels, and if I'd needed anything to convince me of life after death these would have done it. I was a small child when I saw them, but all my life they have been my most vivid memory. They were perfectly lovely. Some were blonde, and some were dark. They were all smiling and they had white robes with a bluish sheen. Some of them had wings. They spoke to me, and their voices were clear and sweet. They seemed to be saying goodbye to me, as one angel said: 'Come, we must leave her now.' They were quite close to me, and I put up my hand to touch the soft cheek of one of them. I could not understand all they said."

In 1933 Miss Sheila Bryant was sleeping in a room by herself in an old house, and at her bedside she had a small-framed picture, which was propped up waiting to be hung. Something wakened her suddenly out of a very deep sleep, and she found it was the picture which had slipped and fallen down. The room was full of a soft golden light, and at the foot of her bed a tall figure was standing, with the most beautiful shining face she could ever have imagined. He wasn't looking at her but towards the fallen picture, and then the eyes turned to her and the whole face lit up even more luminously and smiled. They remained looking at each other, and Miss

345

Bryant says she knew then what is meant in the Bible about there being "no speech nor language" in Heaven. Gradually the vision faded, and she went blissfully to sleep again, knowing she had been allowed to see her Guardian Angel. "There was no halo or anything of that kind," she said, "but there was an intense golden luminosity emanating from this Angelic Being. He was very tall. I did not see his arms or hands, and the lower part of the figure was of course hidden by the bottom of my bed. There was no movement except of the head and the eyes turning from looking at the picture to look and then to smile at me. I do not remember the mouth—only the unspeakably wonderful eyes—first solemn and then smiling."

When Mrs. Norah de Courcy was eight or nine years old, she was sharing a room (in a house in Wiltshire) with her youngest sister, then a baby, who woke easily and cried a lot. She was therefore used to being very quiet even when awake, and as they were put to bed early she often lay awake for a long time. "This evening," she recounted, "I think I had almost slept when [I] opened my eyes to see in the dusk-light an angel standing on the foot of my bed. The figure was short—three to four feet, I would say—and the lovely grey wings were folded, reaching to the feet like a cloak. I remember no surprise, only wonder and a great longing to touch those wings. I started to crawl to the end of the bed, and the angel was gone. I didn't mention the vision for a long time, but when I did tell my mother, she said that, as a child in Ireland, she had once seen a ring of fairies dancing in mid-air, tiny creatures all bright in the dark."

Mrs. Christina Stark, of Washington, USA, said that she had seen a few angels, and she called these beings "emanations of the heavenly spheres." Her friend, Mrs. Evelyn Paxton had been aware of the presence of angels many times. She had awakened in the morning to see by her bed a lovely figure robed in white, just standing guard over her. She has felt a softly moving breeze over her head in a closed room and received the impression of a voice: "I am Michael," then a counter breeze just as gentle but different, followed by "I am Gabriel." She knows the soft touch of their wings, and feels the quietude of their presence, which is external to her personal peace and yet conforms with it.

The following are extracts from letters sent to me by Mrs. G. K. Evason, of Kent. "There are two angels with pure white wings who come and stand one on each side of my private altar. They have been seen by a number of people particularly during the war years, when I used to hold a group meeting here for the sending-out of peace vibrations regularly every week. One of these beings comes and stands behind me at times, and completely enfolds me with his wings for protection. I understand the wings are really unnecessary for flight, but are symbols of a high state of evolution. There appeared about two feet away from me an angel robed in pure white, with long white wings reaching from the shoulders to the heels, but I was not permitted to see the face, which was averted. The whole vibration was that of complete protection and purity. I have had a number of visits from this Angelic Being since then. He has a brilliant golden halo and golden auric radiations.

"Tonight, as I joined in the Silent Minute, the form of the Radiant One appeared at my side, robed, as before, in pure white with trailing over-robe and golden halo. This vision always appears at the same time.

"This last Sunday evening was one never to be forgotten. As I gazed at him he turned towards me and suddenly and deliberately opened out His wings. This was so clear and unmistakeable that I felt it completely answered all questions regarding the reality of the true Angelic Beings. No one can ever shake or destroy my knowledge regarding them."

Mrs. M. O. Weller, of Surrey, had a vision of a very tall, white-robed figure in her garden. The light around the being's head was golden but so bright that she could not look at it. Afterwards, the garden seemed very dark, although it was afternoon.

Mrs. Hilda Litchfield, late of Nottingham, gave me the following account. "As an only child, aged ten, staying in Kandy, Ceylon, with my parents, I slept in a large, lofty room with long window openings and jalousies. These were closed at night, but the light of the very bright moon streamed through between the laths. My father was seriously ill at that time, and one night I awoke to see, between me and the moonlit, a figure poised in the air about four feet from the ground. He was quite nine feet tall, and clothed completely in white. A wreath of leaves circled his head, and one long palm-leaf was held and rested against his right shoulder. The expression on his face was calm and beautiful, and he gazed towards the room where my father lay. I was very frightened and presently managed to cover my face with the sheet. I stayed covered for a long time before I dared to look again. When I did so, the figure was still there and remained for some time without moving, before gradually fading away."

Another account of a bedside vision came from Mrs. J. Burrows, of Nottinghamshire. "One night, while my mother was in a Nursing Home waiting to undergo a serious operation, I wakened suddenly and saw an angel standing at the side of my bed. Her face was lovely, and she had large wings and wore a diaphanous gown. Her feet appeared to be crossed, and as I watched her she slowly raised her arm and pointed heavenwards. It was as though she wished to resign me to the fact that my mother would not be cured. An unsuccessful operation was performed, and after about two years of great suffering, my mother passed on. The beautiful expression on the angel's face will always remain in my memory."

M.K.F. Thornley, a pilgrim in the truest sense of the word, travelled different European countries, largely on foot, to seek out and reinvigorate ancient holy sites and holy springs, once hallowed places, now all too often neglected. In one of her letters to me, she wrote of her exhaustion following five weeks of arduous travel through mountain and valley, seeking out and linking the holy places of St. Michael: "The great enthusiasm underlying the pilgrim's quest consists in *actually* reanimating the holy cosmic centres of the planet in preparation for the new era, strengthening the beneficial powers of the mighty entities through human cooperation, re-consecration, and devotion." There followed two of her experiences with angels: "When I was down at the point of Ballinskelligs, where my objective was a holy well of St. Michael, I knelt on the turf by the well to pray, and saw a 'Shining One' close to me, no taller than a human, and right on the ground, not in the air as I usually see them. It was only for a few moments, and then he vanished but I felt so happy. Then two peasant women came over the field with their pails for water from the well, and welcomed me almost affectionately, talking in their lovely voices as if we had known each other for years. The younger woman said 'Here is the stone called St. Michael's Foot, you can see where the toes was, but the stone's almost wore away with crossing.' She then pushed a little grass aside and showed me a grey stone by the well's edge about eighteen inches long, roughly the shape of a foot, and there were the marks where countless fingers had crossed the stone, wearing away the grey surface and showing white. It was the exact place where I had seen the Shining One standing. We talked more together, and then I said very quietly and naturally: 'And are the Holy Ones ever seen here now?' She replied in the same natural, quiet tones: 'Oh yes! Sometimes.' I didn't speak of my experience, but the naturalness of this short dialogue convinced me of her good faith and that in no sense was she 'playing up' to my question.

"On a glorious summer afternoon in 1909, I was cycling alone on an errand through the lovely stretch of country between Frensham and Haslemere. I paused midway on the journey at a little Church standing on a small green by the side of the lonely road. The building was neither old nor new, and boasted no charm or distinction of style without or within. Yet a precious sense of homeliness and welcome met me on entering. As I knelt at the altar steps praying for some I loved dearly and for my own needs, deep peace flowed into my soul, and the air seemed sweet with blessing. After a space I rose, left the altar, and sank on my knees again in the Chancel. I knelt upright on the floor, my hands hanging clasped in front of me, my head held straight up, and facing East. I mention these details to make it plain that there was no direct sunlight on my face, nor was there any pressure of the hands upon the closed eyes, either of which things may cause optical illusion when combined with a dreamy or devout imagination. Moreover, I had been in the dim church long enough to be accustomed to its contrast with the shining day outside. Deep quietness, gratitude, and happiness enfolded me, and I do not know how long I remained thus before I became aware of a wonderful Presence poised near the altar. I sensed a figure of towering stature clad in azure and white radiance… but wondrous beyond all mystery of dazzling light and mighty height, was the fragrance of Love, which poured out from this Presence; Love so vivid, yet so peaceful and compassionate that no words can begin to describe it. I was held in a depersonalized passion of worship, an adoration so sublime that I could feel my praise blending with the strong rhythm of this great Being's love, and glowing upward like an ardent flame of joy to God. My spirit continued timelessly in this soaring blessedness and then began to sink softly earthward into a sense of calm strength and enrichment indescribable, in which I rested till the beloved Presence seemed to withdraw and the outer appearance of surrounding objects asserted itself once more. I arose and went out of the little church with light step and buoyant heart. Life has never been the same since. A potent memory, an inner certitude of Promise, remain to bless those grey hours, those periods of trial, which are an indispensable part of our daily schooling on earth. Such an abiding treasure is surely proof that this experience was no mere religious daydream but held within it an earnest [promise?] from the realms of Reality."

Mrs. Emma S. King, of Australia, copied out for me the following entries from her diaries.

5 October 1937: "After a healing concentration for my sister-in-law, I felt rather spent with the force that had flowed through me and lay face down on the floor to receive a renewal of strength for myself. A beautiful angel came and stood over me, and my consciousness was raised considerably. The angel was about eight feet tall, and its aura extended the full width of the room. It was radiantly white end luminous, with a golden edge, and within the aura, about two feet deep, were circles of revolving, interlacing golden light. The angel's feet touched my right side, and peace and confidence filled my heart. I lay in absolute comfort, physically, astrally, and mentally. In a few moments I saw on my left side something I never believed existed. About three feet away from me stood an embodiment of the dark forces, though he was a magnificent figure in build and looks. I was thoroughly astonished, and deep in my mind, almost mechanically, I said 'Go hence! Go hence!' Then I

realised that the angel was looking straight at this being of darkness so that, despite all his power, he was incapable of coming nearer. Watching safe within the angel's aura, a sudden realisation of the horror and agony of such a life filled my heart with pity, to think that any beings should live in those conditions. As my prayer of compassion went up, the figure of Our Lord became visible about a foot from my head, and a voice told me to make the Sign of the Cross over the dark one. I obeyed, and he slowly faded away. It was a most weird experience, and I felt I was being taught the power of protection, which is drawn around us when we try continually to turn our thoughts and aspirations upward."

5 November 1939, Healing Service at Liberal Catholic Church (founded in Holland): "Father Farquharson asked the congregation to repeat a verse with him and while this was being done a glorious form of Our Lord completely blotted out the altar. The force flowing from Him was like blue and white opalescent fire, and when Reverend Farquharson invoked the Angel of Healing, this radiant being stood between Our Lord and the two priests officiating. The force from Our Lord came through the angel into and through the two priests to the people who were presenting themselves to be anointed. More and more I am impressed by the work being done by the Invisible Helpers during these services. At this service there were young children on one side of the Church who had passed out through the wars in various countries, and on the other side were dark-robed souls needing help. There were two in particular, very sad and wretched women, brought from the dark side of the astral plane to kneel at the altar rail. My attention was drawn to these two. They knelt sideways, not facing the radiant Angel of Healing, but looking with almost terrified eyes into mine. My heart went out to these two more than all the rest, in love and sympathy."

December 1939, Healing Service, L. C. Church: "At the invocation, an Angel of Our Lord appeared before the altar. It was very tall, taller than the highest point of the altar. The vibrations of its aura were beautiful, like iridescent downy feathers pulsing outward and sending streams of healing force in every direction. During the anointing of the people, the aura of the assistant priest was filled with brilliant blue in which silver stars kept appearing and disappearing."

February 1940, Healing Service, L.C. Church: "During the service, Reverend Farquharson's head was surrounded with radiant yellow vibrations. When I returned to my seat after being anointed, the Angel of Healing became visible to me before the altar. The power from this glorious being flooded the whole church, flowing through the two priests in streams of gold and rose vibrations. My whole consciousness became intently fixed on the angel's face, the glory and beauty of it making completely oblivious all physical-plane movement. My heart filled with longing to paint this vision for all there to see, but at the same time I felt the despair of the artist who knows that even with brushes dipped in light and fire it would be impossible to portray what was before me. Although my attention was riveted on this lovely being, I could still see all around me the poor soul from the dark side of the astral plane, brought there for help. They were all darkly clad, kneeling in the healing vibrations. The more love and sympathy that went from me to those about me, the clearer and more uplifting became the vision of the angel.

"The Angel of Benediction was entirely different, hovering over the 'Host' and raying out vibrations of peace that seemed to crown the work of the Healing Angel."

April 1941, Healing Service, L.C. Church: "This was Palm Sunday, and the Angel of Healing flooded the whole building with beautiful purple rays of light. This light and power came through Reverend Furse-Morrish in a wonderful rose vibration, filling his aura as he anointed the people who came forward. The same force coming through Farquharson was opalescent, with a lot of blue and silver in it."

Melbourne, 1942, Healing Service, L.C. Church: "This is the first Healing Service of the New Year. When I went up for the anointing, I prayed to be just a channel through which healing might pass to my little grandson who was in a hospital in the country with scarlet fever. I saw the power go through me from the angel direct to the child in the bed in the hospital. This healing power passed through an angel who overshadowed the child and the bed. This was interesting, as I saw the extra healing force passing through myself and augmenting the power of the Angel of Healing already caring for the child's welfare."

Melbourne, 1942, Healing Service, L.C.Church: "I particularly wish to try to describe the Healing Angel at this service, as I have never seen an angel just like it before. It was truly magnificent. Radiant silvery light and force poured from it in every direction, with healing and peace and infinite impersonal sympathy reaching out far beyond the confines of the little church. But over and above all these things and stronger than anything else was the abundant power of endurance, and it seemed as though the angel was a gateway to a vast storehouse of this power. Another unusual thing was that this same angel stayed and took charge of the Service of Benediction. This is the first time I have seen this happen, as always when I have been there it has been the Angel of Healing for the Healing Service and a different angel for the Benediction Service. During the following week, however, Mr. Farquharson came to see me and said that Reverend McConkie had been visited by this particular Angel—which in the beginning had been the means of Reverend McConkie starting the Healing Service—and it told him that it had been away to another planet. It had a long talk with him and informed him that it was staying for the Healing Service and the other service being held that day. This accounts for my seeing the same angel officiating at both services. Mr. Farquharson told me this after I had given him my account, and he was very pleased that the two visions tallied."

Mrs. Veronica Maxwell gave the following description of an Angelic Being who seemed to be guarding an ancient shrine. "One day, while staying with some friends who owned a wild island off the Bay of Donegal, I climbed a mountain partly covered with woodland until I reached the top, which had a superb view of seventeen uninhabited islands spread out on the silver waters glittering in the sunshine. I sat down on moss-covered stones and had such an extraordinary feeling that I scraped away some of the moss and saw that the ancient stones were built into something deep down, which might have been an altar or part of a temple. In this magic place, the soft wind blew over the wild thyme with a gentle sound, and I was lost in the remote beauty of it all. Then I became aware of something. There was a Presence standing looking at me, perhaps ten yards away or more. It was very tall, with a most regal bearing and of great beauty. The general impression was of luminous silver and white, and he held in his hand a shining, unsheathed sword. As he stood there I had the feeling of a wonderful benediction flowing round me. I don't know how long it lasted but long enough for my spirit to rejoice, as it has rejoiced ever since."

Mr. H. T. Howard, of Nottingham, sent me the following account of a great angel who guards a sacred place in Northumberland: "[I found myself] being subject to a very high-frequency vibration. (I am an occultist—and there are signs by which this can be perceived.) This continued until I left the place an hour or two later and requested to be 'returned to normal.' In these and in other ways I have formed a kind of magical link with the place, so that it means something special to me. When I am away from it, the place seems to be constantly calling me back, largely for this reason I spend every annual summer holiday at Alnwick—so that I can revisit Dunstanburgh two or three times again. And after the holiday is over, I begin to look forward to the next time. I find, however, I can contact the place and experience its peace to some extent wherever I am; in times of need I find I can also contact the angel of the place."

Mrs. Esme Swainson, of Somerset, has seen the great angels in charge of magnetic centres, at Maiden Castle, the prehistoric hill fort in Dorset, and the Tor at Glastonbury, Somerset. The Maiden Castle Angel is over 30 feet high, and holds what seems to be a rod of power. From my contributor's rough sketch of the angel, I could see that the lines of force flowing from the head are vaguely reminiscent of an Indian's feathered headdress. As regards the Tor Angel, Mrs. Swainson received the impression of fire and sun-power, of gold and rose. "I was reminded of the idea of St. Michael," she said, "more than female, though I don't think these Angels have any sex." She has seen the Deva in charge of a healing group, and also the Angel of the Presence at Mass. The one she saw most clearly at a special meeting had a rather pointed chin and slanting eyes, and from its head streamed lines of force, which gave the appearance of hair.

"This is my experience of seeing an Angel," wrote Mrs. Pauline Young, of Lancashire. "I was lying in my bed feeling very peaceful and looking at the wall in front of me, when two feet appeared in the ceiling, then the whole body just seemed to drop down to my floor. There, standing in front of me, was the figure of an angel who seemed to be female, but I'm not quite sure. She wore a pale grey gown and her hair was jet-black and cut in a bob-style. She looked as if she was talking to someone, and never once saw me, or glanced my way. Her wings were very beautiful; they were about eight feet long to her size of approximately five feet. I just sat there looking at her. She did not glow, or look any different from you and I, except, of course, for the wings. Then after a few minutes she just rose before my very eyes, back up through the ceiling, and was gone."

"Having been a student of music from early childhood," said Mrs. M. K. Thornley of Cornwall, "it is natural that vibrations should interpret themselves to me with form and meaning through sound, at times perhaps subjectively, but at others I verily believe by the actual perception of matters or beings from 'outside' and having no connection whatever with myself. The following instance is perhaps worth recording. During the First World War there was a certain amount of violin playing demanded of me, though hands coarsened by the chemicals and hard work of the hospital wards and a total lack of opportunities for practice made these occasions anything but satisfactory to me. In 1915 I was taken over to a hall somewhere to perform, but it is not of my performance there is anything to say, but of a beautiful lady who sang the old Easter hymn, which is best known as setting to the words 'Ye watchers and ye Holy Ones, bright Seraphs Cherubim and Thrones.' Her voice was clear and golden as transparent amber; large, joyous, sweet; and she sang like an instrumentalist, giving every note its true value and prominence. It was as if the message of the hymn was utterly real and beloved to her uplifted heart and she was giving it out as a treasure to all around. The first verse was to my ears a lovely

355

solo, accompanied by a worn piano. Then, towards the end of it, I seemed to hear other voices in harmony, chiming in among her Alleluias, and during the next verses this effect was cumulative, her lovely voice leading, but amplified and supported by other voices in increasing numbers. Those who are familiar with the magnificent tune know well the opportunities it gives for extended harmony and elaboration, and every thread and maze of sound was appropriated by voices of such angelic clarity and sweetness that the effect was a paean of worship, and utterly beautiful. The thought naturally came to me: 'are there people behind those screens, an unseen chorus?' But that couldn't be the case; I had just been at the back of the little stage with the other performers, and I knew such a thing was out the question. I rather shyly asked an old, intimate friend sitting beside me if she had heard other voices, but she shook her head, and no more was said. I do not know how to explain it, but shall never forget nor cease to be grateful that I heard what seemed to be the sweet, singer's train of heavenly songsters. I have never heard the like before or since."

Mrs. Shirley Eshelby, also of Cornwall, was very deaf, but she said, "There is no deafness in my soul, and I can hear celestial music, which is far more beautiful than anything I have ever heard with physical ears."

In this next account, Mrs. Emma S. King, of Australia, describes how an angel and a group of fairies helped the well-known singer Miss Marjorie Lawrence during a performance at the Melbourne Town Hall in August 1944. This wonderful artist had previously been stricken with poliomyelitis while singing in Mexico City, but eventually she had recovered sufficiently to be able to travel by air in her wheelchair to give concerts in camps and hospitals. At the concert that Mrs. King attended, Miss Lawrence had to sing sitting down, as her legs were still paralysed. "When she was ready to sing, she looked up to a wonderful Angel of Music high above the audience and near the centre of the hall. There was perfect coordination between the angel and herself, and with the downpouring of power came her first notes. When she finished her song, she clearly acknowledged the angel's help before bowing to the applause of the audience. During the heavier items of her programme, the inter-play between her and the angel became more and more complete, until in Brunnhilde's farewell to Siegfried the angel drew closer and closer, and finally remained poised in front of Miss Lawrence on the stage, with its force turned into her to augment her own. "All the evening, around her knees was a circle of very tall fairies, send-ing a continuous stream of vibrations into her legs."

In September 1935, Mrs. King went to a concert by Richard Crooks and combined choirs in the Melbourne Exhibition Build-ing. "The last item on the programme was the 'Hallelujah Chorus.' A huge angel, radiating scintillating white light, appeared beneath the dome, and as the music rose to a climax a circle of small angels formed under the outer edge of the dome. The light emanating from them, which might best be described as white fire without heat, left a feeling of benediction that lasted for some days. Mrs. King felt she had experienced something of what Handel himself saw while he was composing this music, for it is well-known that his servant found him in tears of rapture, exclaiming: 'I did think I did see all Heaven before me, and the great God himself.'"

In her before-mentioned book *Rediscovering the Angels*, Mrs. Flower A. Newhouse wrote that on sacred holidays we should try to hear Handel's "Hallelujah" chorus. "Whenever this music is sung, the angels of the astral and mental worlds join the chorus and their accompaniment is a thousand times more joyous and victorious than the human parts." She also said that the music of the Chil-dren's Prayer in Humperdinck's opera "Hansel and Gretel" was in-spired by the chantings of the Guardian Angels.

The Theosophical lecturer Miss Clara M. Codd told me that as well as two other people she knew in South Africa, her sister could on occasions hear "the music of the spheres." One man, who heard it in the wilds of N. Rhodesia, did not at first know what it was. An-other man heard it in the mountains near Pretoria in South Africa. "I asked my sister," Miss Codd continued, "what was the difference between our music and angel music. She said that with our music one could always hear the instrument, like the tap of the piano or the timbre of the human voice, and that our music was in tones and semi-tones, whereas Deva music had no tones or semi-tones but was liquid sound welling out of the whole body of the Deva. I once heard a famous Hungarian gypsy who played like that, with intervals unknown to ordinary music. I think Nature music is something like the wind in the trees. The first cellist of the Hallé orchestra, Mr. John Foulds, tried to reproduce it in sound for us."

Chapter 17: Group Spirits

It is the group spirits, or group souls, who provide us with the real meaning of that mysterious word "instinct" for they are the directive forces that are present in varying degrees in minerals, plants, insects, birds, and animals and marine life. We use the word as a convenient explanation for the marvellous activities in Nature, which so many of us take for granted, such as the wonders of hibernation and migration; the art of mimicry and camouflage; the engineering feats shown in the construction of beavers' dams and badgers' sets; the ingenious structure of moles' tunnels; the hexagonal formation of bees' cells; the geometrical lattices of mineral crystals and the spiral patterns of snail shells; the mating periods of birds and beasts and the times to produce their offspring, as well as the methods of finding food and shelter; the wonderful courtship dances of certain birds, and the variety of ways in which the different kinds of birds build their nests; and who taught them their own special songs and calls? How do the carrier and racing pigeons manage to find their way home, and the swallows to come back to their old nesting-places? How is it that at the ebb of the tide the limpets can find the same spot on the rocks that they left when the tide was full? How can some dogs and cats trace their owners over miles of unfamiliar territory? Without some superior intelligence or spiritual guidance, how is it that these creatures of land, sea, and air can display such wisdom and resourcefulness when, unlike us, they are supposed to have no free-will power of reasoning? The answer, of course, lies in the work of the group spirits, and Cyril Scott, the composer and occultist, rightly called them the "Guiding Intelligences" and said that each species or group of plants, insects, birds, and animals is ensouled by such a being, who prompts and stimulates the members of its own group.

In *The Rosicrucian Cosmo-Conception* by Max Heindel, who founded the Rosicrucian Fellowship at Oceanside, California, we are told that these group spirits govern their charges from the outside by means of suggestion, working in the blood of the animals through the air inspired, and that the life currents of the group spirits play along the horizontal spines of the animals, while in the case of plants the currents enter from the centre of the earth by way of the roots. He said that migratory birds are guided by the group spirit currents that encircle the earth, and each group spirit directs its charges to fly at the right altitude suitable for that particular group, thus providing the birds with a sort of inner compass.

In a course of lectures "Series 21" published under the title *The Spiritual Beings in the Heavenly Bodies and in the Kingdom of Nature*, Rudolf Steiner, the Founder of the Anthroposophical Society, also mentioned these group spirits, and said that those of the minerals work in the form of rays from without, inwards, streaming from different parts of cosmic space.

Dr. Annie Besant, one of the great leaders of the Theosophical Society, wrote in her book *The Ancient Wisdom* that when the form of one of the members of an animal group perished, the experience that it gained through functioning in that vehicle is stored in the spiritual body of the group soul, whose slightly-increased life is poured into the other forms that compose its group. Thus they continue to share the experiences of all the perished forms and, in this way, a race memory is born in the new forms.

In her book *The Kingdom of the Shining Ones* (Christward Publications, Vista, California), the Rev. Flower A. Newhouse of the Christward Ministry refers to the life currents of the group spirits as "frequencies" or "thought-bands," and says they are known in the Higher Worlds as "mentor waves." She tells us that the more highly-developed animals such as the horse, monkey, elephant, dog, and cat are breaking away from the group souls and reaching the stage of individualisation, and when this is achieved their evolution will be much more rapid than that which human beings have known.

Max Heindel also mentioned this in his aforesaid book and explained that it is accounted for by the spiral path of evolution, but to me it is also some well-deserved recompense for their terrible sufferings at the hands of scientists and other human beings.

In a *Rosicrucian Fellowship Magazine* dated 1954, it was stated that we had no need to feel "superior" to the animals, for each human of the present period of Earth-manifestation was at one time in the "animals status," while each animal now is potentially a human, so the difference between us is simply one of evolutionary timing.

Many animals are psychic, for at times they seem able to see things and people that we cannot see, and they can also sense danger. There are many instances where humans have been rescued from house fires through being warned by their pets, and I have a true, heart-warming account of a sheepdog that rescued several hundred sheep from a blazing barn.

If we have loved a pet sincerely and deeply, we are sometimes able to see its spirit after its so-called death, for the link of love is never broken. Many books have been written about the life after death, and it is comforting to know that our animal or bird friends are there to greet us when we ourselves pass from the terrestrial to the spiritual planes of existence.

My contributor Mrs. Clara Clayton said that a group spirit knows when any help is given by humans to its own particular group, and it is also very much aware of human cruelty towards its charges. Max Heindel went further than this and said that the group spirit suffers when any members of its group are hurt.

Animals are sent to Earth in physical forms, just as we are, in order to gain experience that will help them to evolve, and since the same divine life animates us all, we have no right to hinder their evolution by killing, ill-treating, or mutilating them, any more than we have the right to kill and ill-treat each other.

White Eagle, the North American Indian who inspired the founding of the White Eagle Lodge and its teachings, said that no good can ever come to mankind from cruel experiments with animals because it is against divine law.

Sathya Sai Baba, the cosmic avatar of Prasanthi Nilayam, India, declared that there is neither need nor justification for vivisection, and that the solution of every physical problem and the ultimate explanation of every material phenomenon can only be discovered by research into super-physical worlds.

The following is a Teaching Angel's message to Geoffrey Hodson, who was able to tune in to the angel's higher vibrations: "Why is the intellect, which is so keen when concentrated on material things, so blind to the eternal truths of life? Disease has been with you through countless ages, and is even now a growing menace to your lives; with all your knowledge and your intellect you cannot see wherein the causes lie. You torture animals, you make your horrid antidotes, you saturate your bodies with poisons and with drugs until the temple of the living God, which is your Self, is no more worthy of its Hierophant... When war, oppression, exploitation, cruelty, and selfishness cease upon earth, disease will disappear within one generation, and not before. Cease, then, the nameless horrors of the research department of your hospitals; emancipate yourselves from the ghastly superstition that by causing pain to others you may keep it from yourselves..."

Cruelty of any kind to birds and animals is abhorrent, and this includes factory farming, which is against the laws of Nature, and should be entirely abandoned in time to avert the dire consequences that we humans are bringing upon ourselves.

"None, not the tiniest insect, the smallest plant, the most insect mineral, is outside of the life of the Creator," said an un-named writer in the before-mentioned *Rosicrucian Fellowship Magazine*. That is why the group spirits, whose great work for the inhabitants of the other kingdoms of Nature is unceasing, deserve more of our compassion, understanding, and cooperation, for to them all the different forms of the One Life are sacred.